VIZ GRAPHIC NOVEL

From Far Away™

Vol.1

Story and Art by
Kyoko Hikawa

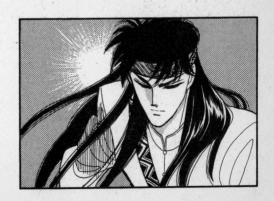

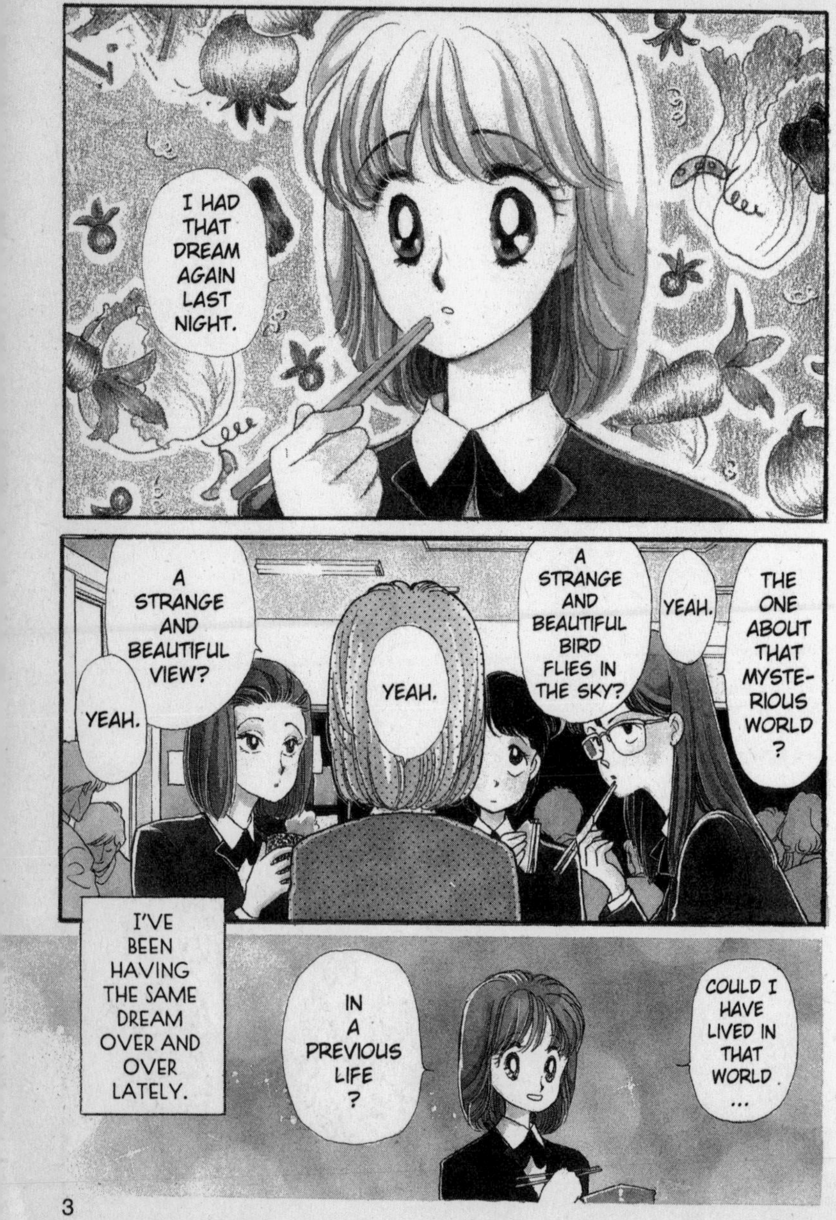
I HAD THAT DREAM AGAIN LAST NIGHT.
THE ONE ABOUT THAT MYSTE-RIOUS WORLD?
YEAH.
A STRANGE AND BEAUTIFUL BIRD FLIES IN THE SKY?
YEAH.
A STRANGE AND BEAUTIFUL VIEW?
YEAH.
COULD I HAVE LIVED IN THAT WORLD ...
IN A PREVIOUS LIFE?
I'VE BEEN HAVING THE SAME DREAM OVER AND OVER LATELY.

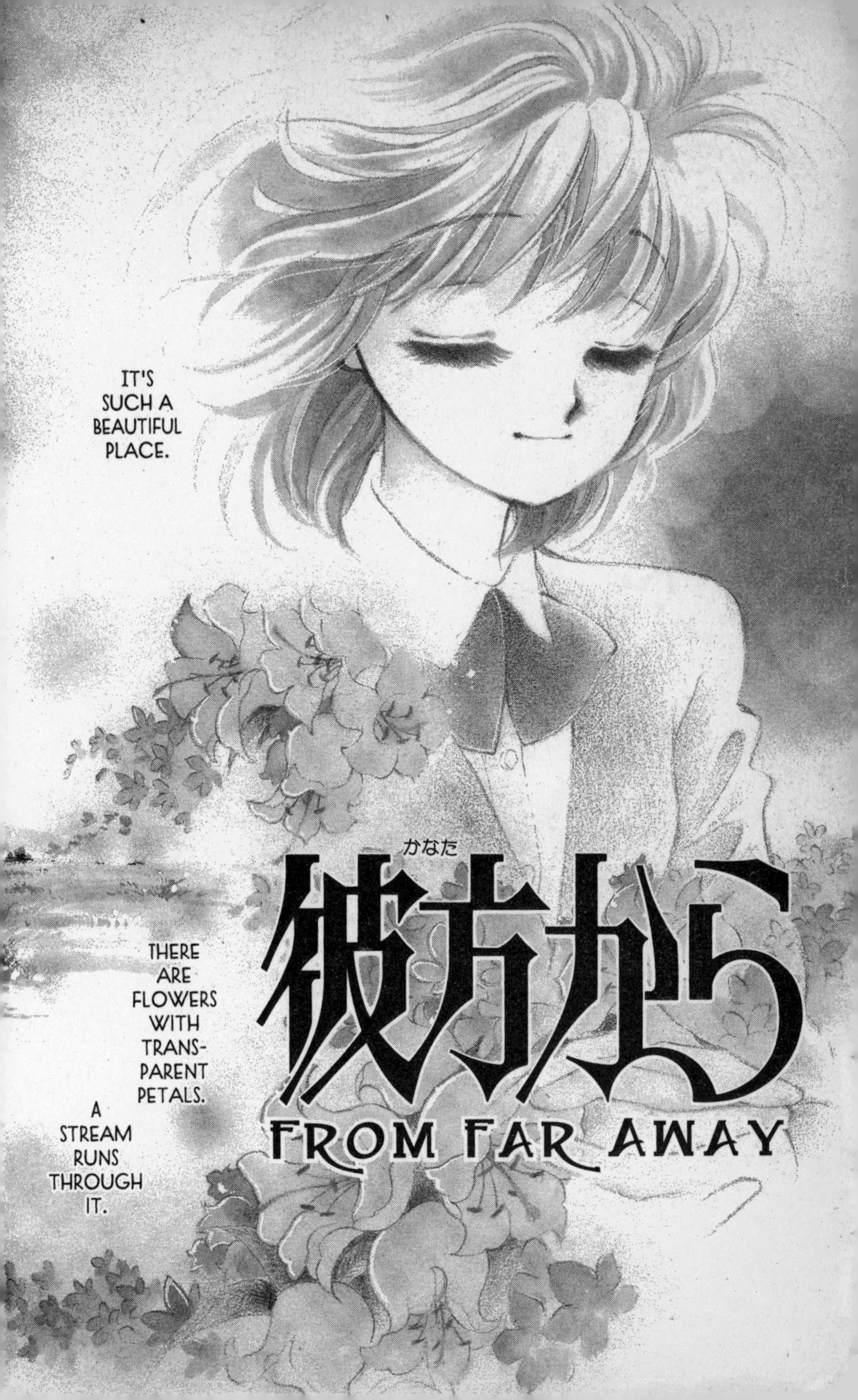
IT'S SUCH A BEAUTIFUL PLACE.
THERE ARE FLOWERS WITH TRANS-PARENT PETALS.
A STREAM RUNS THROUGH IT.
かなた
彼方から
FROM FAR AWAY

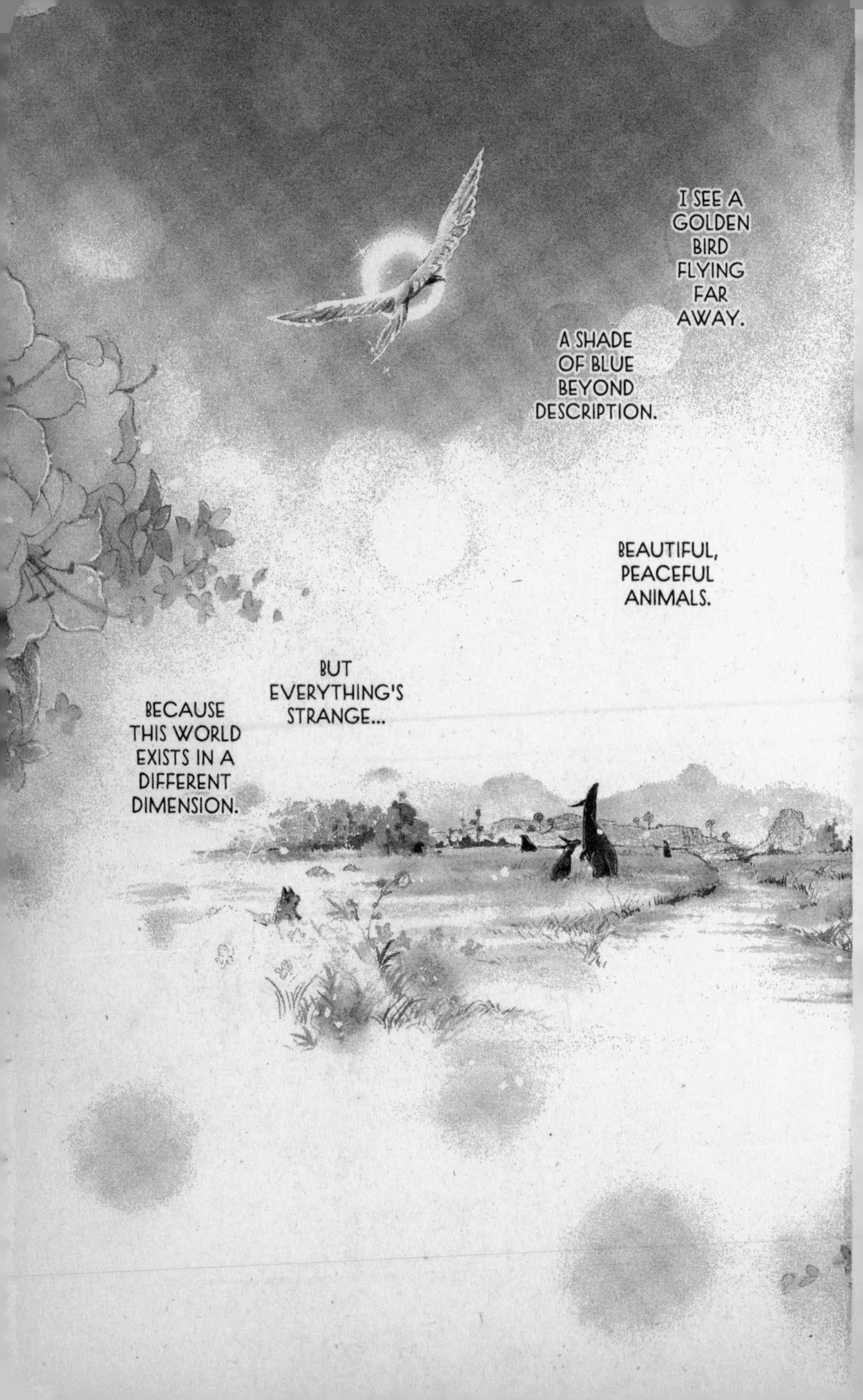
I SEE A GOLDEN BIRD FLYING FAR AWAY.
A SHADE OF BLUE BEYOND DESCRIPTION.
BEAUTIFUL, PEACEFUL ANIMALS.
BUT EVERYTHING'S STRANGE...
BECAUSE THIS WORLD EXISTS IN A DIFFERENT DIMENSION.

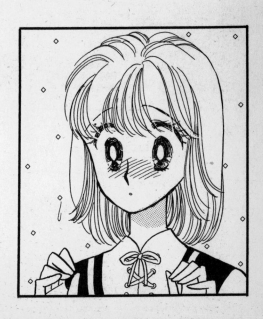

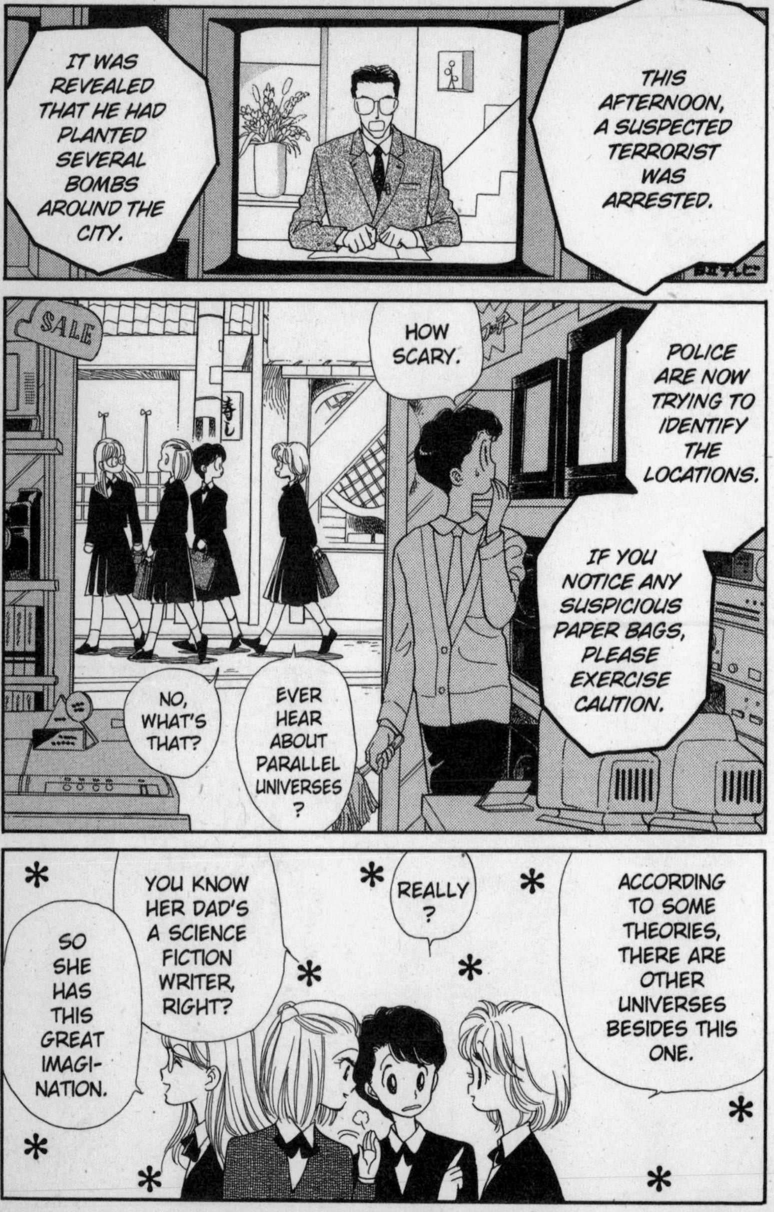
THIS AFTERNOON, A SUSPECTED TERRORIST WAS ARRESTED.
IT WAS REVEALED THAT HE HAD PLANTED SEVERAL BOMBS AROUND THE CITY.
POLICE ARE NOW TRYING TO IDENTIFY THE LOCATIONS.
HOW SCARY.
SALE
IF YOU NOTICE ANY SUSPICIOUS PAPER BAGS, PLEASE EXERCISE CAUTION.
EVER HEAR ABOUT PARALLEL UNIVERSES?
NO, WHAT'S THAT?
ACCORDING TO SOME THEORIES, THERE ARE OTHER UNIVERSES BESIDES THIS ONE.
REALLY?
YOU KNOW HER DAD'S A SCIENCE FICTION WRITER, RIGHT?
SO SHE HAS THIS GREAT IMAGINATION.

✱ This story is pure fiction. Any resemblance to real people, organizations or incidents is coincidental.

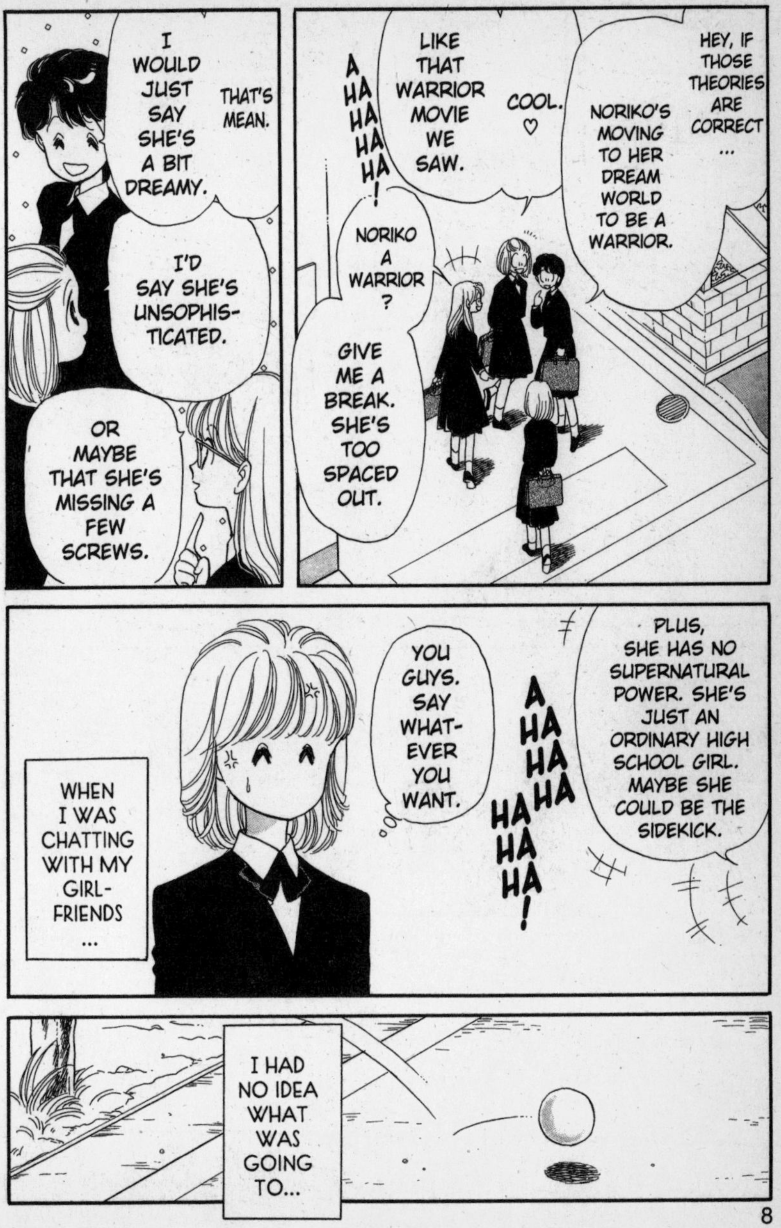
HEY, IF THOSE THEORIES ARE CORRECT ...
NORIKO'S MOVING TO HER DREAM WORLD TO BE A WARRIOR.
COOL. ♡
LIKE THAT WARRIOR MOVIE WE SAW.
AHAHAHAHA!
NORIKO A WARRIOR?
GIVE ME A BREAK. SHE'S TOO SPACED OUT.
THAT'S MEAN.
I WOULD JUST SAY SHE'S A BIT DREAMY.
I'D SAY SHE'S UNSOPHIS-TICATED.
OR MAYBE THAT SHE'S MISSING A FEW SCREWS.
PLUS, SHE HAS NO SUPERNATURAL POWER. SHE'S JUST AN ORDINARY HIGH SCHOOL GIRL. MAYBE SHE COULD BE THE SIDEKICK.
AHAHAHA HAHAHA!
YOU GUYS. SAY WHAT-EVER YOU WANT.
WHEN I WAS CHATTING WITH MY GIRL-FRIENDS ...
I HAD NO IDEA WHAT WAS GOING TO...

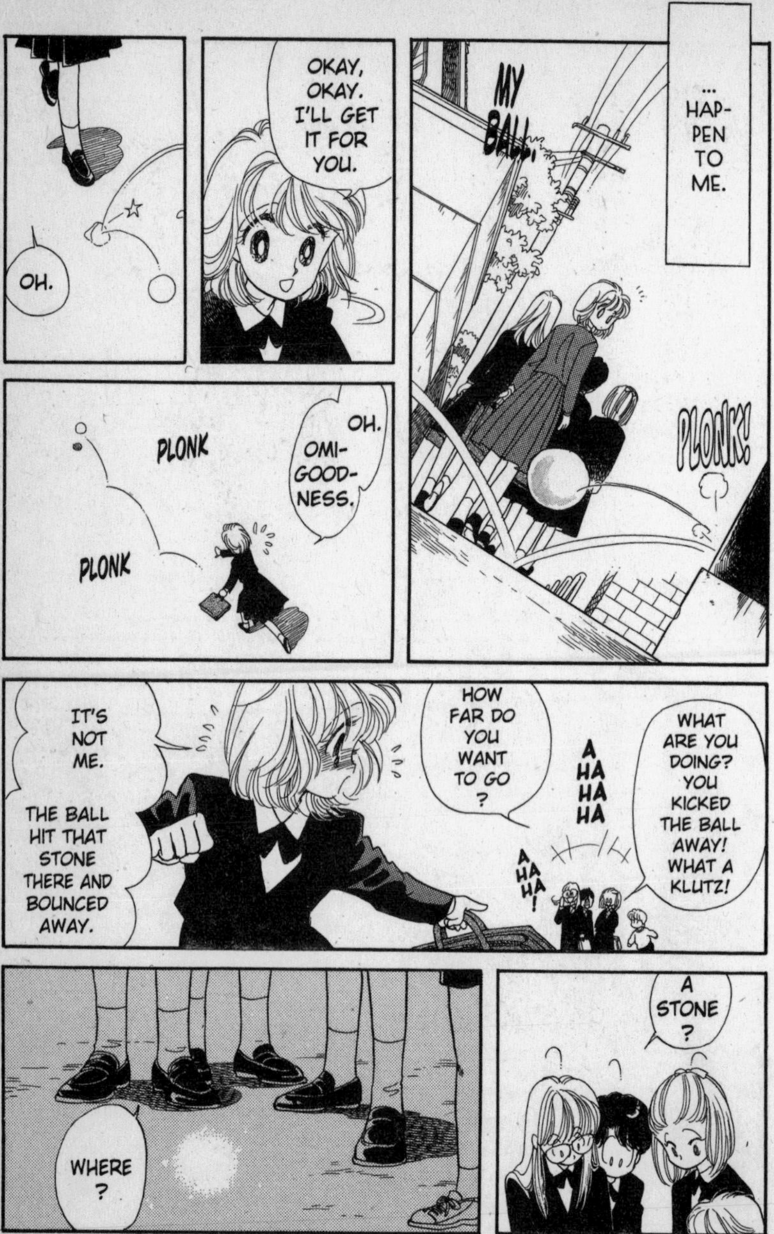
... HAP-PEN TO ME.
MY BALL.
PLONK!
OKAY, OKAY. I'LL GET IT FOR YOU.
OH.
OH. OMI-GOOD-NESS.
PLONK
PLONK
WHAT ARE YOU DOING? YOU KICKED THE BALL AWAY! WHAT A KLUTZ!
AHAHAHAHA
HOW FAR DO YOU WANT TO GO ?
AHAHA!
IT'S NOT ME.
THE BALL HIT THAT STONE THERE AND BOUNCED AWAY.
A STONE ?
WHERE ?

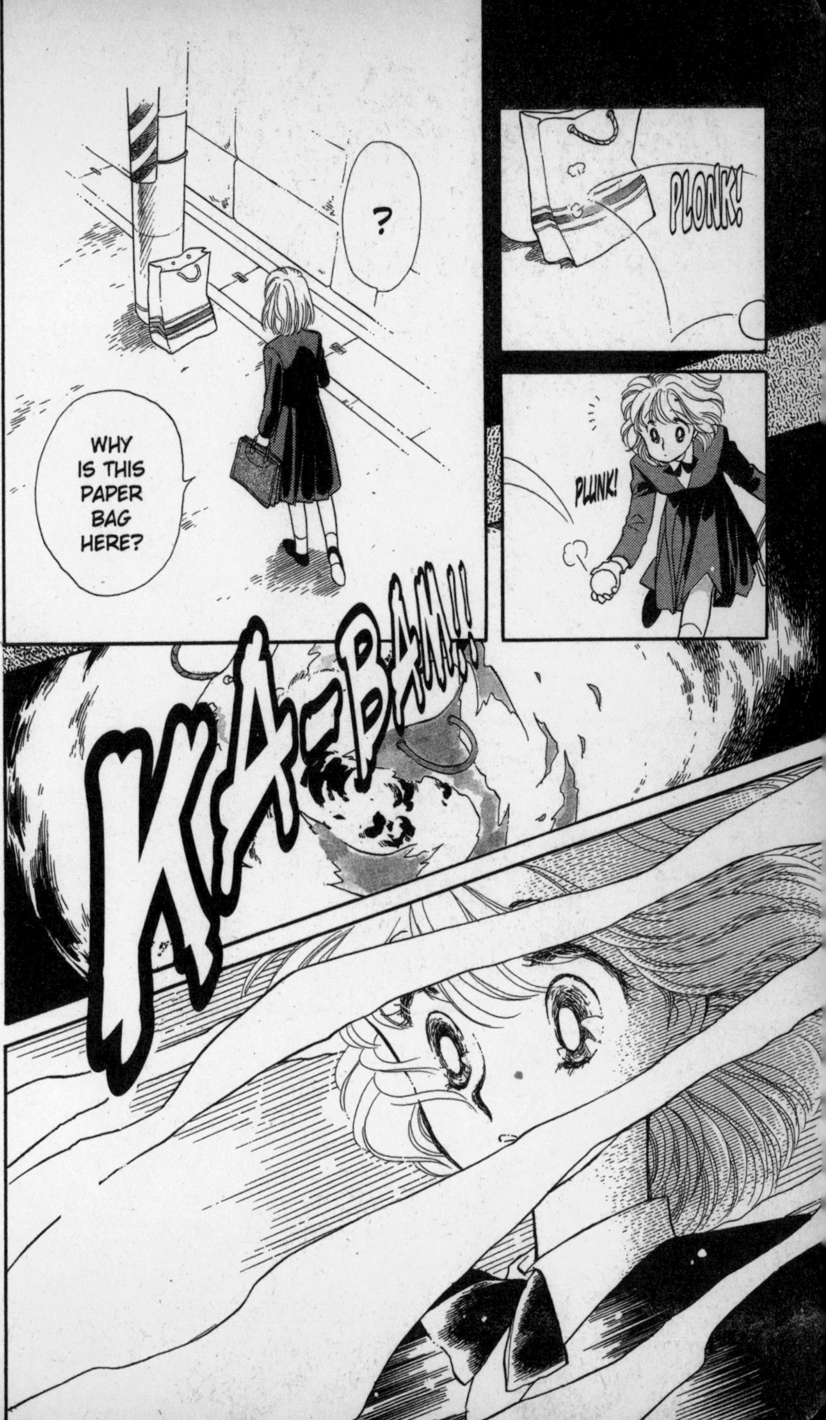
PLONK!
PLUNK!
?
WHY IS THIS PAPER BAG HERE?
KA-BAM!!

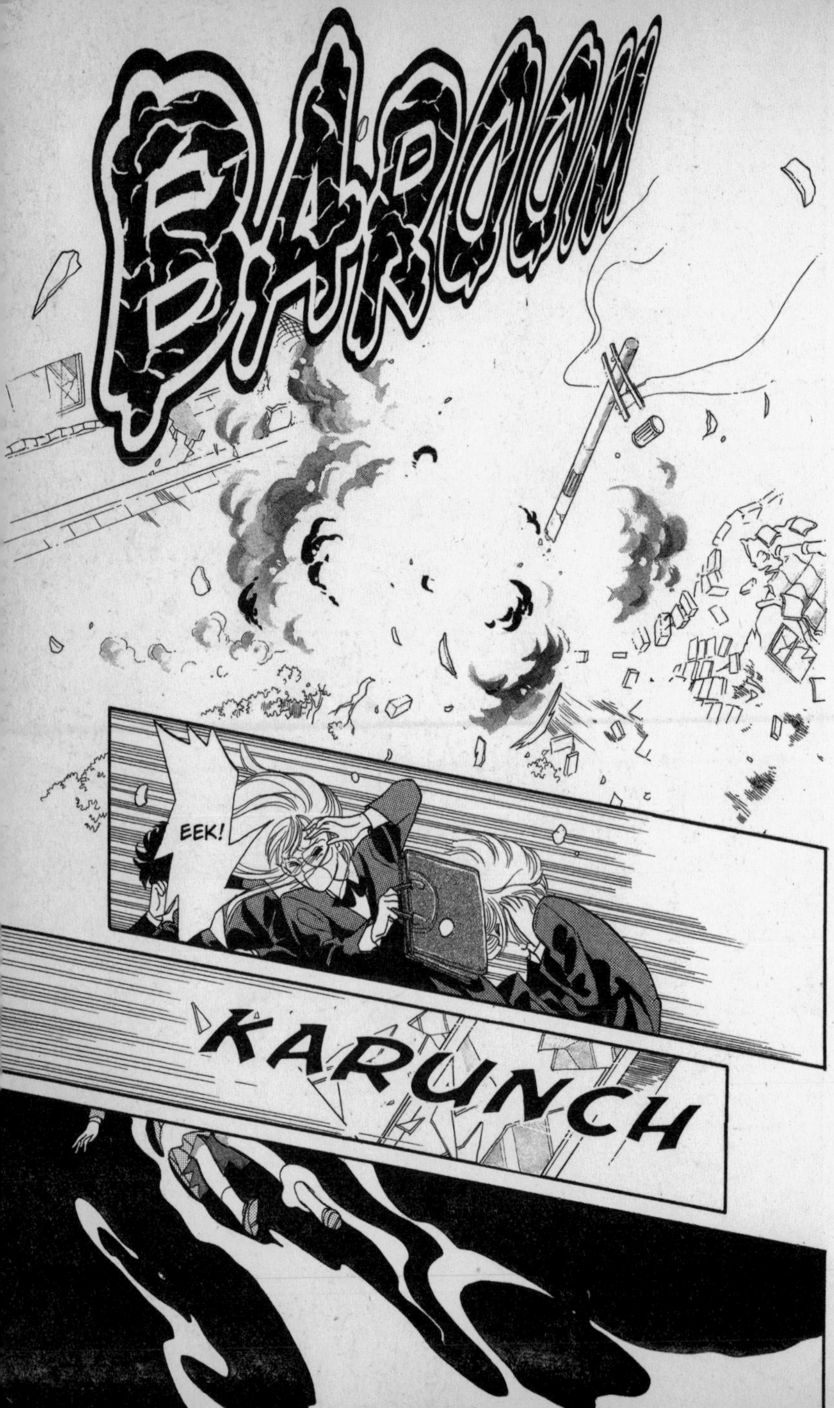
BABOOM
EEK!
KARUNCH

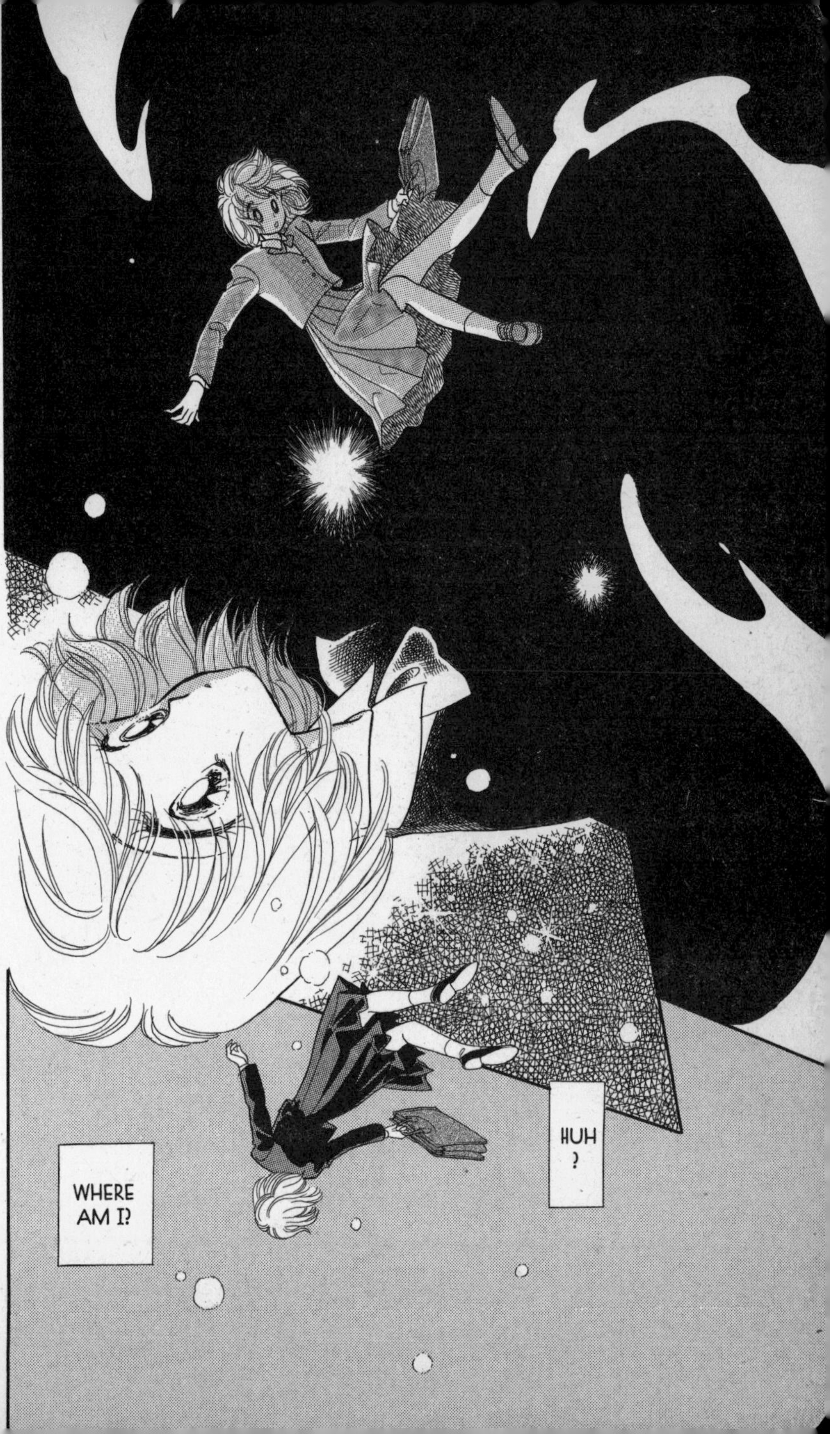
HUH?
WHERE AM I?

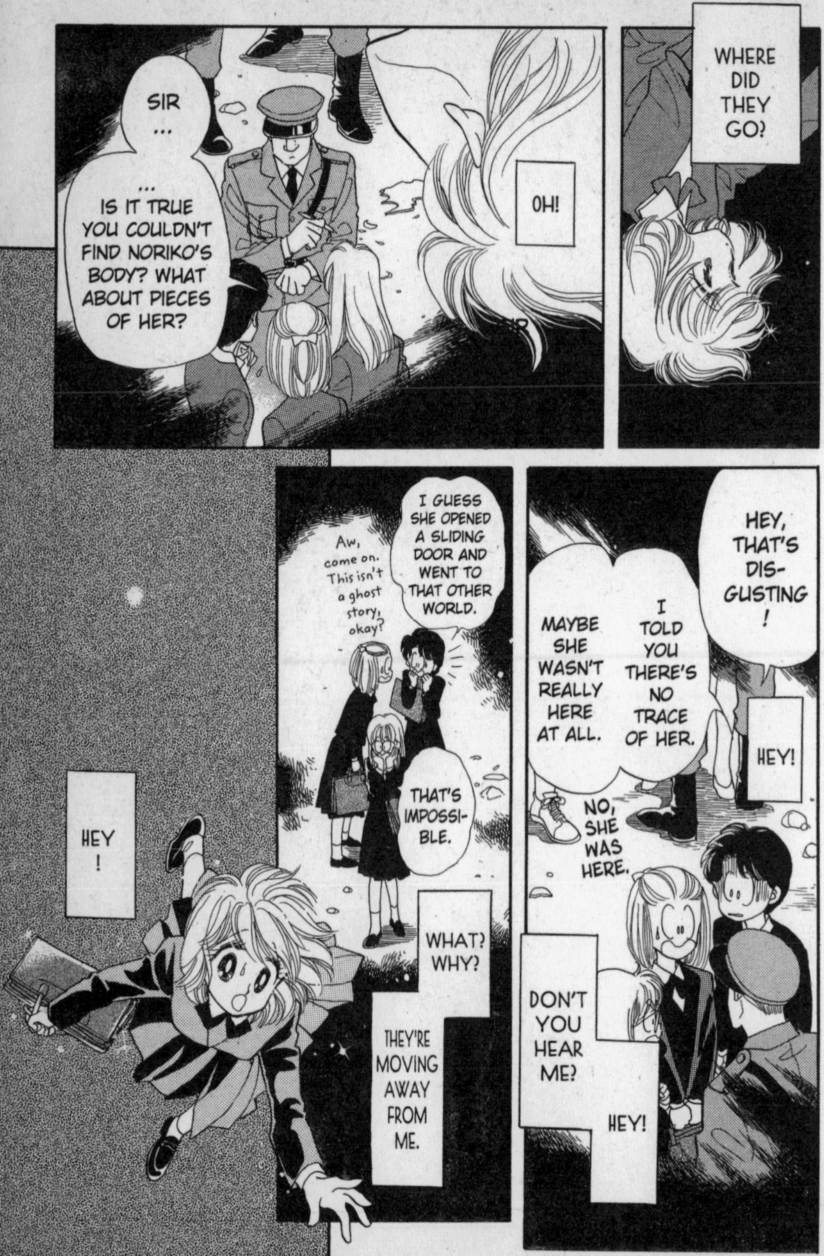
WHERE DID THEY GO?
OH!
SIR ... ... IS IT TRUE YOU COULDN'T FIND NORIKO'S BODY? WHAT ABOUT PIECES OF HER?
HEY, THAT'S DIS-GUSTING!
HEY!
I TOLD YOU THERE'S NO TRACE OF HER.
MAYBE SHE WASN'T REALLY HERE AT ALL.
NO, SHE WAS HERE.
DON'T YOU HEAR ME?
HEY!
I GUESS SHE OPENED A SLIDING DOOR AND WENT TO THAT OTHER WORLD.
Aw, come on. This isn't a ghost story, okay?
THAT'S IMPOSSI-BLE.
WHAT? WHY?
THEY'RE MOVING AWAY FROM ME.
HEY!

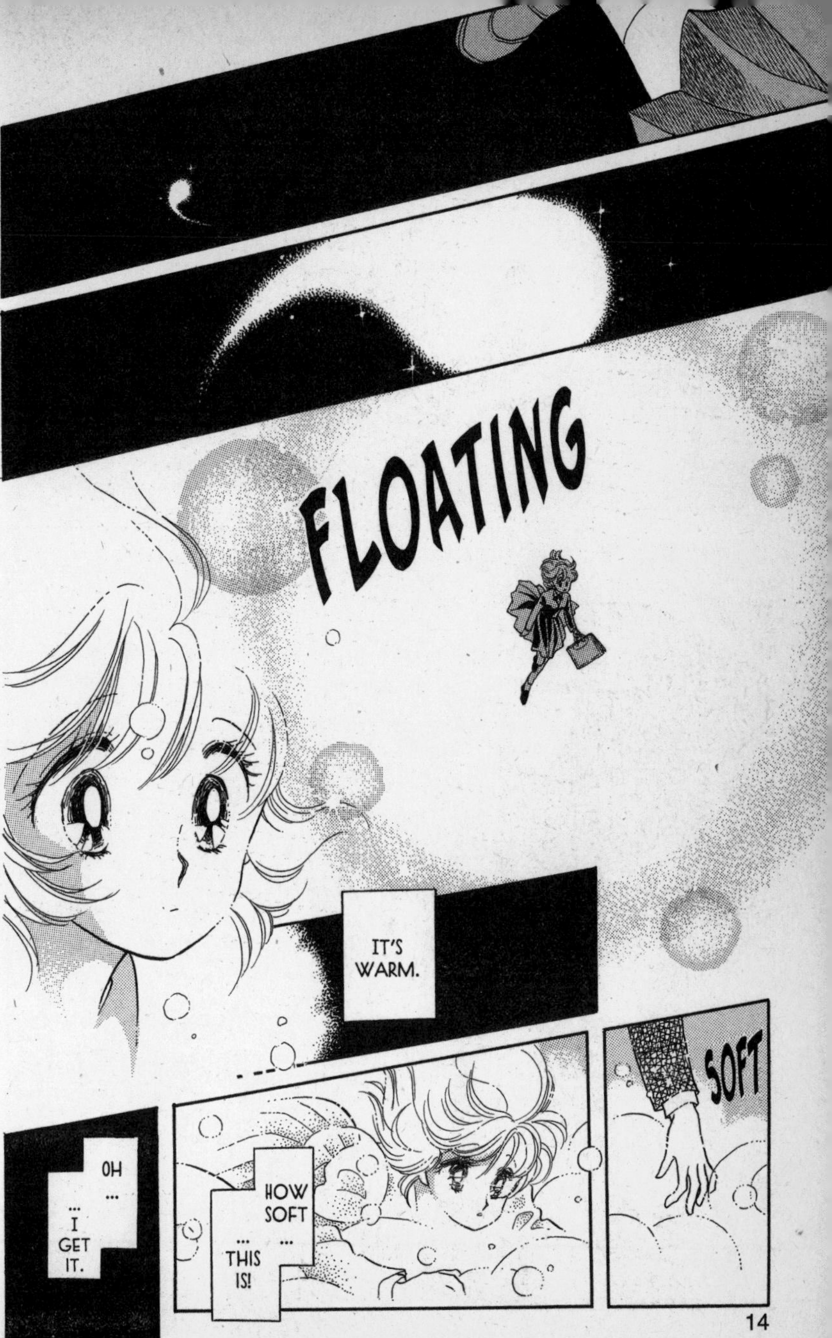
FLOATING
IT'S WARM.
SOFT
HOW SOFT ... ... THIS IS!
OH ... ... I GET IT.

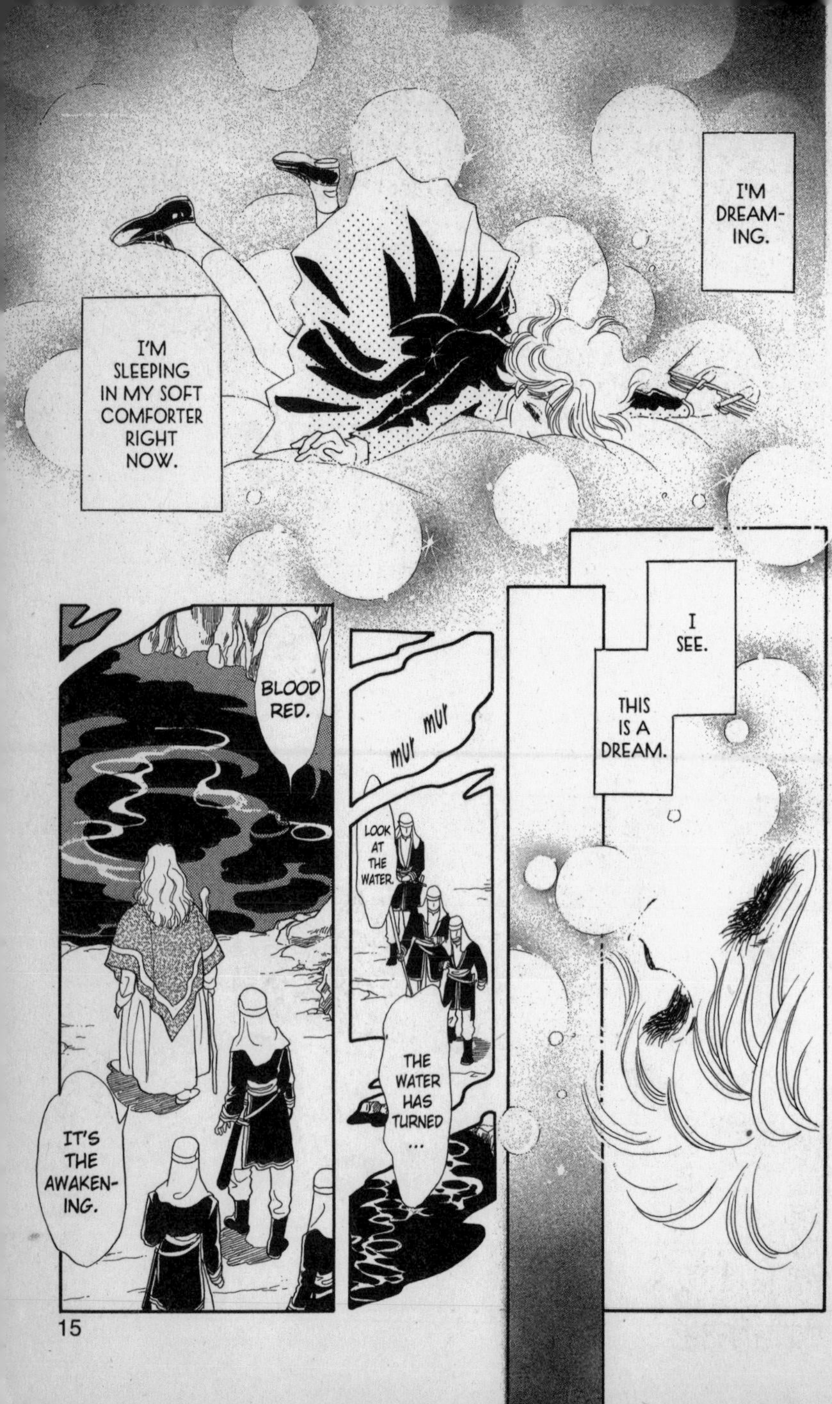
I'M DREAMING.
I'M SLEEPING IN MY SOFT COMFORTER RIGHT NOW.
I SEE.
THIS IS A DREAM.
mur mur
LOOK AT THE WATER.
THE WATER HAS TURNED ...
BLOOD RED.
IT'S THE AWAKENING.

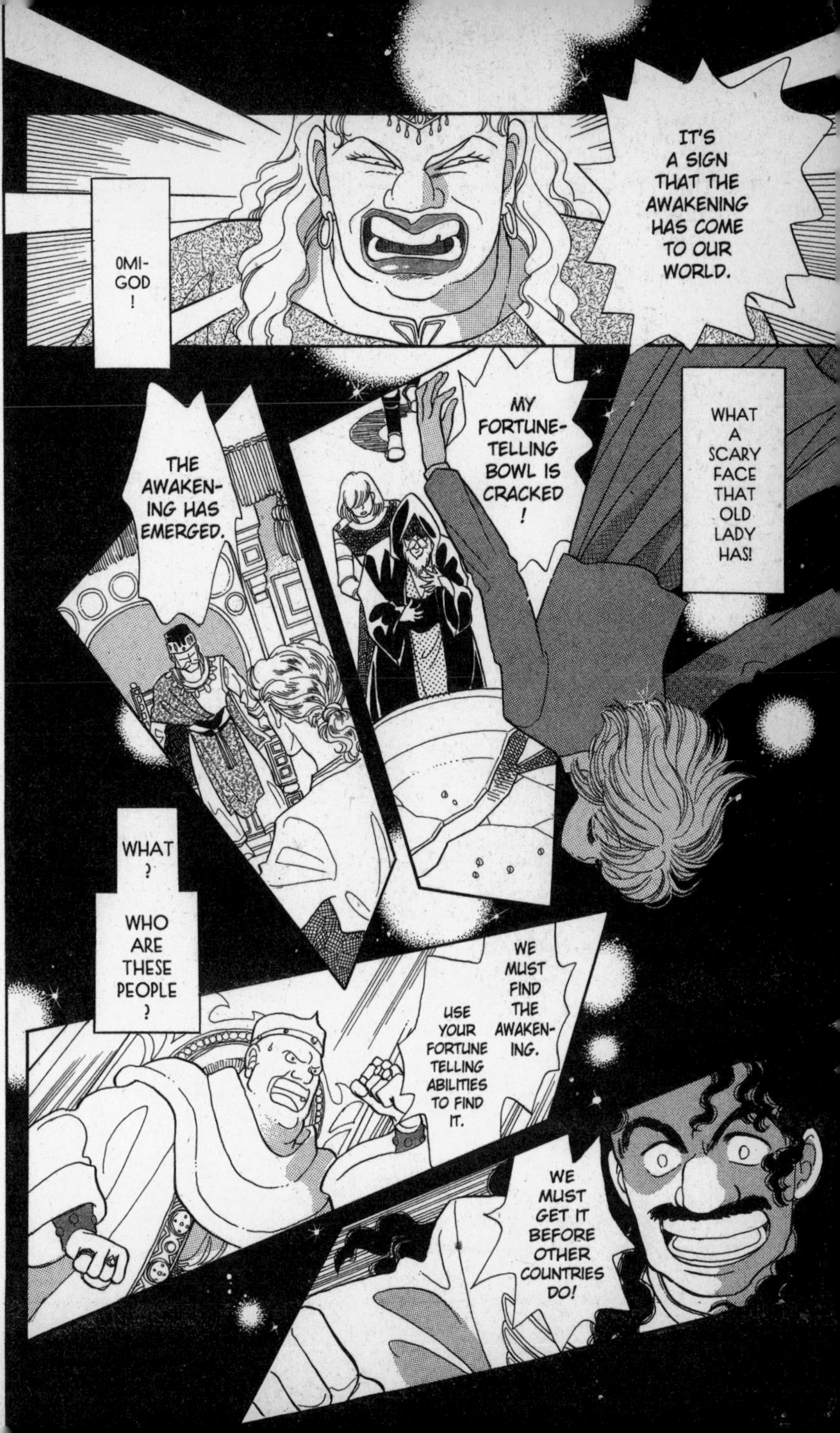
IT'S A SIGN THAT THE AWAKENING HAS COME TO OUR WORLD.
OMI-GOD!
WHAT A SCARY FACE THAT OLD LADY HAS!
MY FORTUNE-TELLING BOWL IS CRACKED!
THE AWAKEN-ING HAS EMERGED.
WHAT?
WHO ARE THESE PEOPLE?
WE MUST FIND THE AWAKEN-ING.
USE YOUR FORTUNE TELLING ABILITIES TO FIND IT.
WE MUST GET IT BEFORE OTHER COUNTRIES DO!

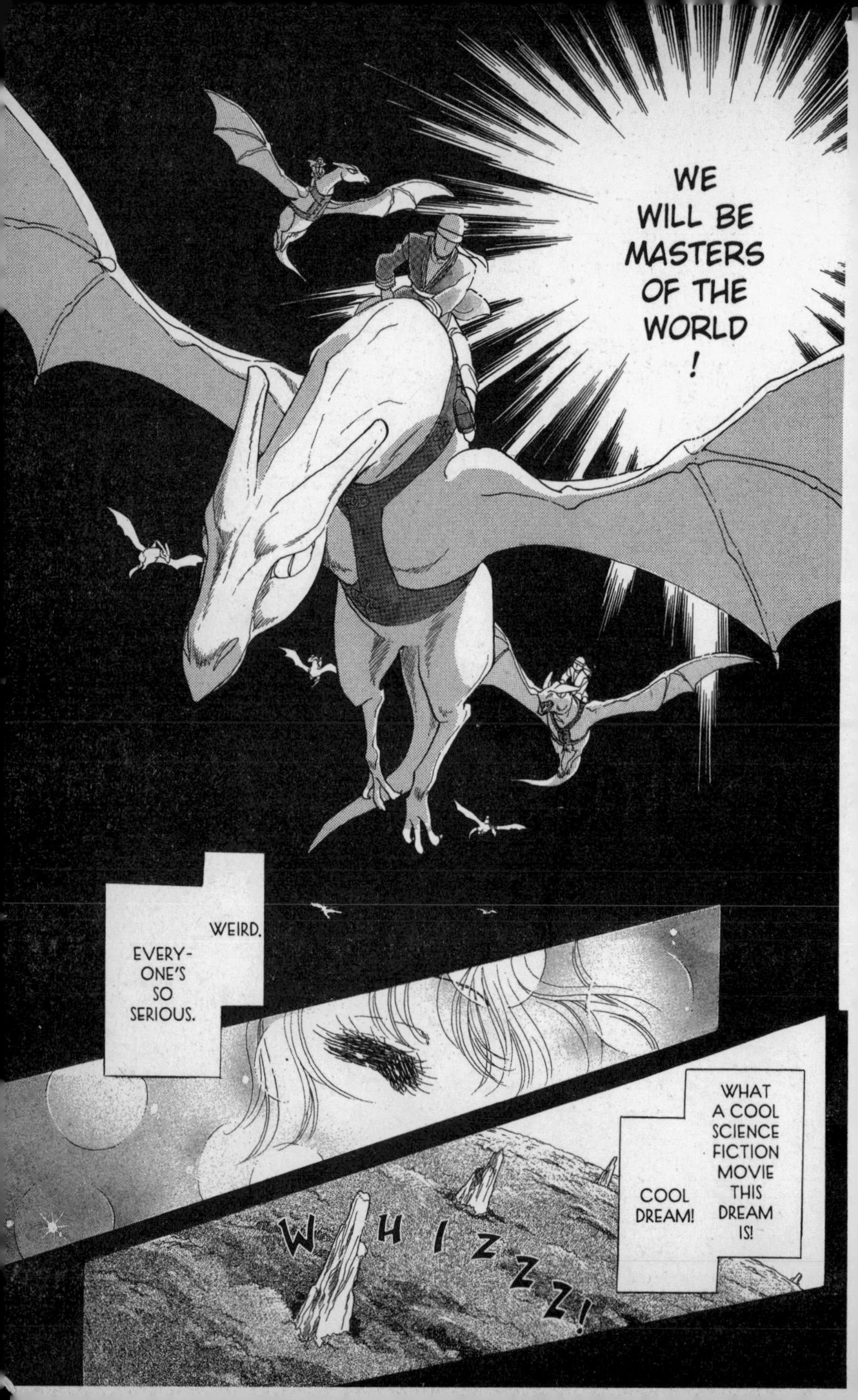
WE WILL BE MASTERS OF THE WORLD!
WEIRD.
EVERYONE'S SO SERIOUS.
WHAT A COOL SCIENCE FICTION MOVIE THIS DREAM IS!
COOL DREAM!
WHIZZZZ!

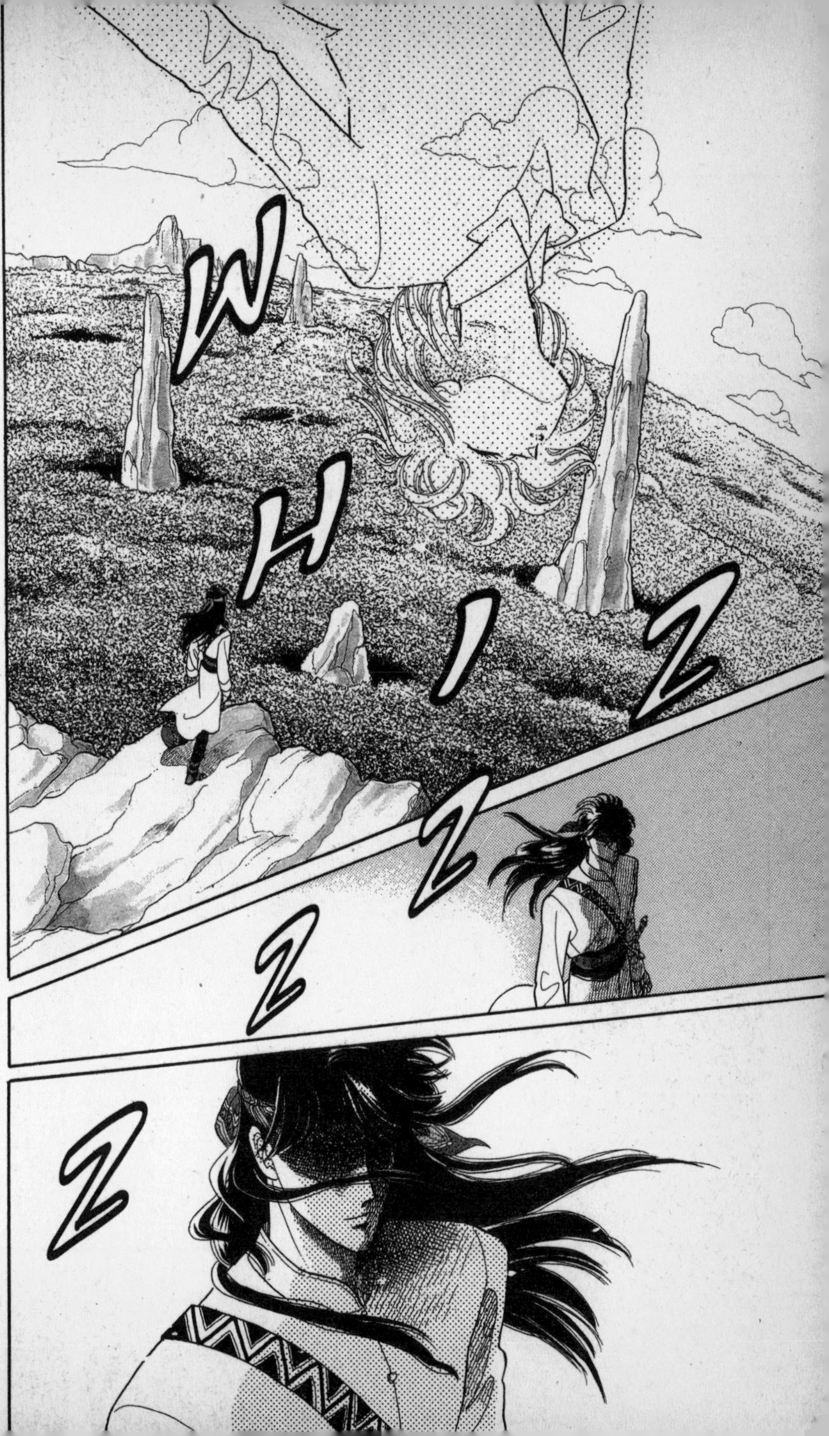
WHIZZZZ

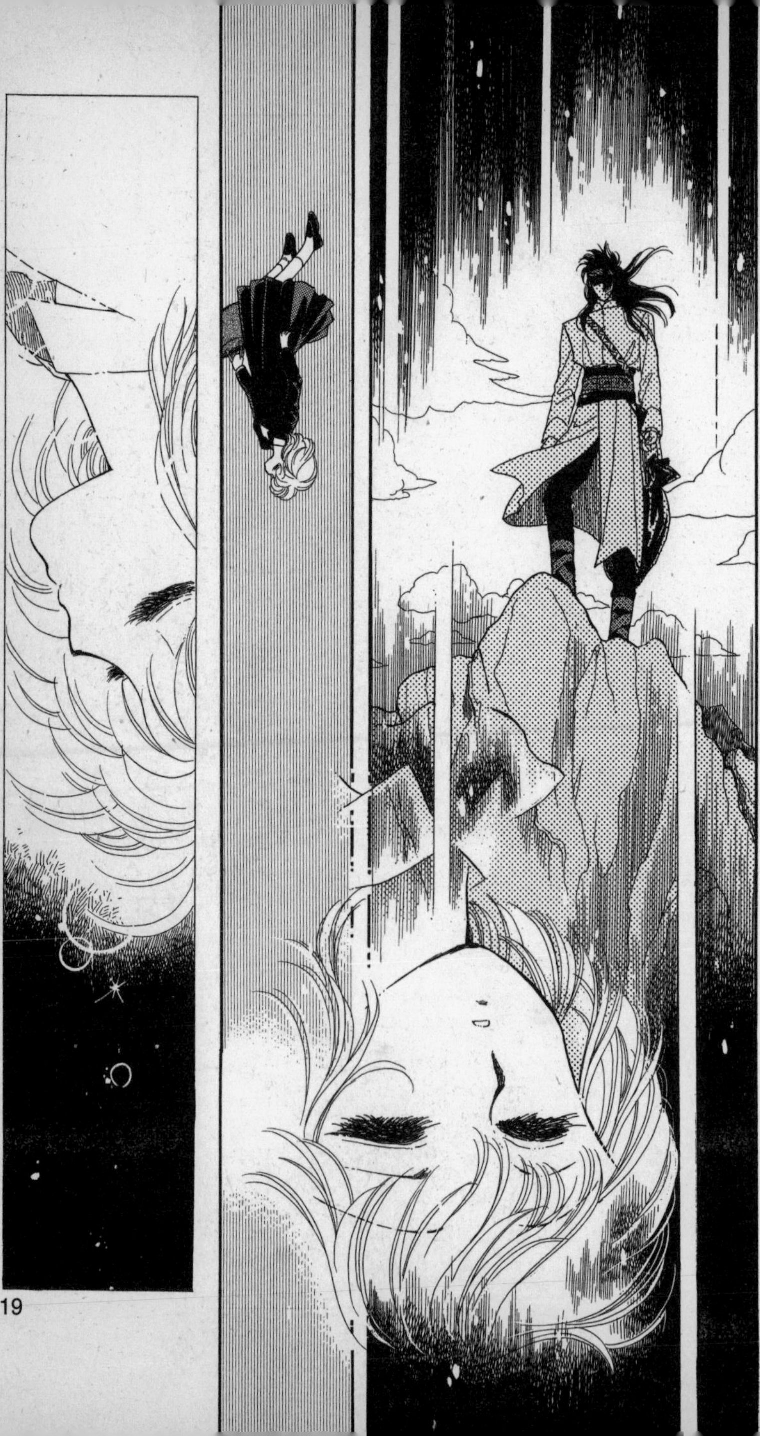

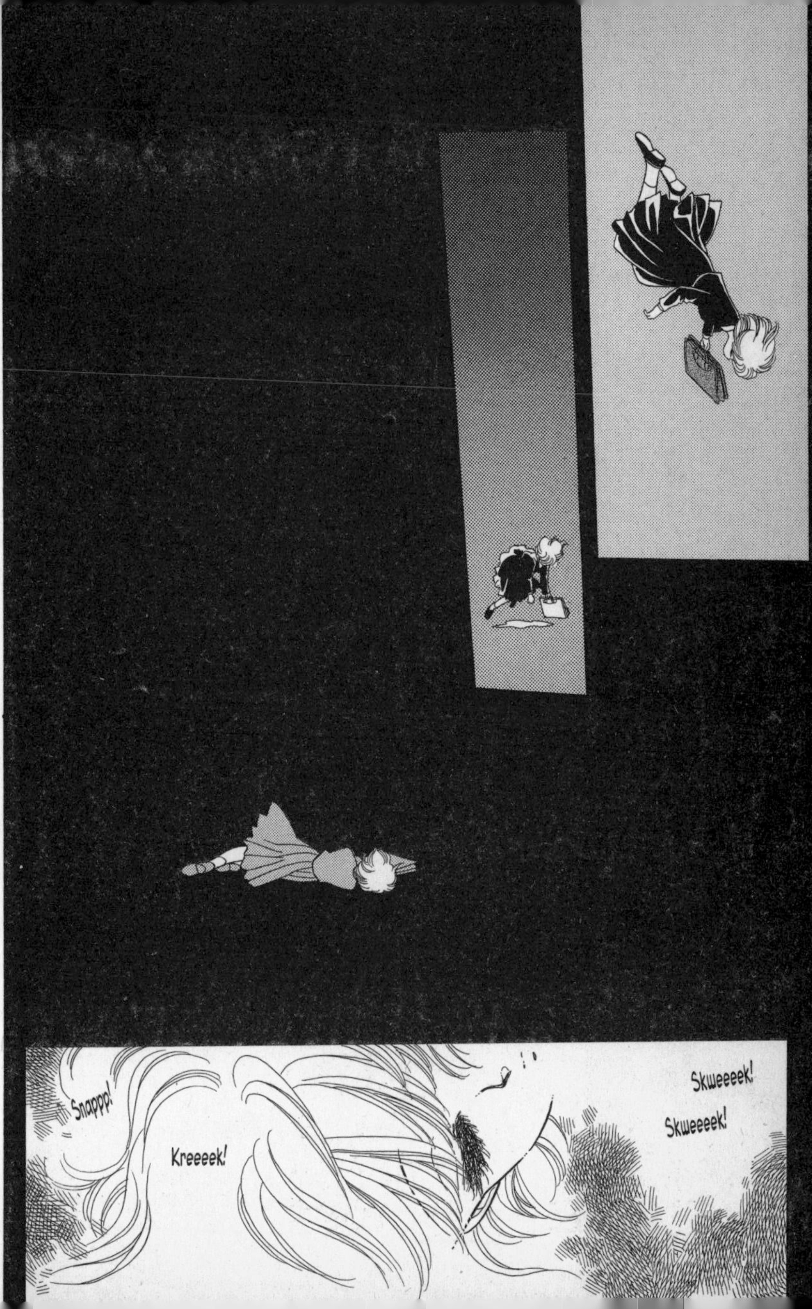
Skweeeek!
Skweeeek!
Snappp!
Kreeeek!

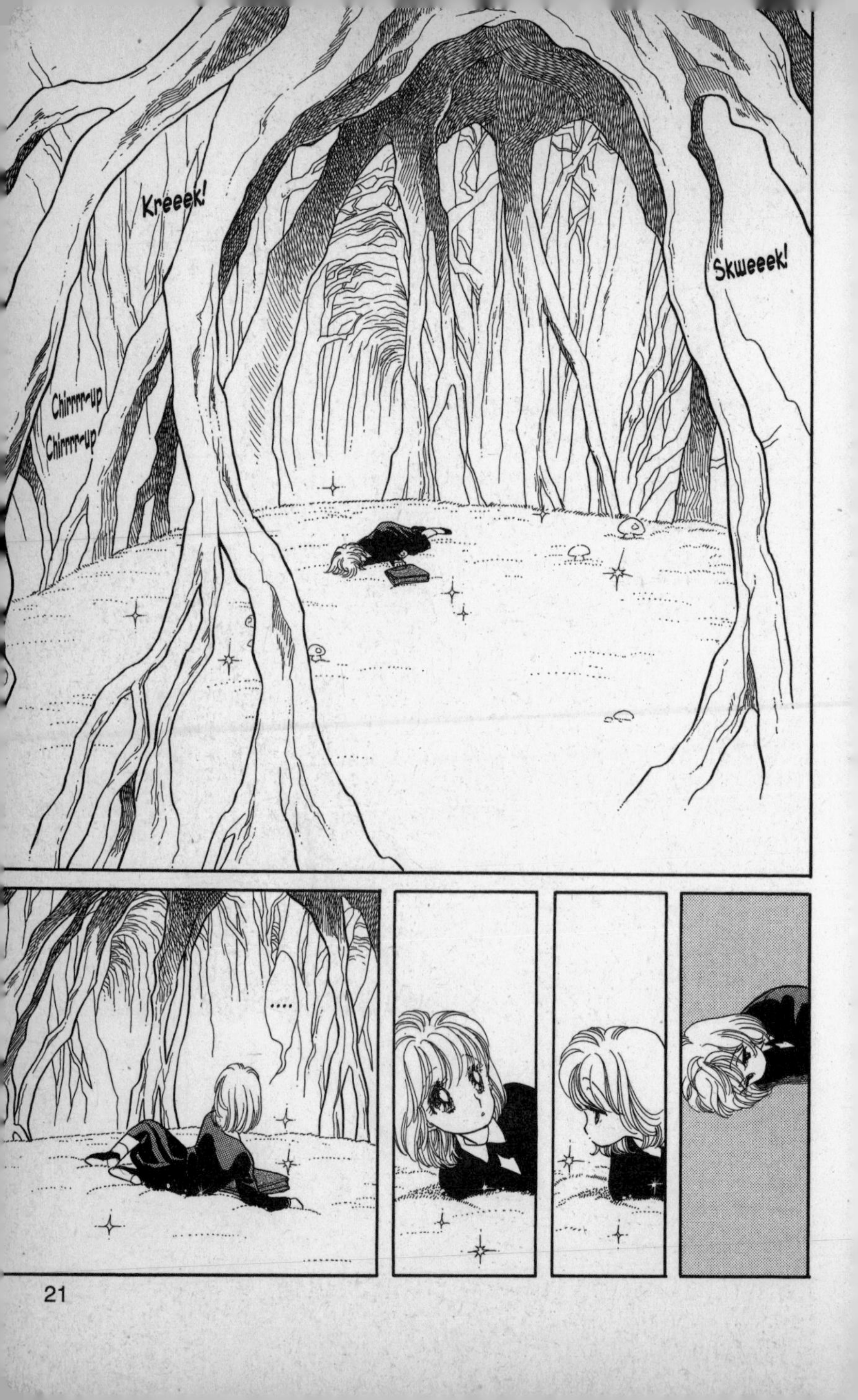
Skweeek!
Kreeek!
Chirrrr-up
Chirrrr-up
....

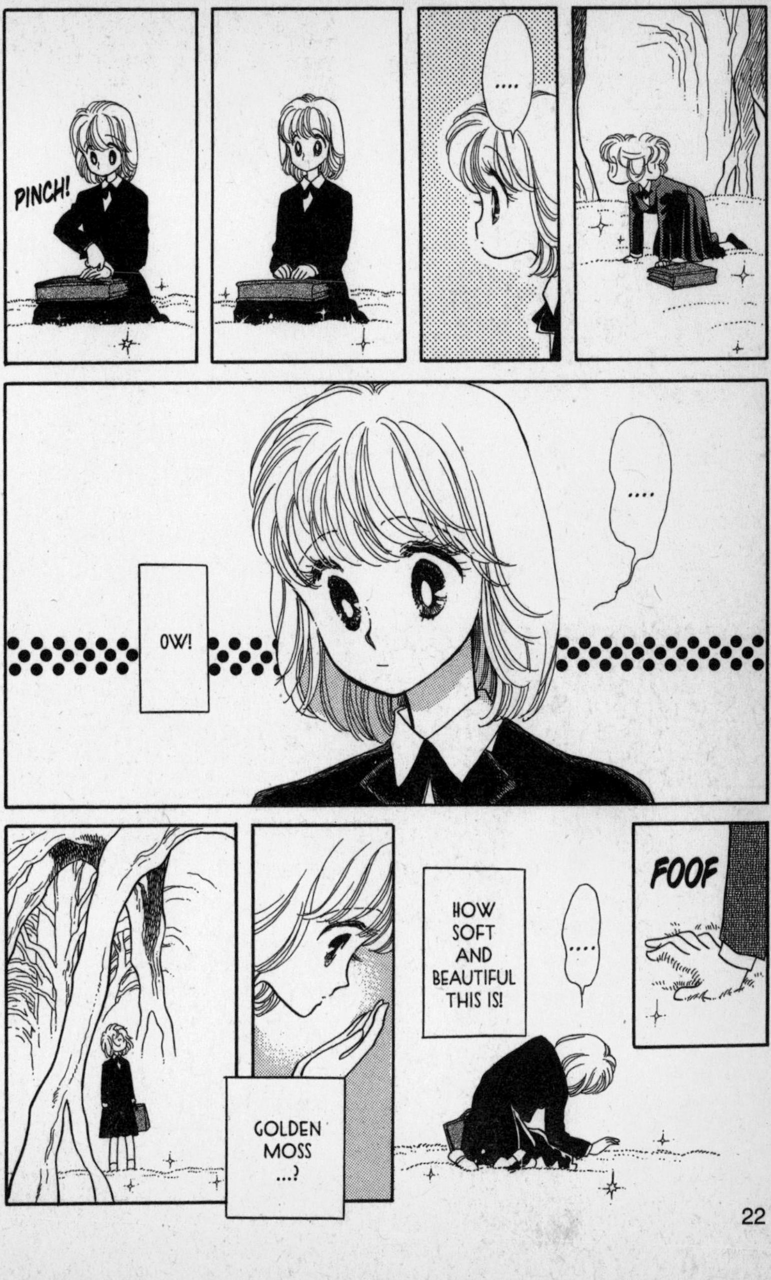
....
PINCH!
....
OW!
FOOF
....
HOW SOFT AND BEAUTIFUL THIS IS!
GOLDEN MOSS ...?

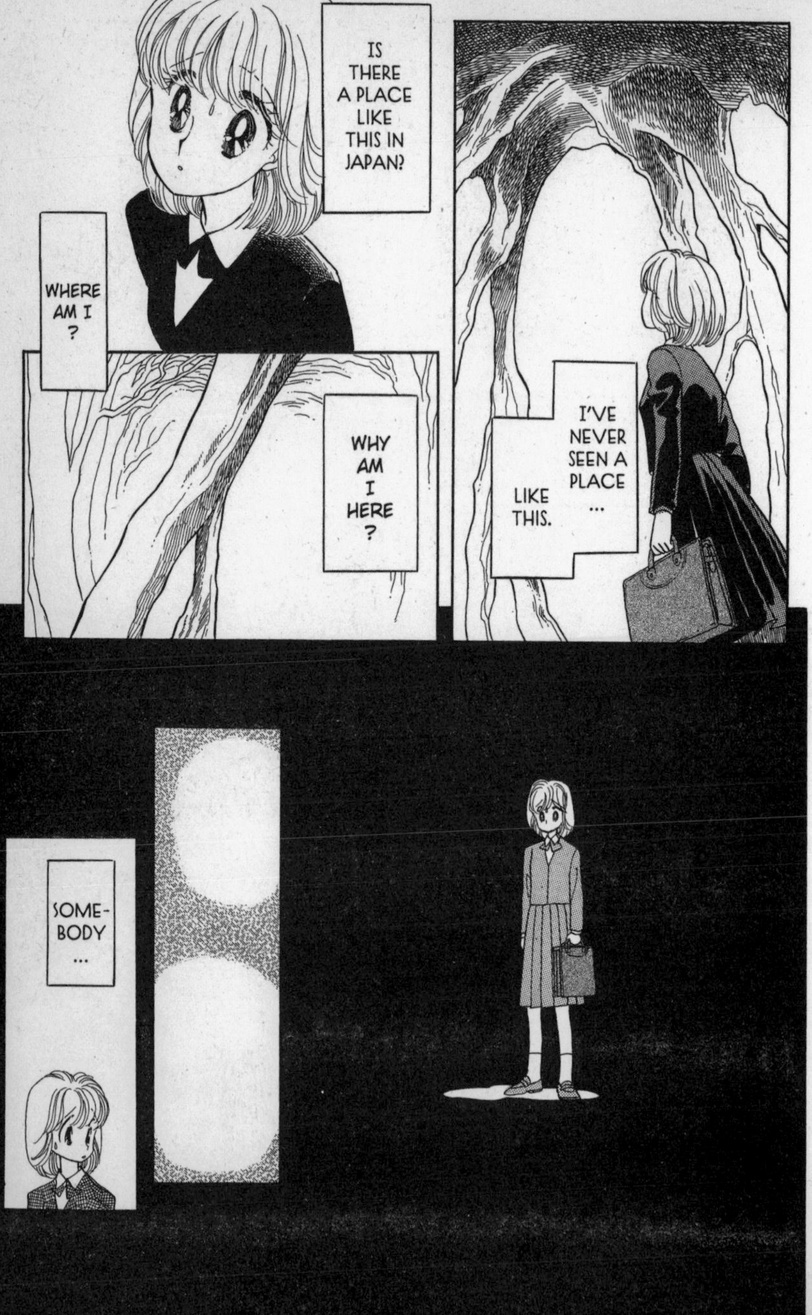
I'VE NEVER SEEN A PLACE ... LIKE THIS.
IS THERE A PLACE LIKE THIS IN JAPAN?
WHERE AM I ?
WHY AM I HERE ?
SOME-BODY ...

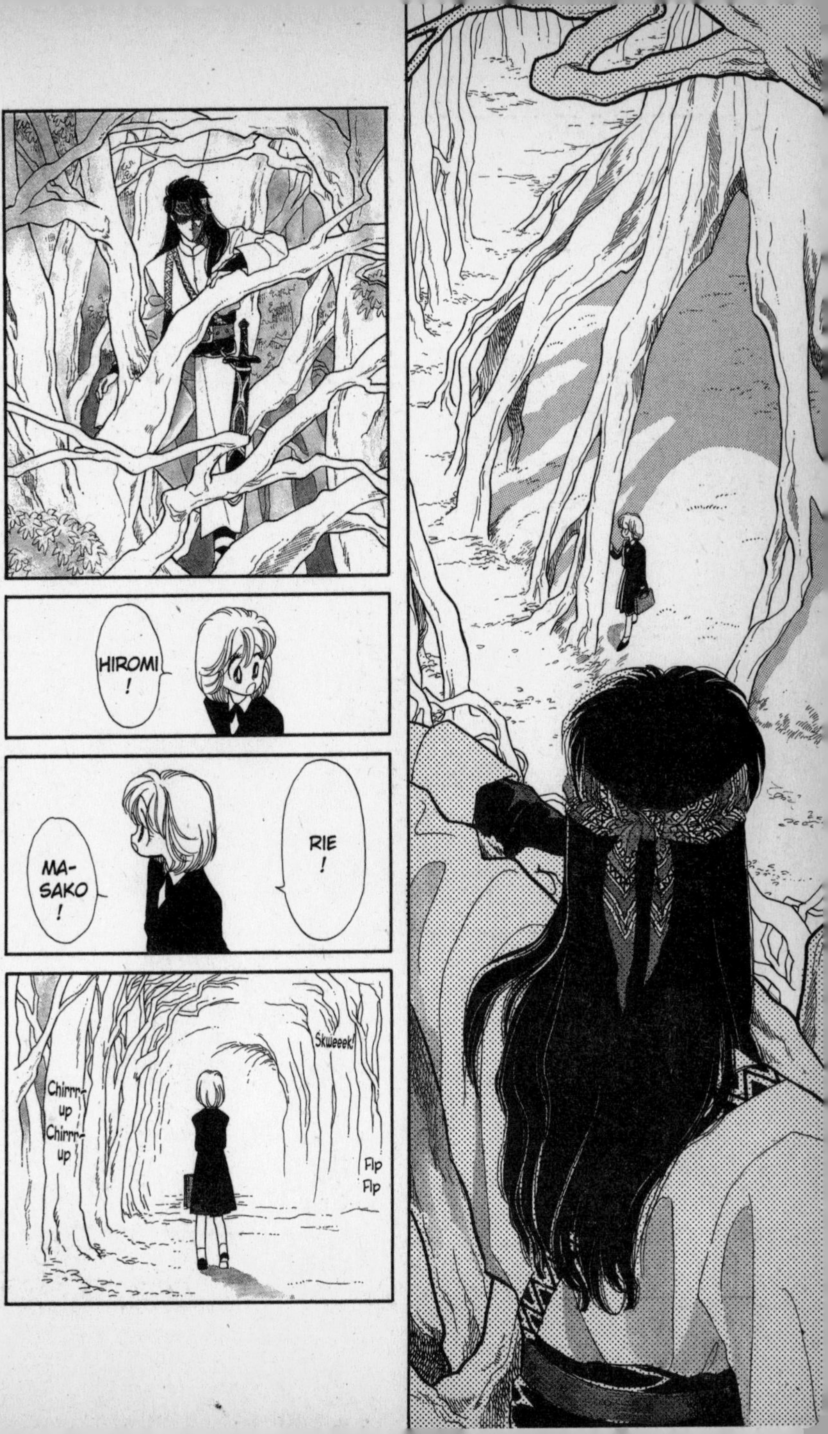
HIROMI!
RIE!
MA-SAKO!
Skweeek!
Chirrr-up Chirrr-up
Flp Flp

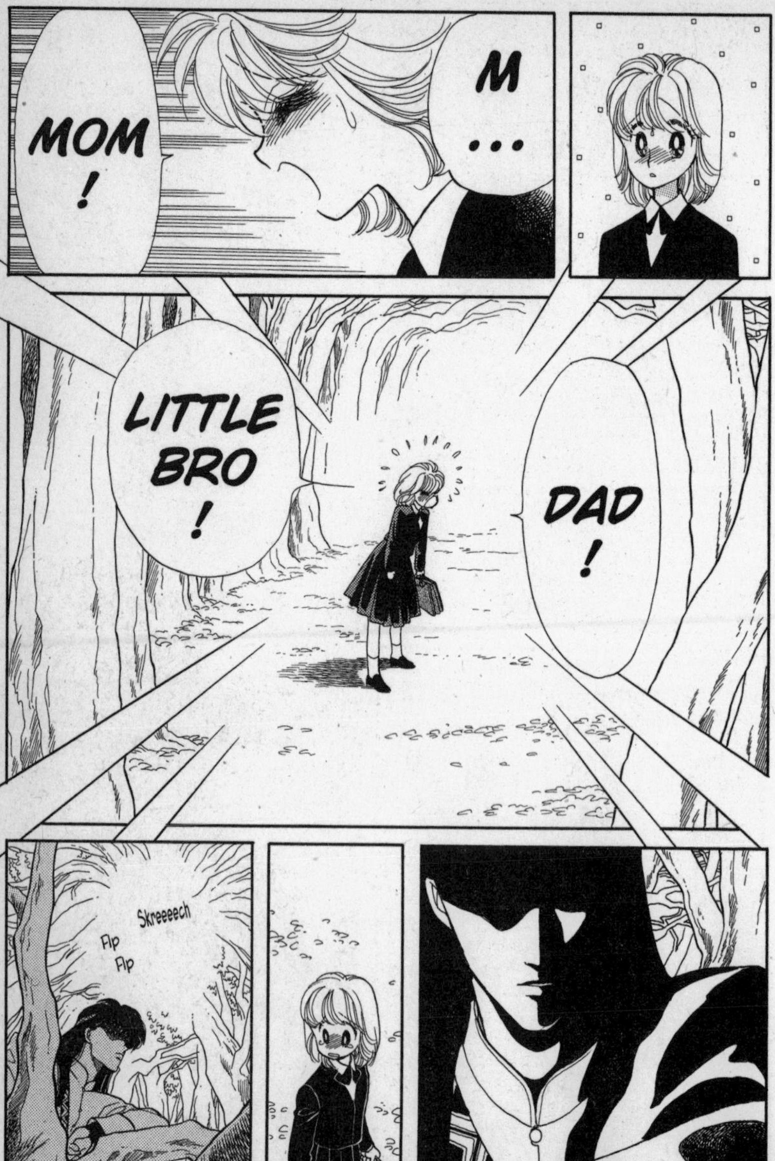
M ...
MOM !
DAD !
LITTLE BRO !
Skreeeech
Flp
Flp

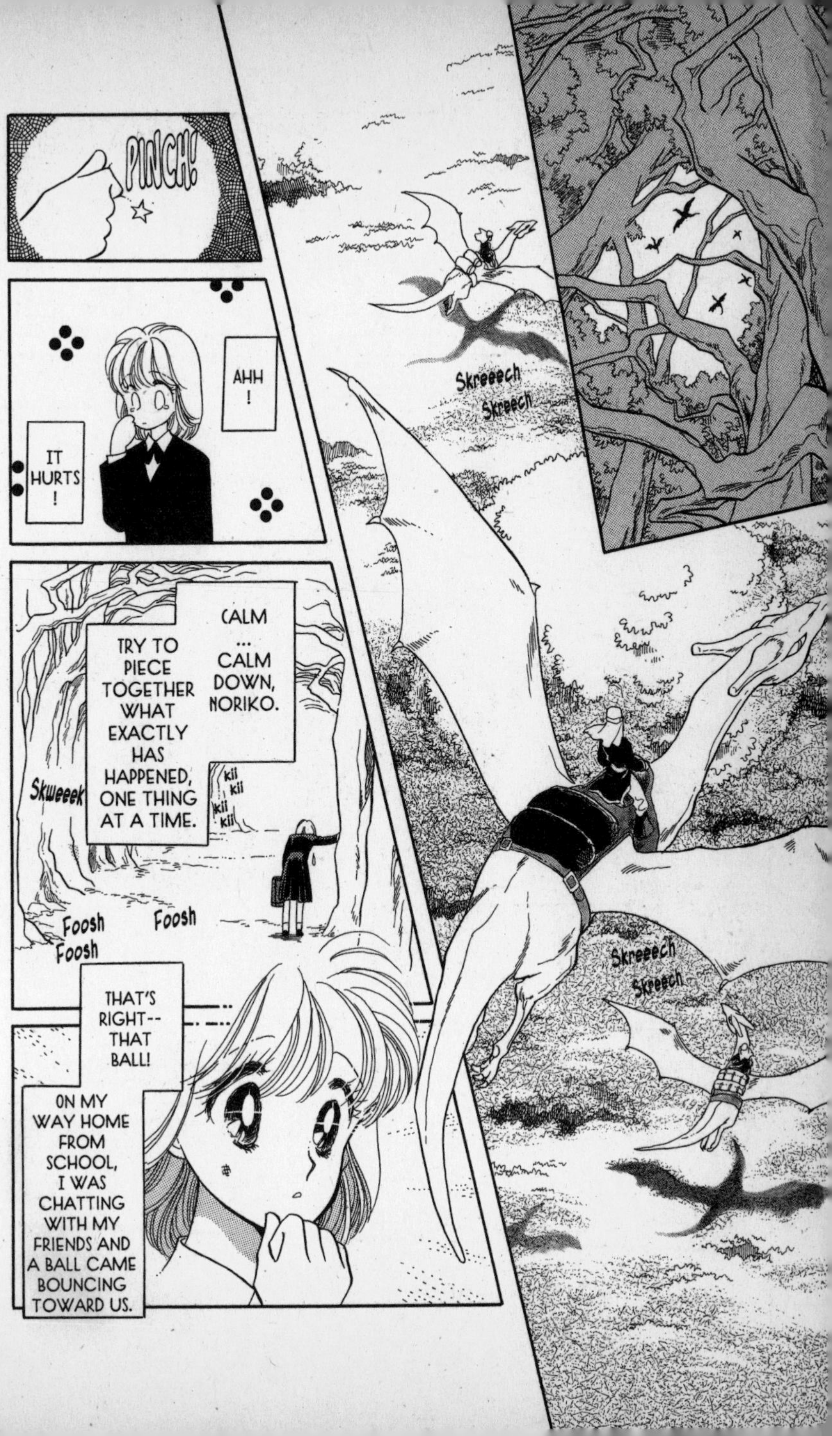
Skreeech
Skreech
Skreeech
Skreech
PINCH!
AHH!
IT HURTS!
CALM ... CALM DOWN, NORIKO.
TRY TO PIECE TOGETHER WHAT EXACTLY HAS HAPPENED, ONE THING AT A TIME.
kii kii kii kii
Skweeek
Foosh
Foosh
Foosh
THAT'S RIGHT-- THAT BALL!
ON MY WAY HOME FROM SCHOOL, I WAS CHATTING WITH MY FRIENDS AND A BALL CAME BOUNCING TOWARD US.

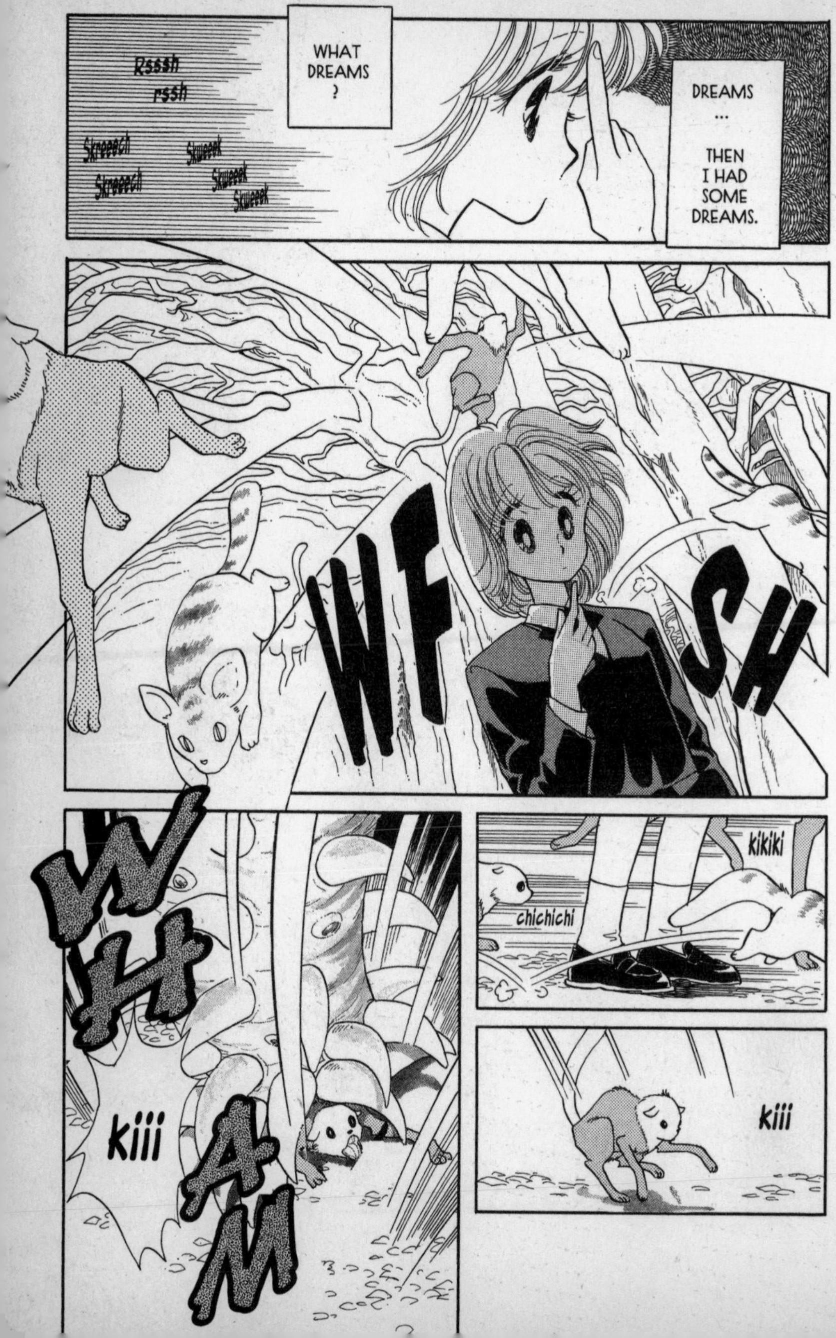
DREAMS ... THEN I HAD SOME DREAMS.
WHAT DREAMS ?
Rsssh rssh
Skweeek Skweeek Skweeek
Skreeech Skreeech
WFSH
kikiki
chichichi
kiii
WHAM
kiii

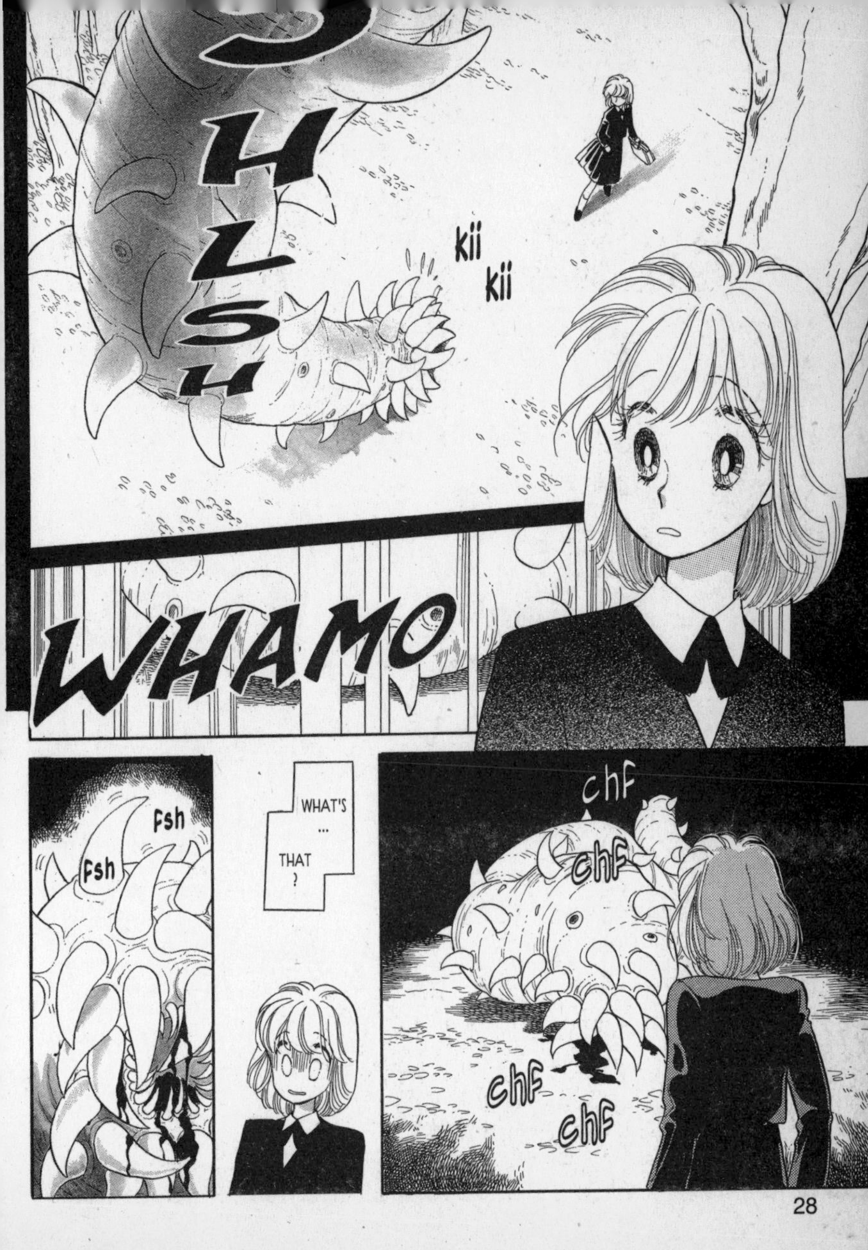
HLSH
kii
kii
WHAMO
chF
chF
chF
chF
WHAT'S ... THAT ?
Fsh
Fsh

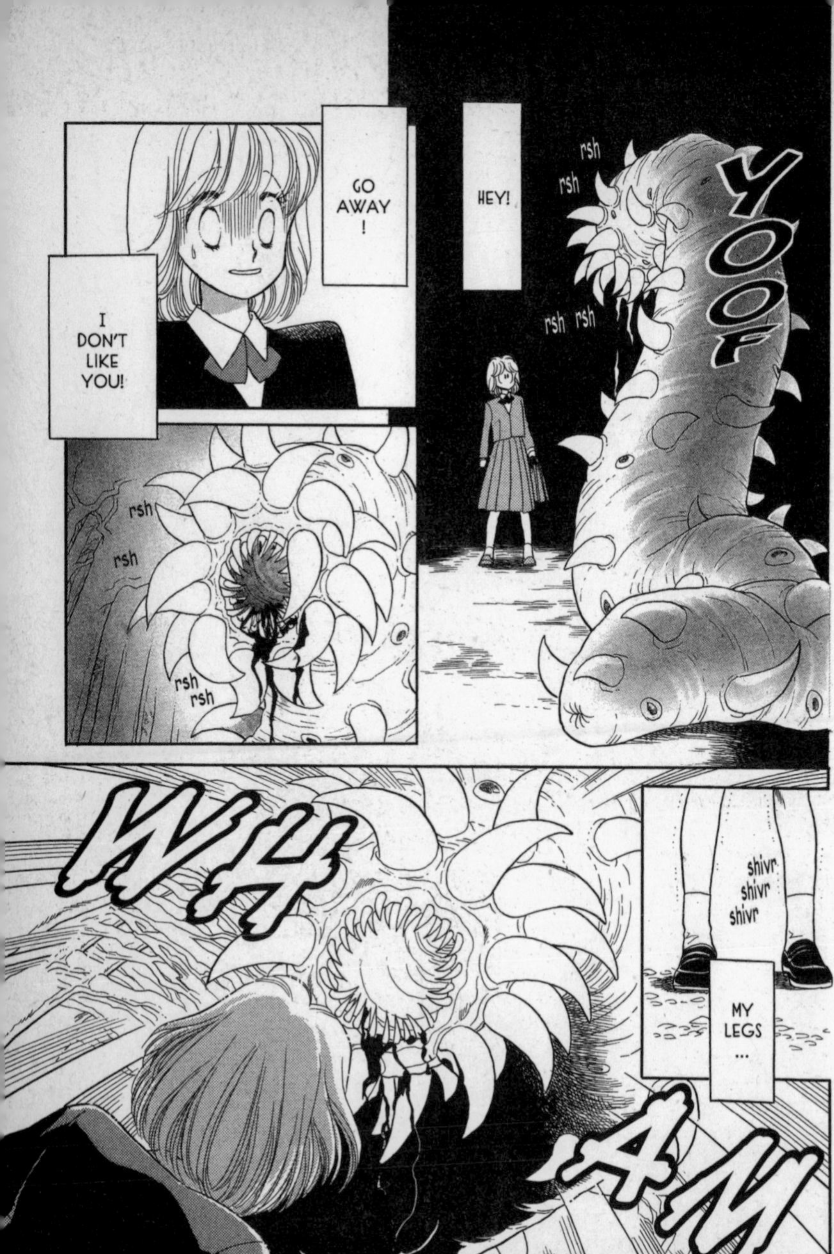
HEY!
rsh
rsh
YOOF
rsh rsh
GO AWAY!
I DON'T LIKE YOU!
rsh
rsh
rsh
rsh
shivr
shivr
shivr
MY LEGS ...
WHAM

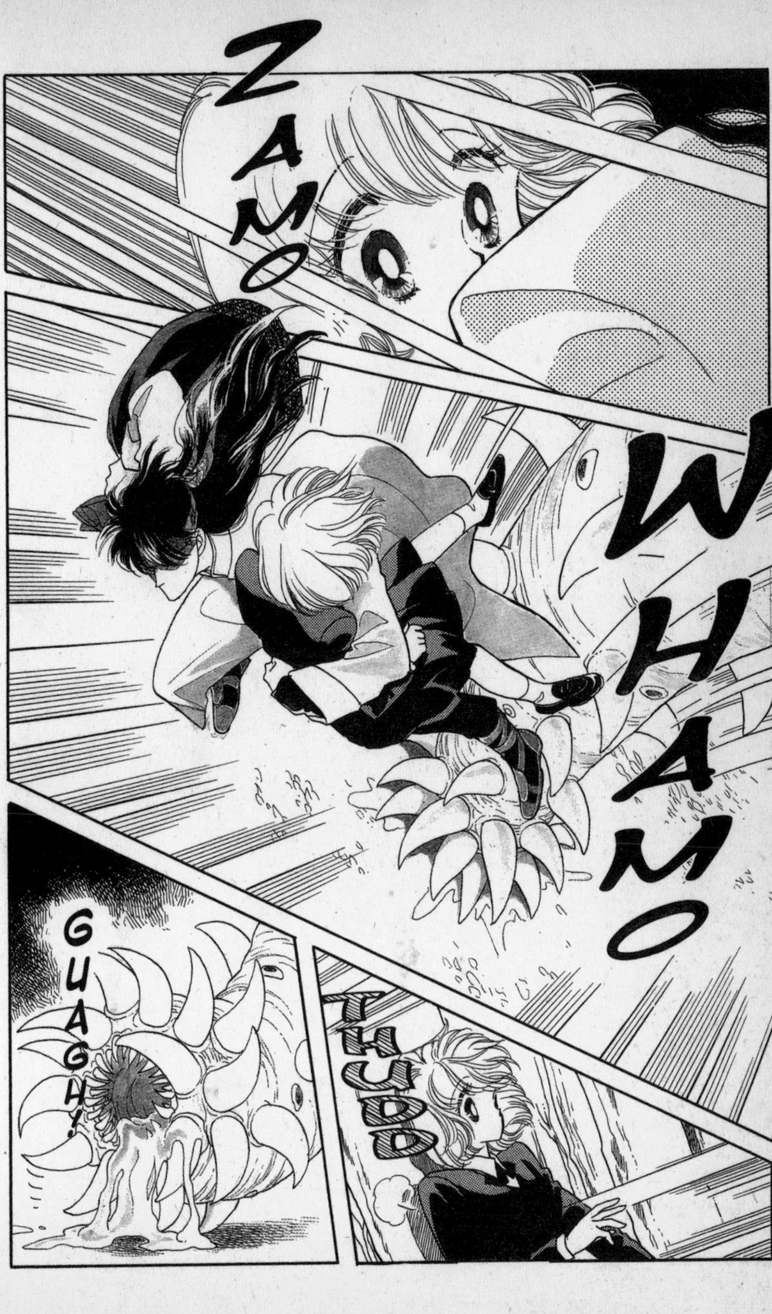
ZAMO
WHAMO
THUDD
GUAGH!

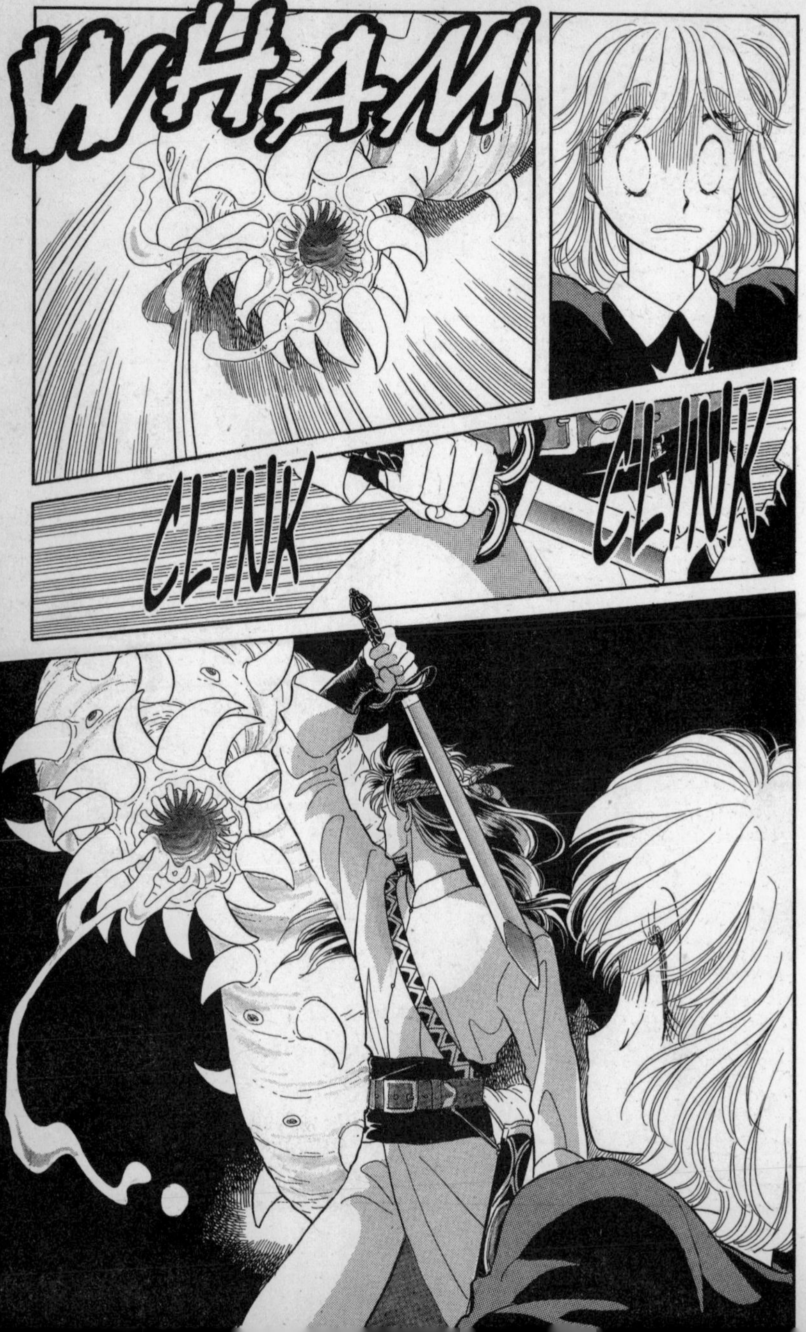
WHAM
CLINK
CLINK

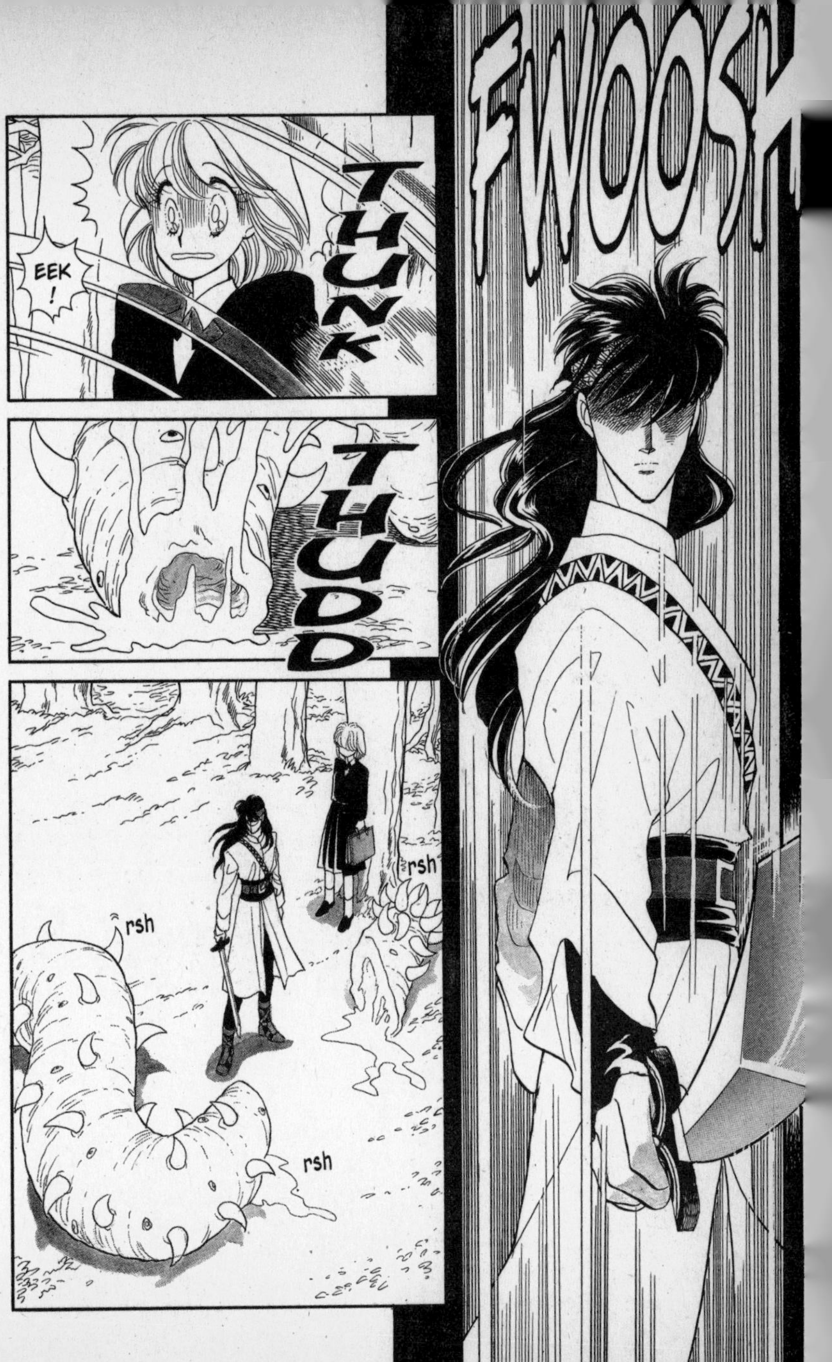
FWOOSH
THUNK
EEK!
THUDD
rsh
rsh
rsh

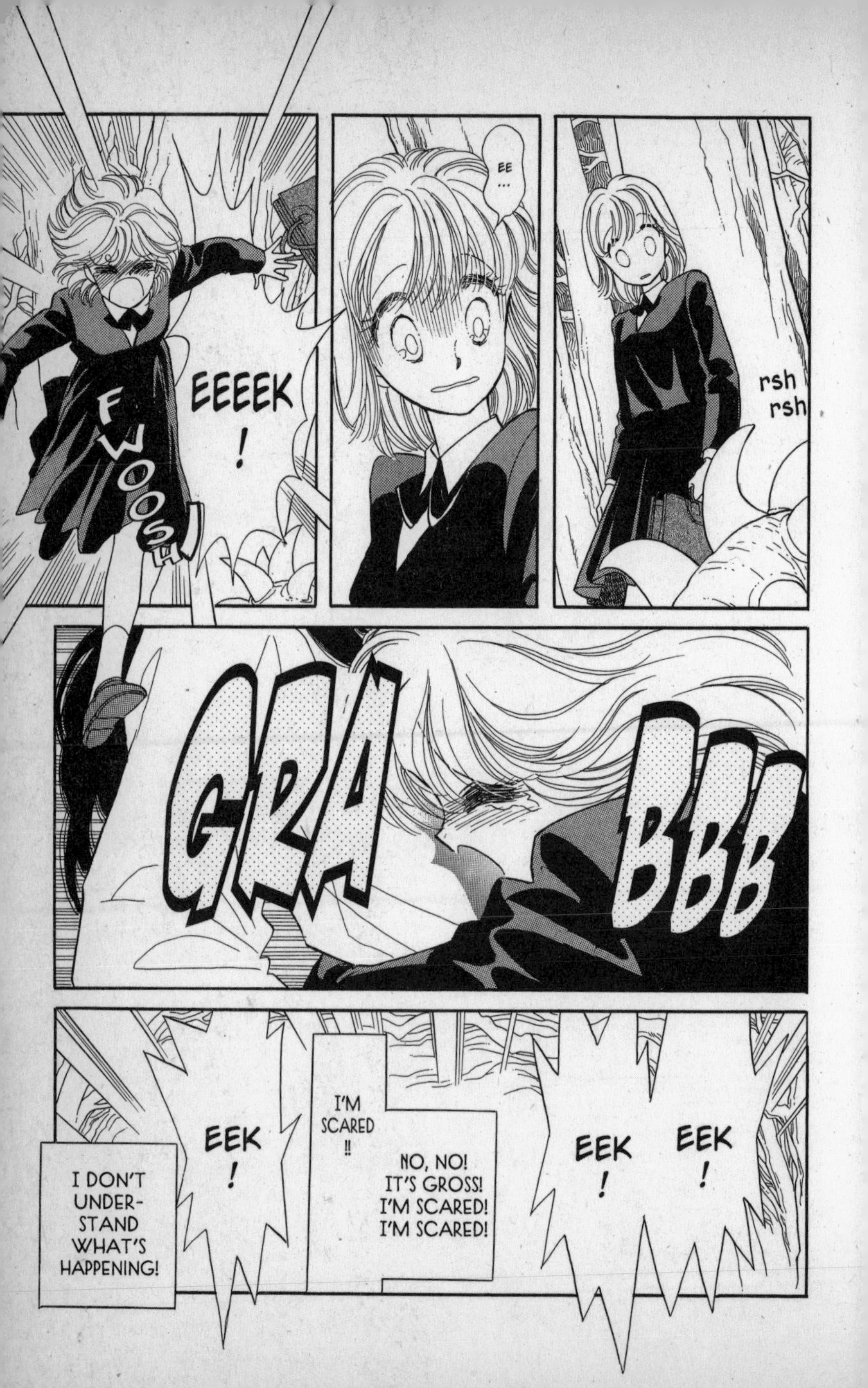
rsh rsh
EE...
EEEEK!
FWOOSH
GRABBB
EEK!
EEK!
I'M SCARED!!
NO, NO! IT'S GROSS! I'M SCARED! I'M SCARED!
EEK!
I DON'T UNDER-STAND WHAT'S HAPPENING!

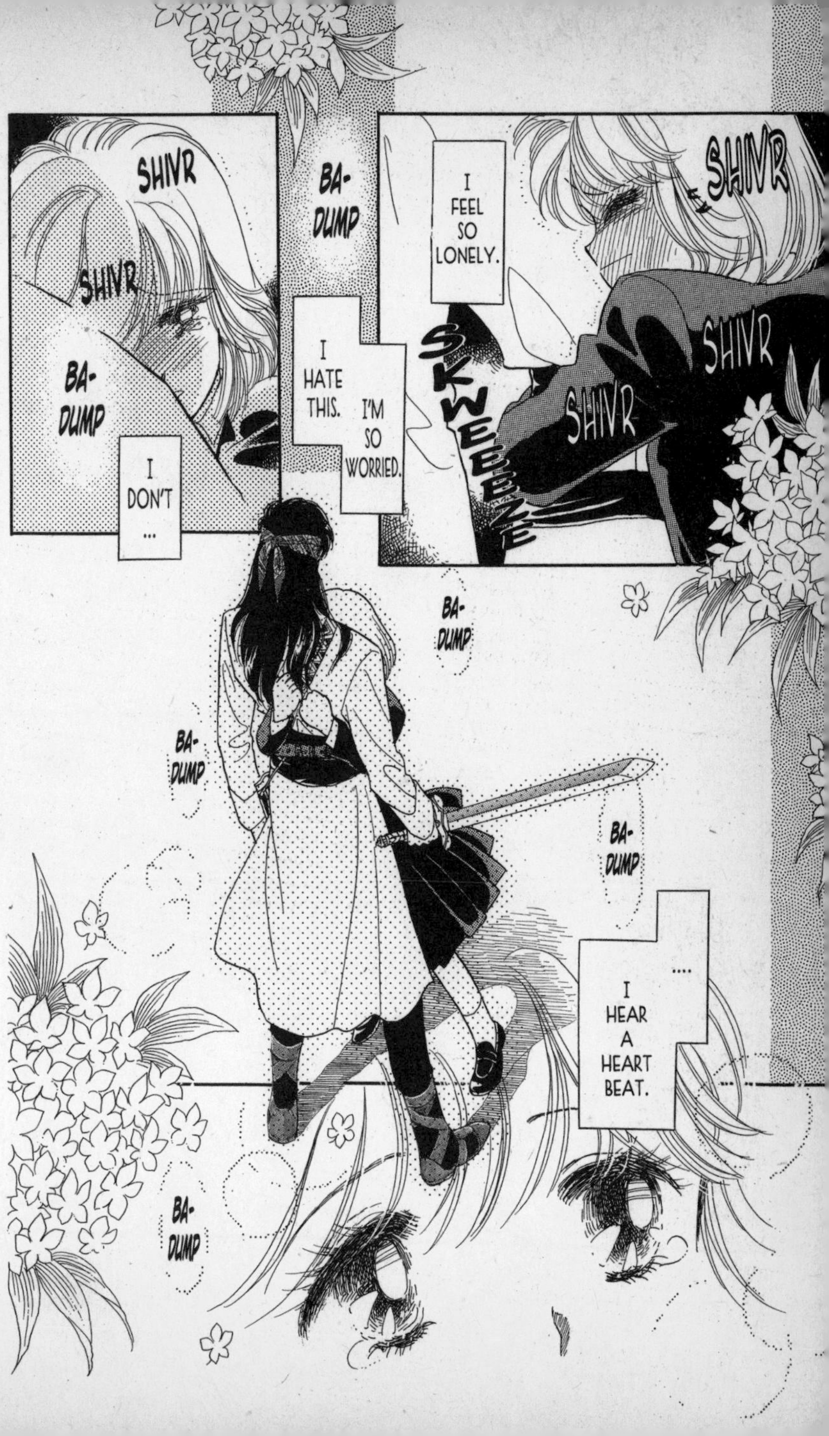
SHIVR
I FEEL SO LONELY.
SKWEEEZE
SHIVR
SHIVR
BA-DUMP
I HATE THIS.
I'M SO WORRIED.
SHIVR
SHIVR
BA-DUMP
I DON'T ...
BA-DUMP
BA-DUMP
.... I HEAR A HEART BEAT.
BA-DUMP
BA-DUMP

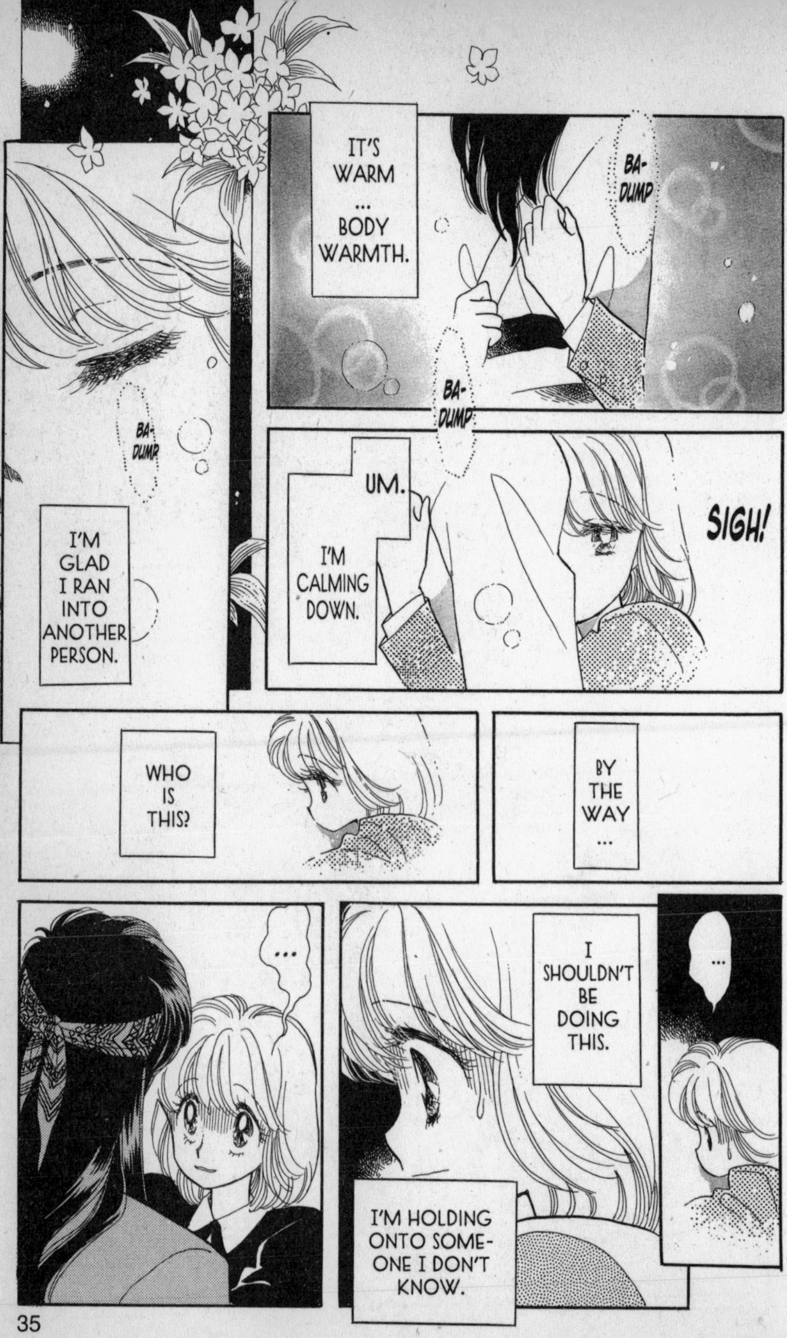
BA-DUMP
IT'S WARM ... BODY WARMTH.
BA-DUMP
SIGH!
UM.
I'M CALMING DOWN.
BA-DUMP
I'M GLAD I RAN INTO ANOTHER PERSON.
BY THE WAY ...
WHO IS THIS?
...
I SHOULDN'T BE DOING THIS.
I'M HOLDING ONTO SOME-ONE I DON'T KNOW.
...

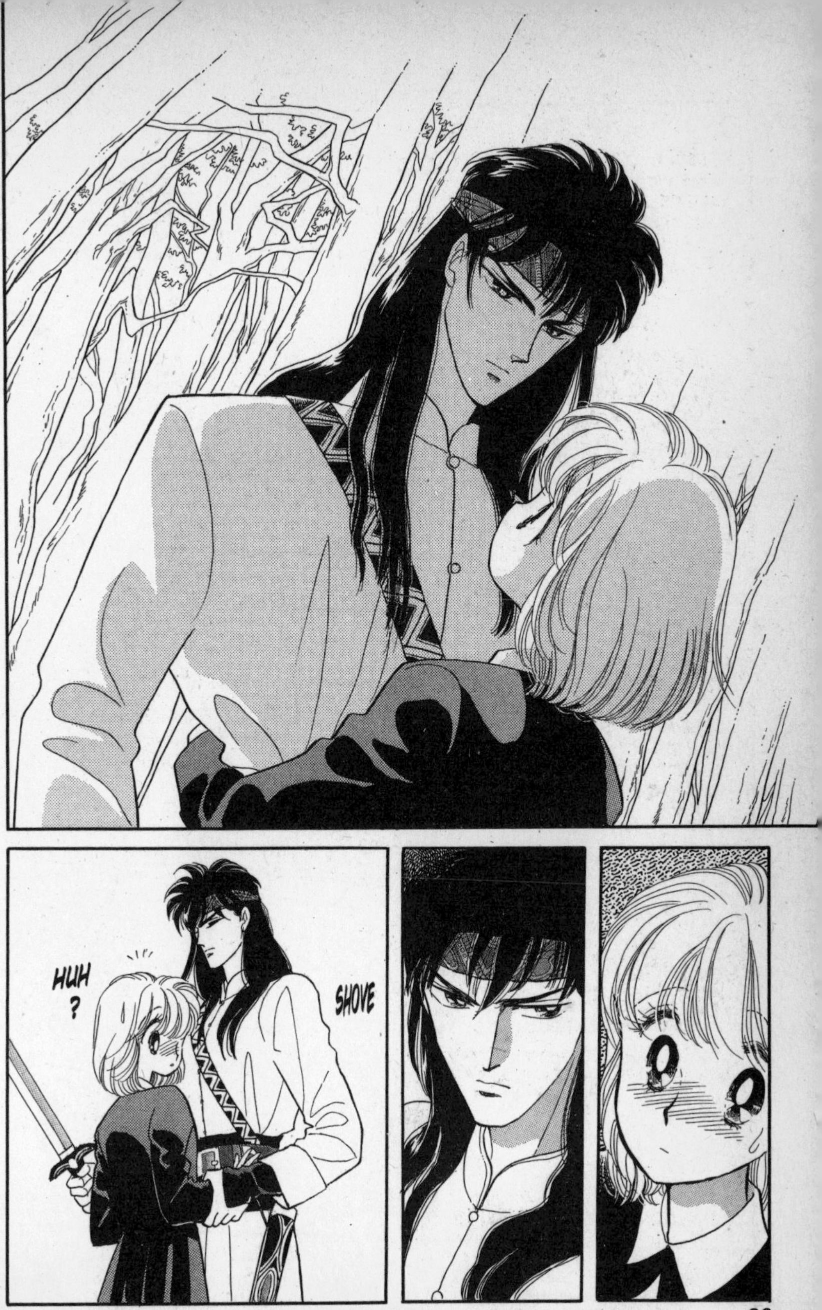
SHOVE
HUH ?

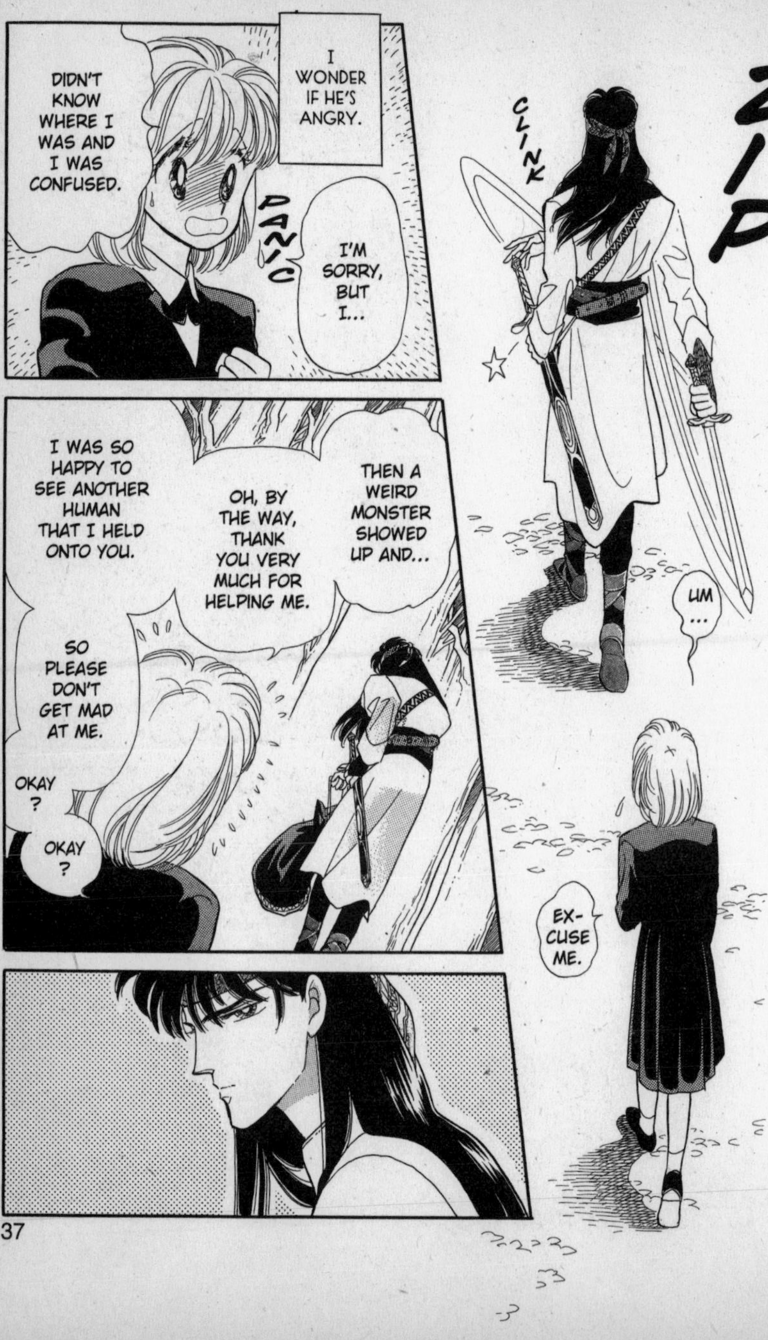

ZIP
CLINK
UM...
EX-CUSE ME.
I WONDER IF HE'S ANGRY.
I'M SORRY, BUT I...
PANIC
DIDN'T KNOW WHERE I WAS AND I WAS CONFUSED.
THEN A WEIRD MONSTER SHOWED UP AND...
OH, BY THE WAY, THANK YOU VERY MUCH FOR HELPING ME.
I WAS SO HAPPY TO SEE ANOTHER HUMAN THAT I HELD ONTO YOU.
SO PLEASE DON'T GET MAD AT ME.
OKAY?
OKAY?

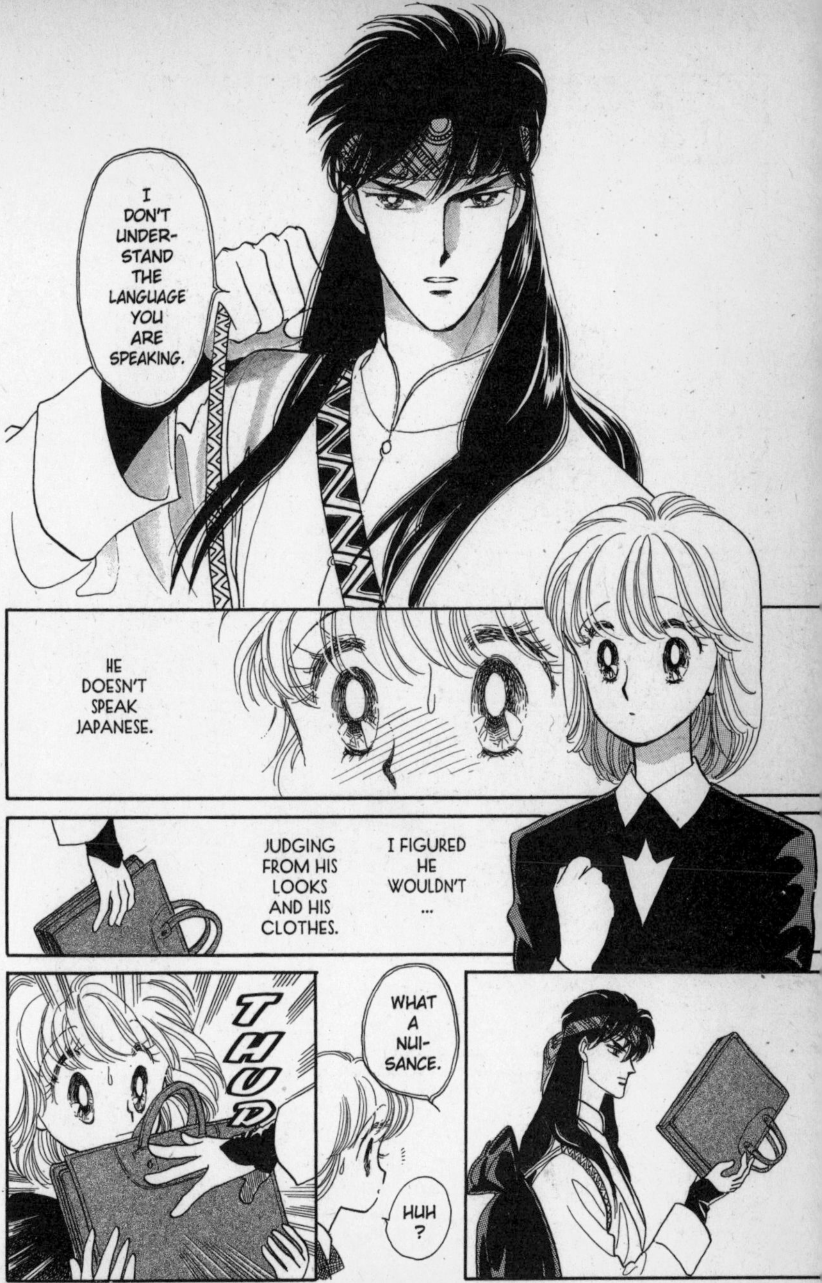
I DON'T UNDERSTAND THE LANGUAGE YOU ARE SPEAKING.
HE DOESN'T SPEAK JAPANESE.
I FIGURED HE WOULDN'T ...
JUDGING FROM HIS LOOKS AND HIS CLOTHES.
WHAT A NUISANCE.
THUD
HUH?

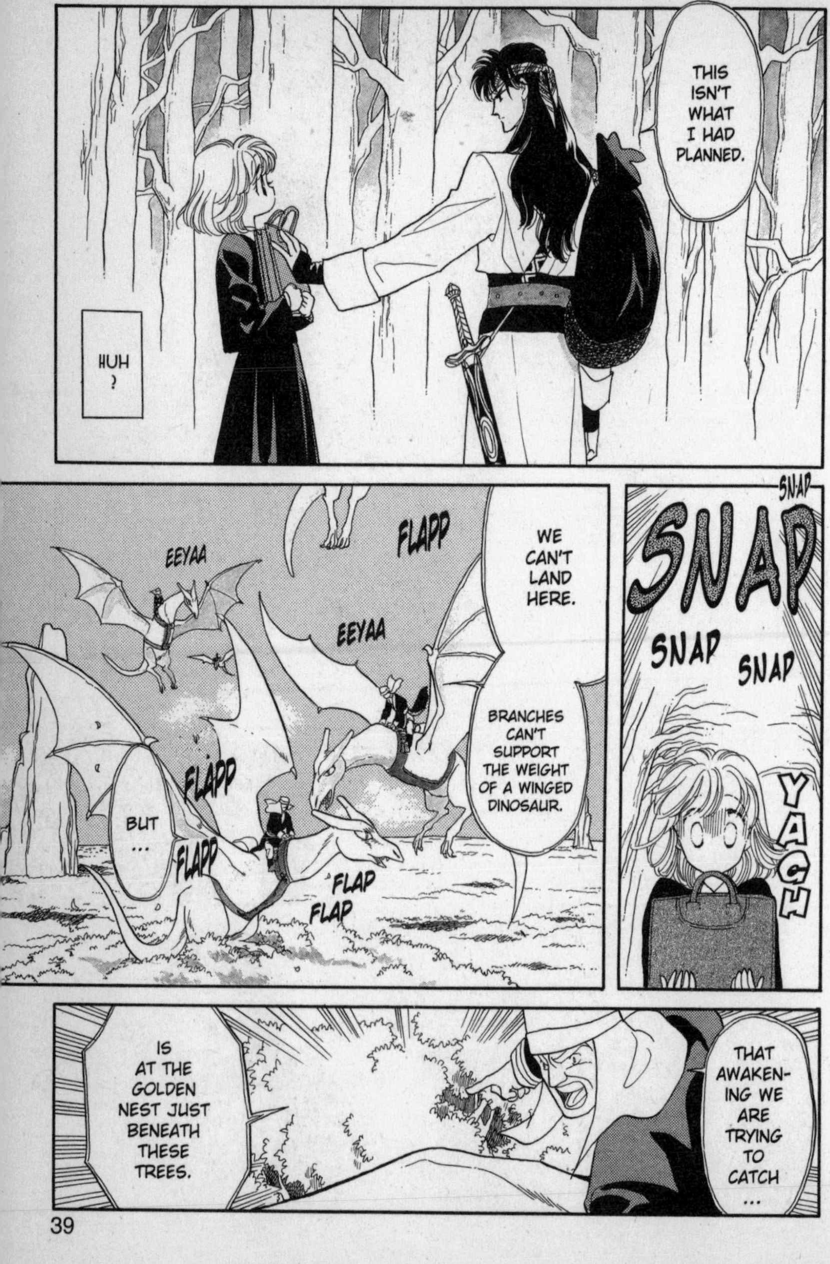
THIS ISN'T WHAT I HAD PLANNED.
HUH?
SN-AP
SNAP
SNAP
SNAP
YACH
FLAPP
WE CAN'T LAND HERE.
EEYAA
EEYAA
BRANCHES CAN'T SUPPORT THE WEIGHT OF A WINGED DINOSAUR.
FLAPP
BUT...
FLAPP
FLAP
FLAP
THAT AWAKEN-ING WE ARE TRYING TO CATCH...
IS AT THE GOLDEN NEST JUST BENEATH THESE TREES.

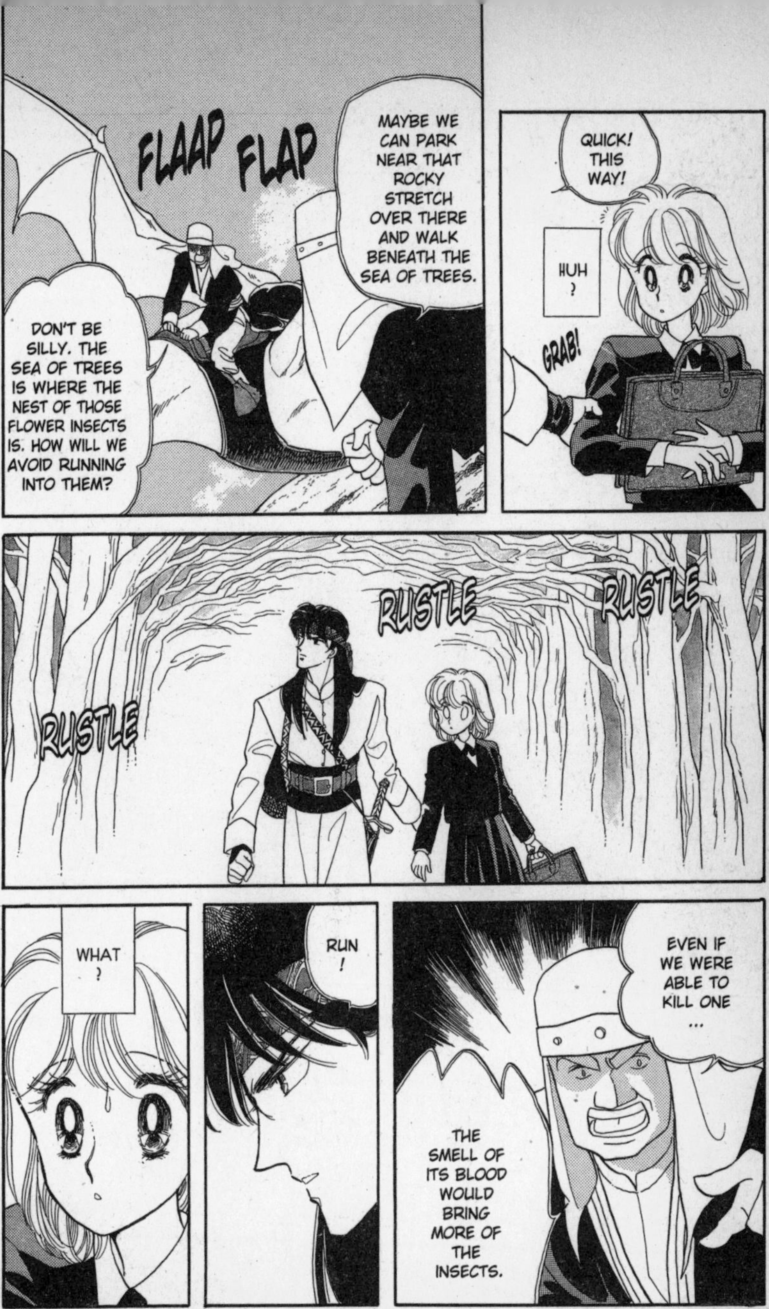
QUICK! THIS WAY!
HUH ?
GRAB!
MAYBE WE CAN PARK NEAR THAT ROCKY STRETCH OVER THERE AND WALK BENEATH THE SEA OF TREES.
FLAAP FLAP
DON'T BE SILLY. THE SEA OF TREES IS WHERE THE NEST OF THOSE FLOWER INSECTS IS. HOW WILL WE AVOID RUNNING INTO THEM?
RUSTLE
RUSTLE
RUSTLE
EVEN IF WE WERE ABLE TO KILL ONE ...
THE SMELL OF ITS BLOOD WOULD BRING MORE OF THE INSECTS.
RUN !
WHAT ?

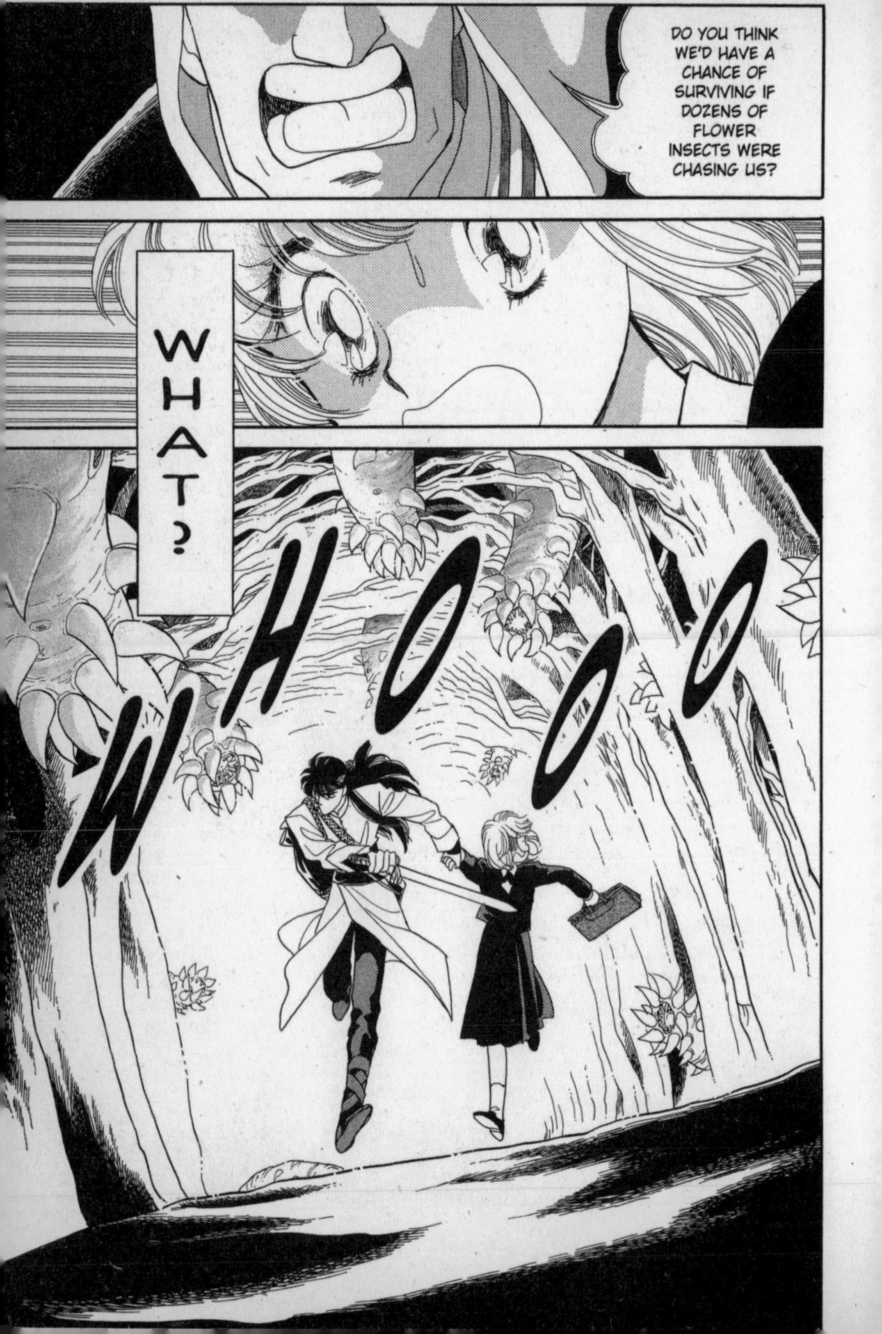

DO YOU THINK WE'D HAVE A CHANCE OF SURVIVING IF DOZENS OF FLOWER INSECTS WERE CHASING US?
WHAT?
WHOOOO

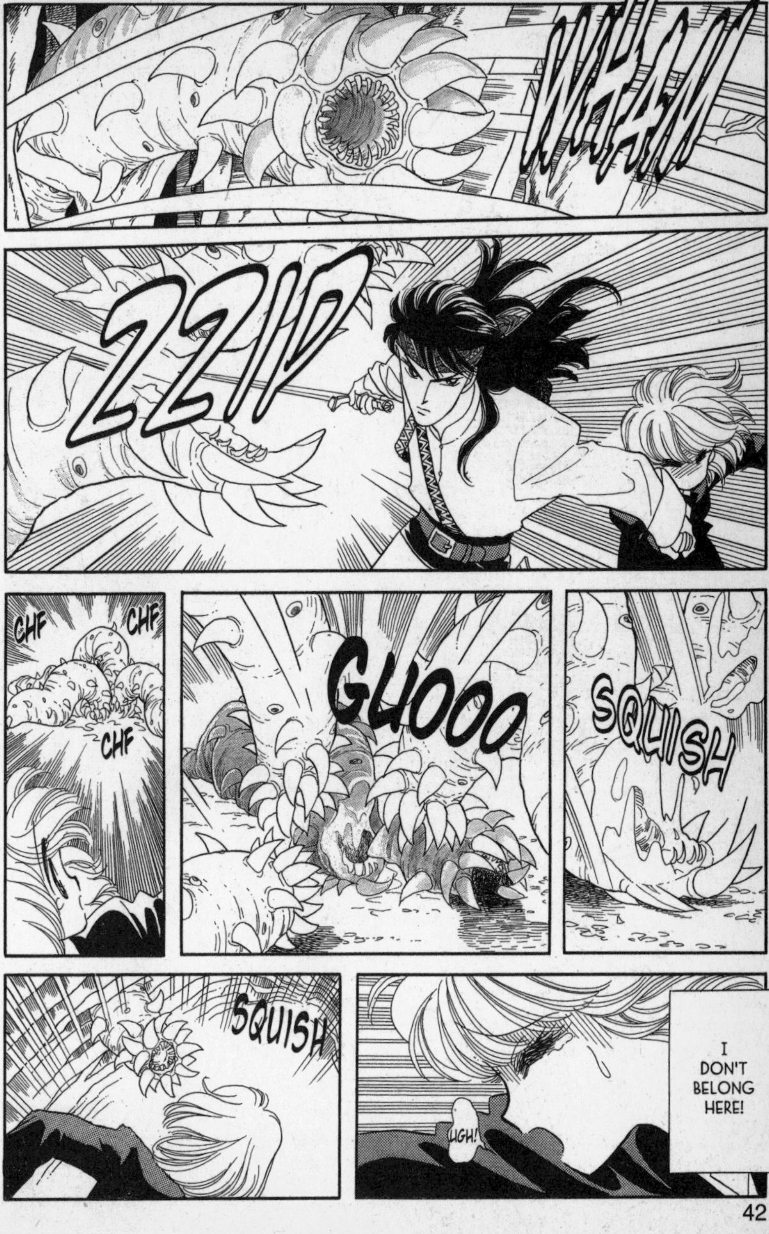
WHAM
ZZIP
SQUISH
GUOOO
CHF
CHF
CHF
I DON'T BELONG HERE!
UGH!
SQUISH

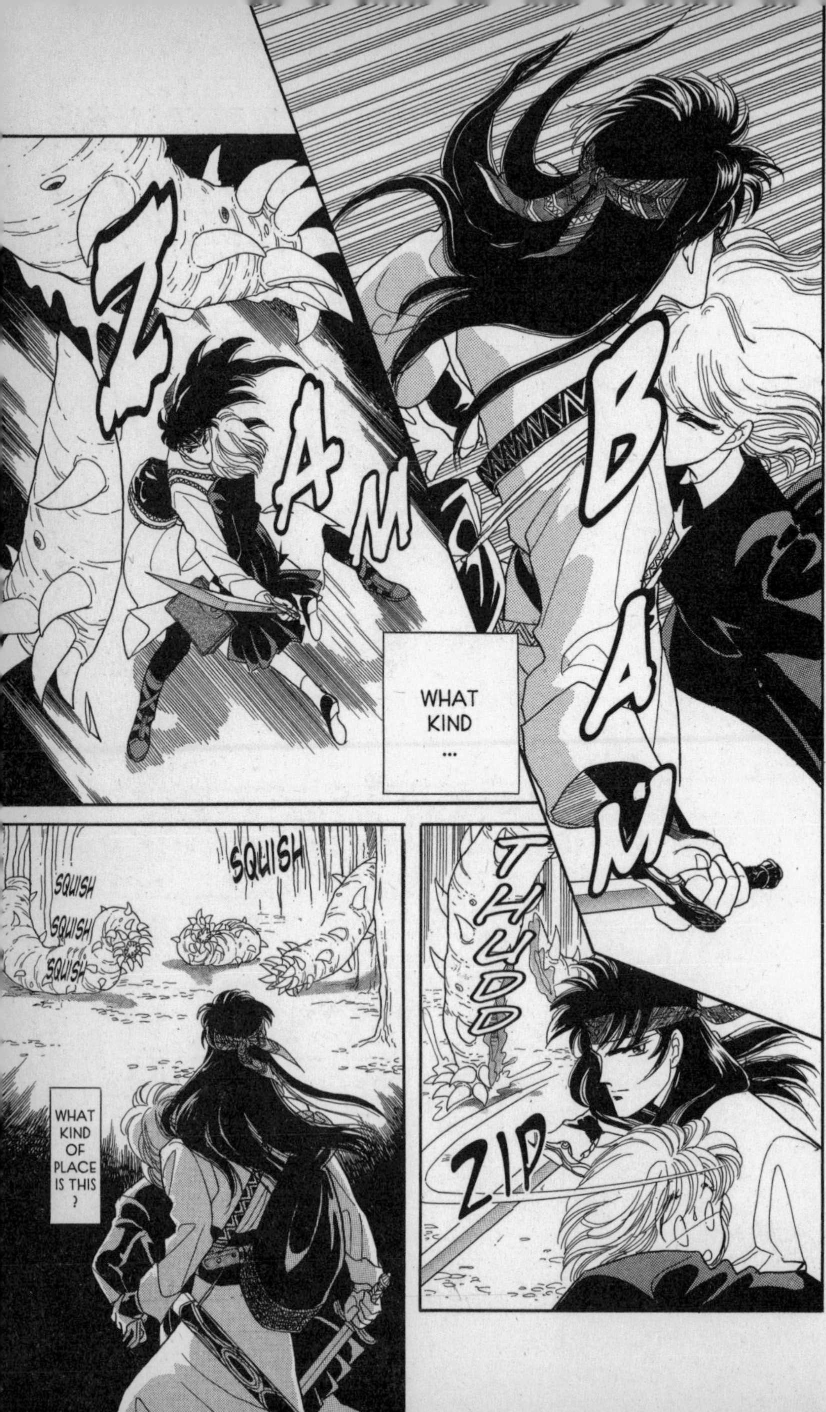

BAM
WHAT KIND ...
ZAM
THUDD
ZIP
SQUISH
SQUISH
SQUISH
SQUISH
WHAT KIND OF PLACE IS THIS ?

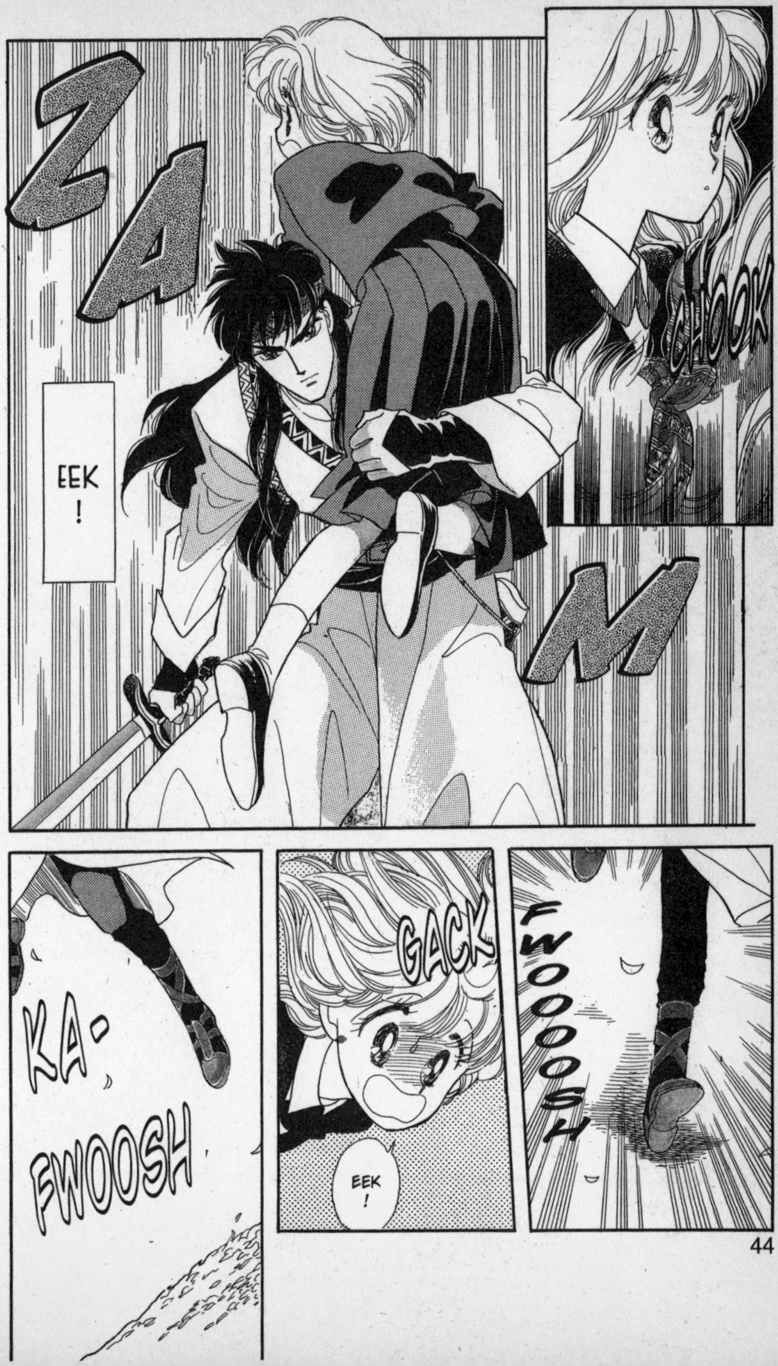
CHOOK
ZA
M
EEK!
FWOOOOOSH
GACK
EEK!
KA-FWOOSH

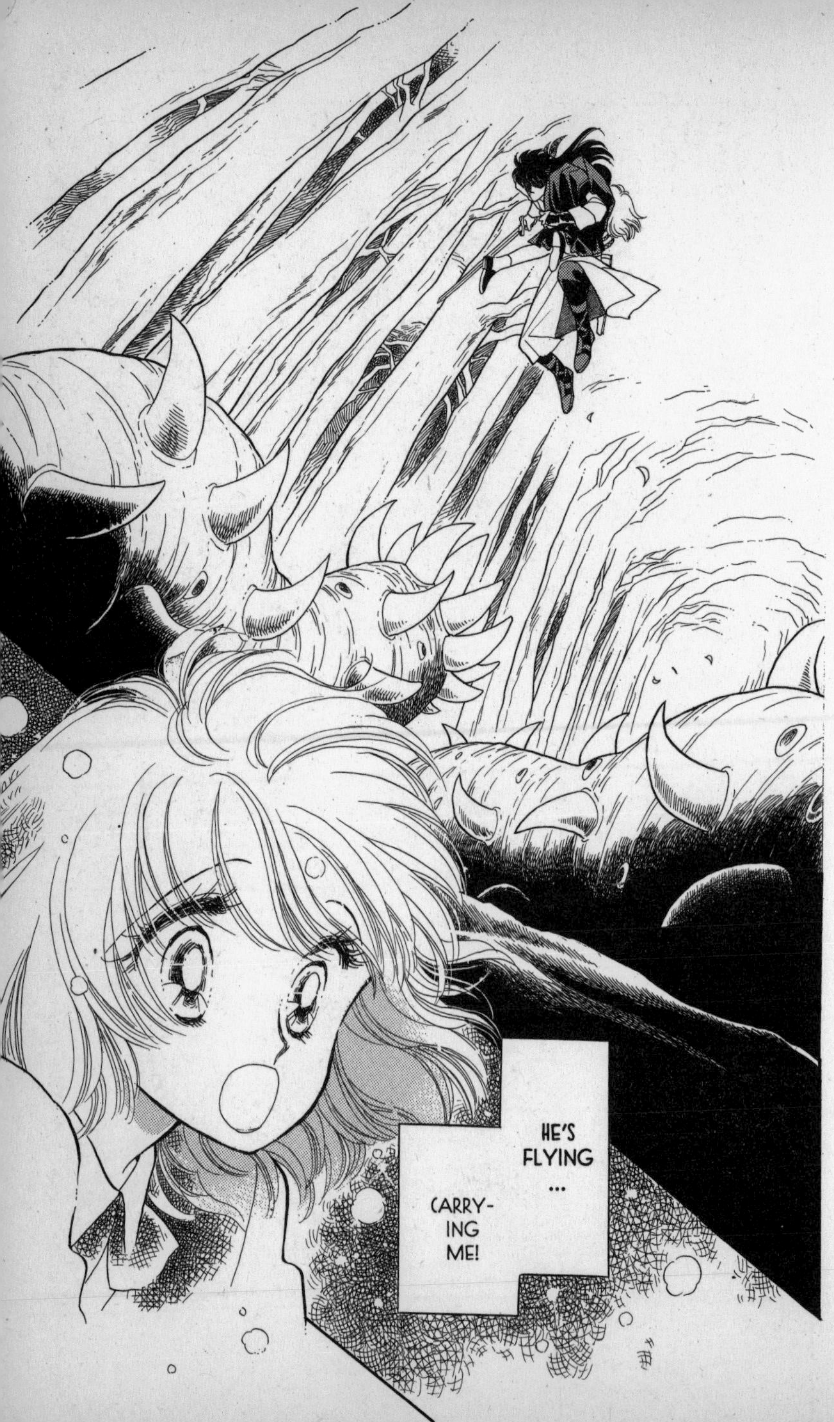
HE'S FLYING ...
CARRY-ING ME!

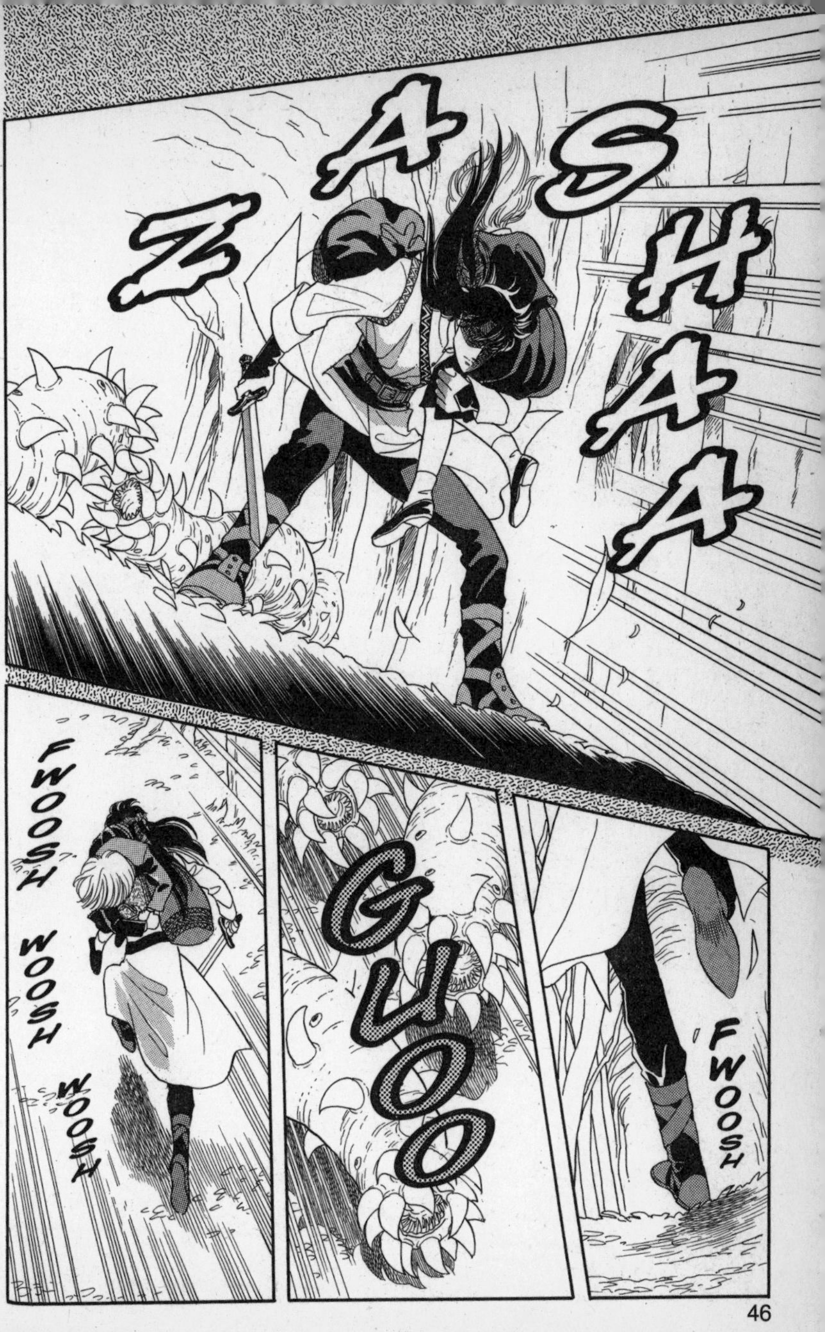
ZASHAAA
FWOOSH
GUOOO
FWOOSH
WOOSH
WOOSH

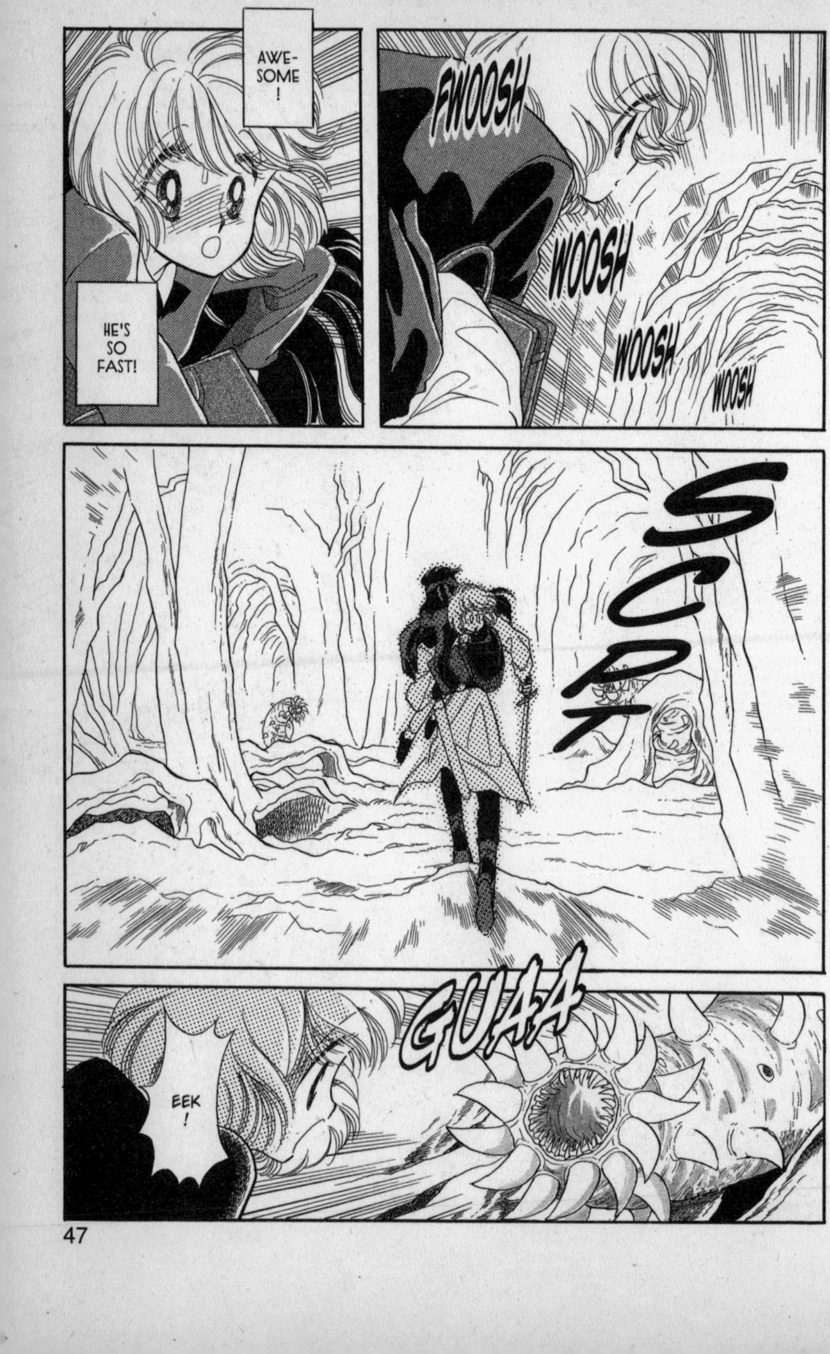
FWOOSH
WOOSH
WOOSH
WOOSH
AWE-SOME!
HE'S SO FAST!
SCPT
GUAA
EEK!

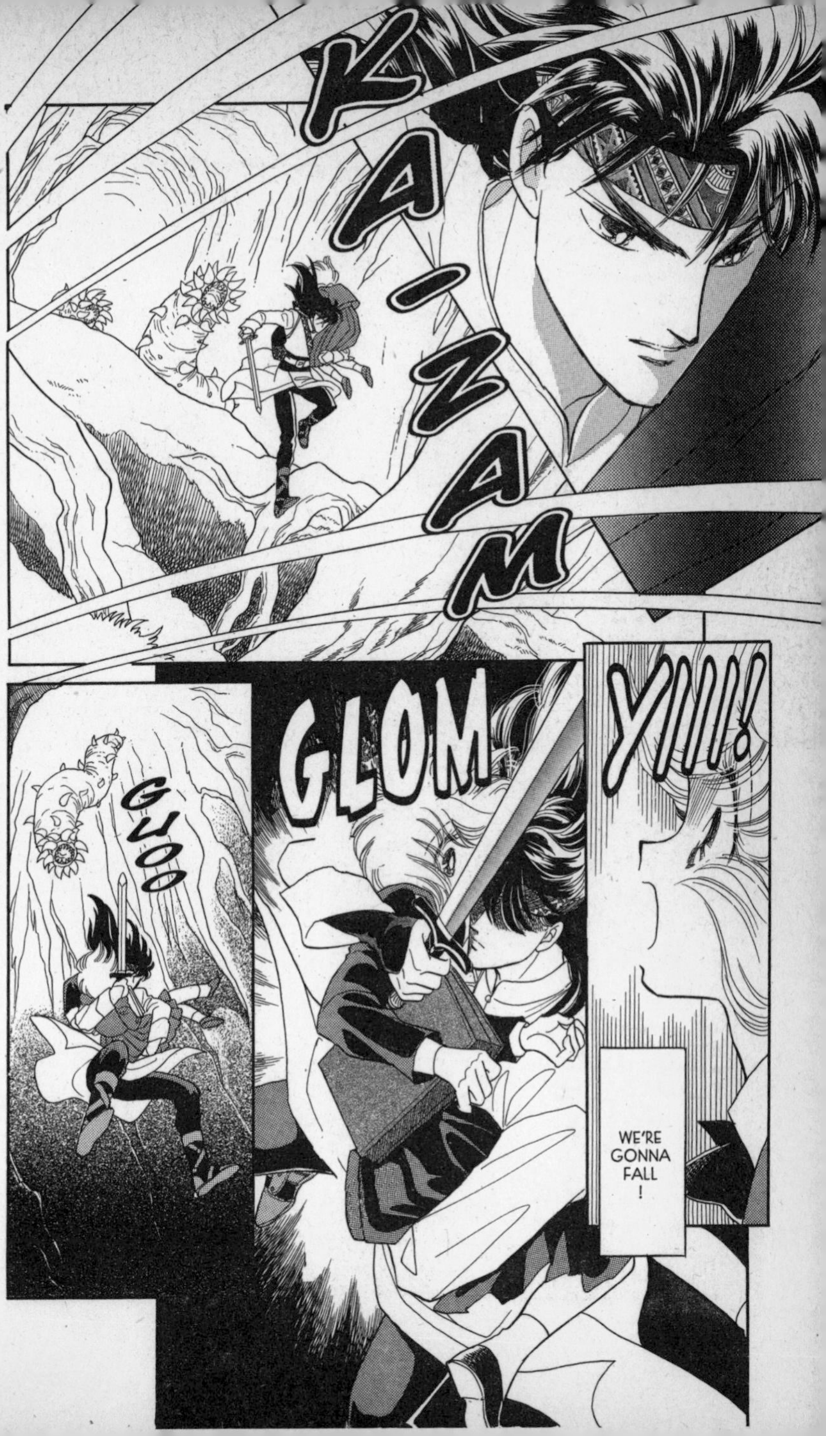
KA-NAM
YIII!
WE'RE GONNA FALL!
GLOM
GUOO

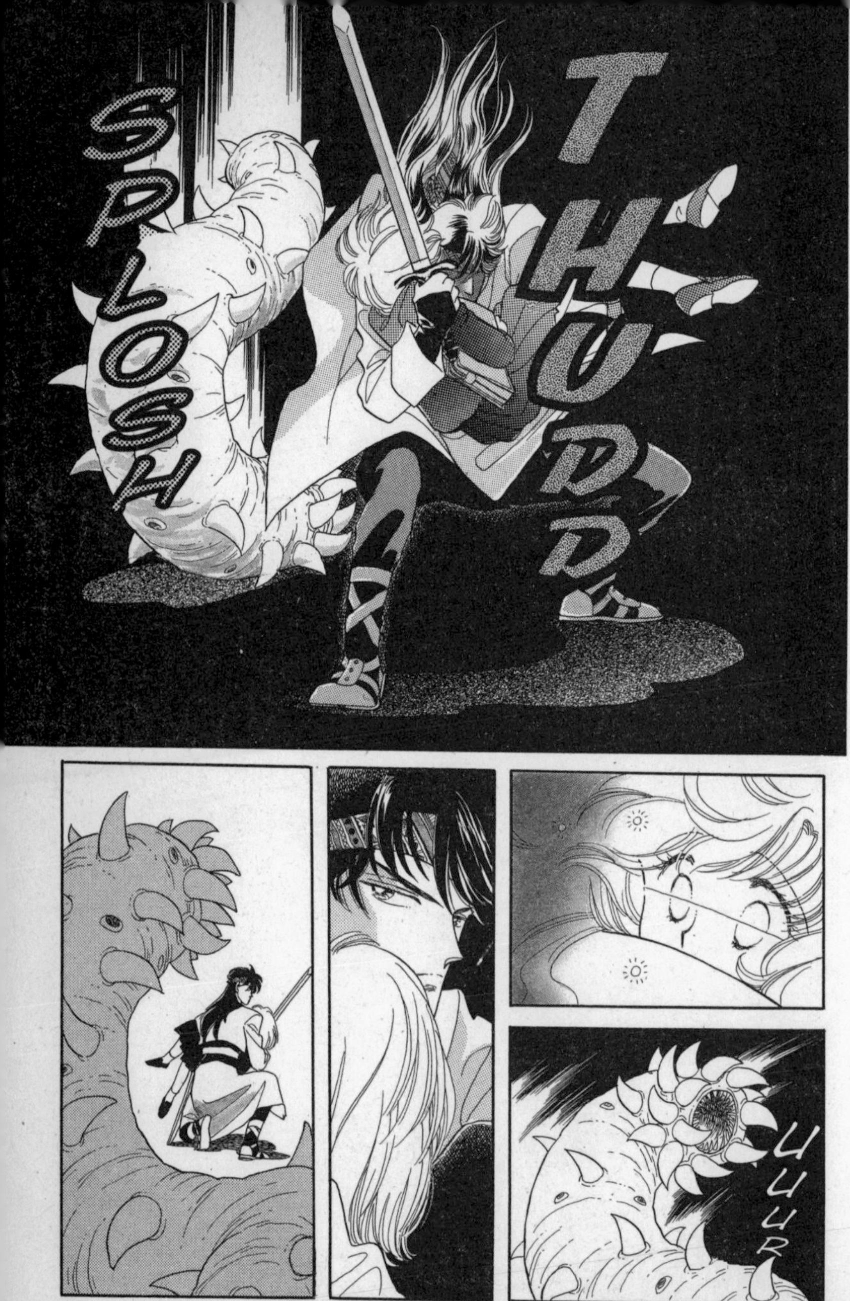
THUDD
SPLOSH
UUUR

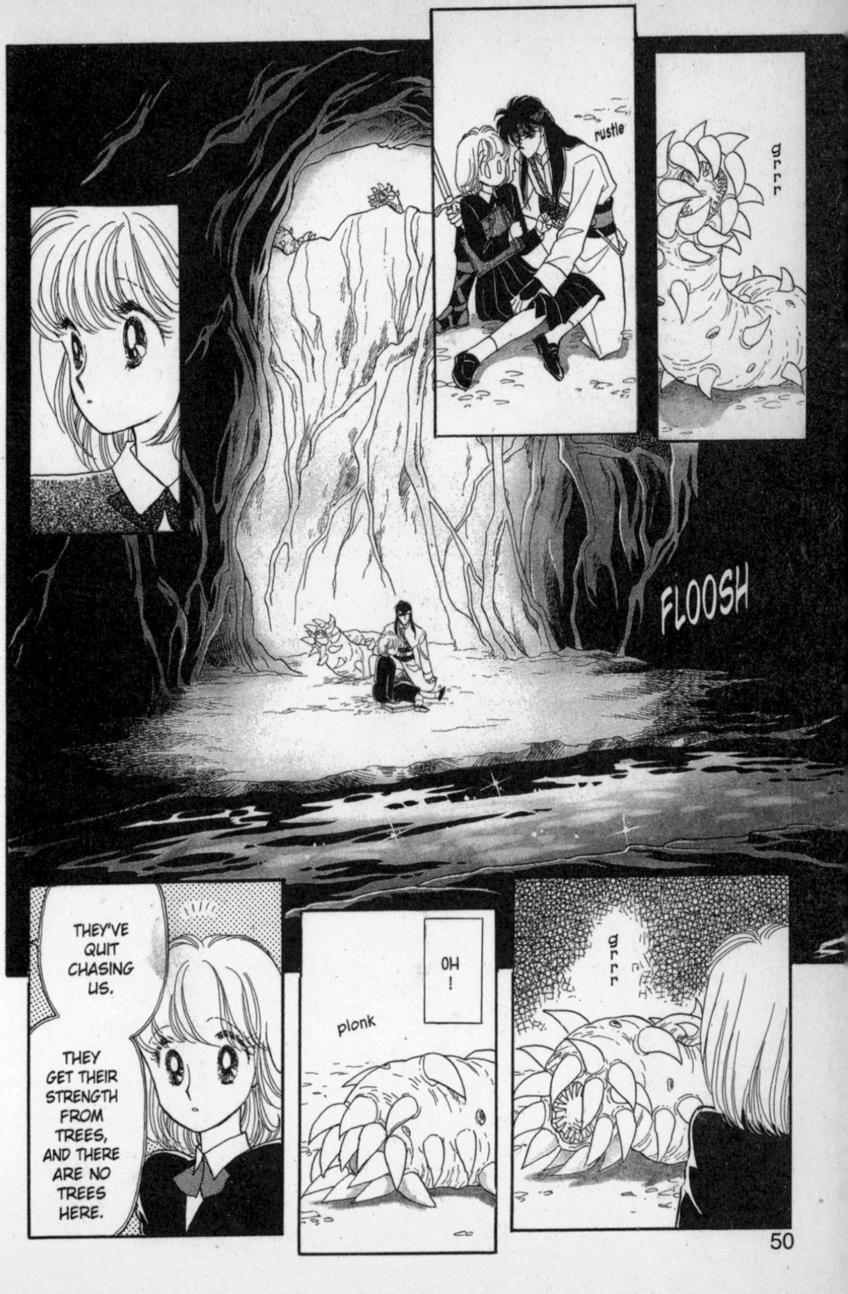
grrr
rustle
FLOOSH
grrr
OH!
plonk
THEY'VE QUIT CHASING US.
THEY GET THEIR STRENGTH FROM TREES, AND THERE ARE NO TREES HERE.

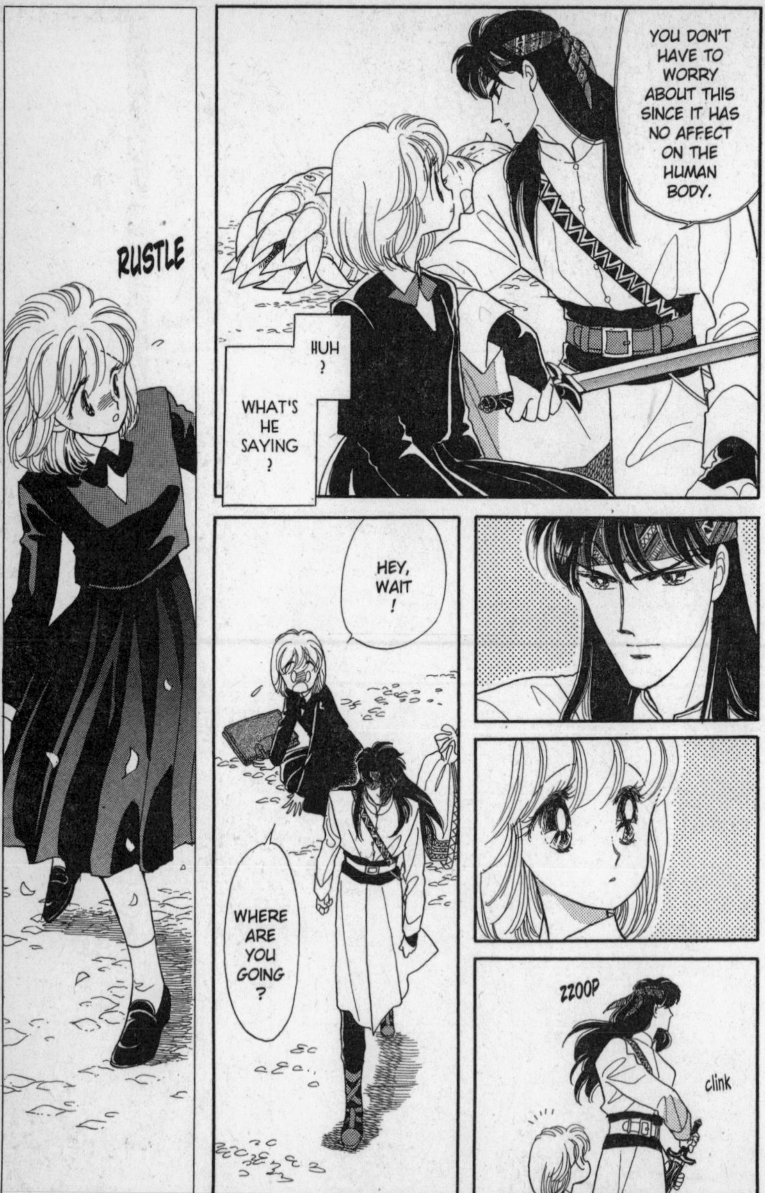

YOU DON'T HAVE TO WORRY ABOUT THIS SINCE IT HAS NO AFFECT ON THE HUMAN BODY.
HUH?
WHAT'S HE SAYING?
ZZOOP
clink
HEY, WAIT!
WHERE ARE YOU GOING?
RUSTLE

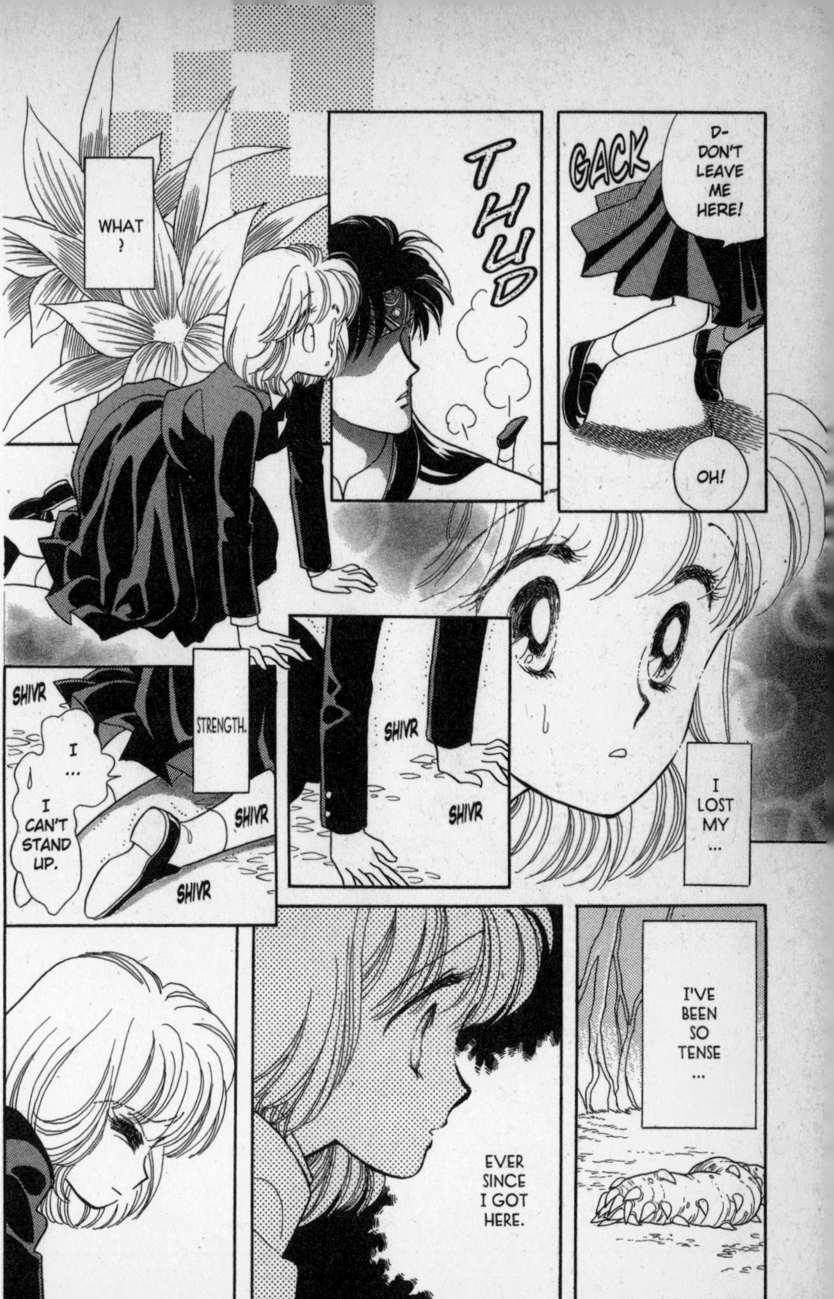
GACK
D-DON'T LEAVE ME HERE!
OH!
THUD
WHAT?
I LOST MY ...
SHIVR
SHIVR
STRENGTH.
SHIVR
I ...
I CAN'T STAND UP.
SHIVR
SHIVR
I'VE BEEN SO TENSE ...
EVER SINCE I GOT HERE.

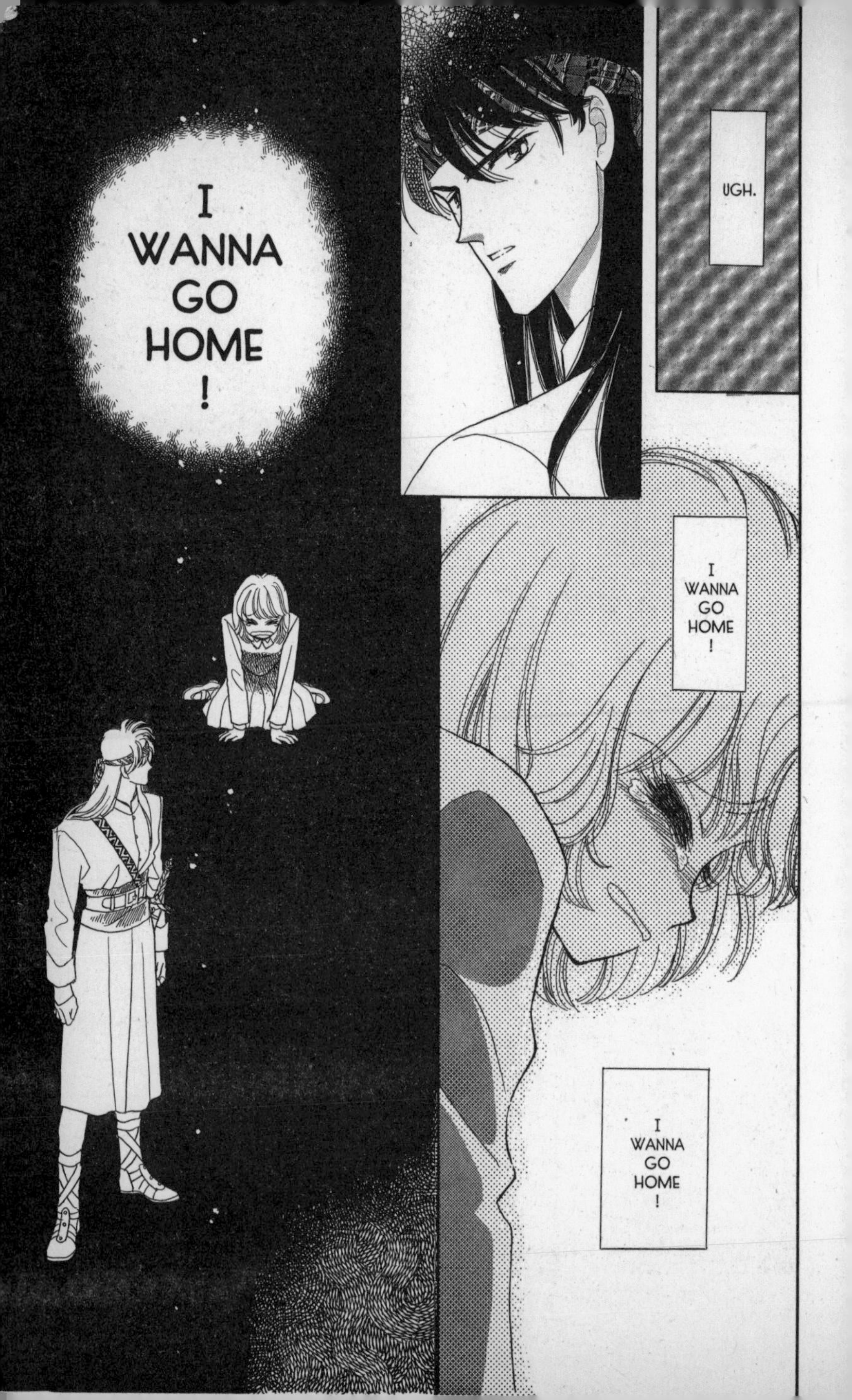
UGH.
I WANNA GO HOME!
I WANNA GO HOME!
I WANNA GO HOME!

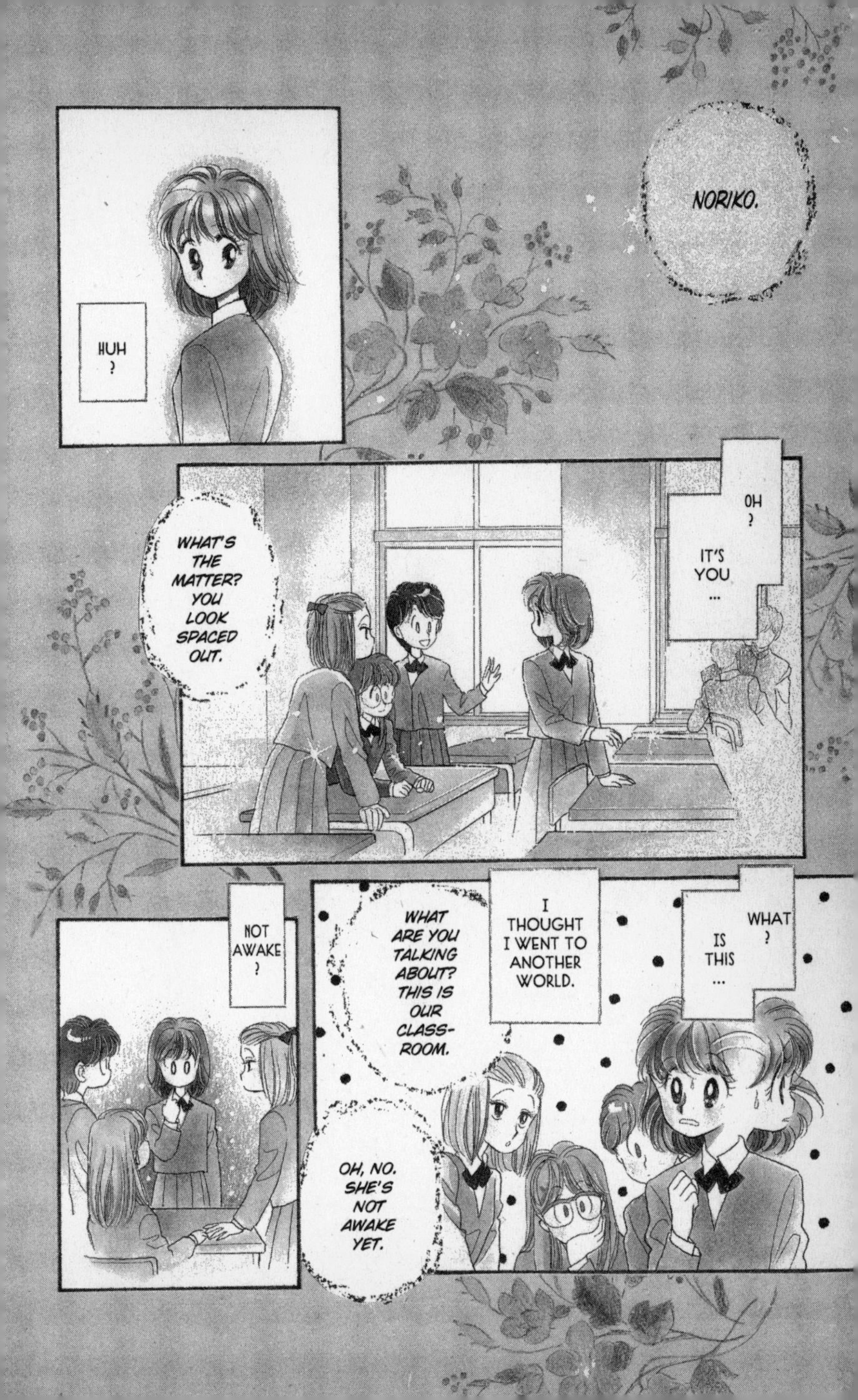

NORIKO.
HUH?
OH? IT'S YOU...
WHAT'S THE MATTER? YOU LOOK SPACED OUT.
WHAT? IS THIS...
I THOUGHT I WENT TO ANOTHER WORLD.
WHAT ARE YOU TALKING ABOUT? THIS IS OUR CLASSROOM.
OH, NO. SHE'S NOT AWAKE YET.
NOT AWAKE?

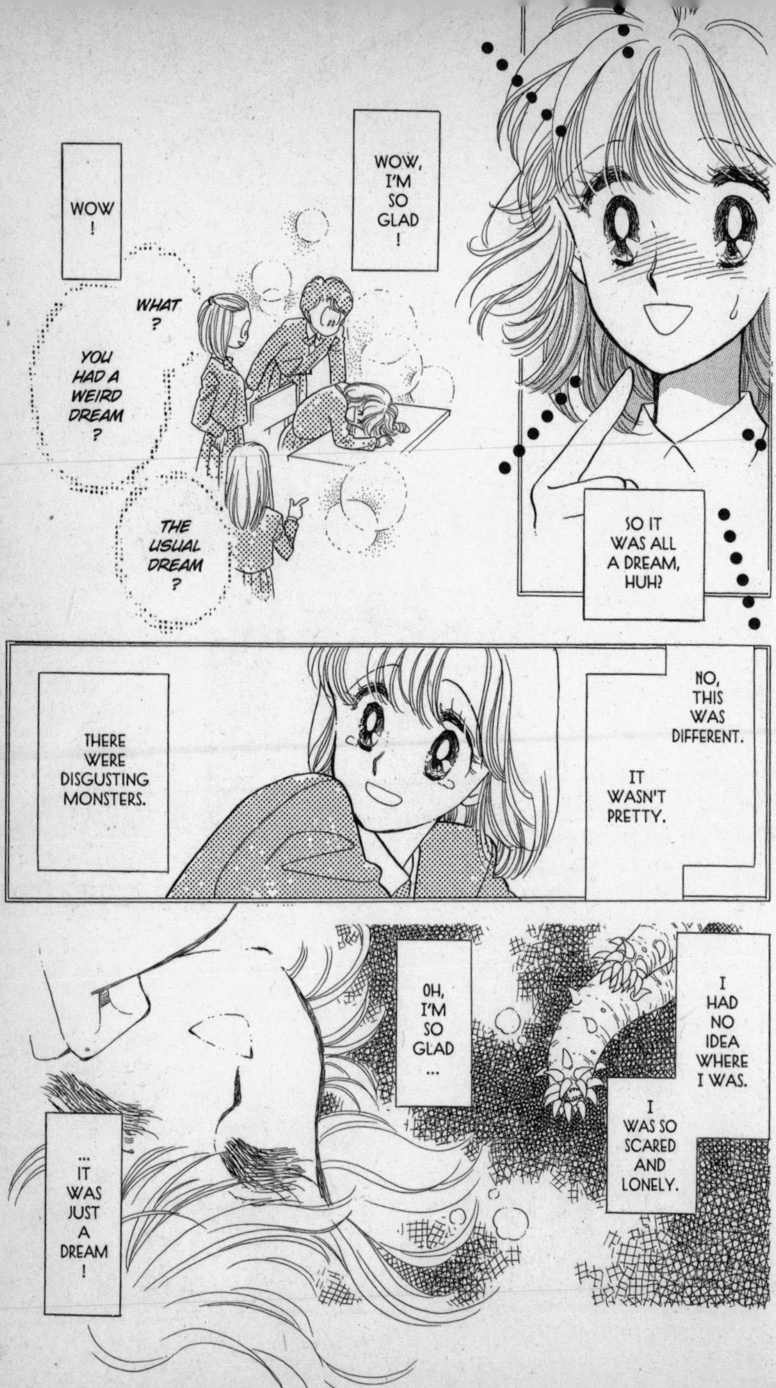
SO IT WAS ALL A DREAM, HUH?
WOW, I'M SO GLAD!
WOW!
WHAT? YOU HAD A WEIRD DREAM?
THE USUAL DREAM?
NO, THIS WAS DIFFERENT.
IT WASN'T PRETTY.
THERE WERE DISGUSTING MONSTERS.
I HAD NO IDEA WHERE I WAS.
I WAS SO SCARED AND LONELY.
OH, I'M SO GLAD...
...IT WAS JUST A DREAM!

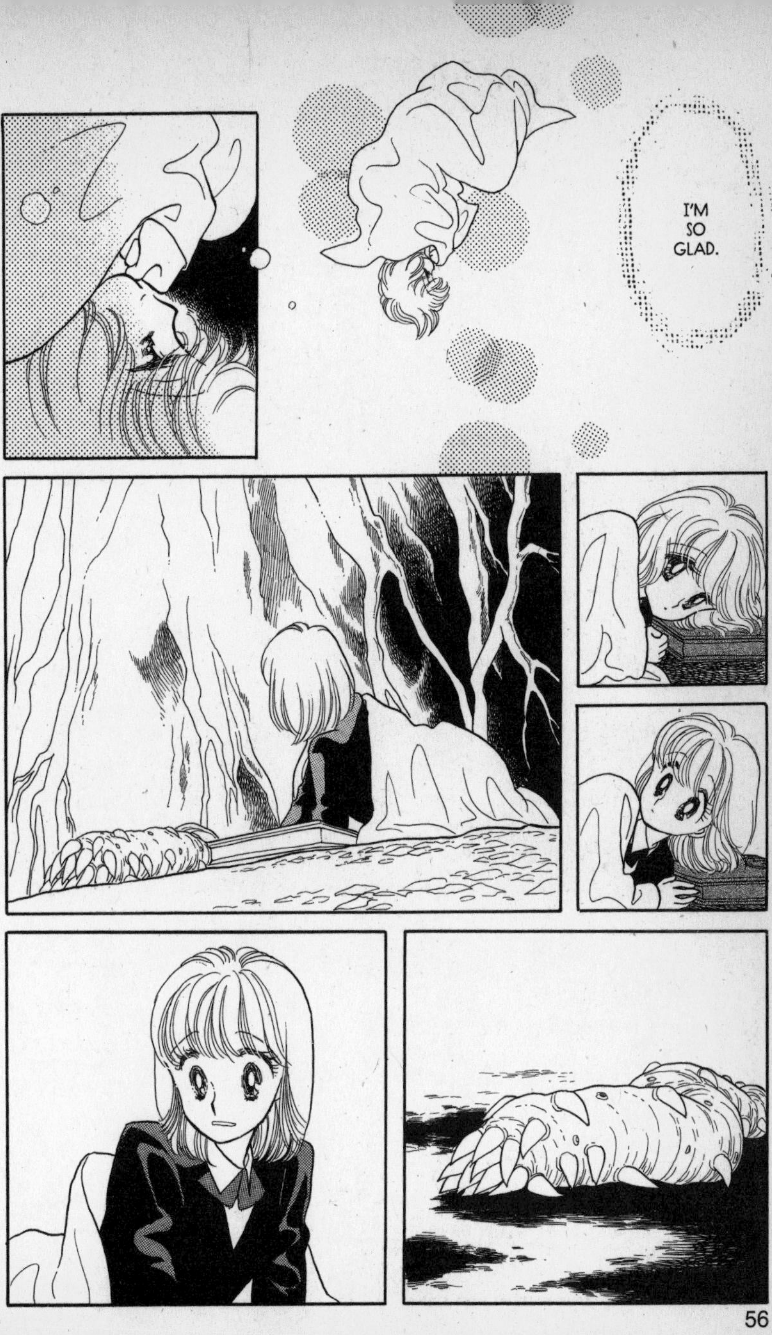
I'M SO GLAD.

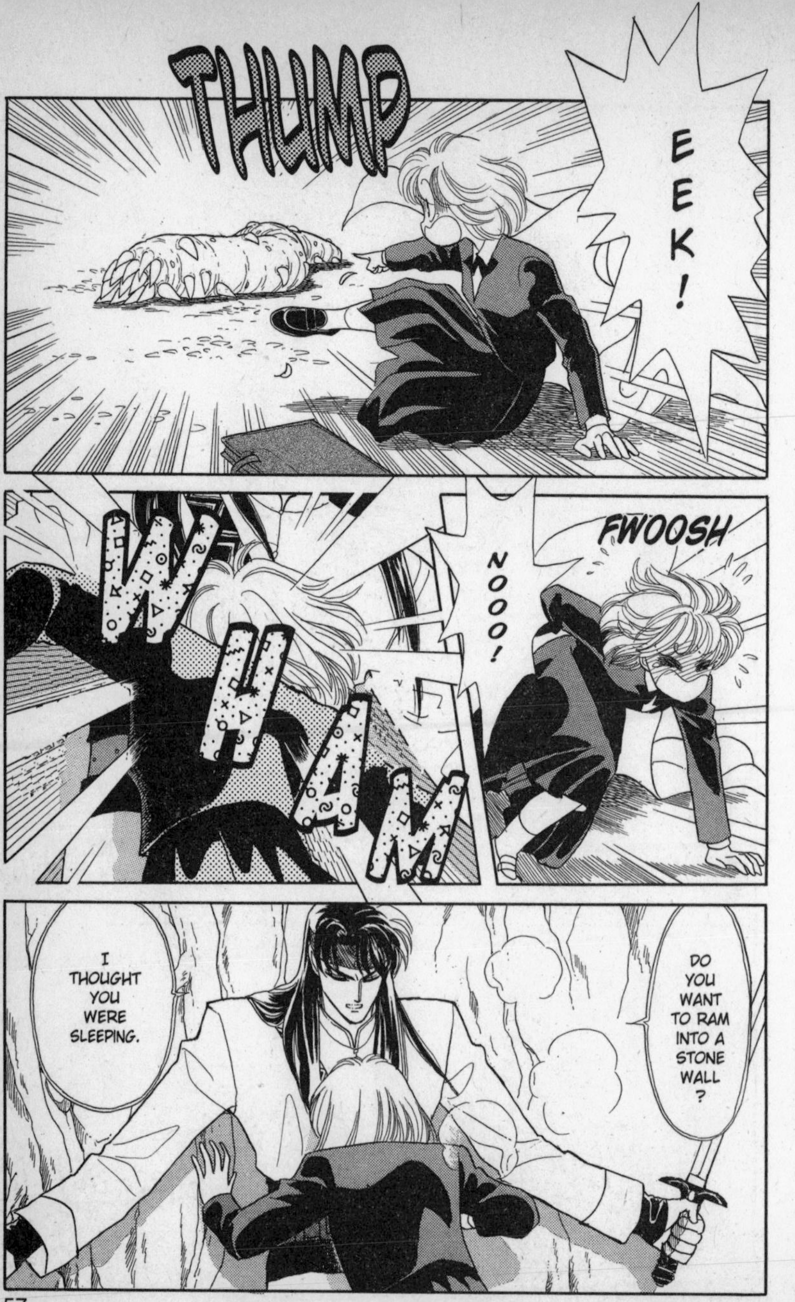
EEK!
THUMP
FWOOSH
NOOOO!
WHAM
DO YOU WANT TO RAM INTO A STONE WALL?
I THOUGHT YOU WERE SLEEPING.

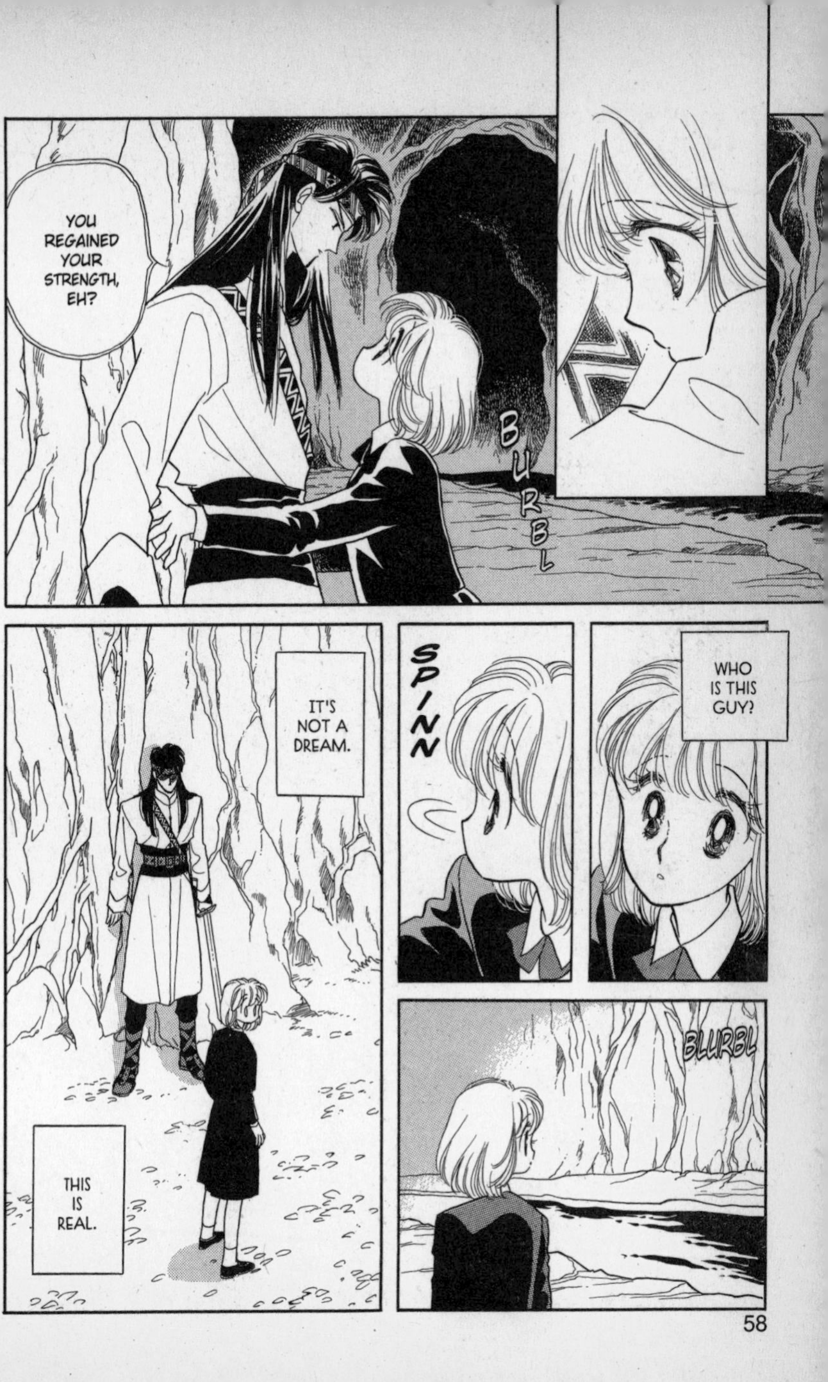
YOU REGAINED YOUR STRENGTH, EH?
BURBL
WHO IS THIS GUY?
SPINN
BLURBL
IT'S NOT A DREAM.
THIS IS REAL.

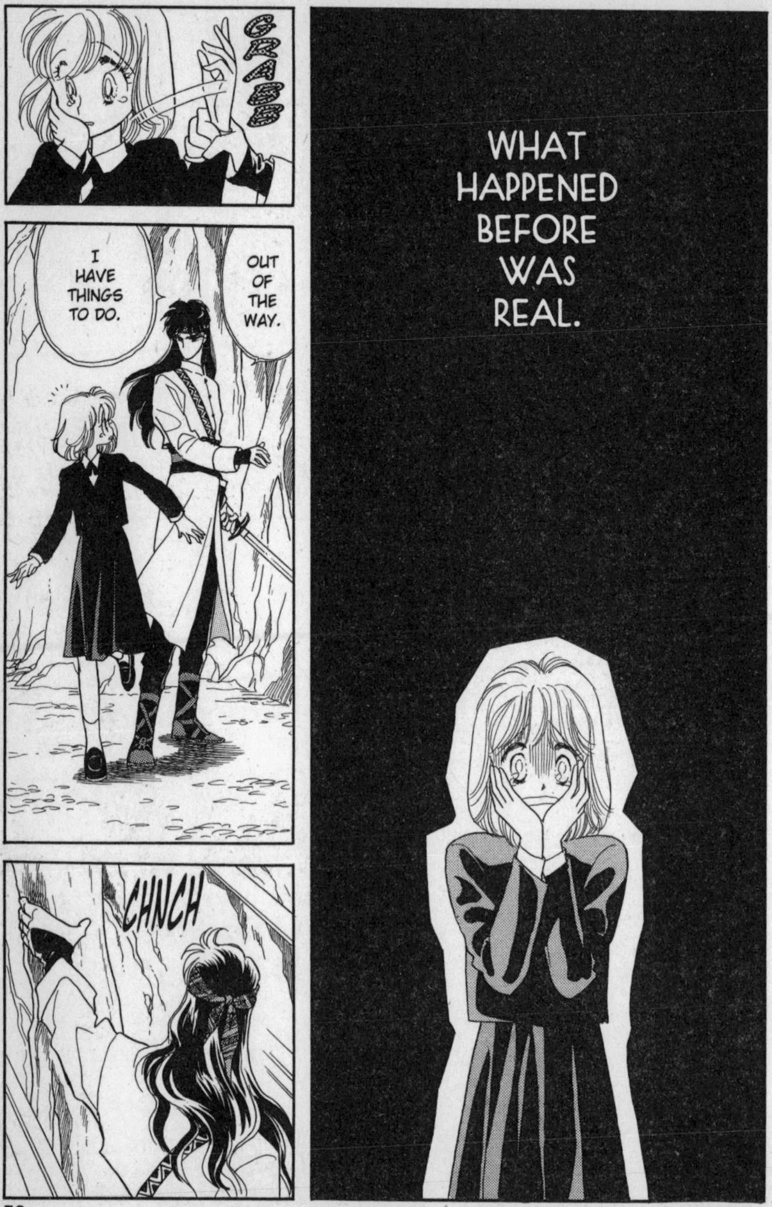
WHAT HAPPENED BEFORE WAS REAL.
GRABB
OUT OF THE WAY.
I HAVE THINGS TO DO.
CHNCH

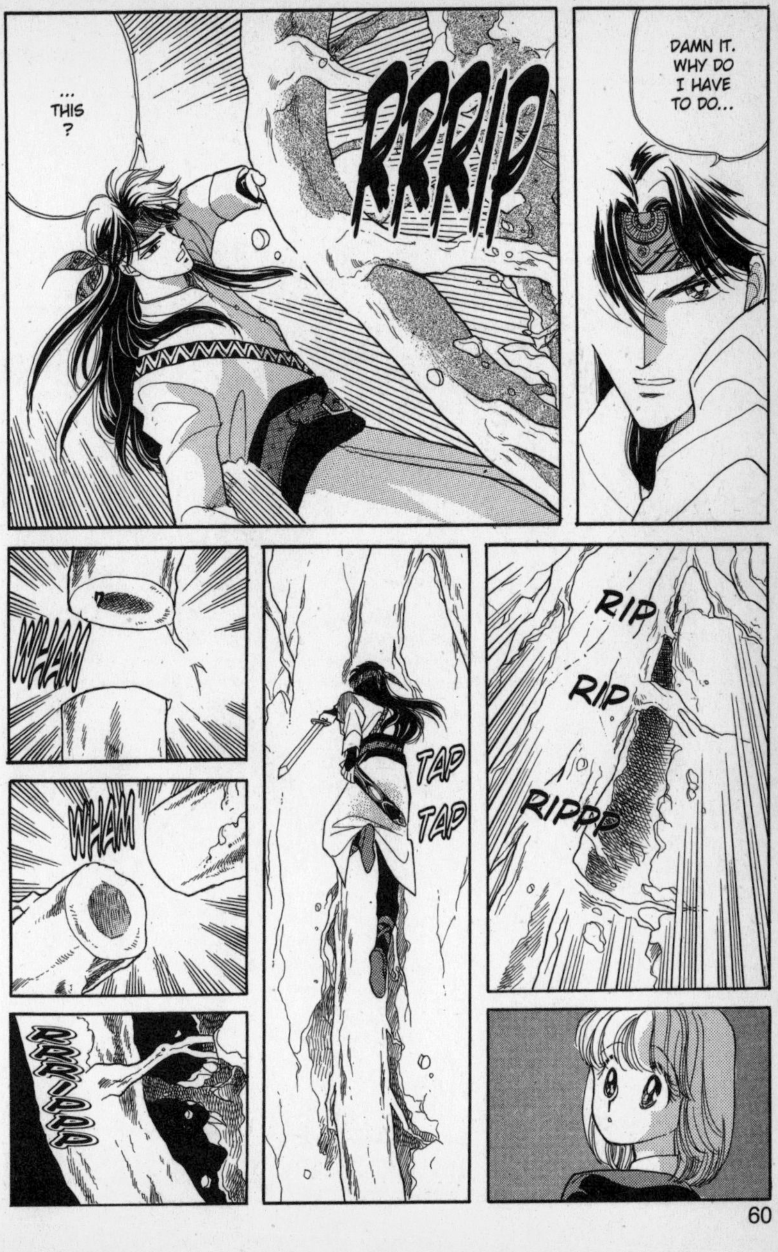
DAMN IT. WHY DO I HAVE TO DO...
... THIS ?
RRRIP
RIP
RIP
RIPPP
TAP TAP
WHAM
WHAM
RRRIPPP

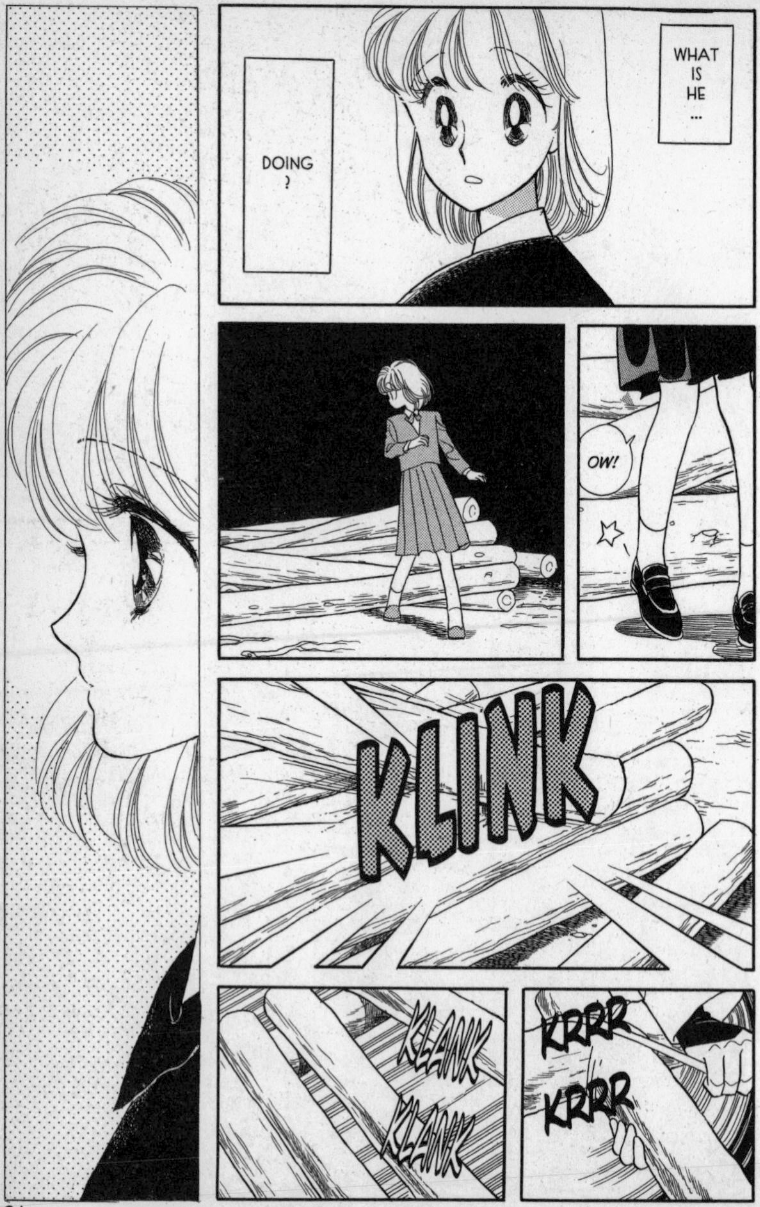
WHAT IS HE ...
DOING ?
OW!
KLINK
KRRR
KRRR
KLANK
KLANK

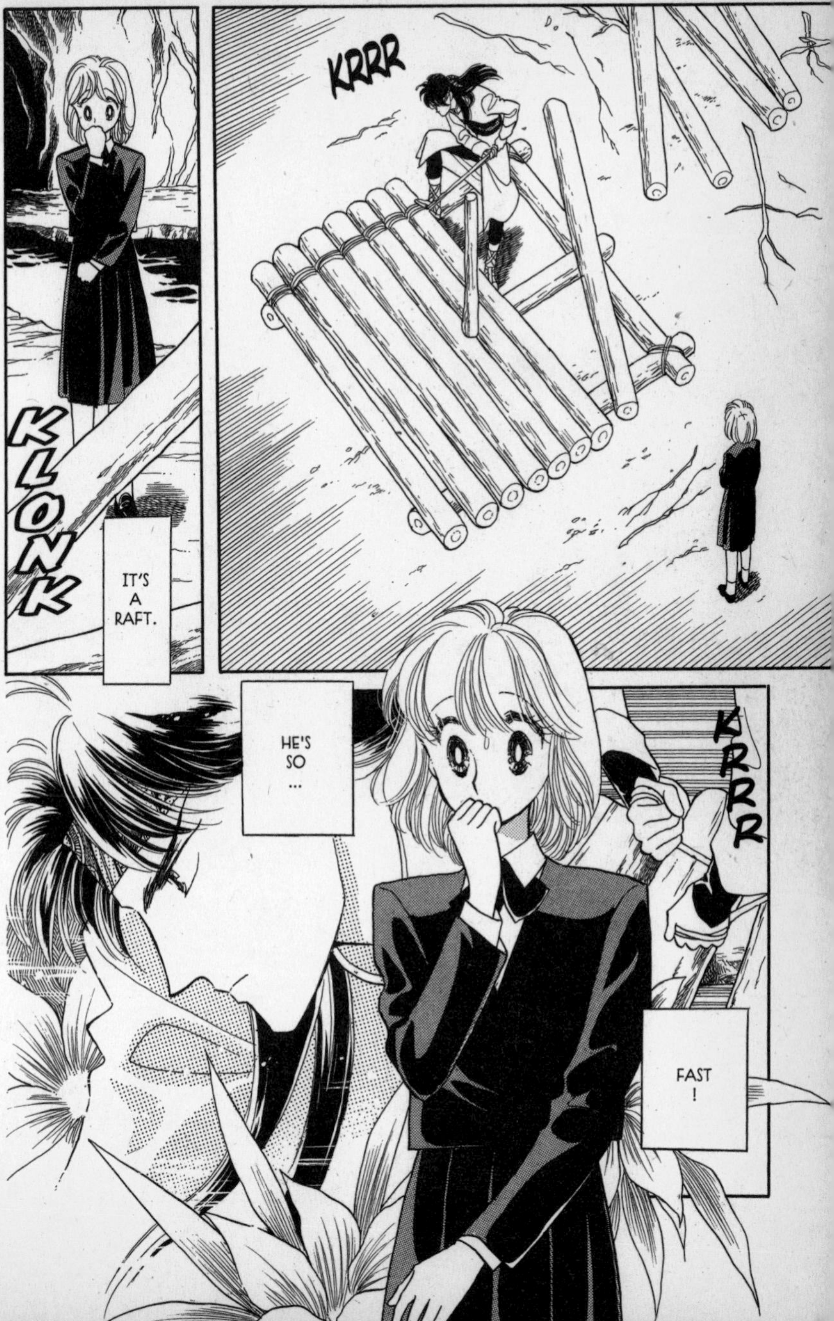
KRRR
KLONK
IT'S A RAFT.
KRRR
HE'S SO ...
FAST !

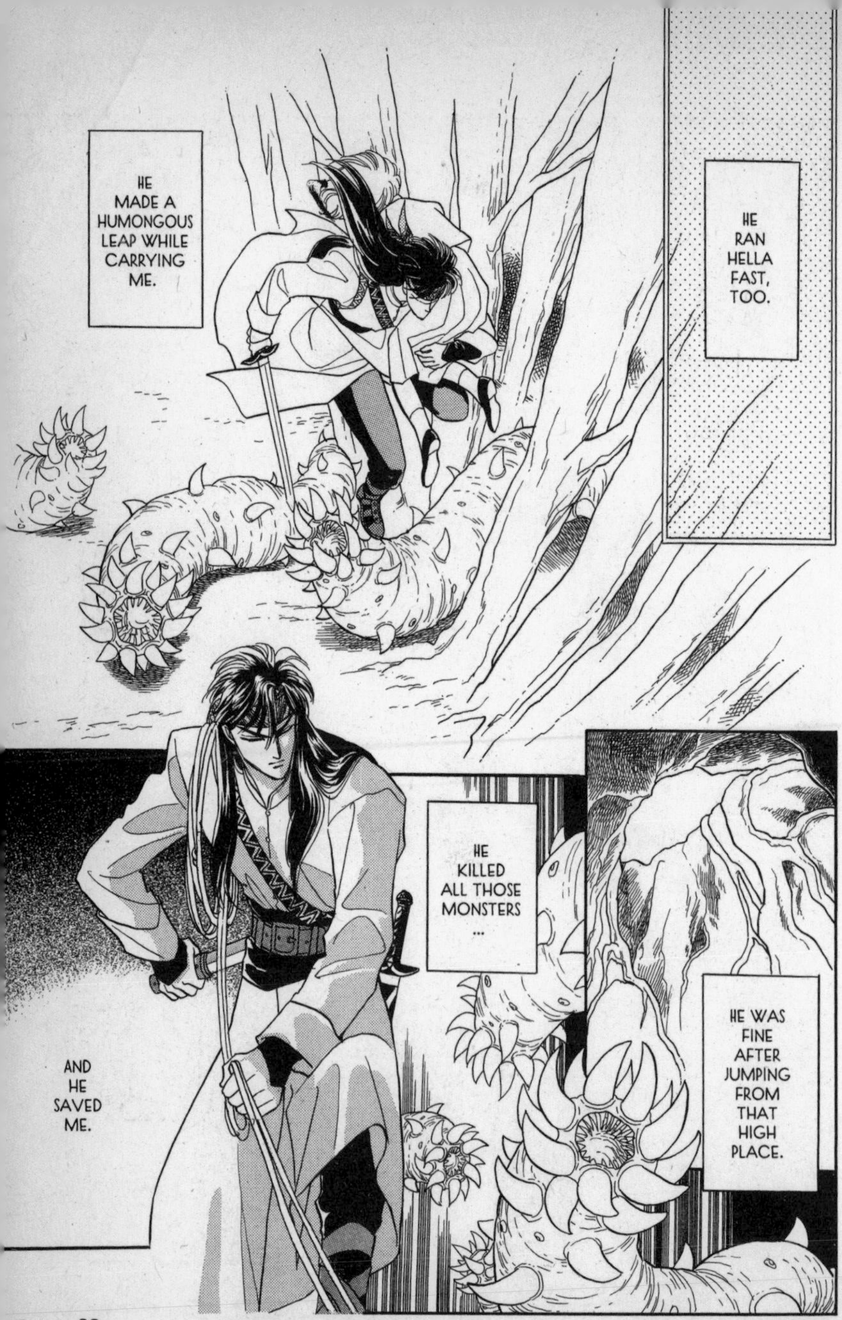

HE RAN HELLA FAST, TOO.
HE MADE A HUMONGOUS LEAP WHILE CARRYING ME.
HE WAS FINE AFTER JUMPING FROM THAT HIGH PLACE.
HE KILLED ALL THOSE MONSTERS ...
AND HE SAVED ME.

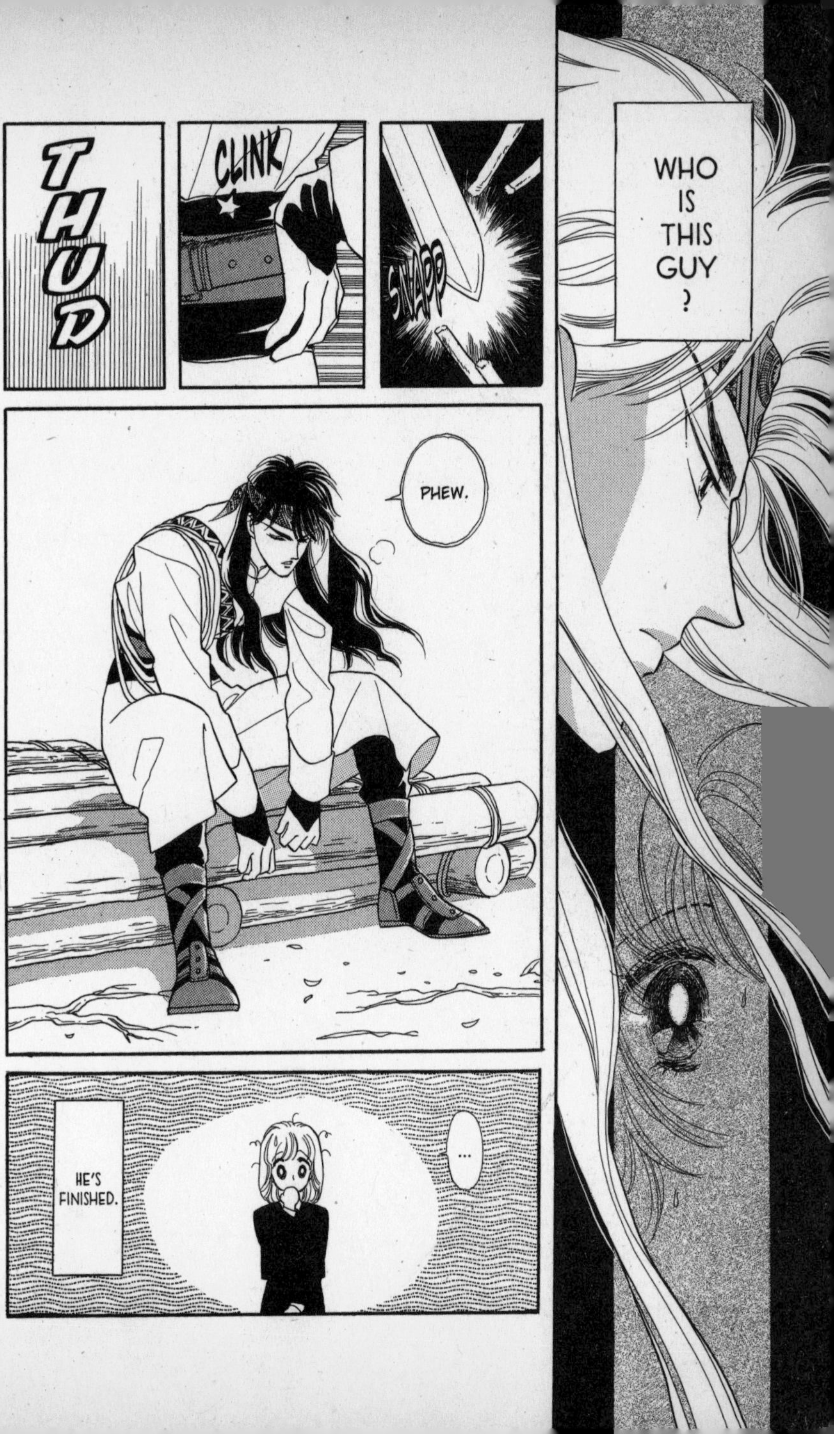
WHO IS THIS GUY?
SNAPP
CLINK
THUD
PHEW.
...
HE'S FINISHED.

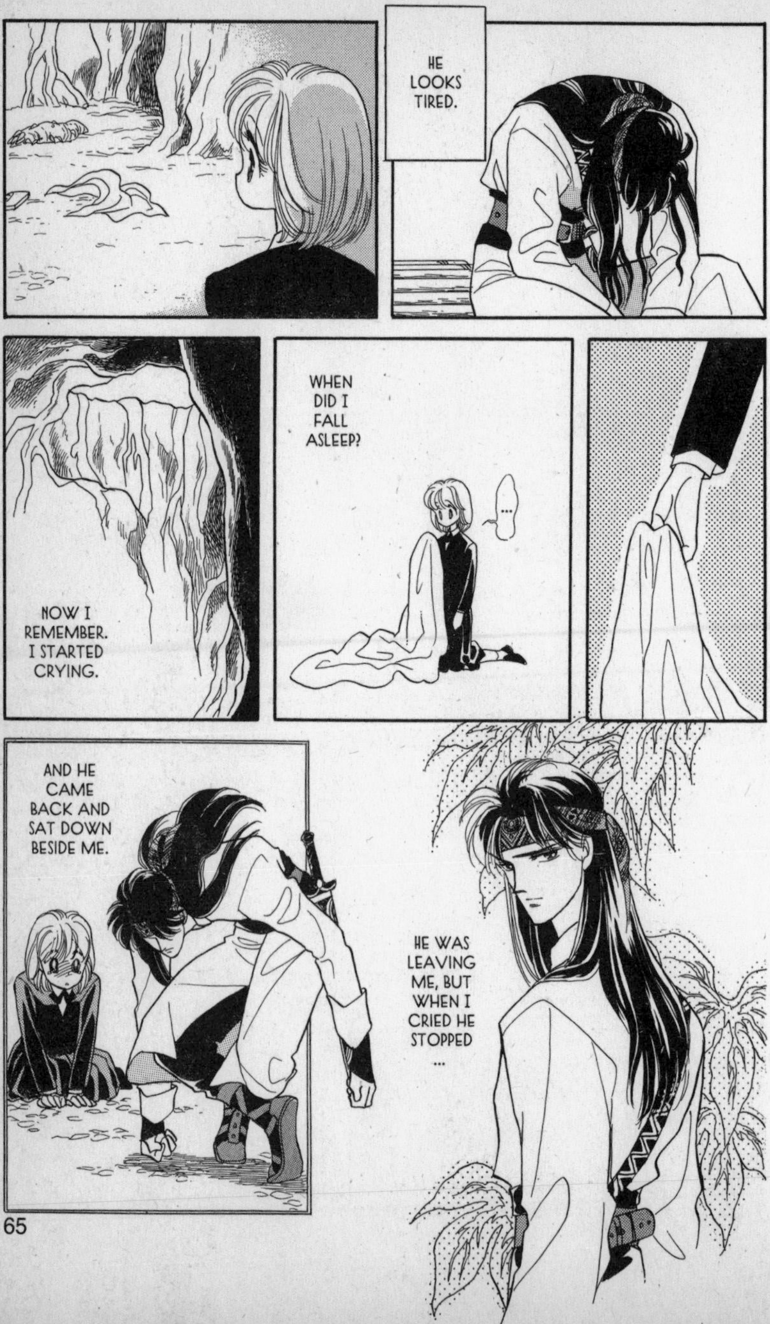
HE LOOKS TIRED.
WHEN DID I FALL ASLEEP?
...
NOW I REMEMBER. I STARTED CRYING.
HE WAS LEAVING ME, BUT WHEN I CRIED HE STOPPED ...
AND HE CAME BACK AND SAT DOWN BESIDE ME.

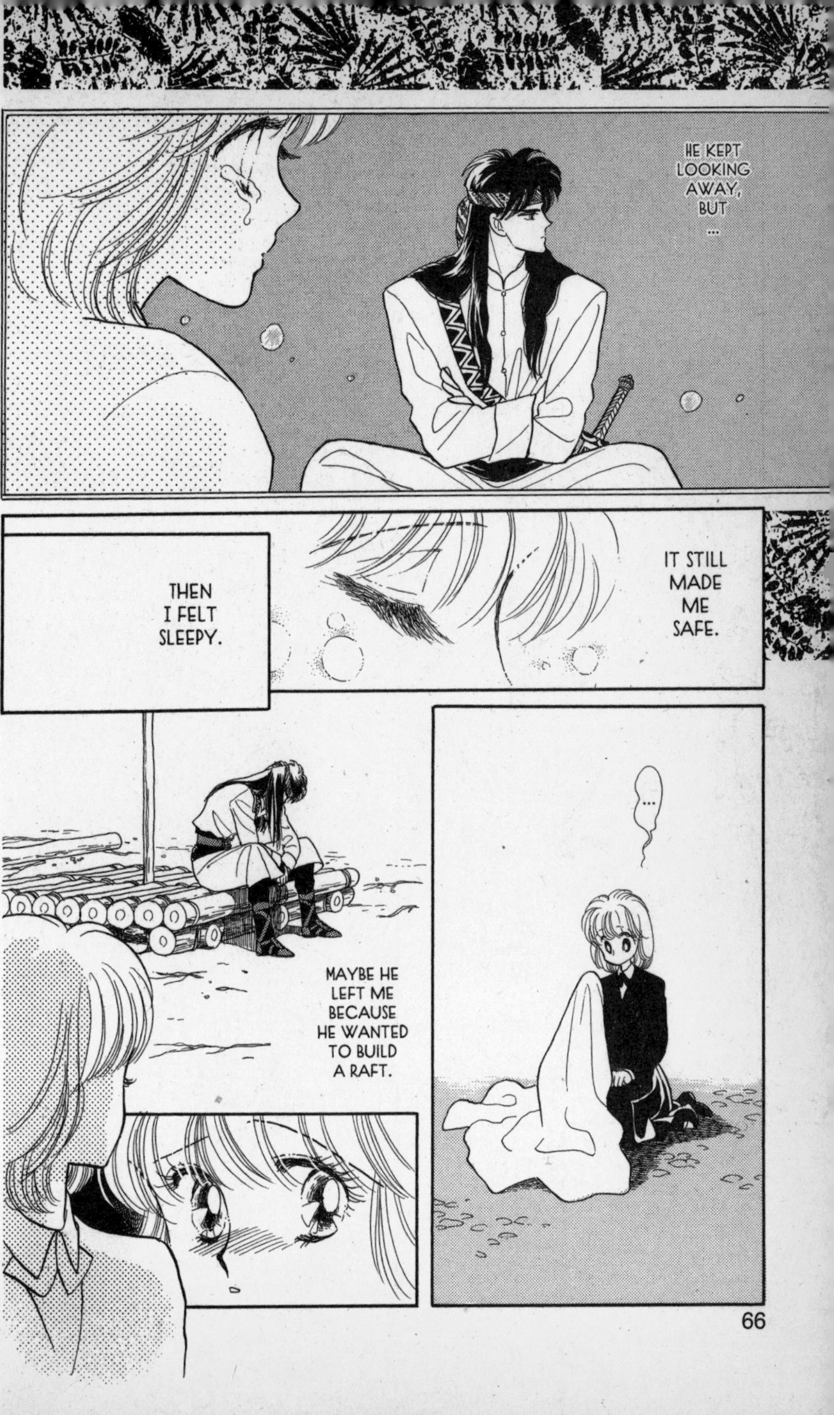
HE KEPT LOOKING AWAY, BUT ...
IT STILL MADE ME SAFE.
THEN I FELT SLEEPY.
...
MAYBE HE LEFT ME BECAUSE HE WANTED TO BUILD A RAFT.

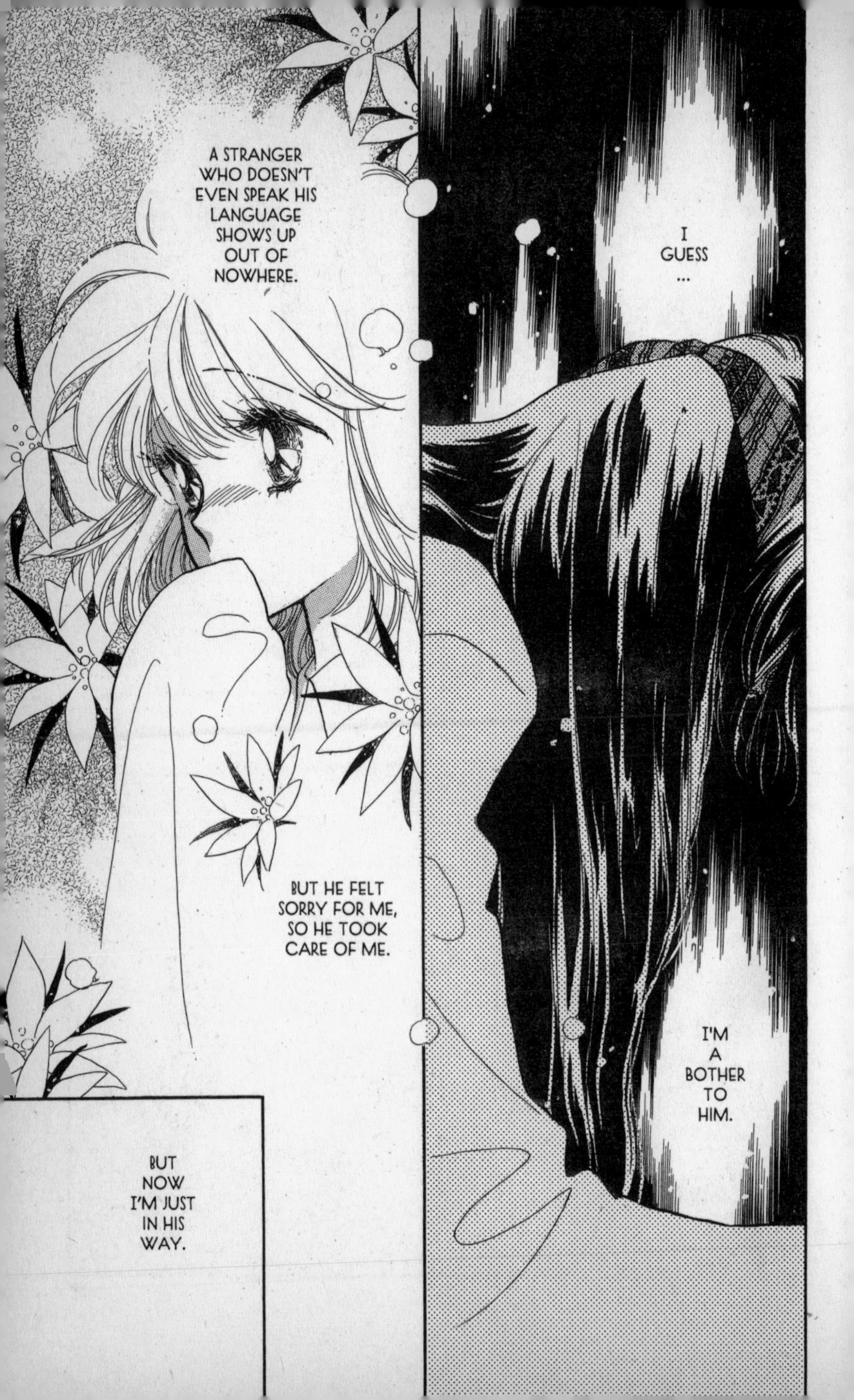
I GUESS ...
I'M A BOTHER TO HIM.
A STRANGER WHO DOESN'T EVEN SPEAK HIS LANGUAGE SHOWS UP OUT OF NOWHERE.
BUT HE FELT SORRY FOR ME, SO HE TOOK CARE OF ME.
BUT NOW I'M JUST IN HIS WAY.

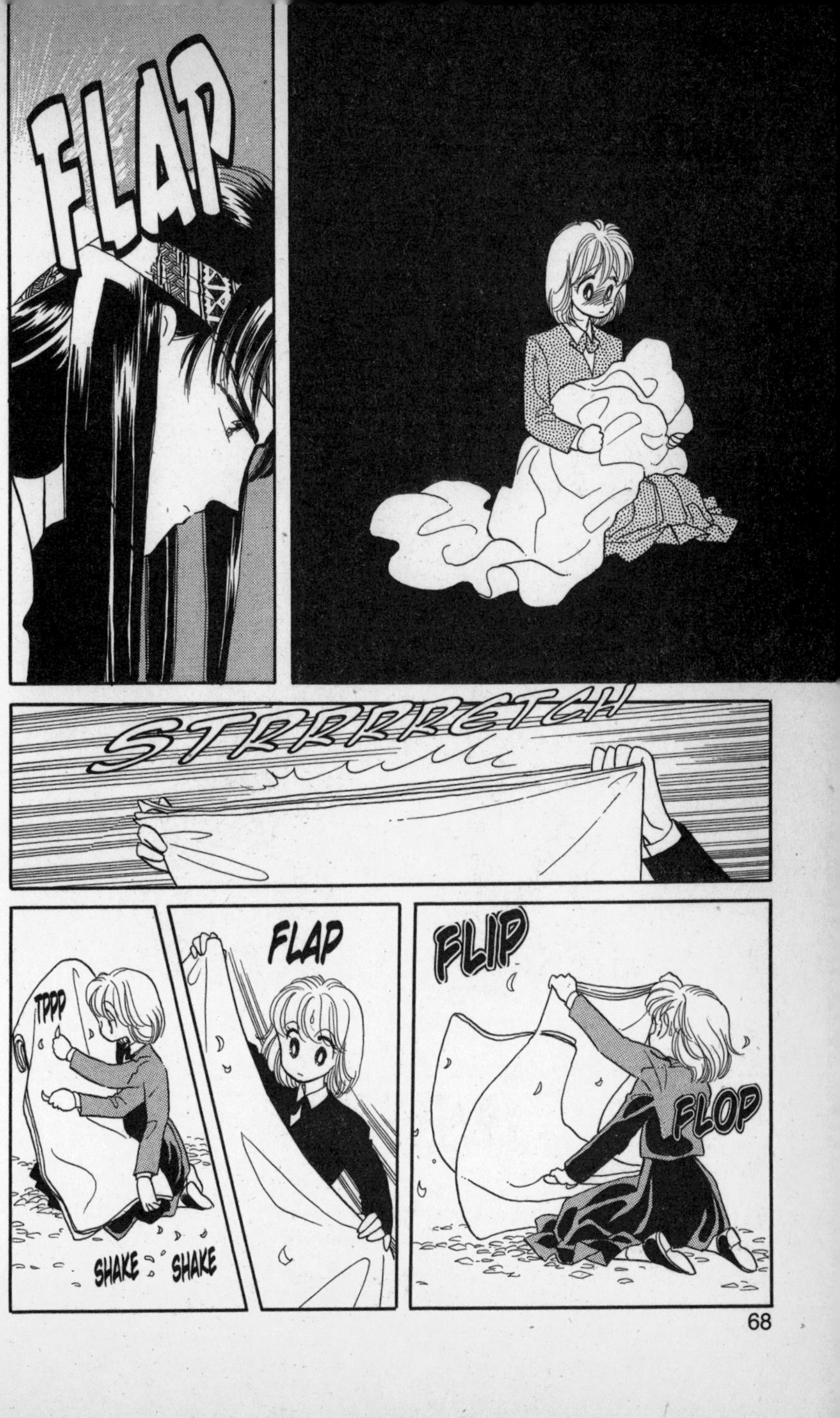
FLAP
STRRRRETCH
FLIP
FLOP
FLAP
TPPP
SHAKE
SHAKE

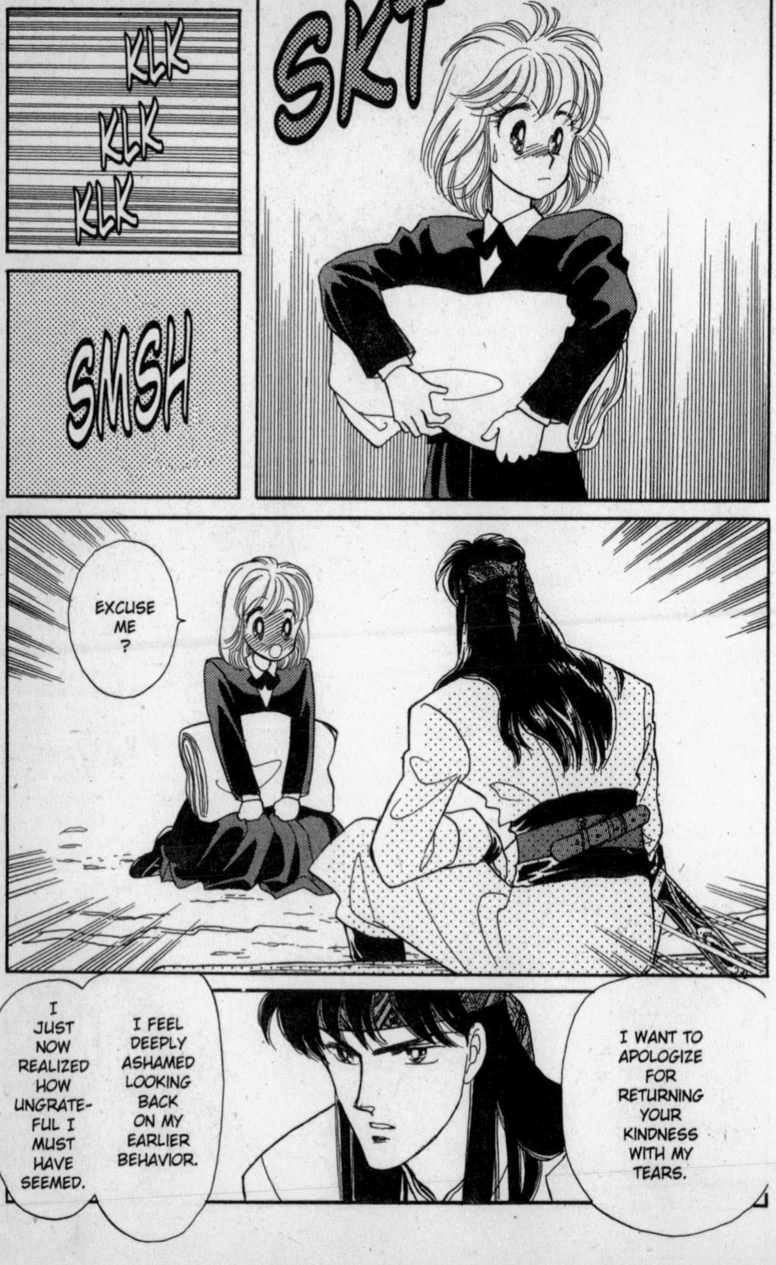
SKT
KLK
KLK
KLK
SMSH
EXCUSE ME ?
I WANT TO APOLOGIZE FOR RETURNING YOUR KINDNESS WITH MY TEARS.
I FEEL DEEPLY ASHAMED LOOKING BACK ON MY EARLIER BEHAVIOR.
I JUST NOW REALIZED HOW UNGRATE-FUL I MUST HAVE SEEMED.

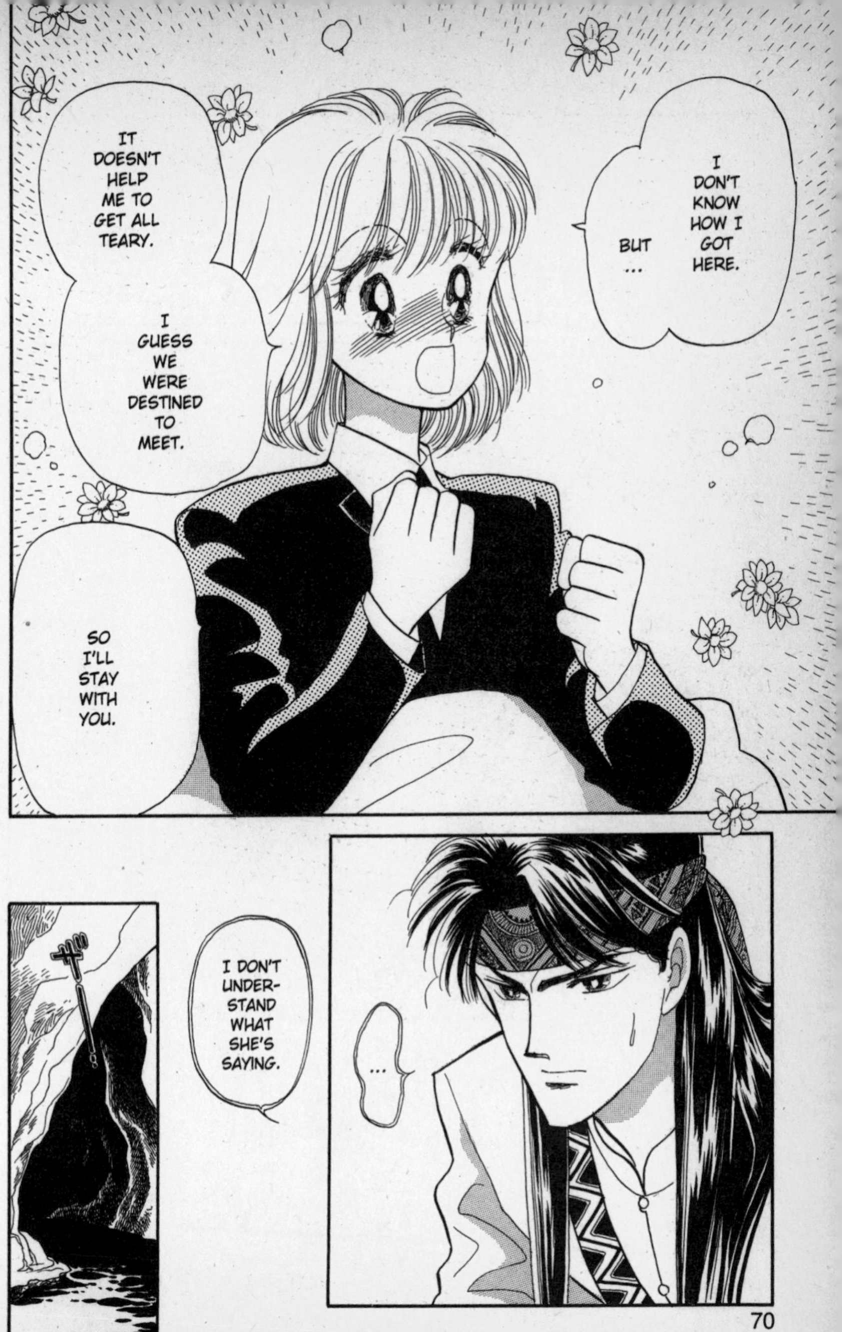
I DON'T KNOW HOW I GOT HERE.
BUT ...
IT DOESN'T HELP ME TO GET ALL TEARY.
I GUESS WE WERE DESTINED TO MEET.
SO I'LL STAY WITH YOU.
...
I DON'T UNDER-STAND WHAT SHE'S SAYING.

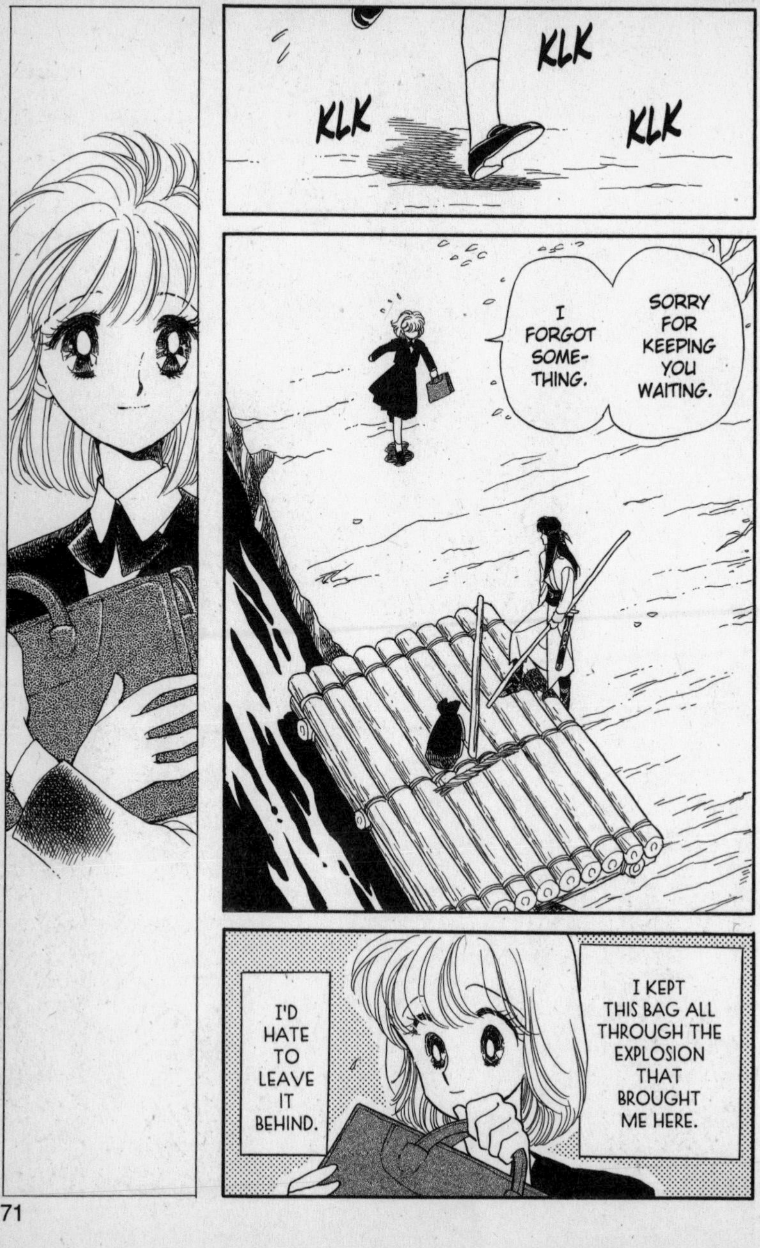
KLK
KLK
KLK
SORRY FOR KEEPING YOU WAITING.
I FORGOT SOME-THING.
I KEPT THIS BAG ALL THROUGH THE EXPLOSION THAT BROUGHT ME HERE.
I'D HATE TO LEAVE IT BEHIND.

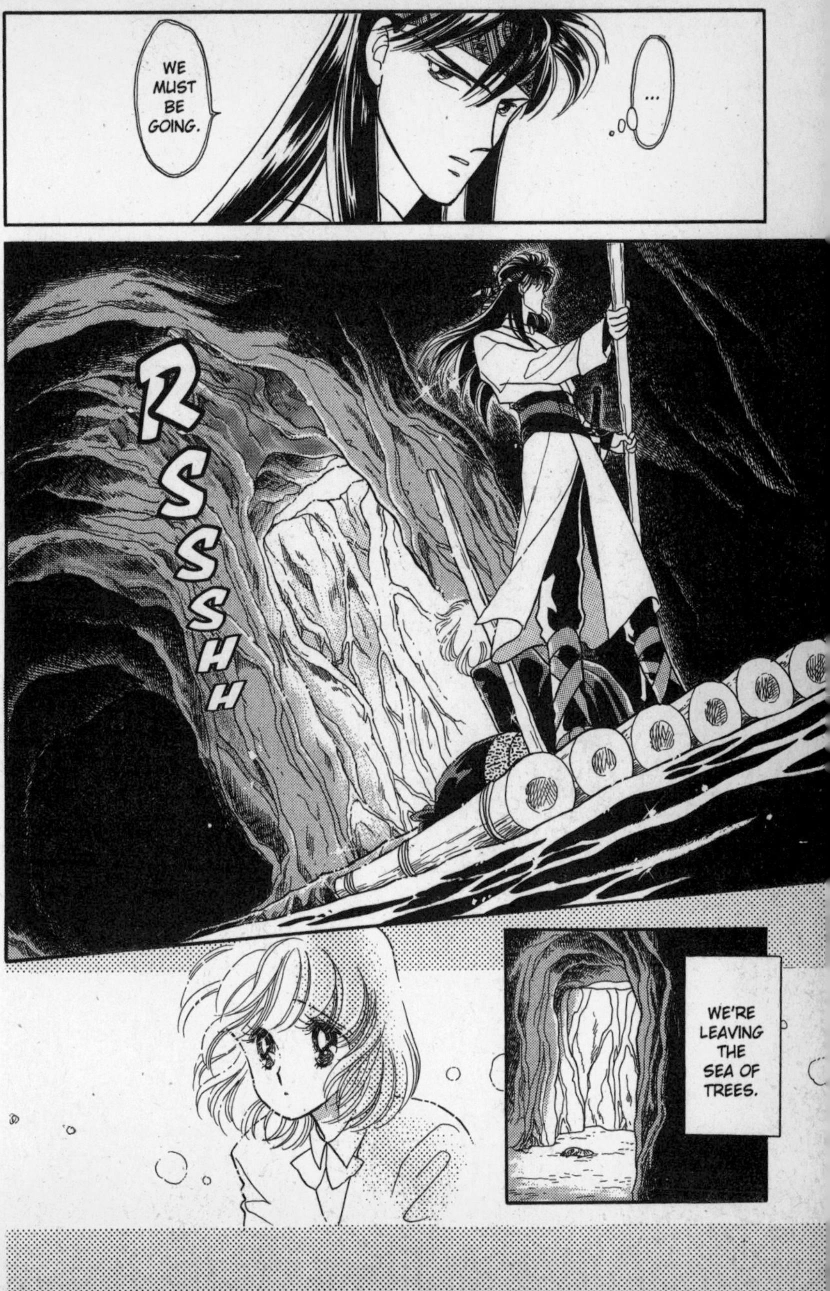
...
WE MUST BE GOING.
RSSSSHH
WE'RE LEAVING THE SEA OF TREES.

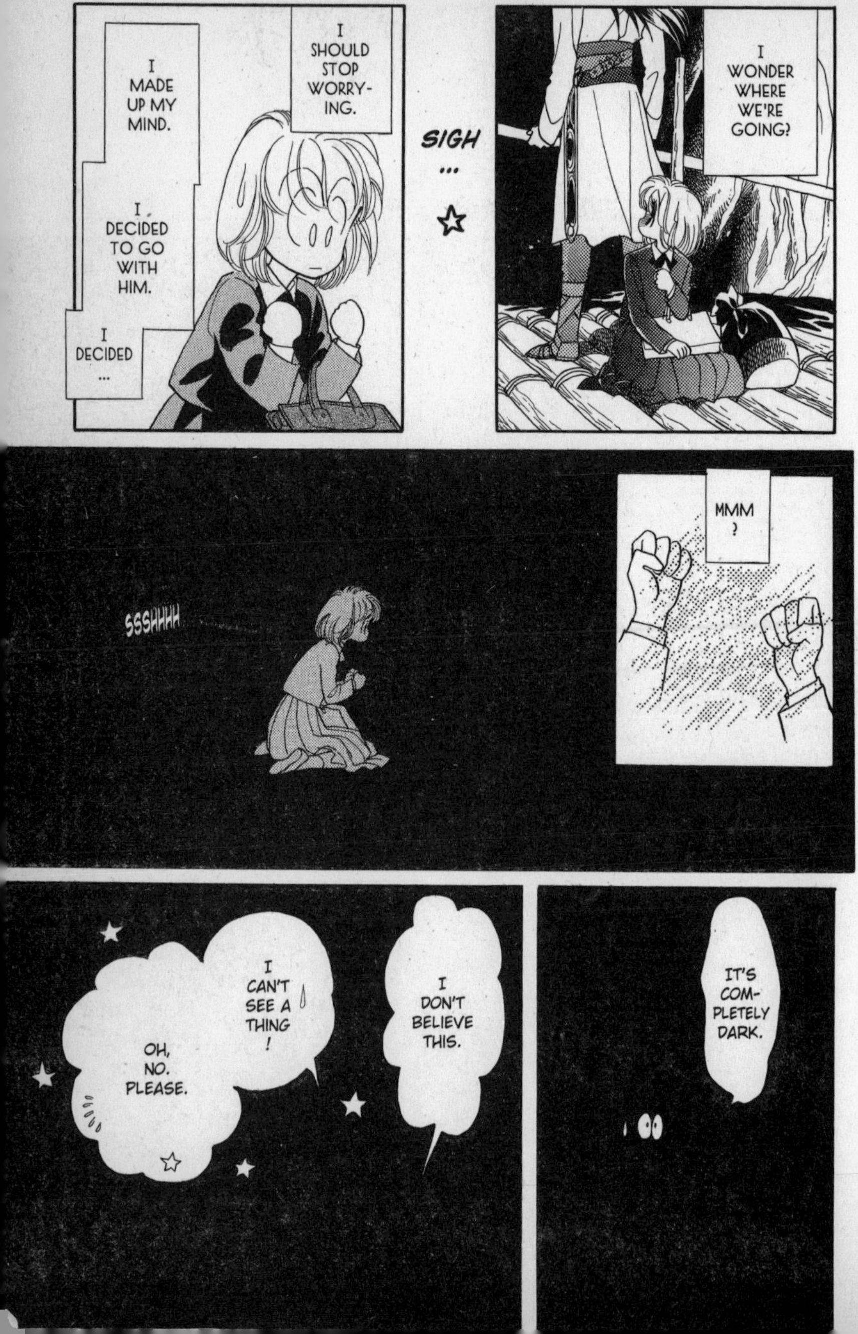
I WONDER WHERE WE'RE GOING?
SIGH ... ☆
I SHOULD STOP WORRY-ING.
I MADE UP MY MIND.
I DECIDED TO GO WITH HIM.
I DECIDED ...
MMM ?
SSSHHHH
IT'S COM-PLETELY DARK.
I DON'T BELIEVE THIS.
I CAN'T SEE A THING !
OH, NO. PLEASE.

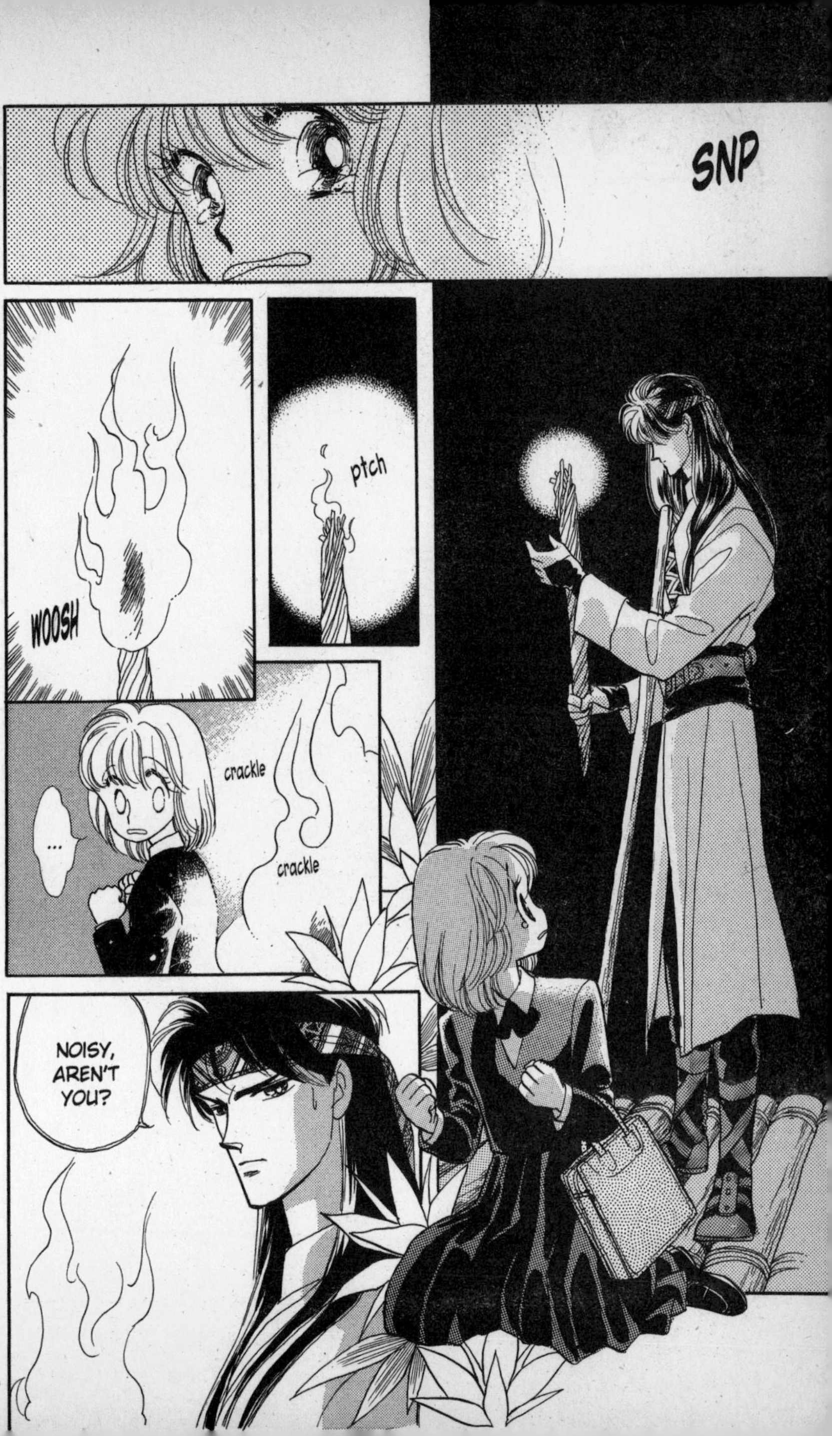
SNP
ptch
WOOSH
crackle
crackle
...
NOISY, AREN'T YOU?

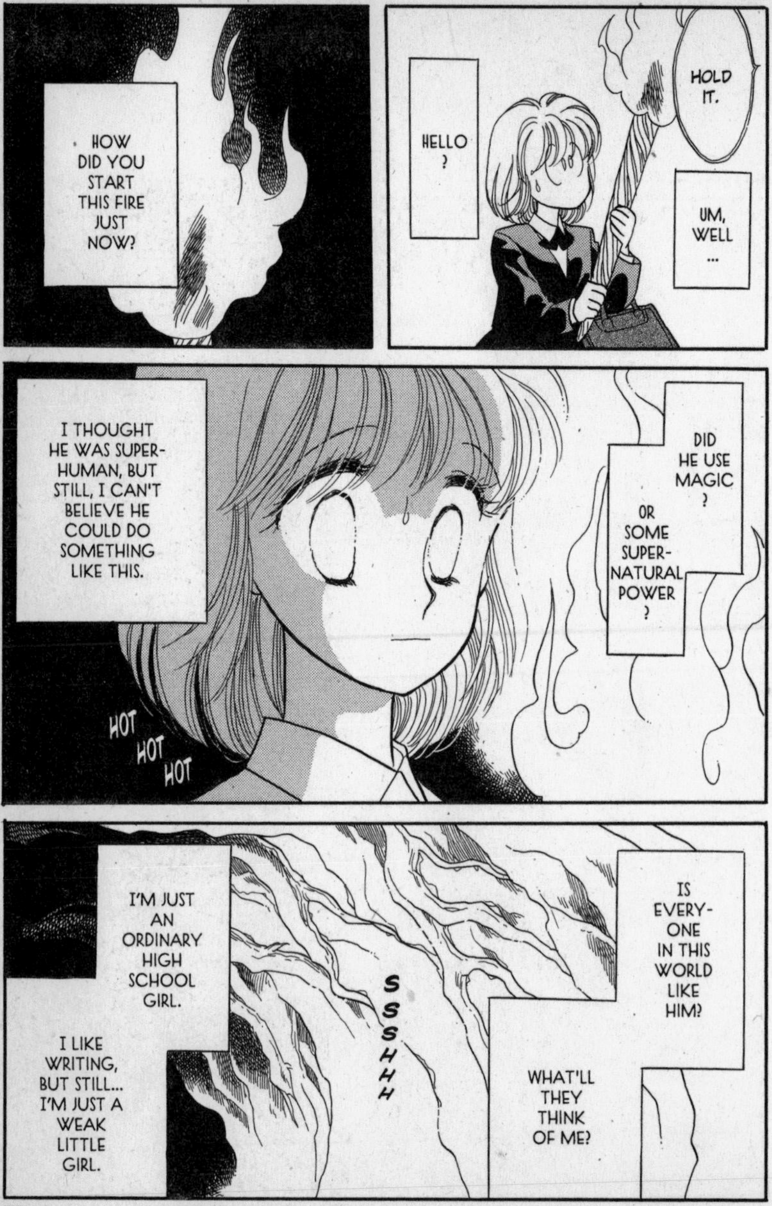
HOLD IT.
HELLO ?
UM, WELL ...
HOW DID YOU START THIS FIRE JUST NOW?
DID HE USE MAGIC ?
OR SOME SUPER-NATURAL POWER ?
I THOUGHT HE WAS SUPER-HUMAN, BUT STILL, I CAN'T BELIEVE HE COULD DO SOMETHING LIKE THIS.
HOT HOT HOT
IS EVERY-ONE IN THIS WORLD LIKE HIM?
WHAT'LL THEY THINK OF ME?
I'M JUST AN ORDINARY HIGH SCHOOL GIRL.
SSSHHH
I LIKE WRITING, BUT STILL... I'M JUST A WEAK LITTLE GIRL.

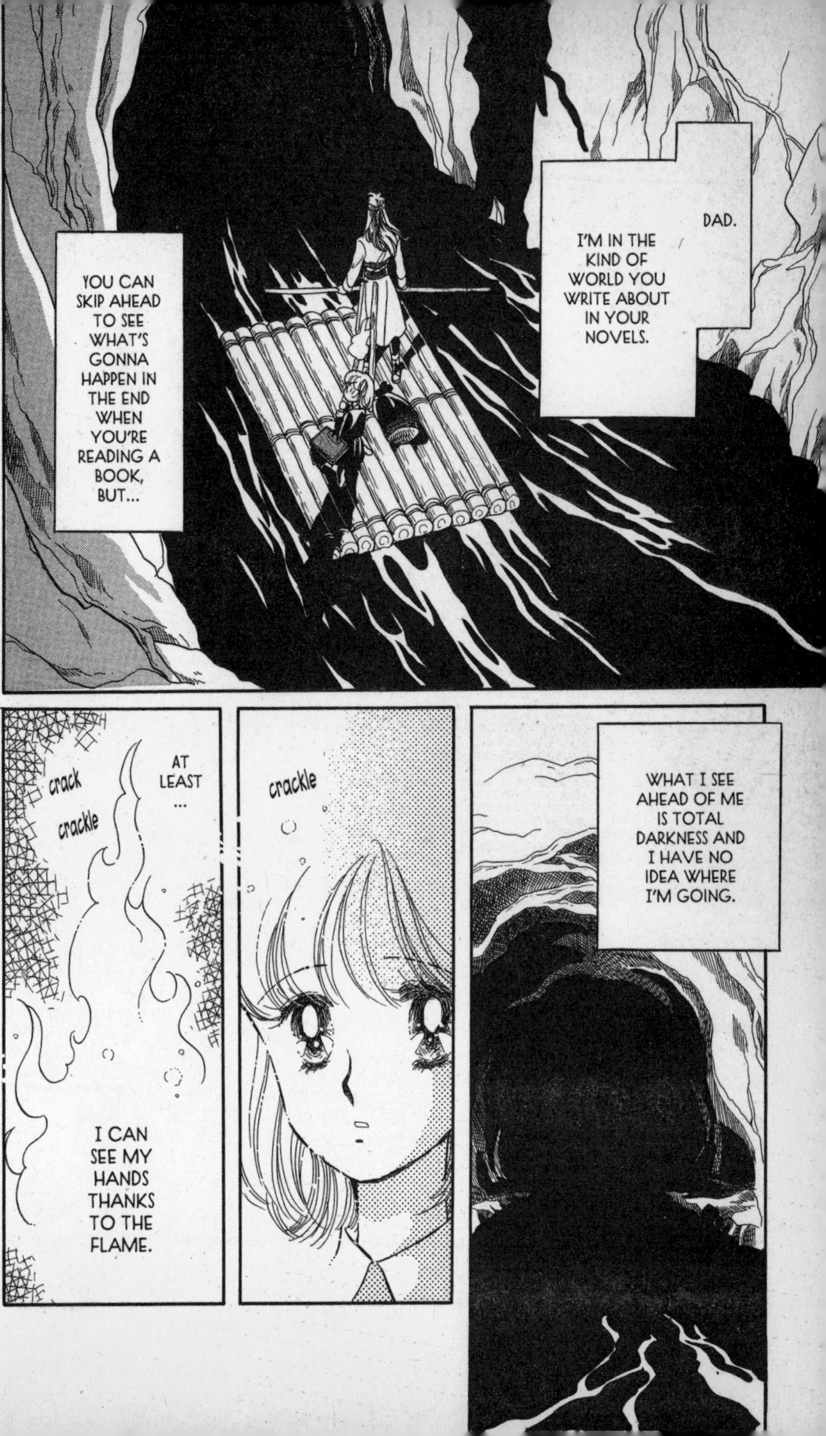
DAD.
I'M IN THE KIND OF WORLD YOU WRITE ABOUT IN YOUR NOVELS.
YOU CAN SKIP AHEAD TO SEE WHAT'S GONNA HAPPEN IN THE END WHEN YOU'RE READING A BOOK, BUT...
WHAT I SEE AHEAD OF ME IS TOTAL DARKNESS AND I HAVE NO IDEA WHERE I'M GOING.
crackle
AT LEAST ...
crack
crackle
I CAN SEE MY HANDS THANKS TO THE FLAME.

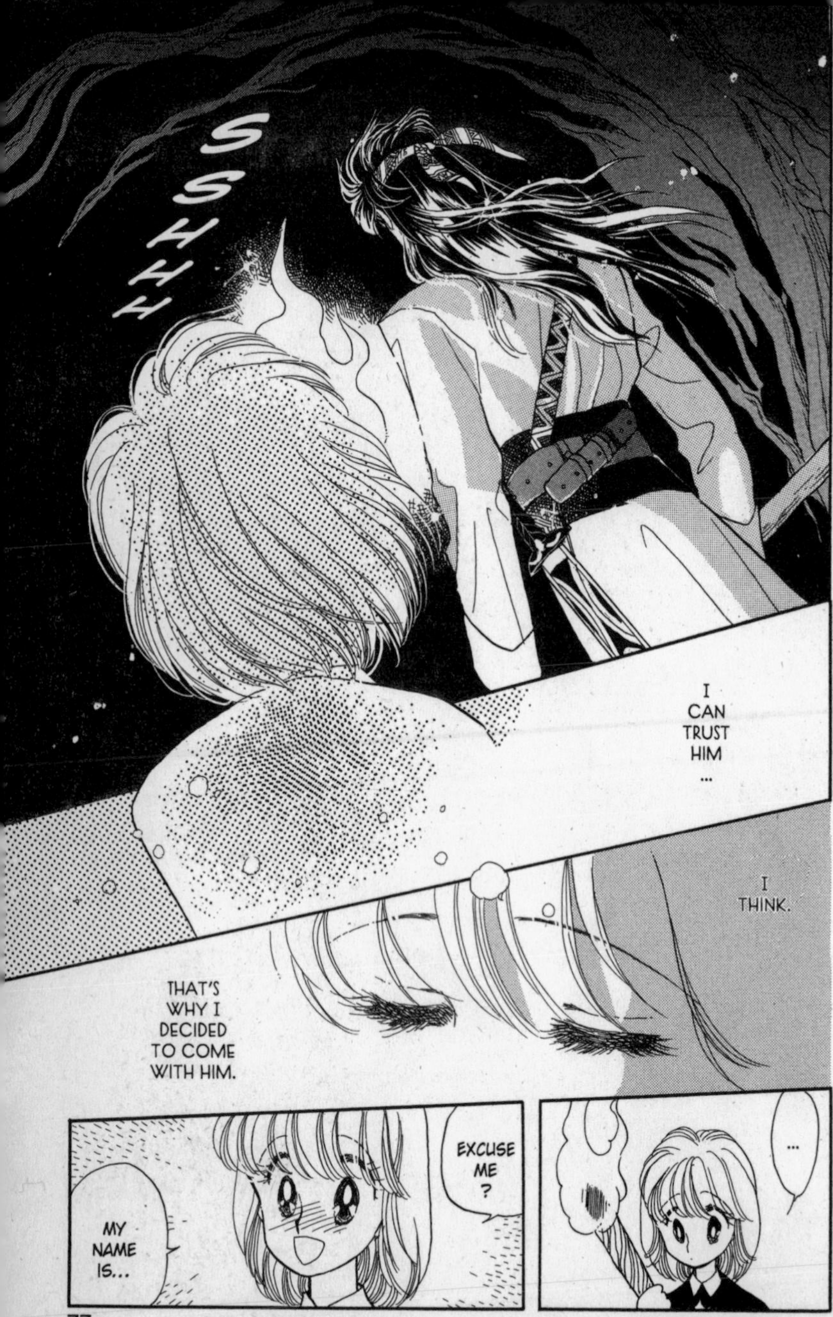
SSHHH
I CAN TRUST HIM ...
I THINK.
THAT'S WHY I DECIDED TO COME WITH HIM.
...
EXCUSE ME ?
MY NAME IS...

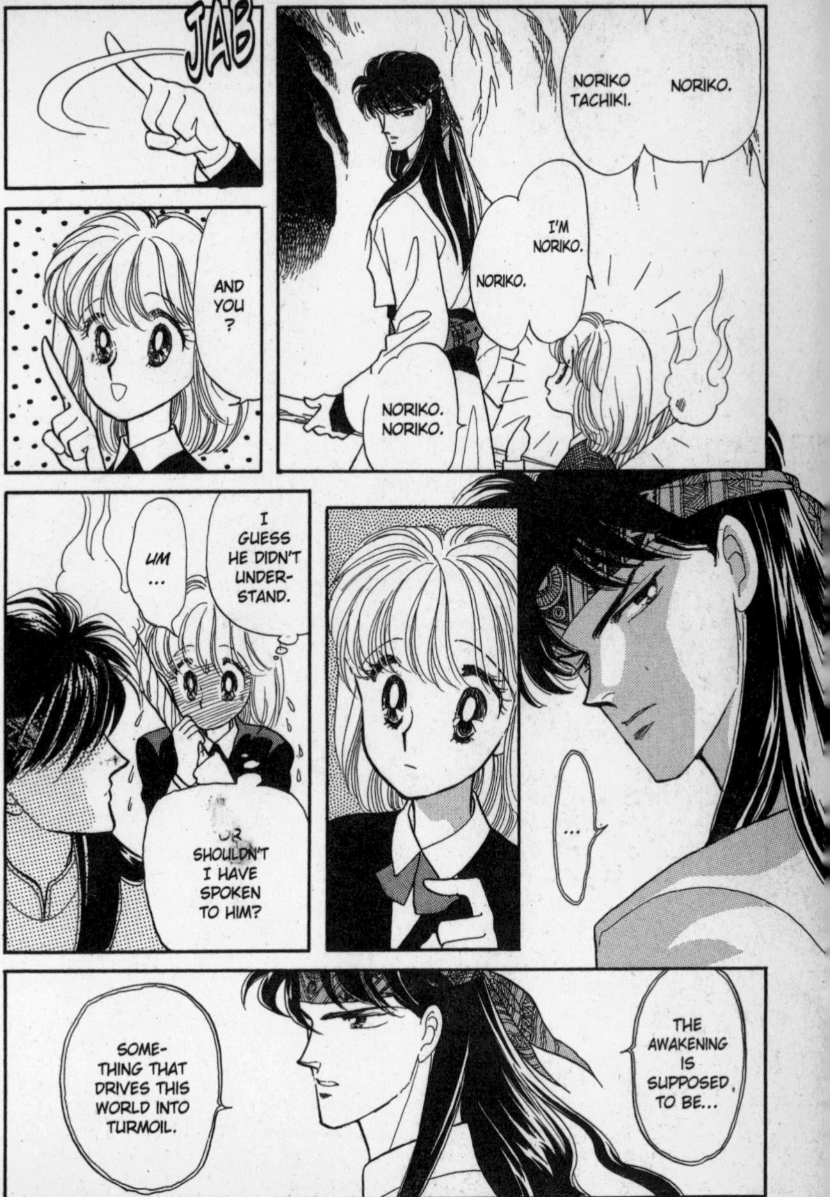
NORIKO TACHIKI. NORIKO.
I'M NORIKO.
NORIKO.
NORIKO. NORIKO.
JAB
AND YOU ?
...
I GUESS HE DIDN'T UNDER-STAND.
UM ...
SHOULDN'T I HAVE SPOKEN TO HIM?
THE AWAKENING IS SUPPOSED TO BE...
SOME-THING THAT DRIVES THIS WORLD INTO TURMOIL.

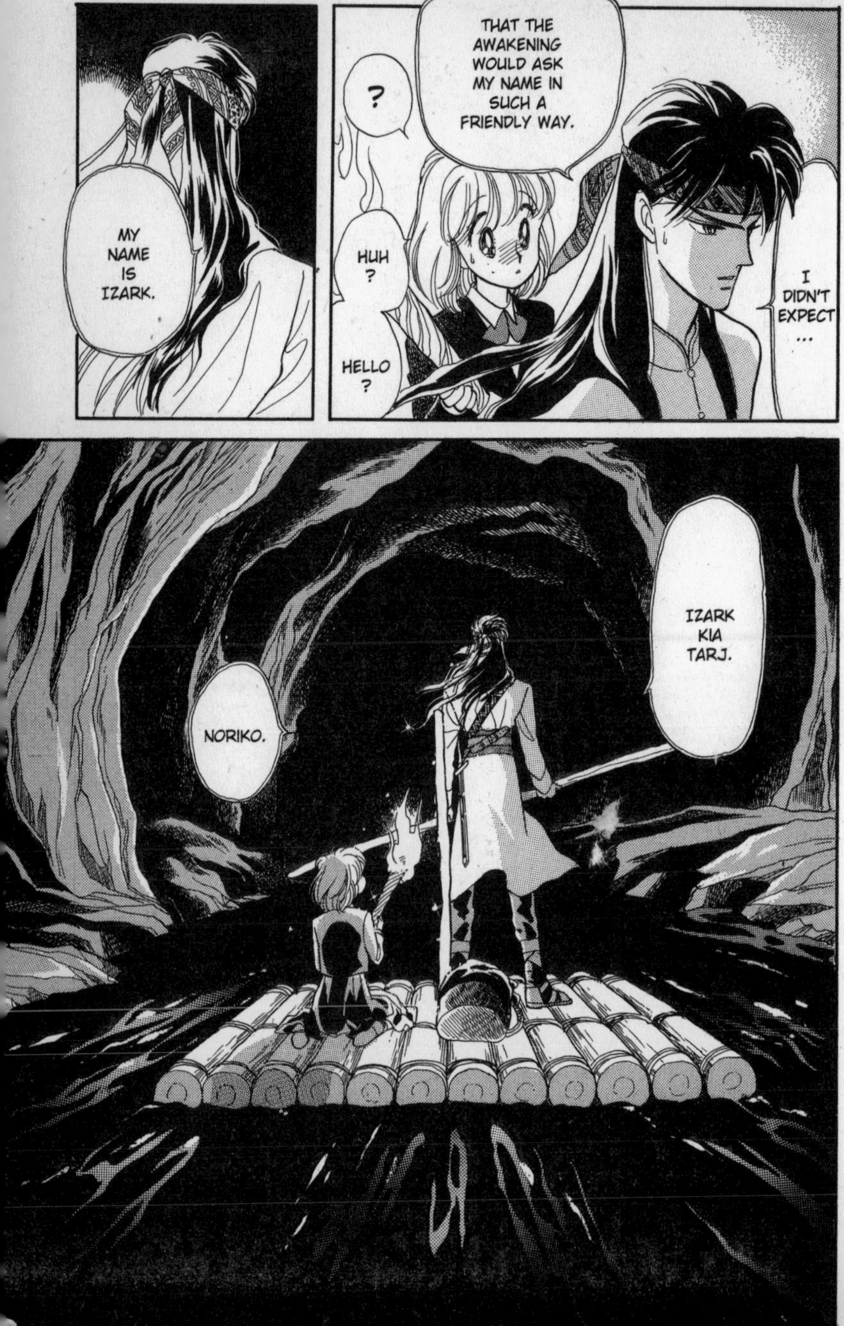
I DIDN'T EXPECT ...
THAT THE AWAKENING WOULD ASK MY NAME IN SUCH A FRIENDLY WAY.
?
HUH?
HELLO?
MY NAME IS IZARK.
IZARK KIA TARJ.
NORIKO.

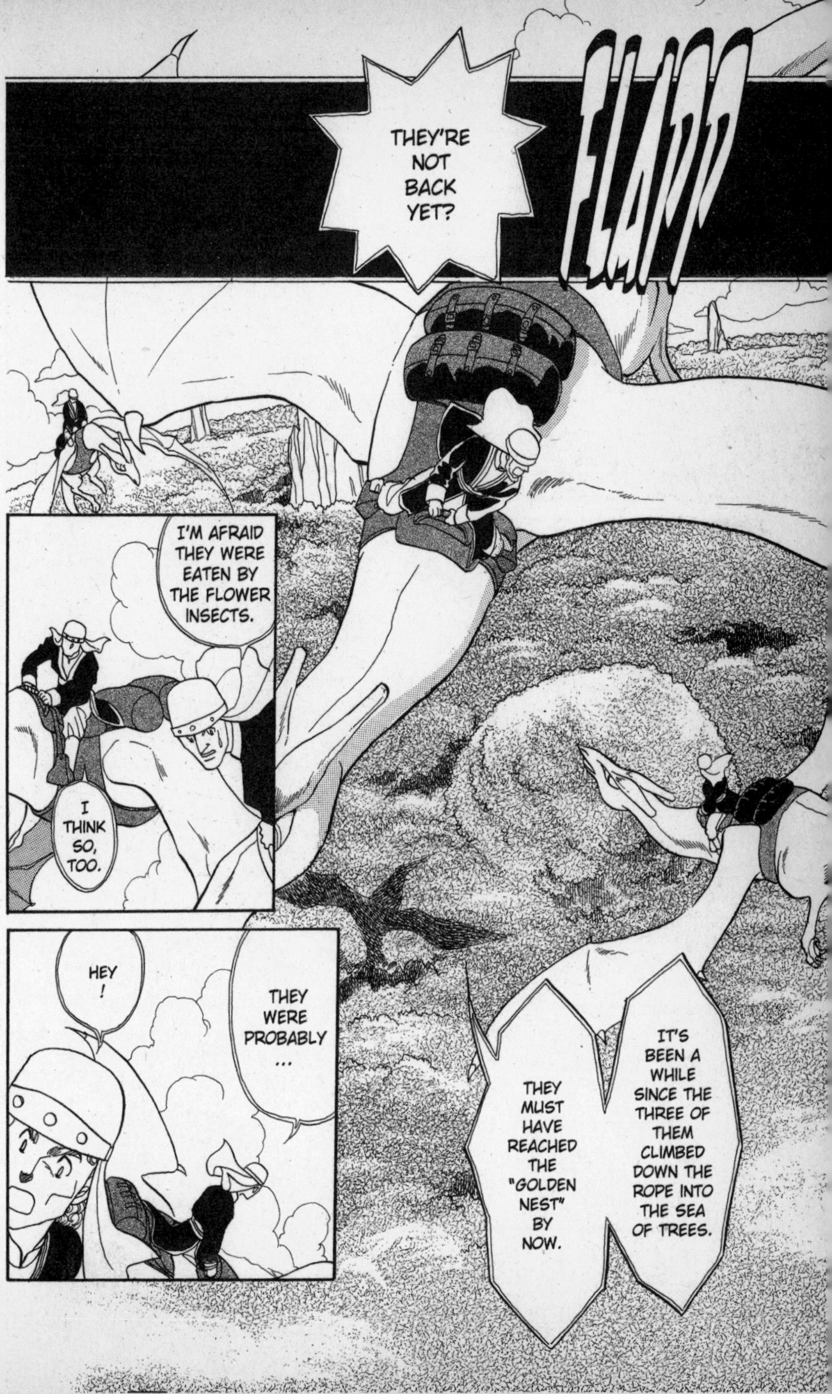
FLAPP
THEY'RE NOT BACK YET?
IT'S BEEN A WHILE SINCE THE THREE OF THEM CLIMBED DOWN THE ROPE INTO THE SEA OF TREES.
THEY MUST HAVE REACHED THE "GOLDEN NEST" BY NOW.
I'M AFRAID THEY WERE EATEN BY THE FLOWER INSECTS.
I THINK SO, TOO.
THEY WERE PROBABLY ...
HEY!

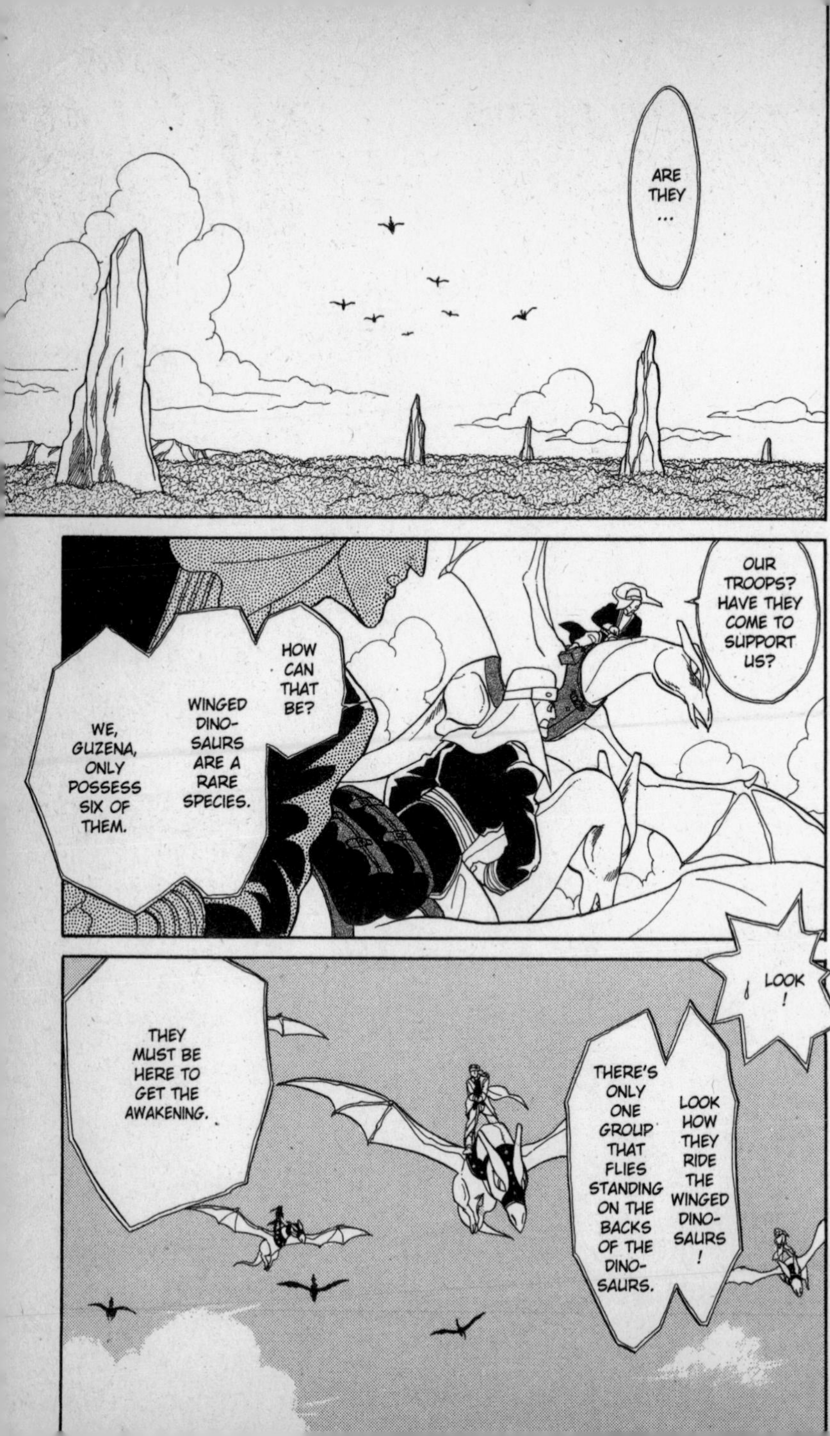
ARE THEY ...
OUR TROOPS? HAVE THEY COME TO SUPPORT US?
HOW CAN THAT BE?
WINGED DINO-SAURS ARE A RARE SPECIES.
WE, GUZENA, ONLY POSSESS SIX OF THEM.
LOOK!
LOOK HOW THEY RIDE THE WINGED DINO-SAURS!
THERE'S ONLY ONE GROUP THAT FLIES STANDING ON THE BACKS OF THE DINO-SAURS.
THEY MUST BE HERE TO GET THE AWAKENING.

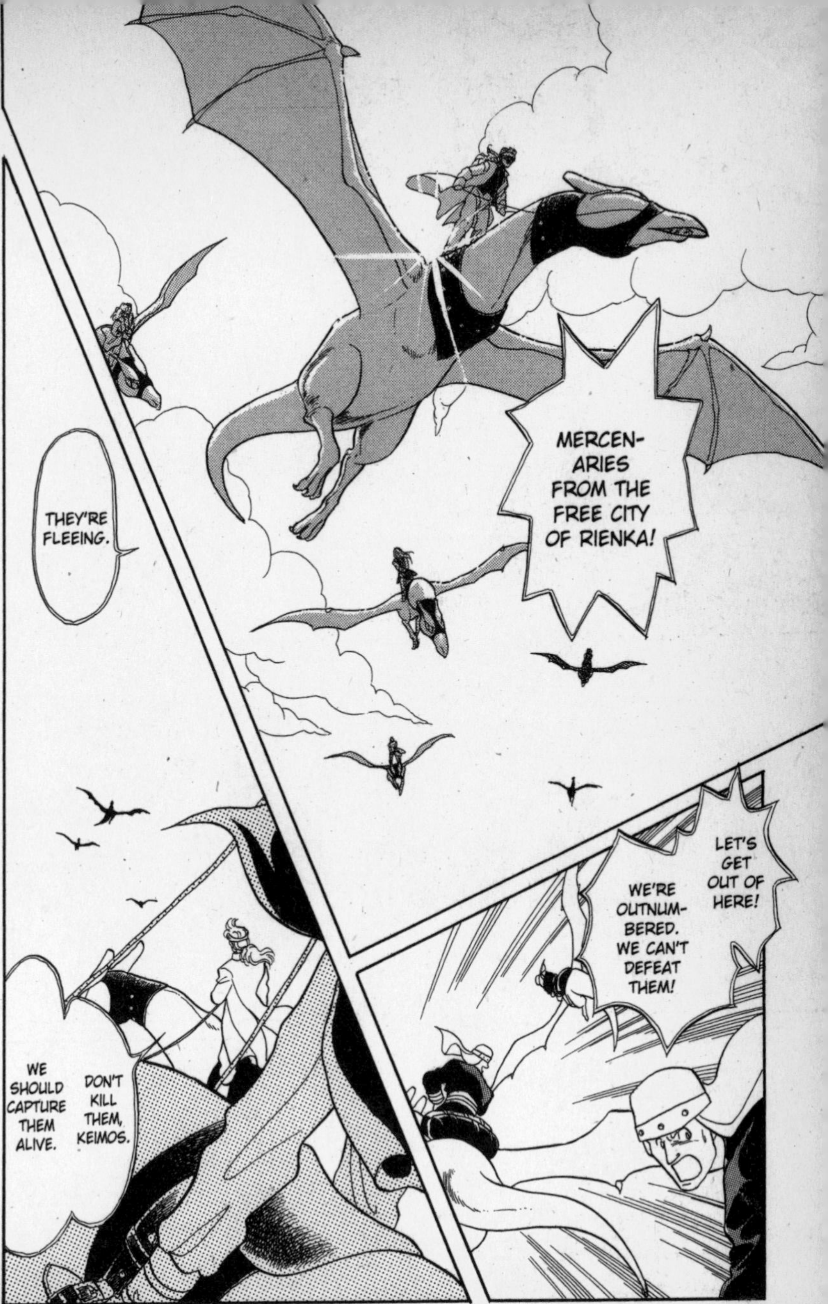
MERCEN-ARIES FROM THE FREE CITY OF RIENKA!
LET'S GET OUT OF HERE!
WE'RE OUTNUMBERED. WE CAN'T DEFEAT THEM!
THEY'RE FLEEING.
DON'T KILL THEM, KEIMOS.
WE SHOULD CAPTURE THEM ALIVE.

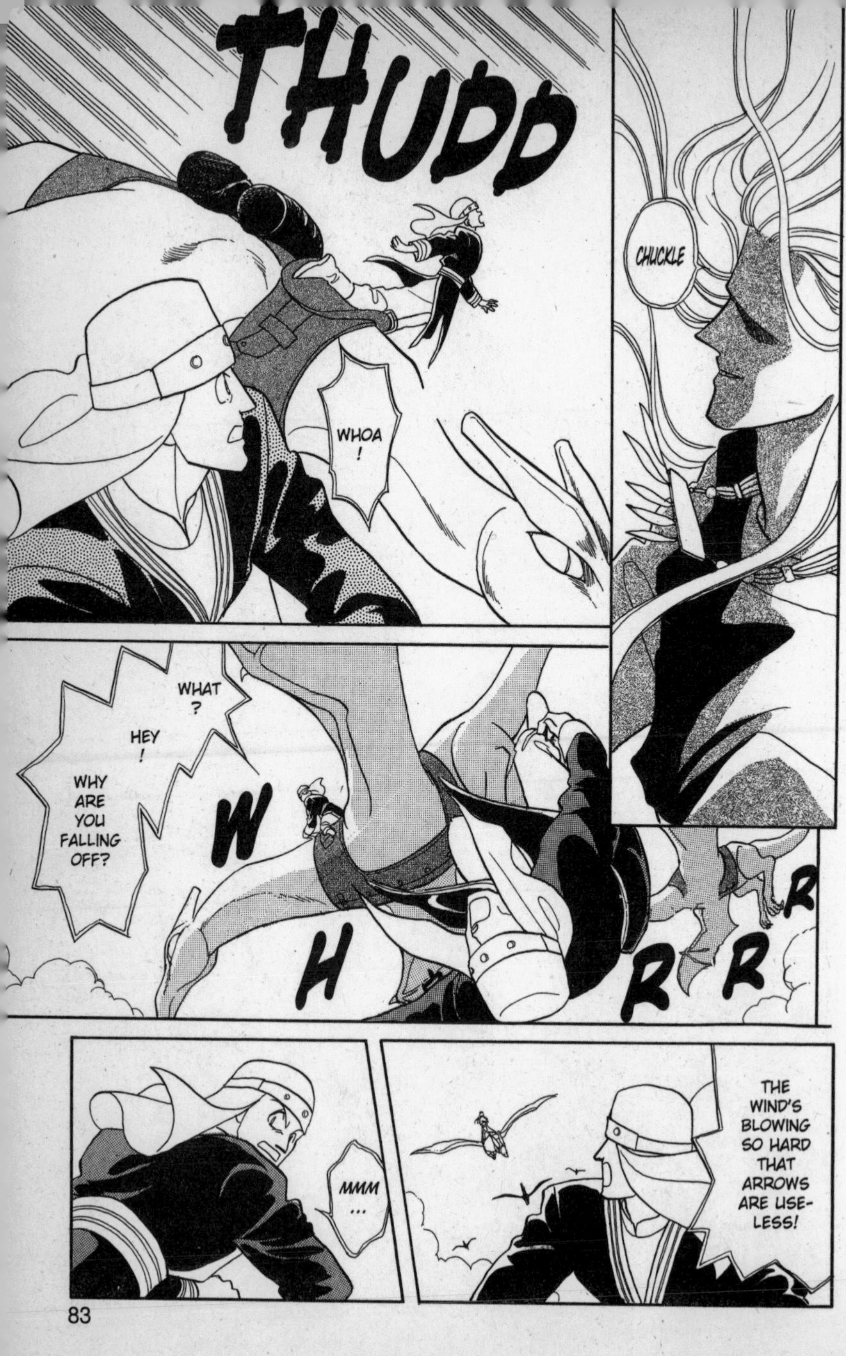
CHUCKLE
THUDD
WHOA!
WHAT?
HEY!
WHY ARE YOU FALLING OFF?
WHRRRR
THE WIND'S BLOWING SO HARD THAT ARROWS ARE USELESS!
MMM...

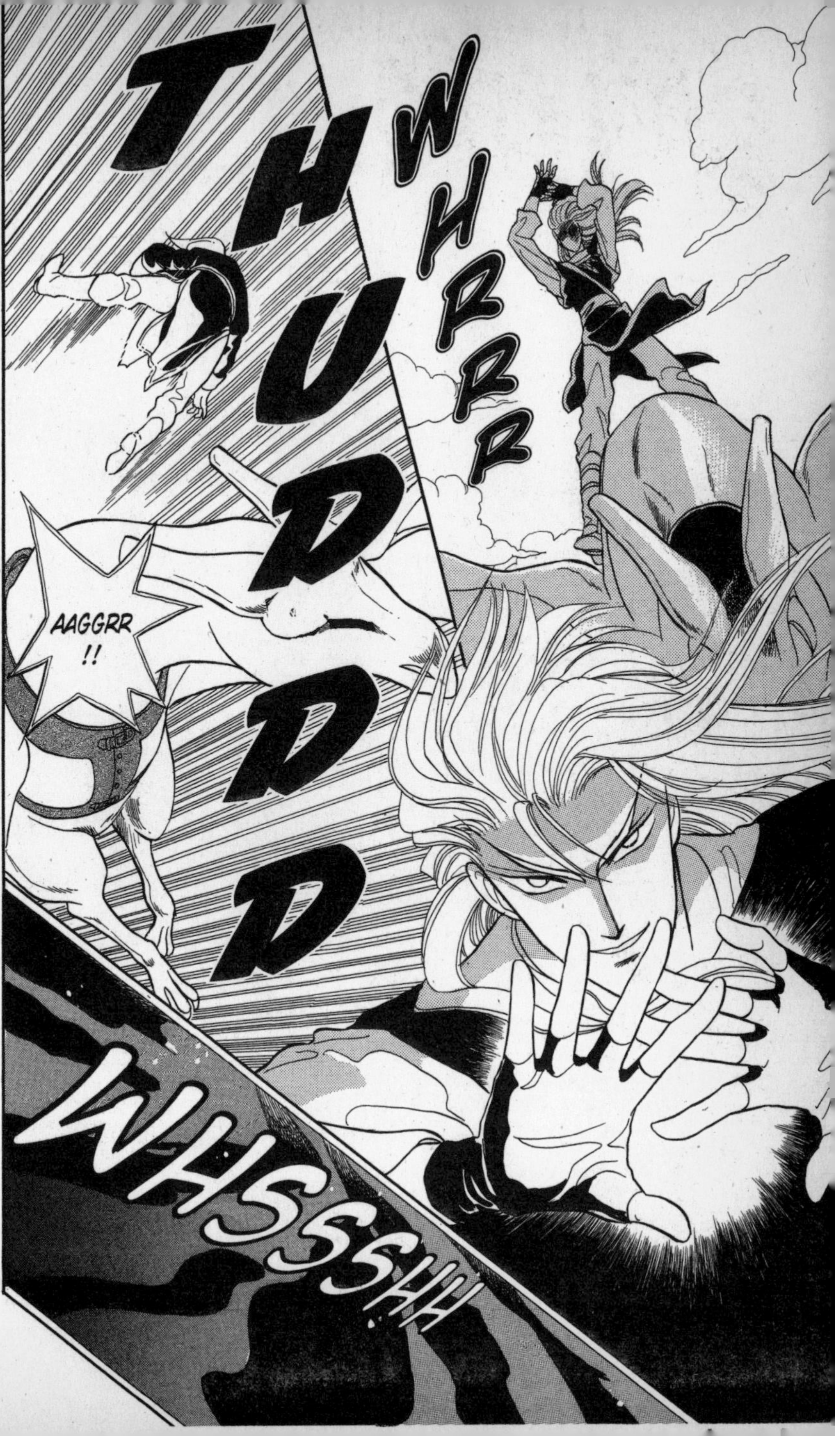
WHRRR
THUDDD
AAGGRR !!
WHSSSHH

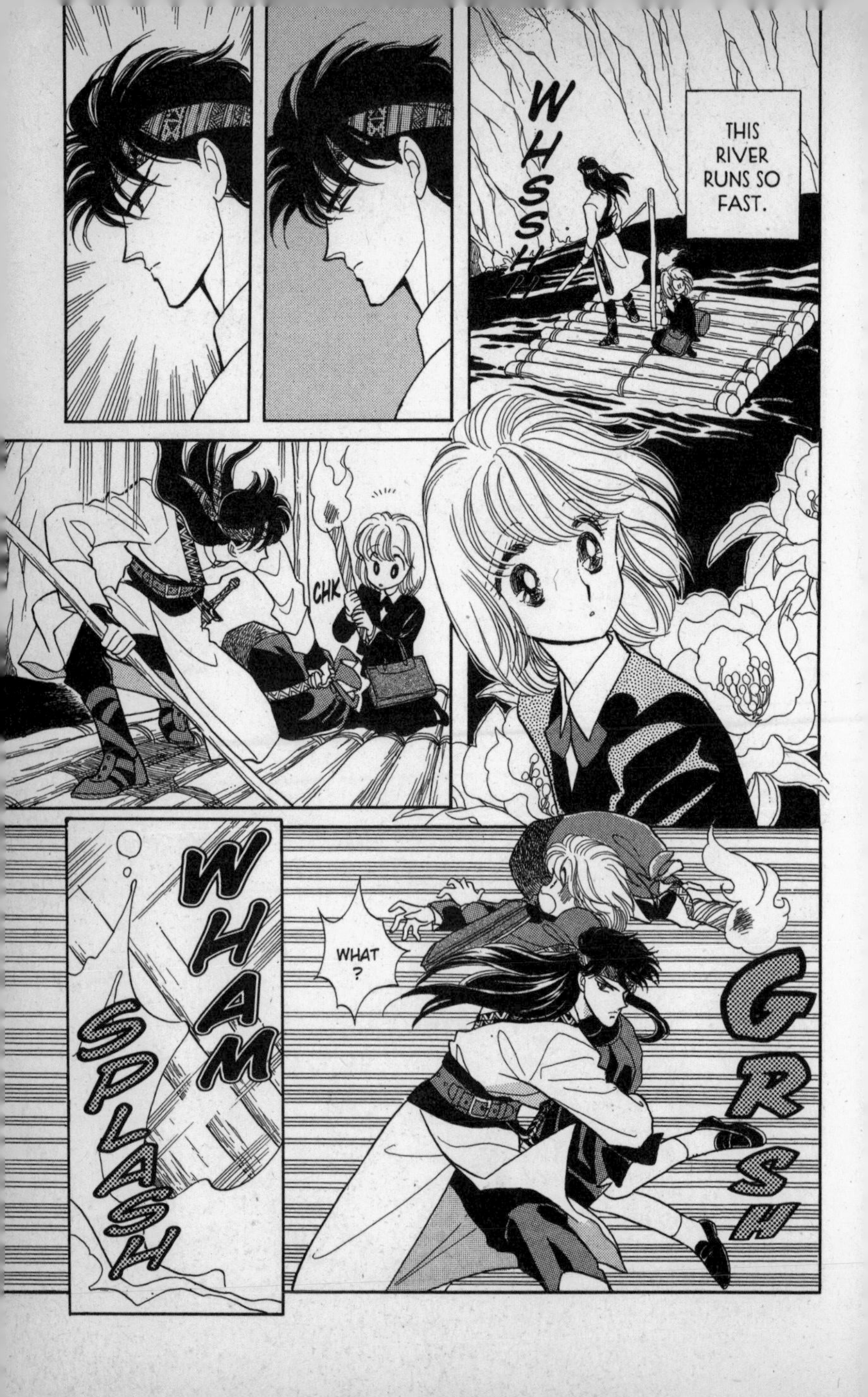
THIS RIVER RUNS SO FAST.
WHSSHH
CHK
GRSH
WHAT?
WHAM
SPLASH

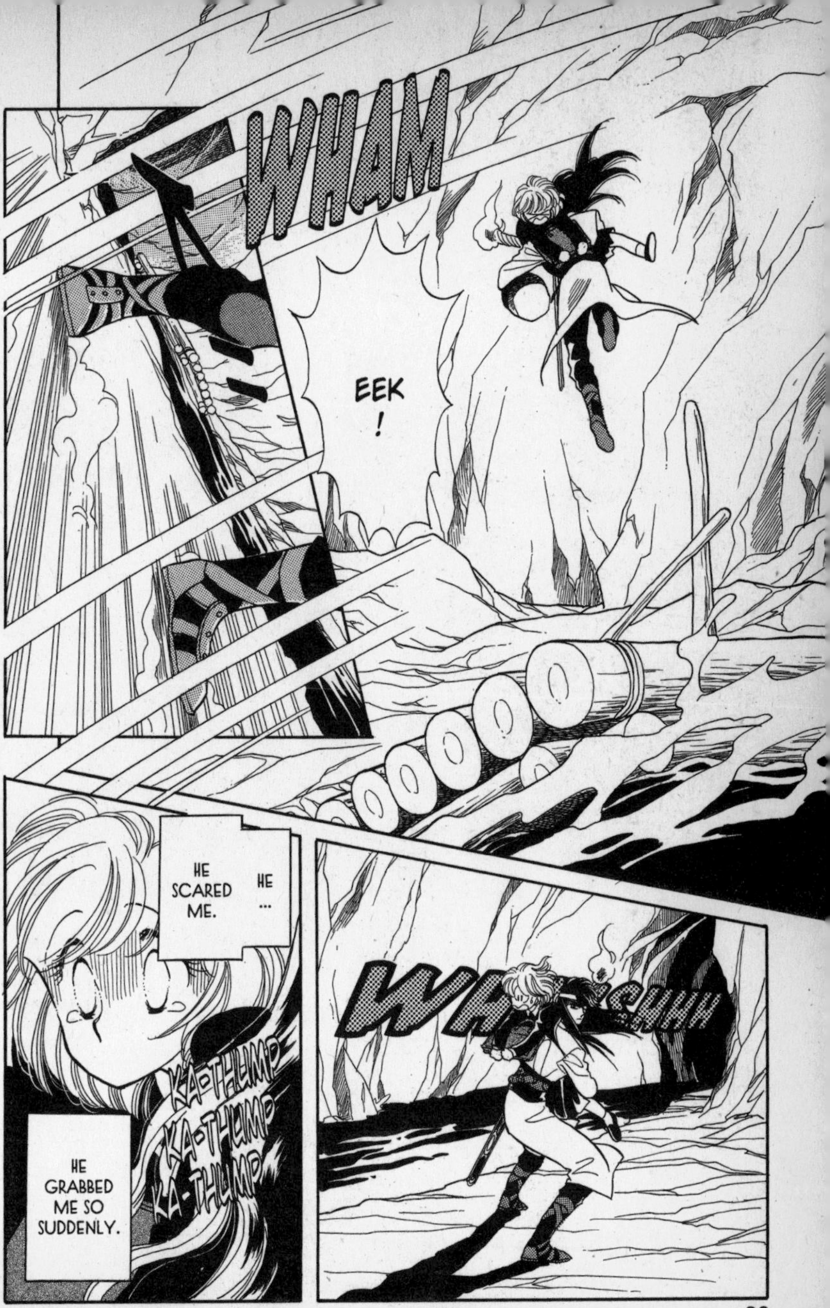
WHAM
EEK !
HE SCARED ME. HE ...
KA-THUMP
KA-THUMP
KA-THUMP
HE GRABBED ME SO SUDDENLY.

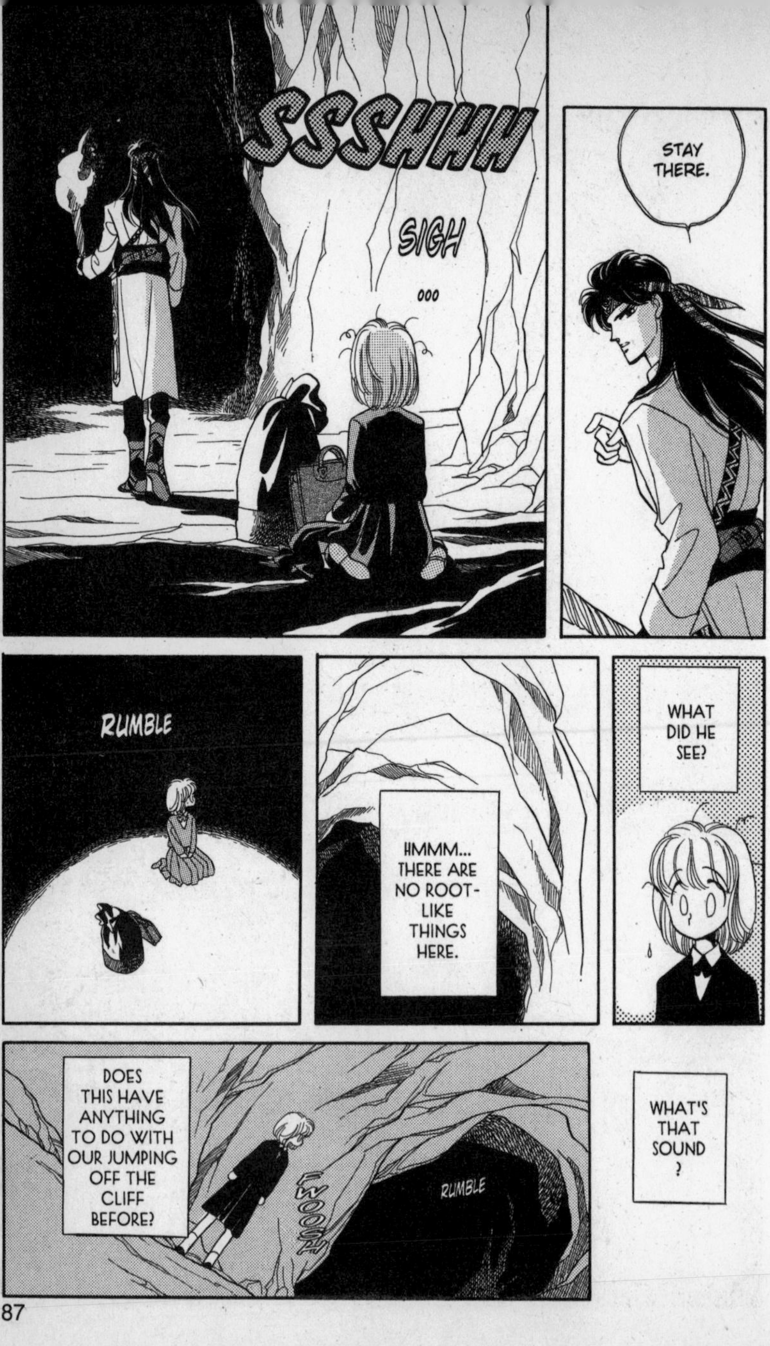
STAY THERE.
SSSHHH
SIGH
ooo
WHAT DID HE SEE?
HMMM... THERE ARE NO ROOT-LIKE THINGS HERE.
RUMBLE
WHAT'S THAT SOUND ?
DOES THIS HAVE ANYTHING TO DO WITH OUR JUMPING OFF THE CLIFF BEFORE?
RUMBLE

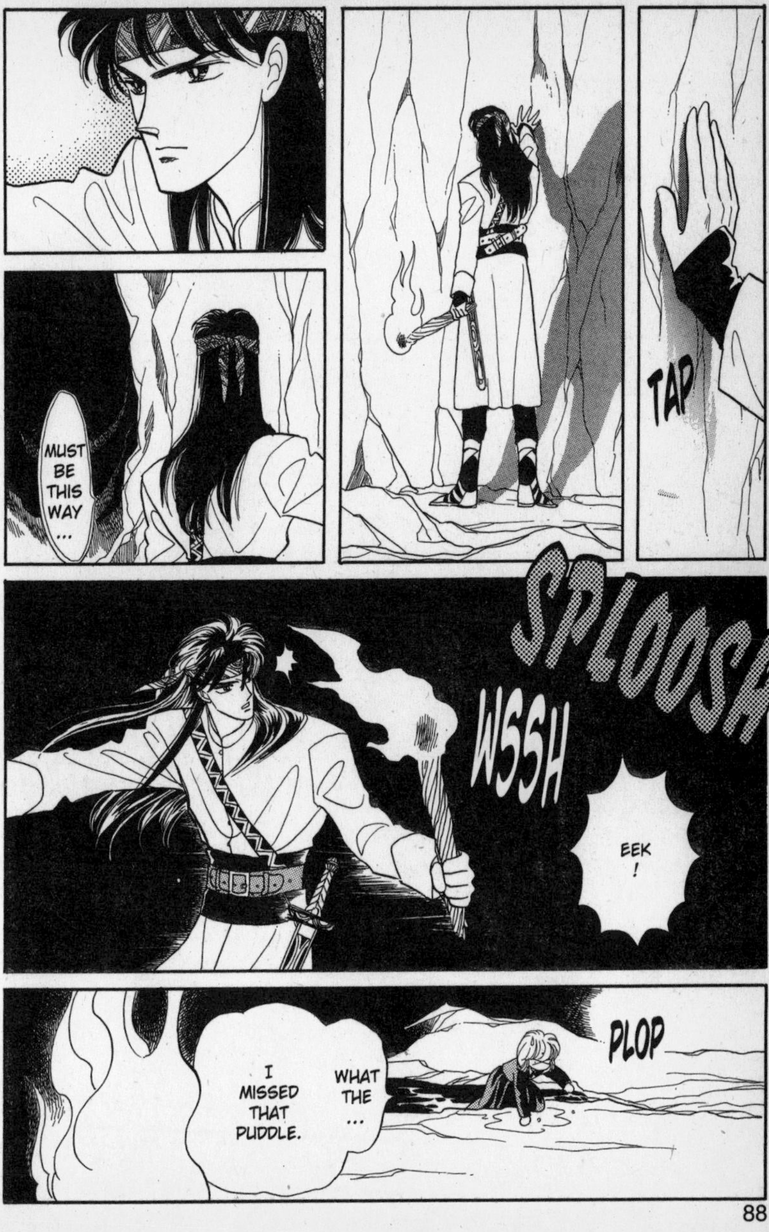
TAP
MUST BE THIS WAY ...
SPLOOSH
WSSH
EEK !
PLOP
WHAT THE ...
I MISSED THAT PUDDLE.

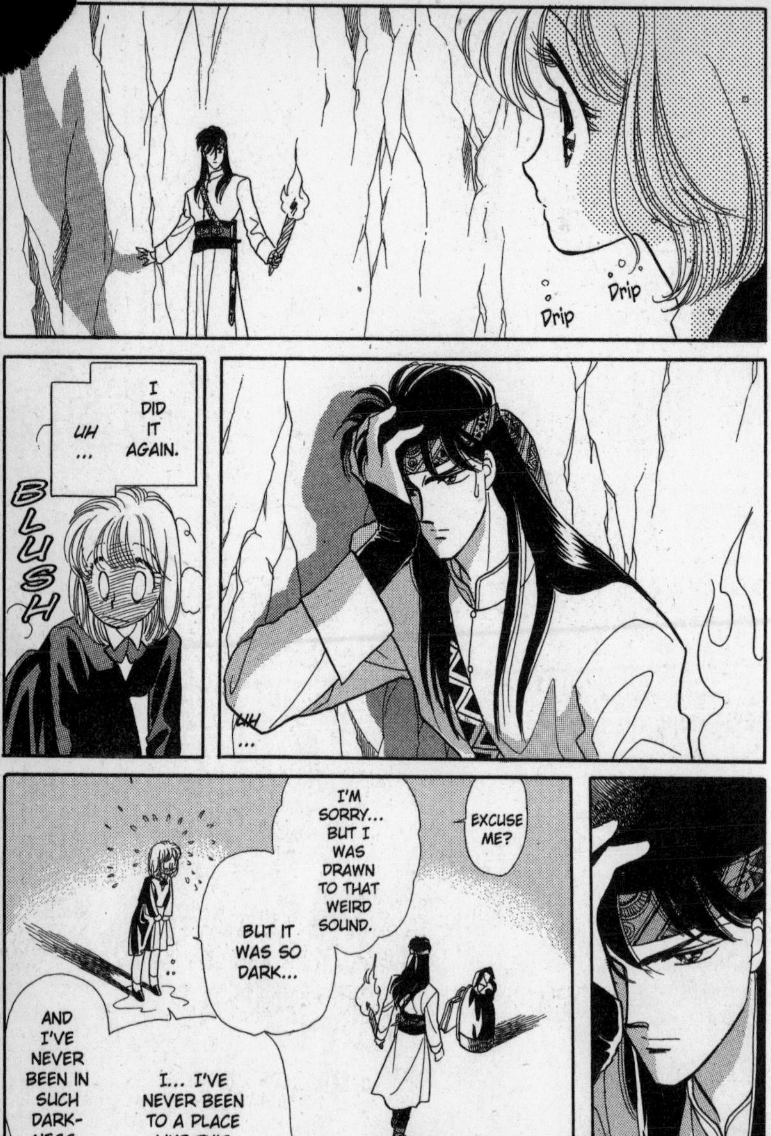
Drip
Drip
UH ...
UH ...
I DID IT AGAIN.
BLUSH
EXCUSE ME?
I'M SORRY... BUT I WAS DRAWN TO THAT WEIRD SOUND.
BUT IT WAS SO DARK...
I... I'VE NEVER BEEN TO A PLACE LIKE THIS IN MY LIFE.
AND I'VE NEVER BEEN IN SUCH DARKNESS.

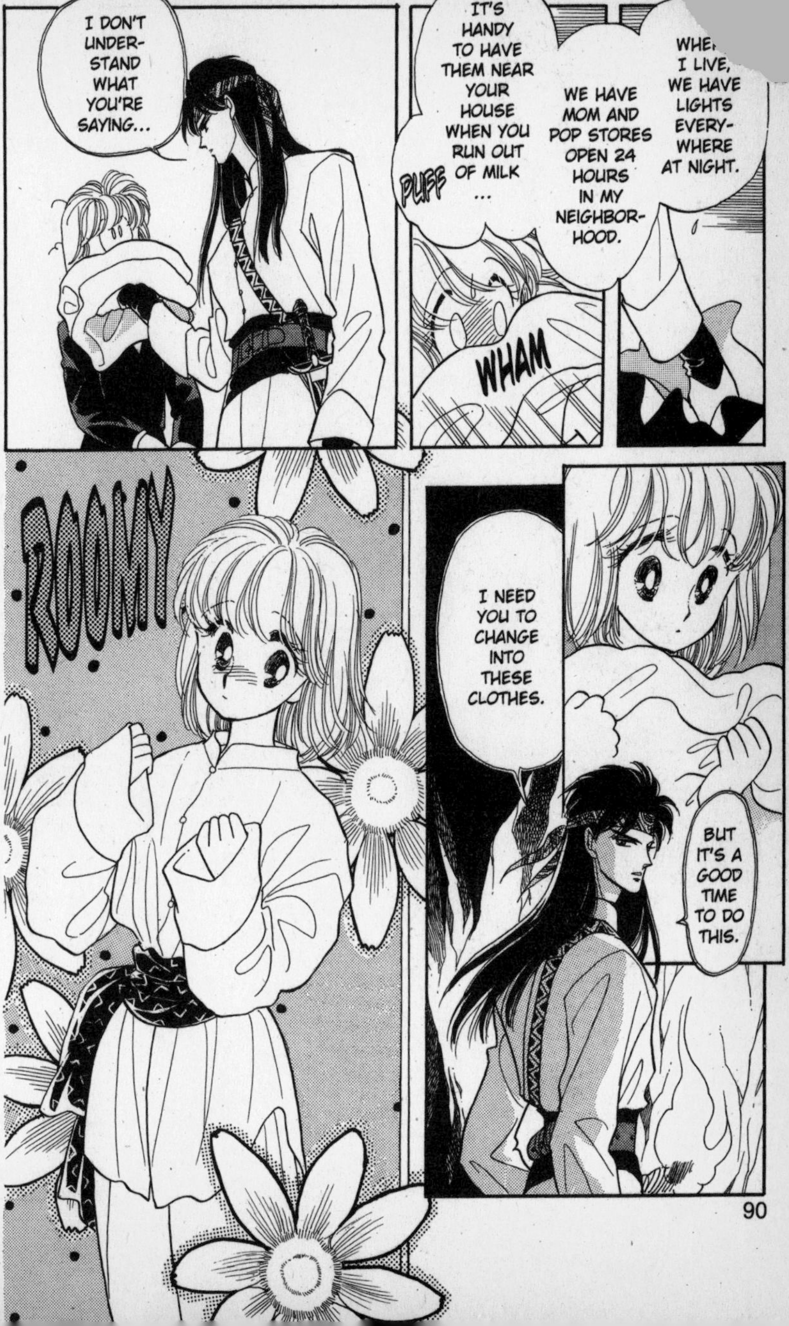
WHE
I LIVE, WE HAVE LIGHTS EVERY-WHERE AT NIGHT.
WE HAVE MOM AND POP STORES OPEN 24 HOURS IN MY NEIGHBOR-HOOD.
IT'S HANDY TO HAVE THEM NEAR YOUR HOUSE WHEN YOU RUN OUT OF MILK ...
PUFF
WHAM
I DON'T UNDER-STAND WHAT YOU'RE SAYING...
I NEED YOU TO CHANGE INTO THESE CLOTHES.
BUT IT'S A GOOD TIME TO DO THIS.
ROOMY

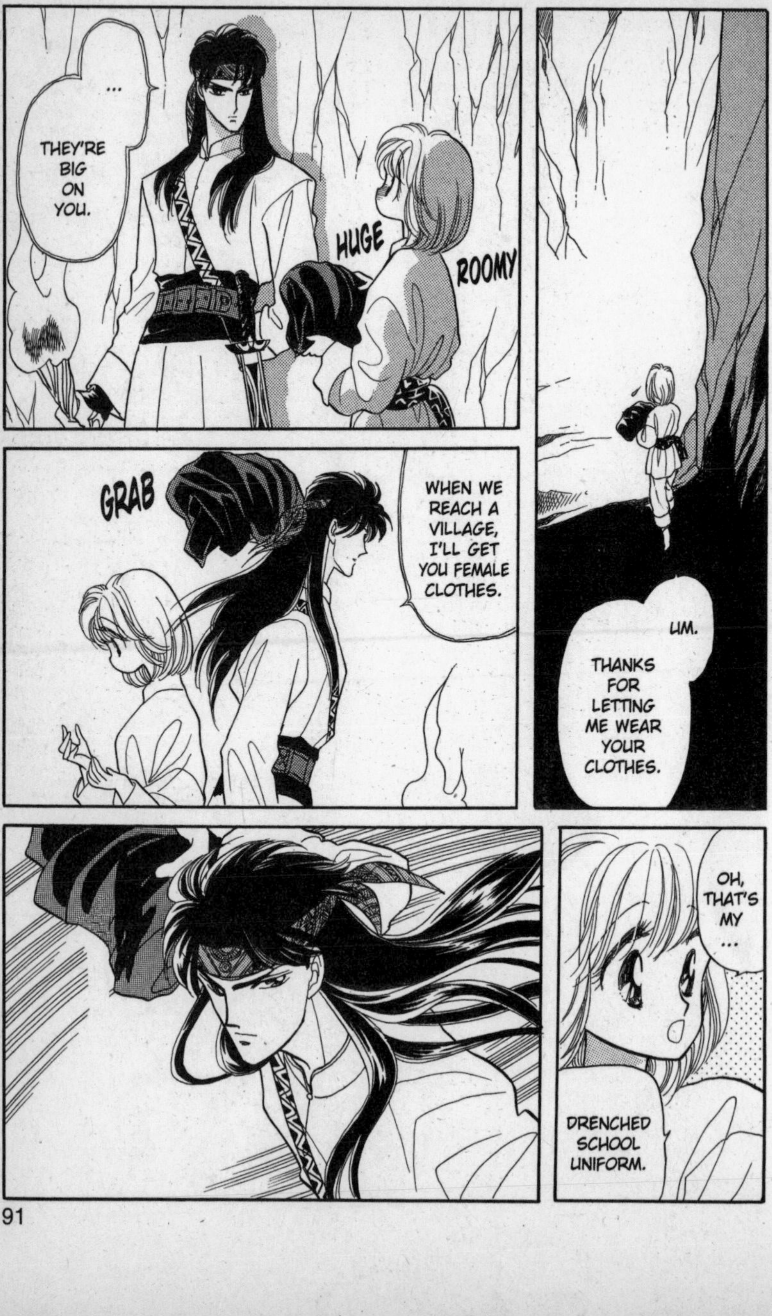
UM.
THANKS FOR LETTING ME WEAR YOUR CLOTHES.
...
THEY'RE BIG ON YOU.
ROOMY
HUGE
WHEN WE REACH A VILLAGE, I'LL GET YOU FEMALE CLOTHES.
GRAB
OH, THAT'S MY ...
DRENCHED SCHOOL UNIFORM.

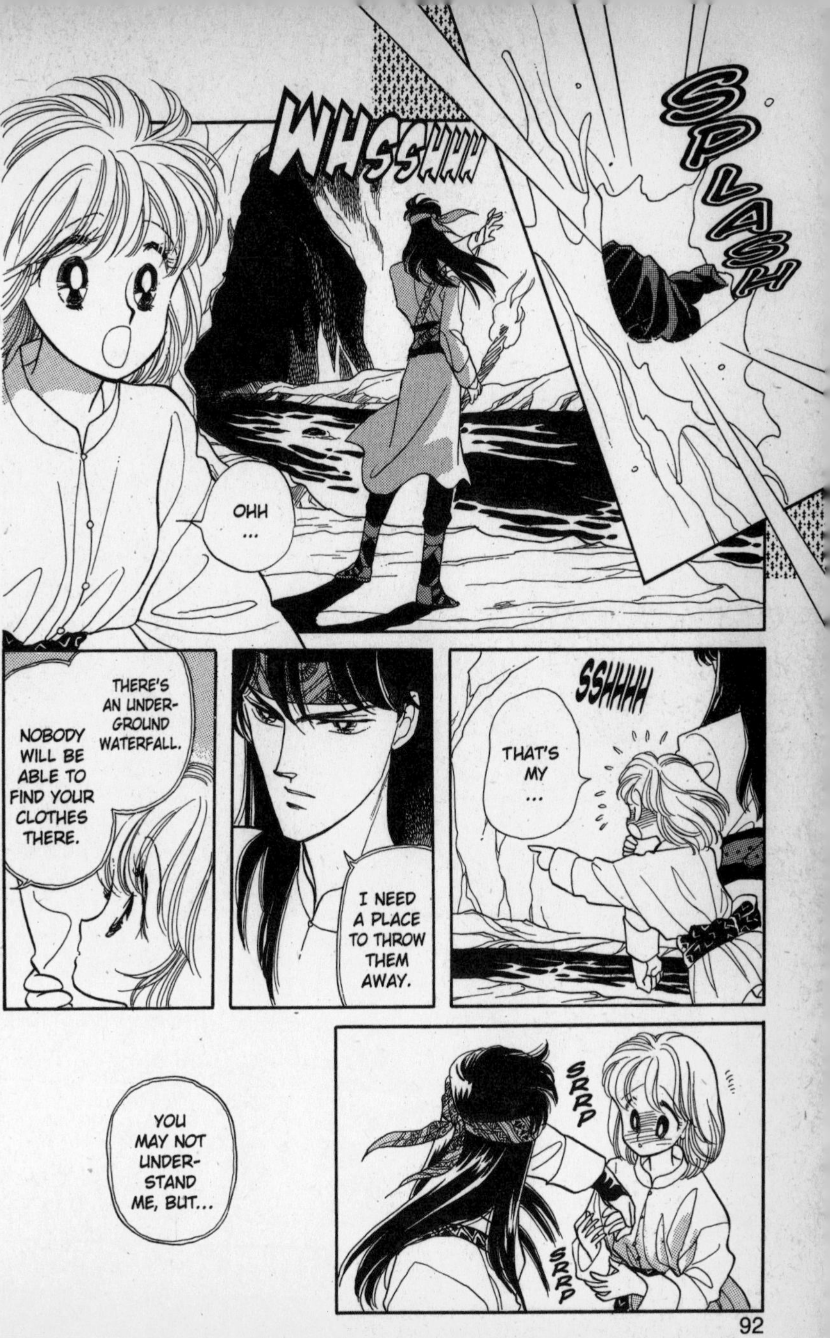
SPLASH
WHSSHHH
OHH ...
SSHHHH
THAT'S MY ...
I NEED A PLACE TO THROW THEM AWAY.
THERE'S AN UNDER-GROUND WATERFALL.
NOBODY WILL BE ABLE TO FIND YOUR CLOTHES THERE.
SRRP
SRRP
YOU MAY NOT UNDER-STAND ME, BUT...

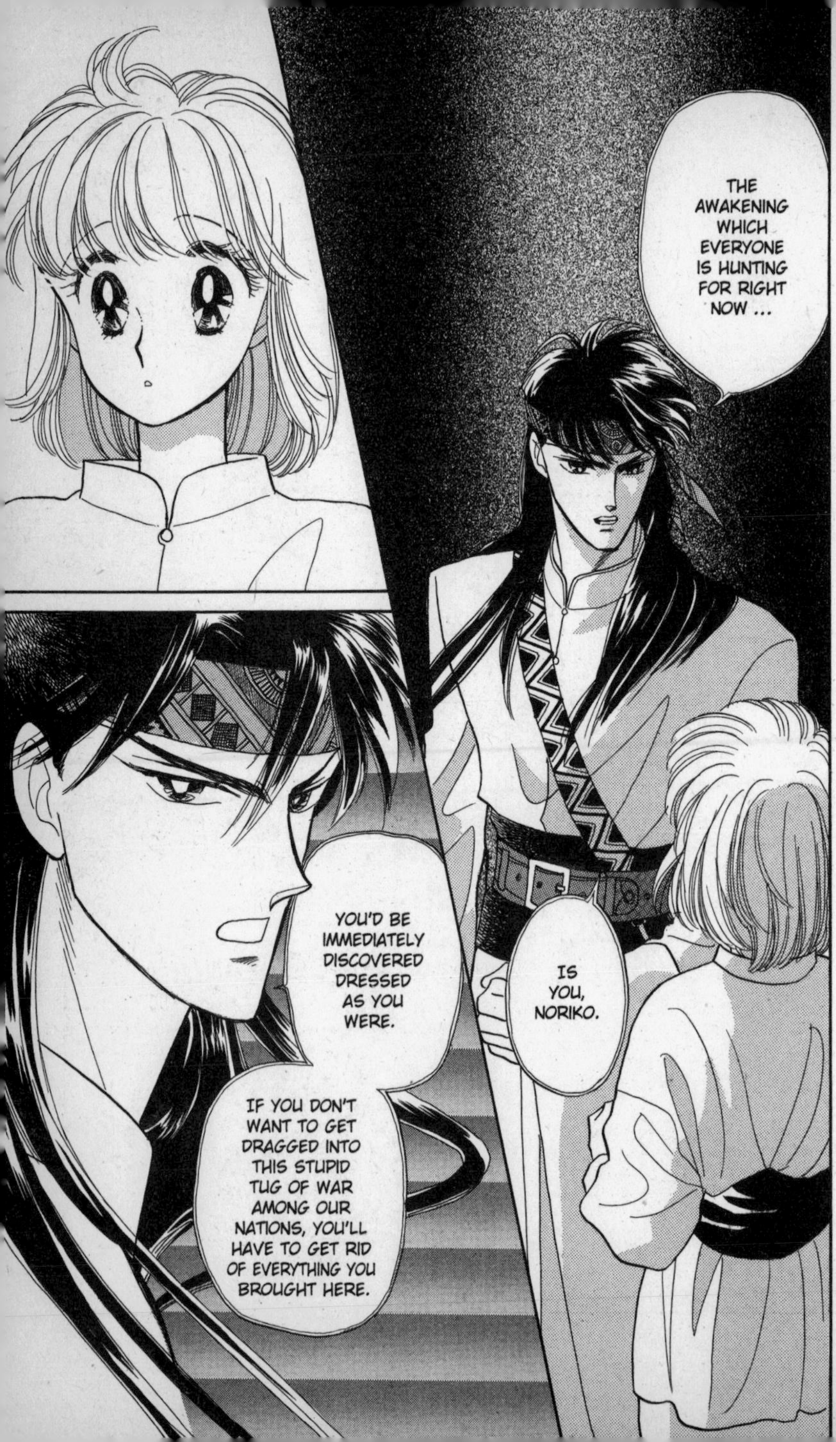
THE AWAKENING WHICH EVERYONE IS HUNTING FOR RIGHT NOW ...
IS YOU, NORIKO.
YOU'D BE IMMEDIATELY DISCOVERED DRESSED AS YOU WERE.
IF YOU DON'T WANT TO GET DRAGGED INTO THIS STUPID TUG OF WAR AMONG OUR NATIONS, YOU'LL HAVE TO GET RID OF EVERYTHING YOU BROUGHT HERE.

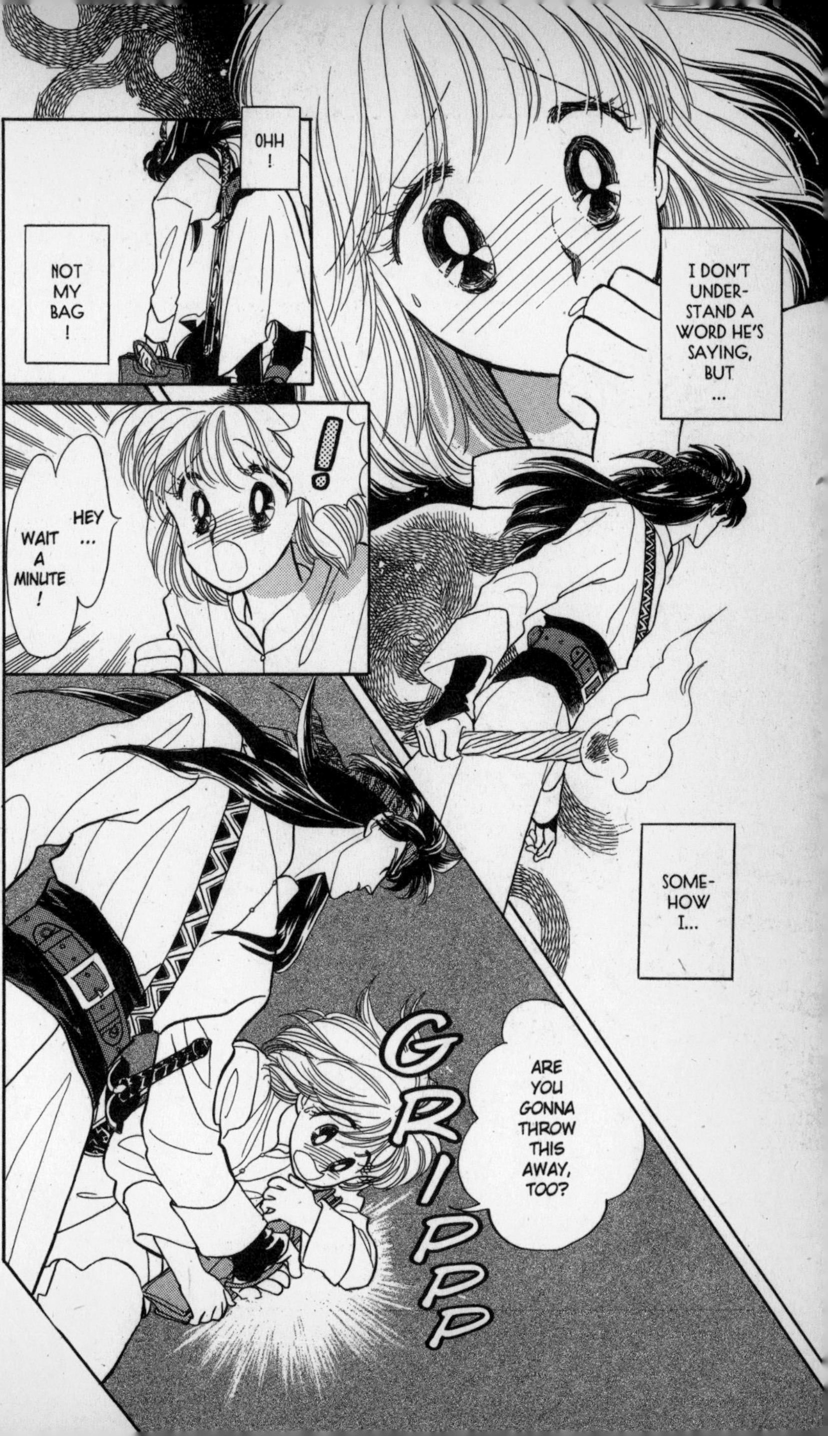
I DON'T UNDER-STAND A WORD HE'S SAYING, BUT ...
OHH!
NOT MY BAG!
!
HEY ... WAIT A MINUTE!
SOME-HOW I...
ARE YOU GONNA THROW THIS AWAY, TOO?
GRIPP

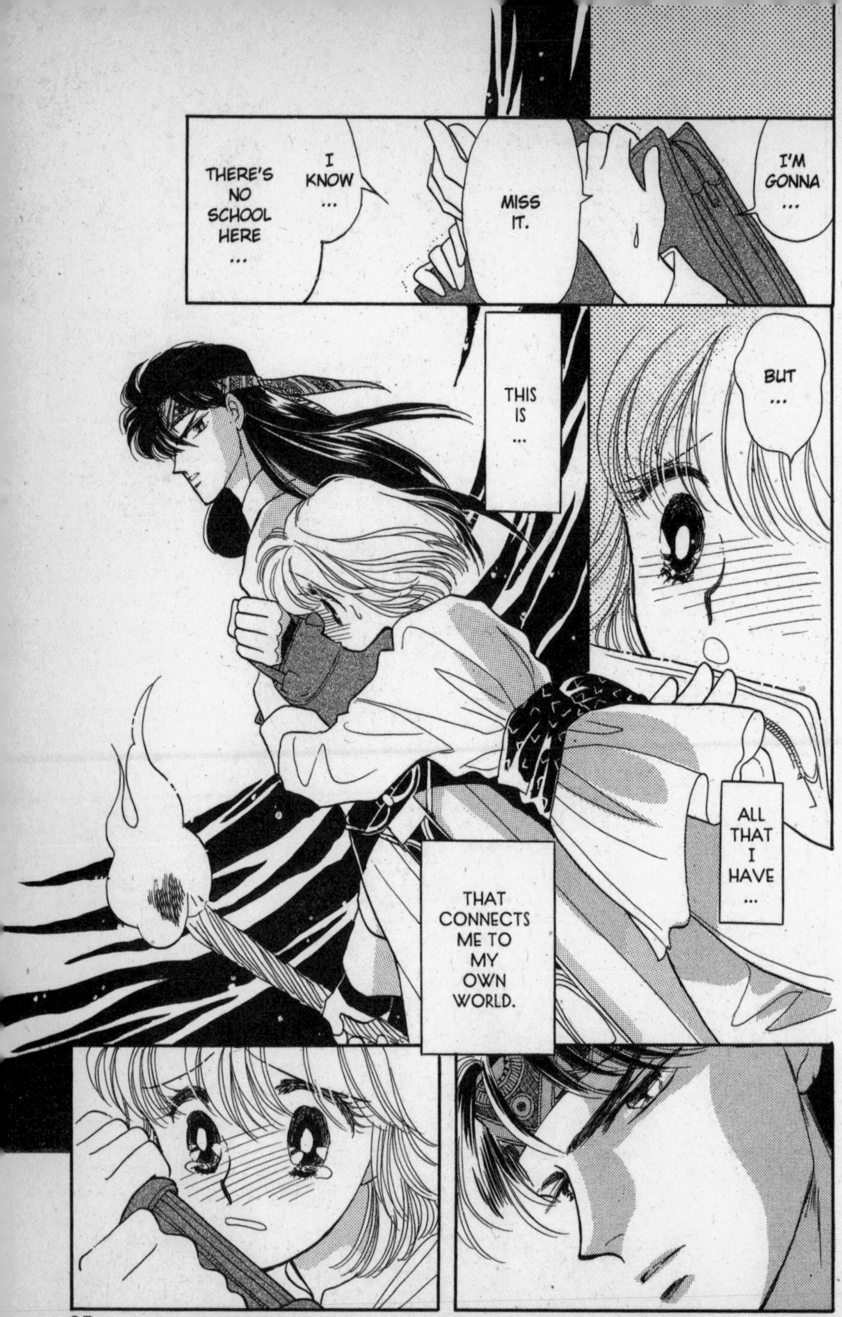
I'M GONNA ...
MISS IT.
I KNOW ...
THERE'S NO SCHOOL HERE ...
BUT ...
THIS IS ...
ALL THAT I HAVE ...
THAT CONNECTS ME TO MY OWN WORLD.

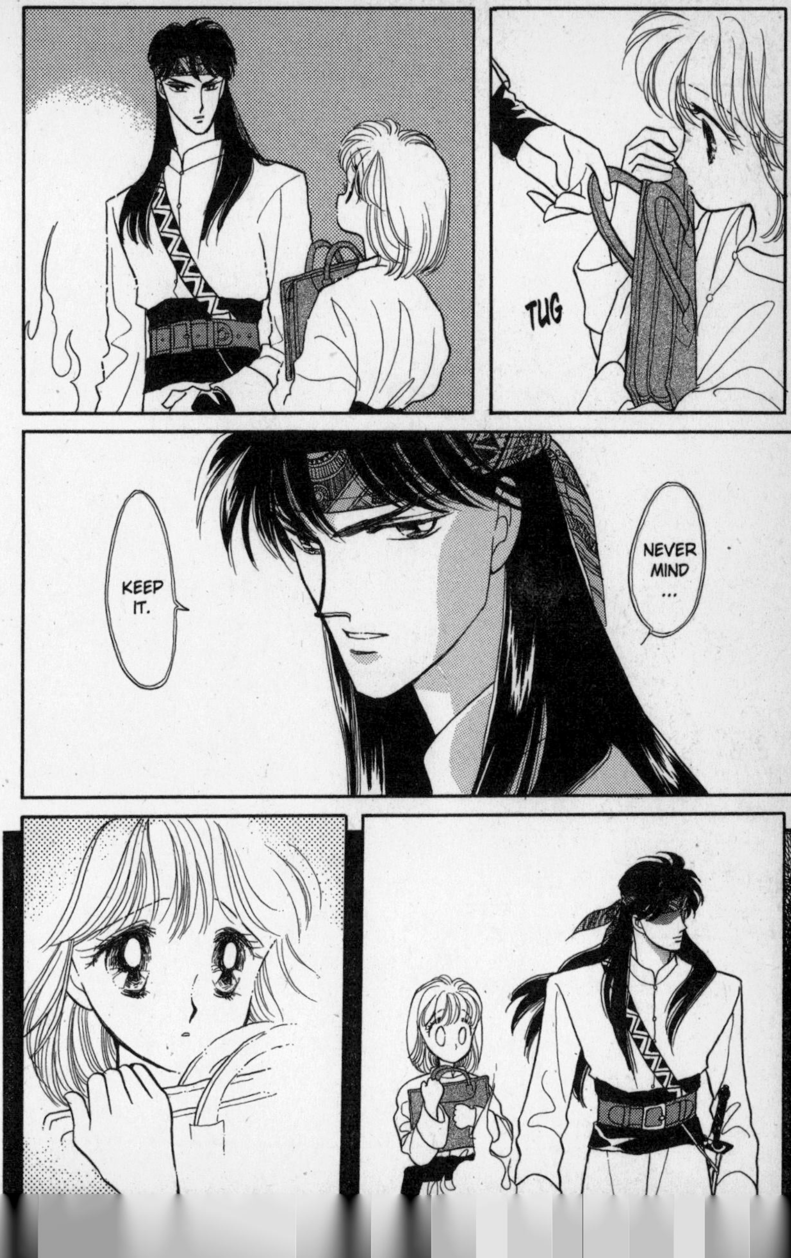
TUG
NEVER MIND ...
KEEP IT.

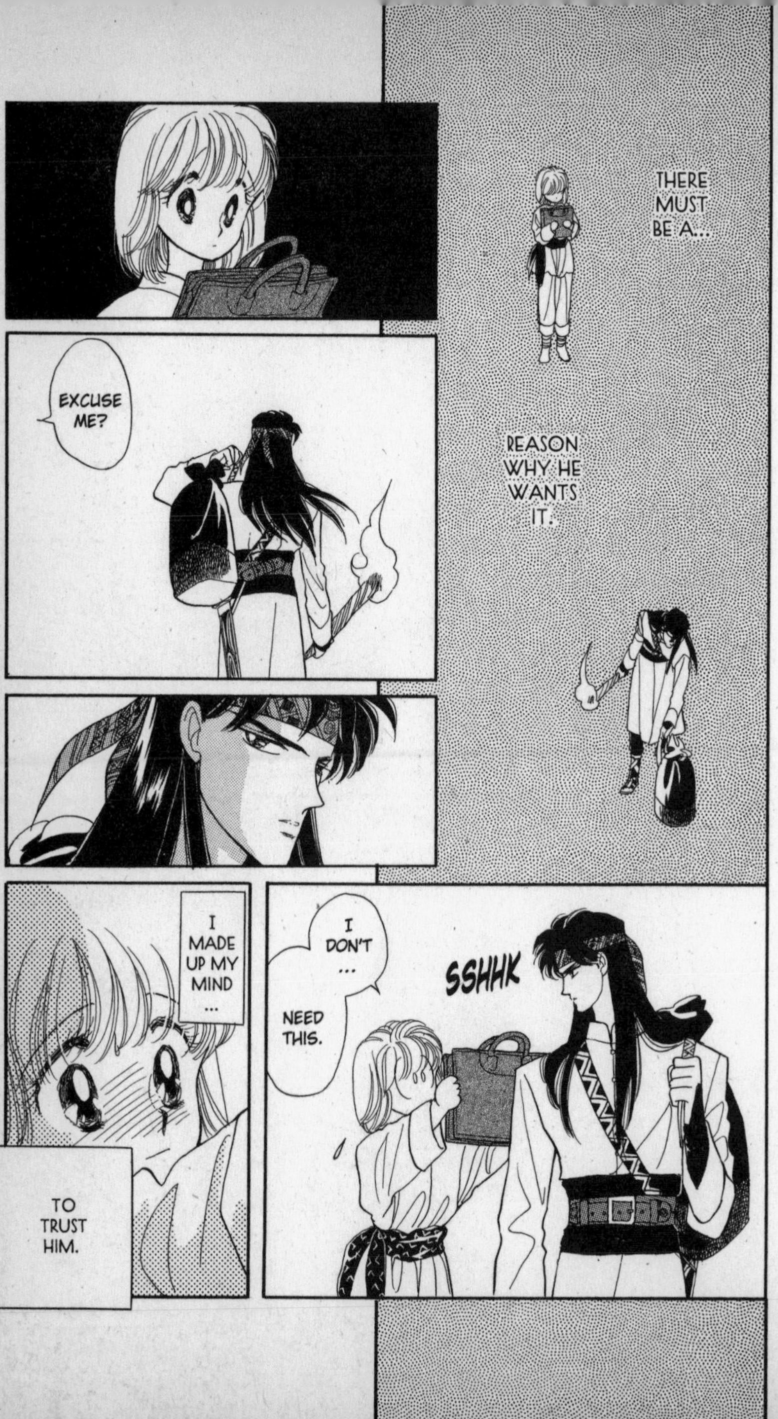
THERE MUST BE A...
REASON WHY HE WANTS IT.
EXCUSE ME?
I DON'T ...
NEED THIS.
SSHHK
I MADE UP MY MIND ...
TO TRUST HIM.

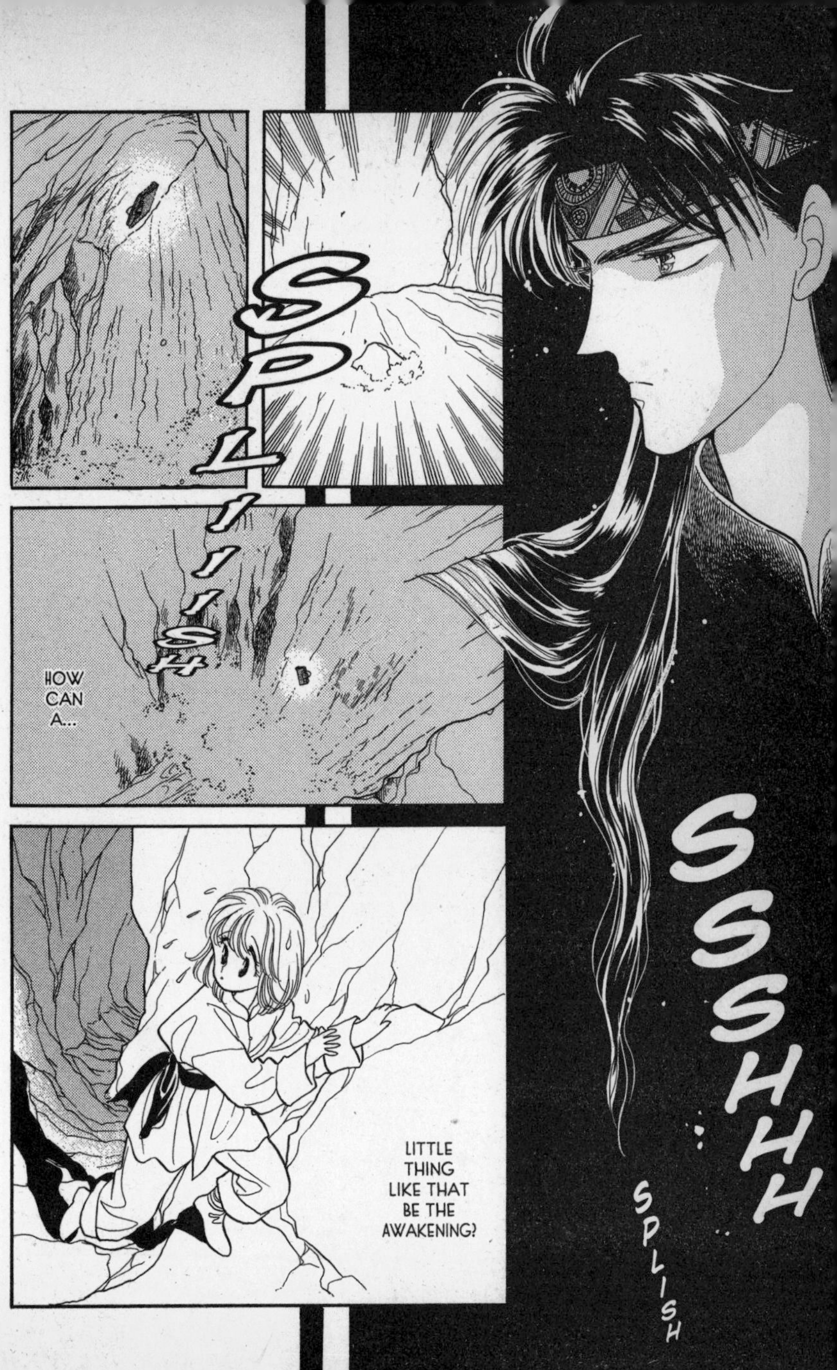
SSSHHH
SPLISH
SPLIIISH
HOW CAN A...
LITTLE THING LIKE THAT BE THE AWAKENING?

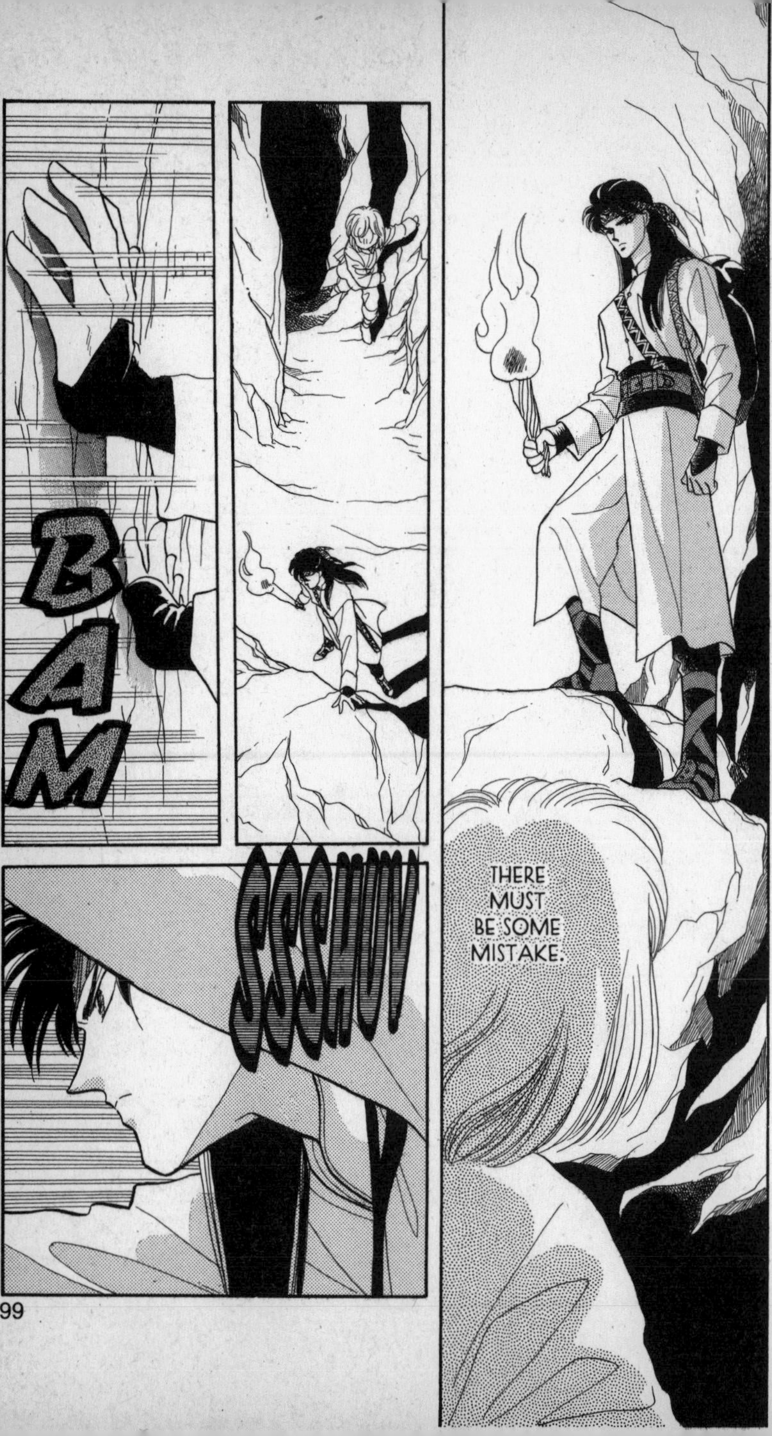
THERE MUST BE SOME MISTAKE.
BAM
SSSHUV

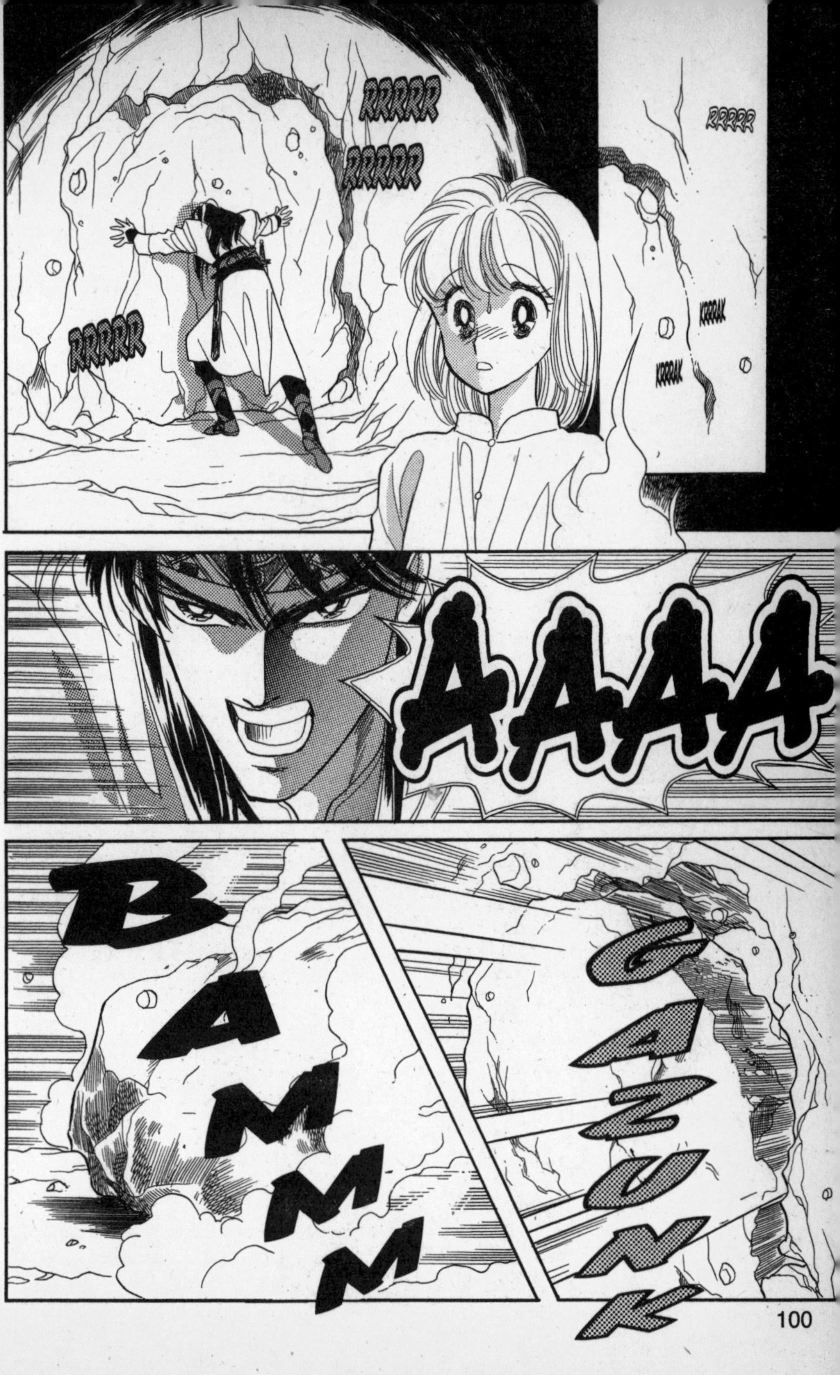
RRRRR
KRRRAK
KRRRAK
RRRRR
RRRRR
RRRRR
AAAA
GAZUNK
BAMMM

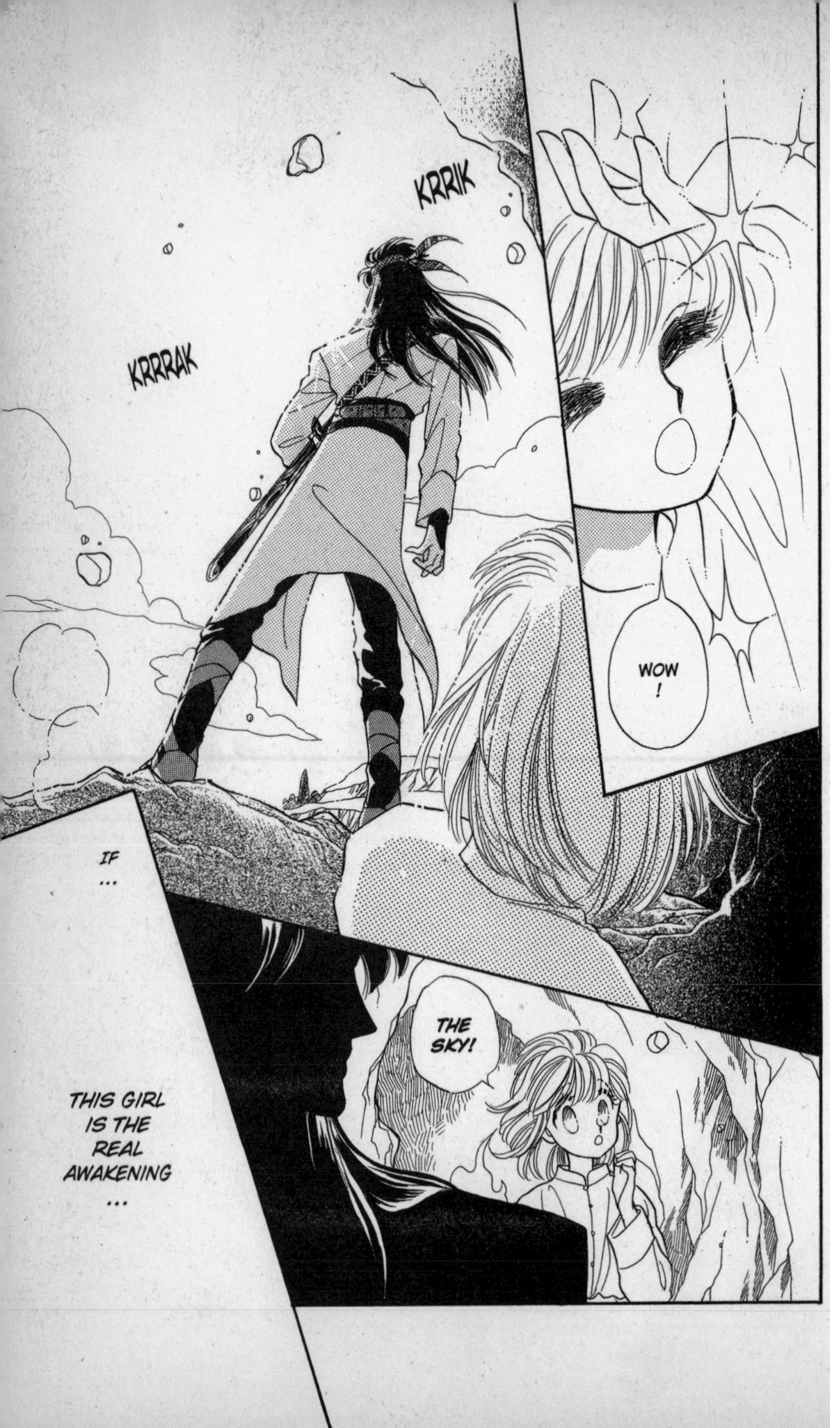
WOW!
KRRIK
KRRRAK
THE SKY!
IF...
THIS GIRL IS THE REAL AWAKENING...

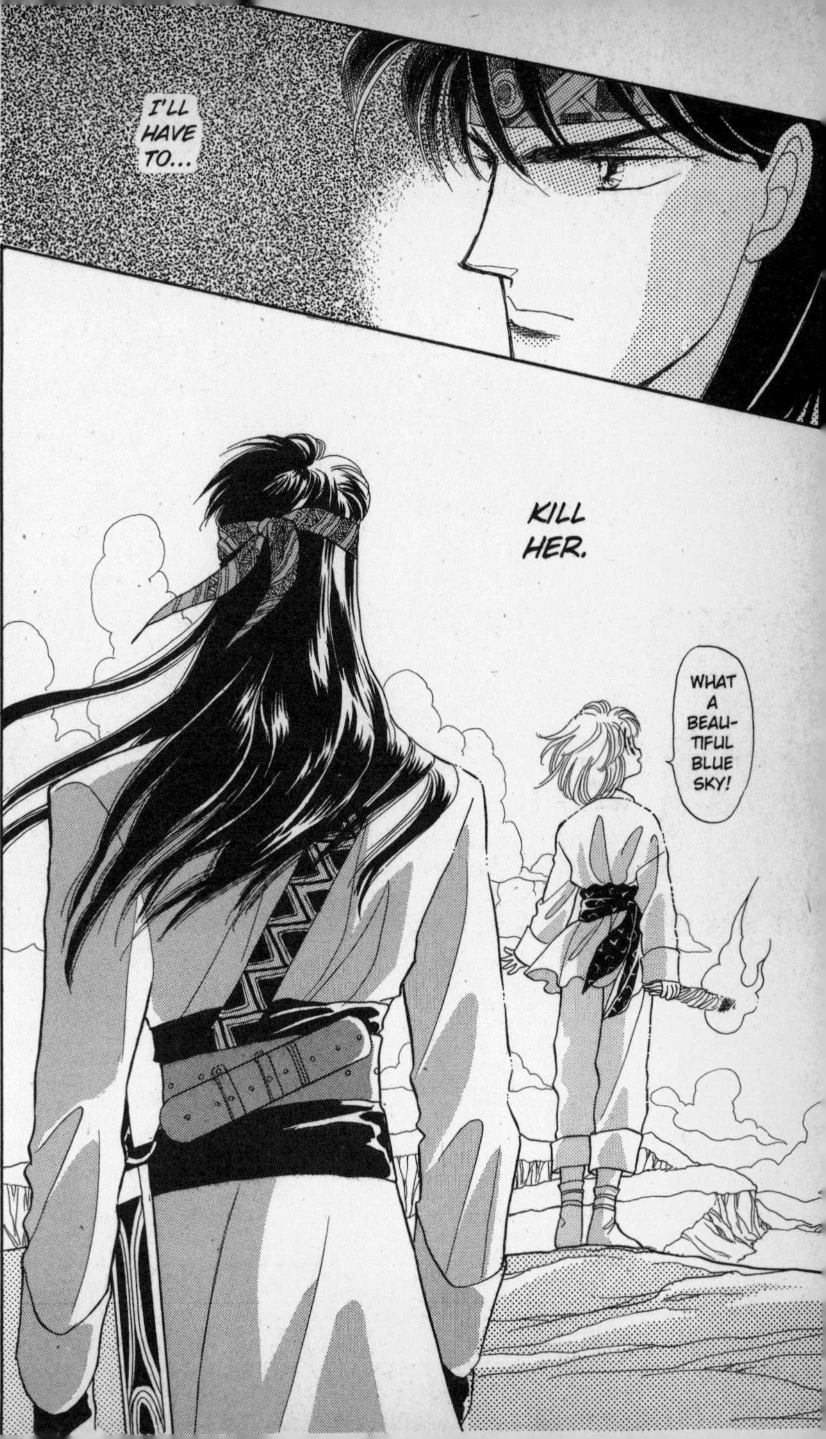
I'LL HAVE TO...
KILL HER.
WHAT A BEAU-TIFUL BLUE SKY!

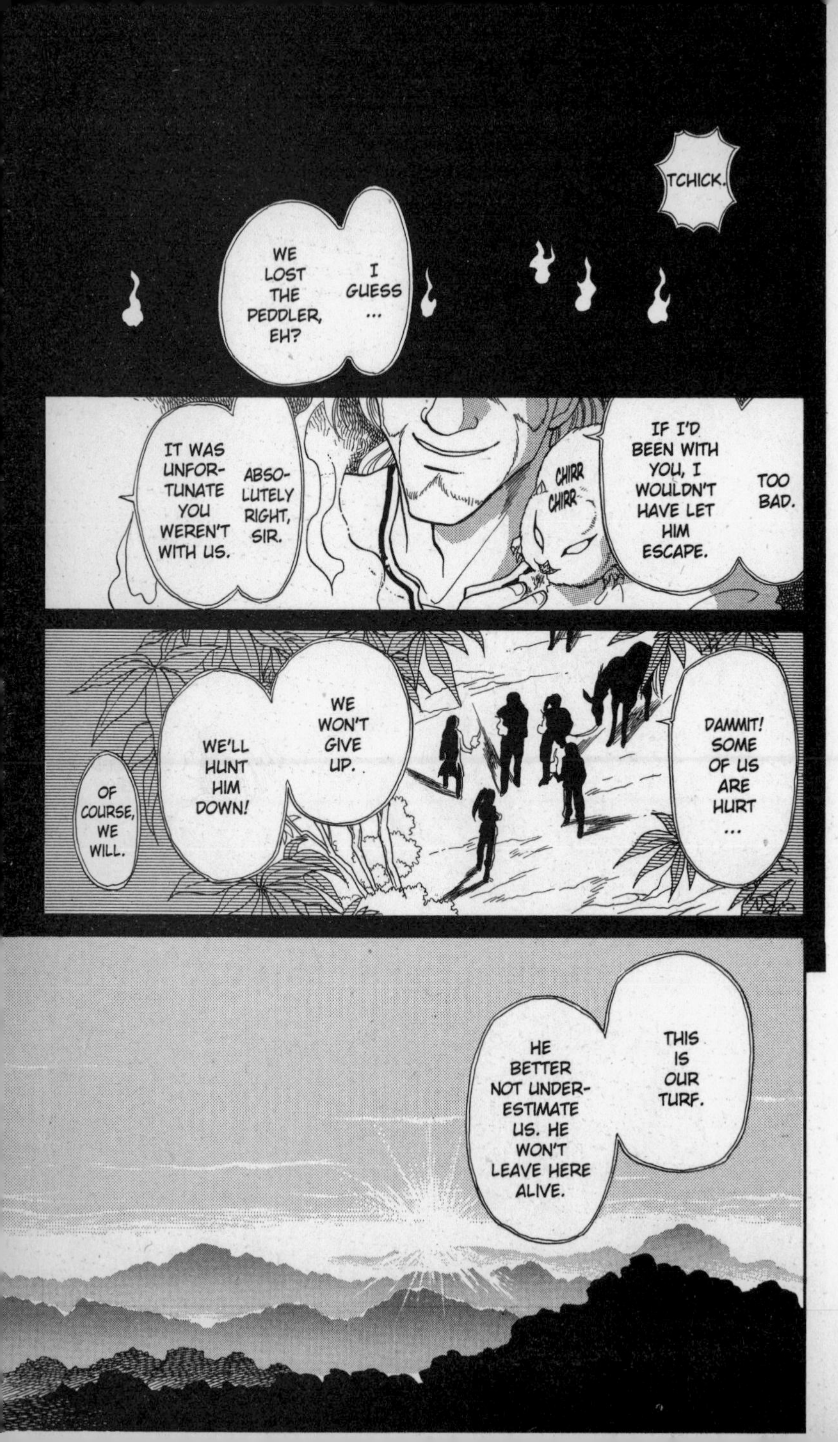
TCHICK.
WE LOST THE PEDDLER, EH? I GUESS...
IF I'D BEEN WITH YOU, I WOULDN'T HAVE LET HIM ESCAPE. TOO BAD.
CHIRR CHIRR
IT WAS UNFORTUNATE YOU WEREN'T WITH US. ABSOLUTELY RIGHT, SIR.
DAMMIT! SOME OF US ARE HURT...
WE'LL HUNT HIM DOWN! WE WON'T GIVE UP.
OF COURSE, WE WILL.
HE BETTER NOT UNDER-ESTIMATE US. HE WON'T LEAVE HERE ALIVE. THIS IS OUR TURF.

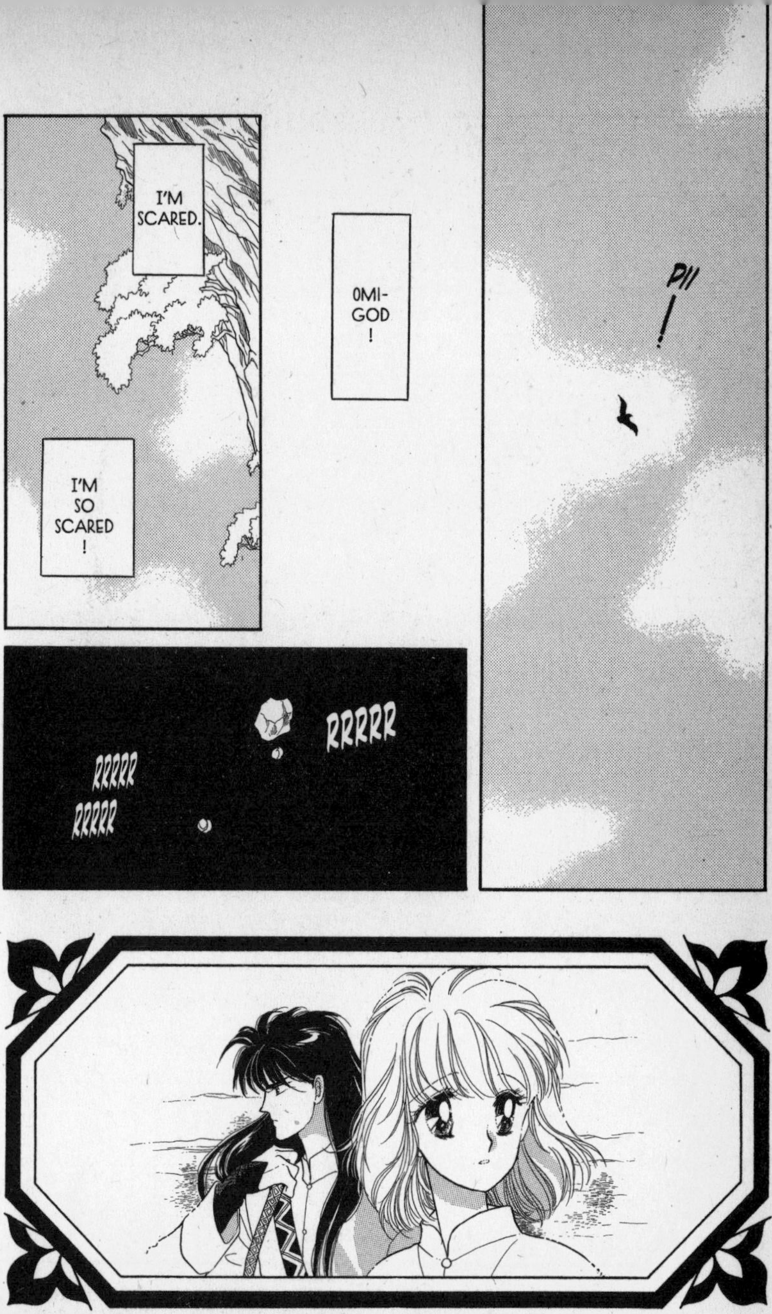
PII!
OMI-GOD!
I'M SCARED.
I'M SO SCARED!
RRRRR
RRRRR
RRRRR

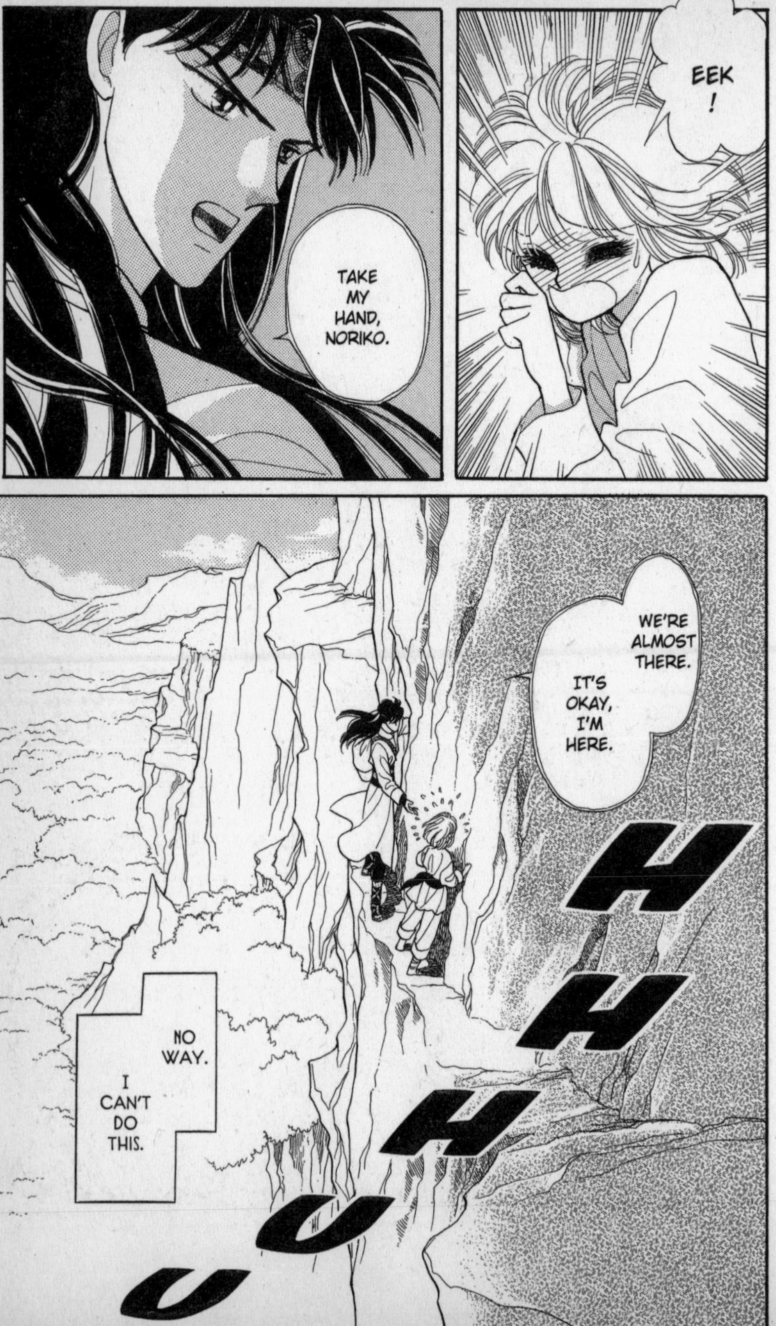
EEK!
TAKE MY HAND, NORIKO.
WE'RE ALMOST THERE.
IT'S OKAY, I'M HERE.
NO WAY.
I CAN'T DO THIS.
UUHHH

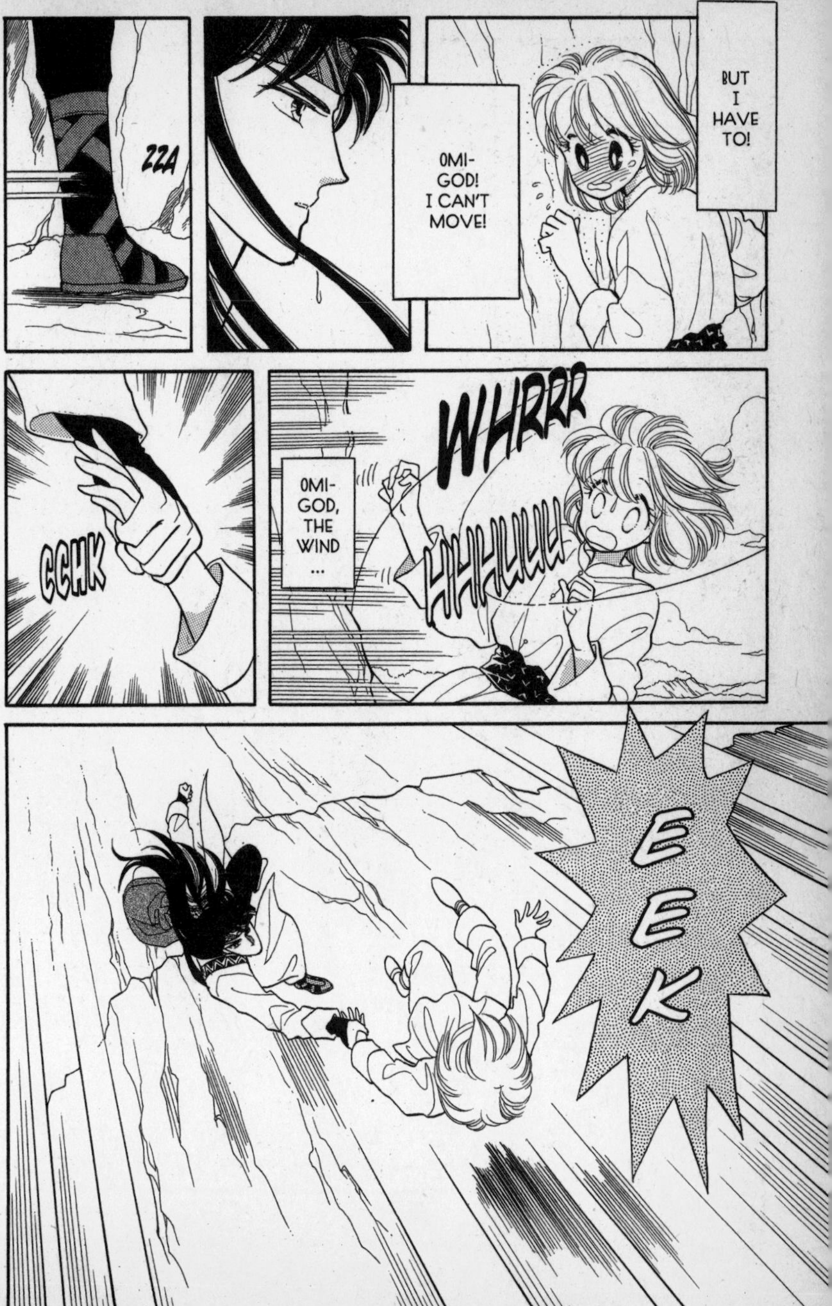
BUT I HAVE TO!
OMI-GOD! I CAN'T MOVE!
ZZA
WHRRR
OMI-GOD, THE WIND ...
HHHUUUU
CCHK
EEEK

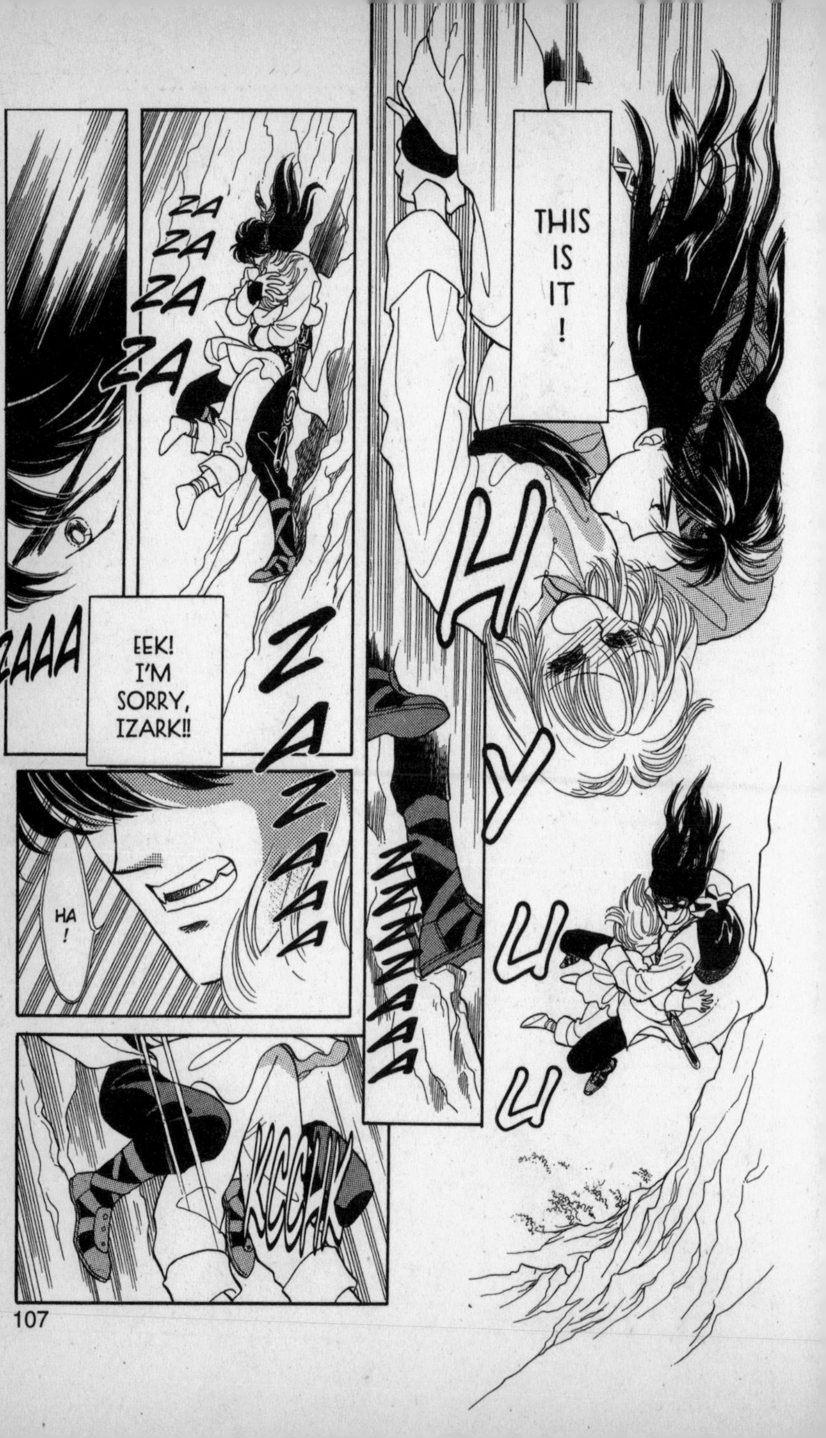
THIS IS IT!
HYUUU
ZAAAAAAAAA
ZA ZA ZA ZA
ZAAA
EEK! I'M SORRY, IZARK!!
ZAAAAA
HA!

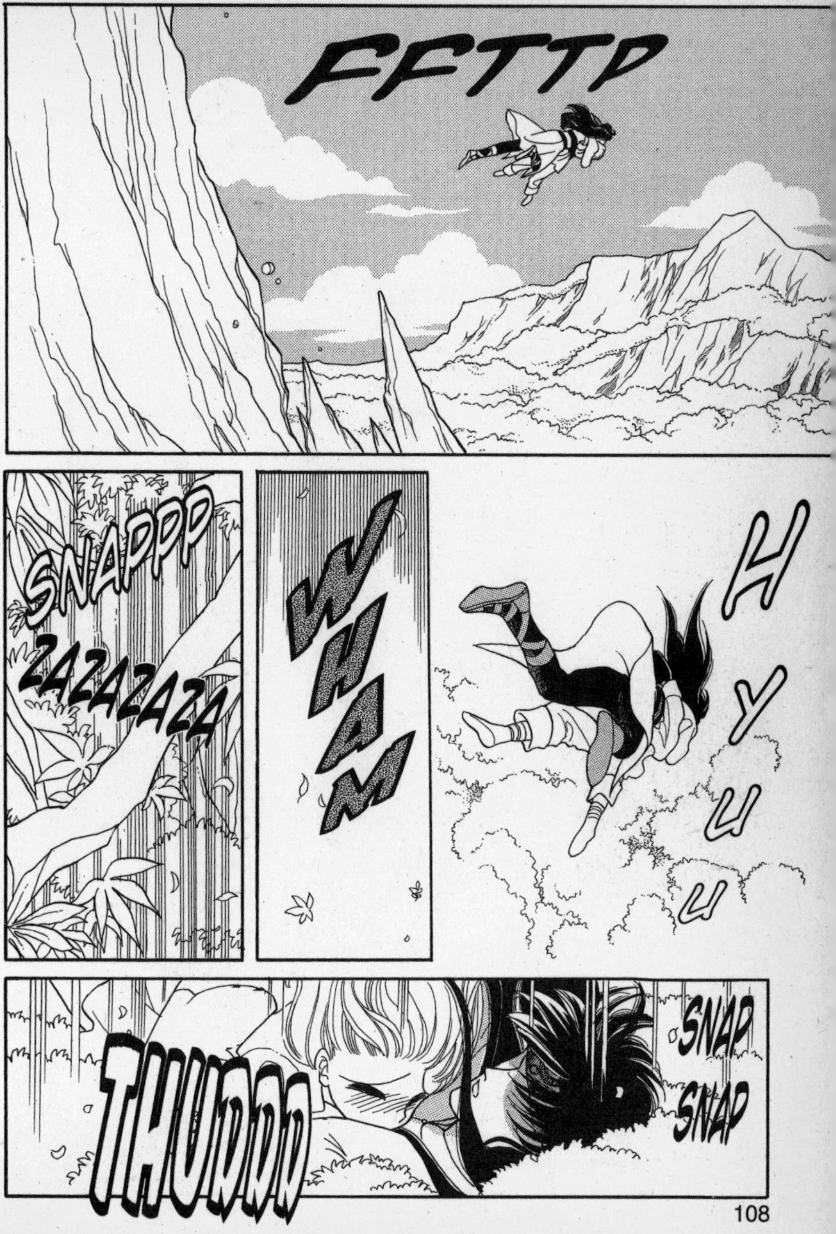
FFTTP
HYUUU
WHAM
SNAPPP
ZAZAZAZA
SNAP
SNAP
THUDDD

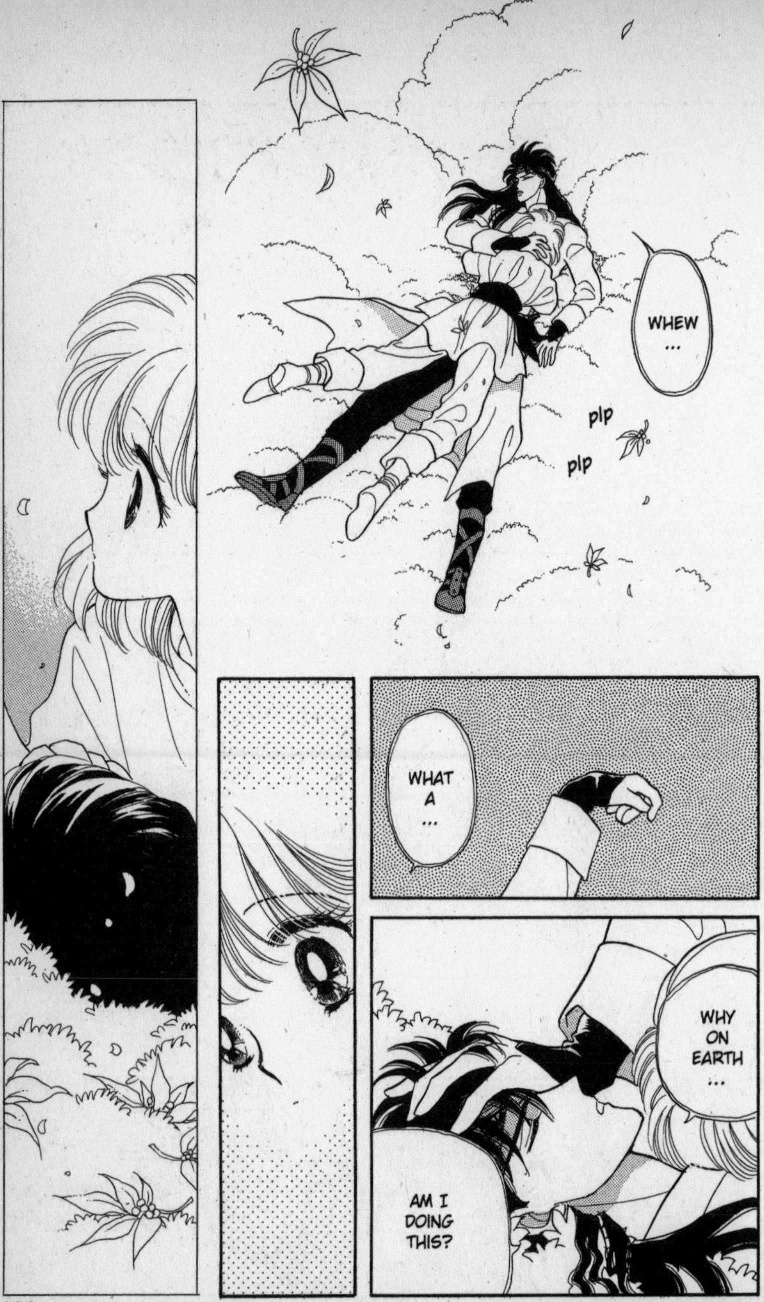
WHEW ...
plp
plp
WHAT A ...
WHY ON EARTH ...
AM I DOING THIS?

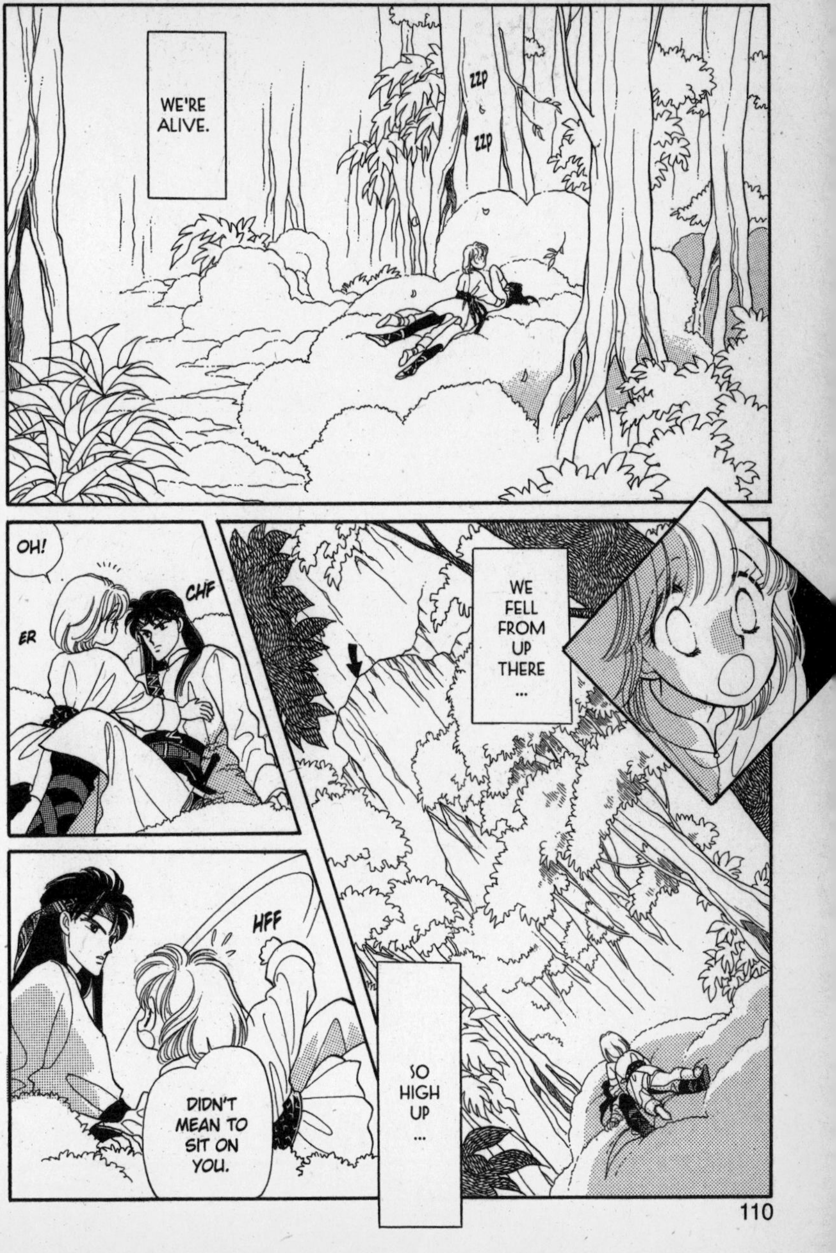

WE'RE ALIVE.
ZZP & ZZP
WE FELL FROM UP THERE ...
SO HIGH UP ...
OH!
CHF
ER
HFF
DIDN'T MEAN TO SIT ON YOU.

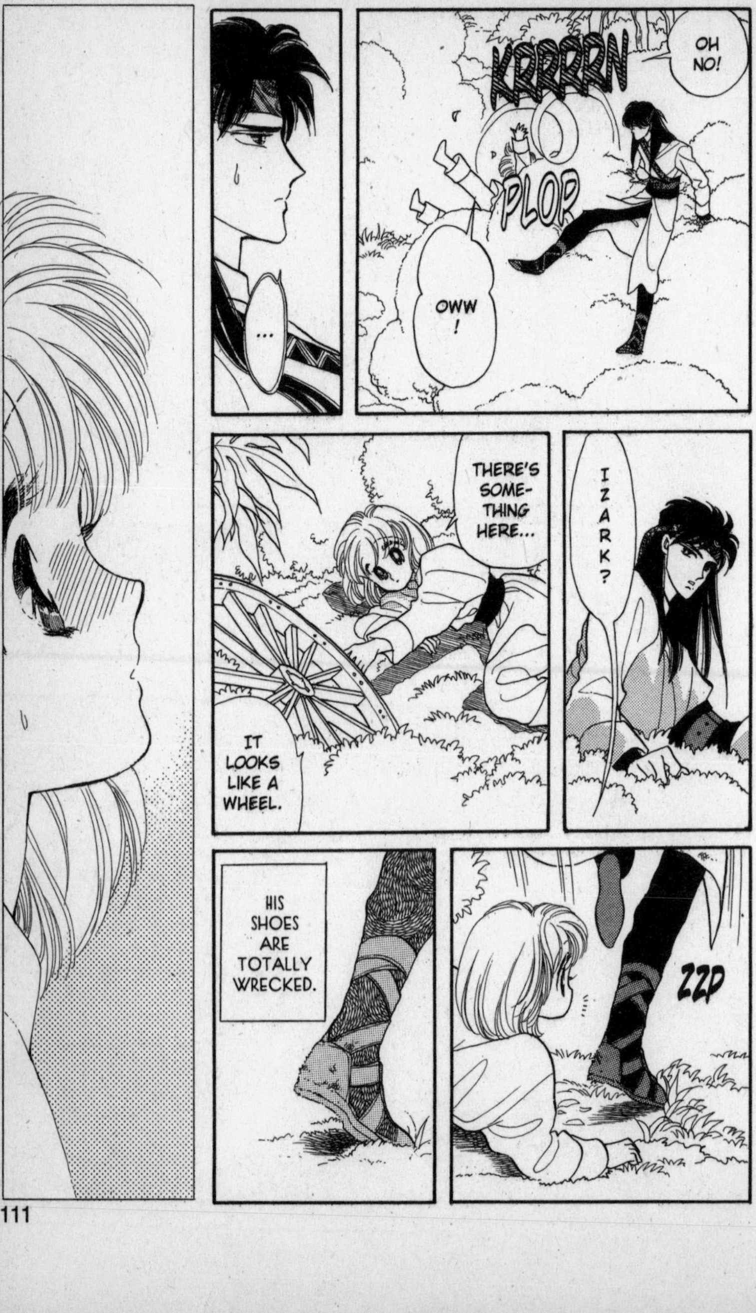

OH NO!
KRRRRN
PLOP
OWW!
...
IZARK?
THERE'S SOME-THING HERE...
IT LOOKS LIKE A WHEEL.
ZZP
HIS SHOES ARE TOTALLY WRECKED.

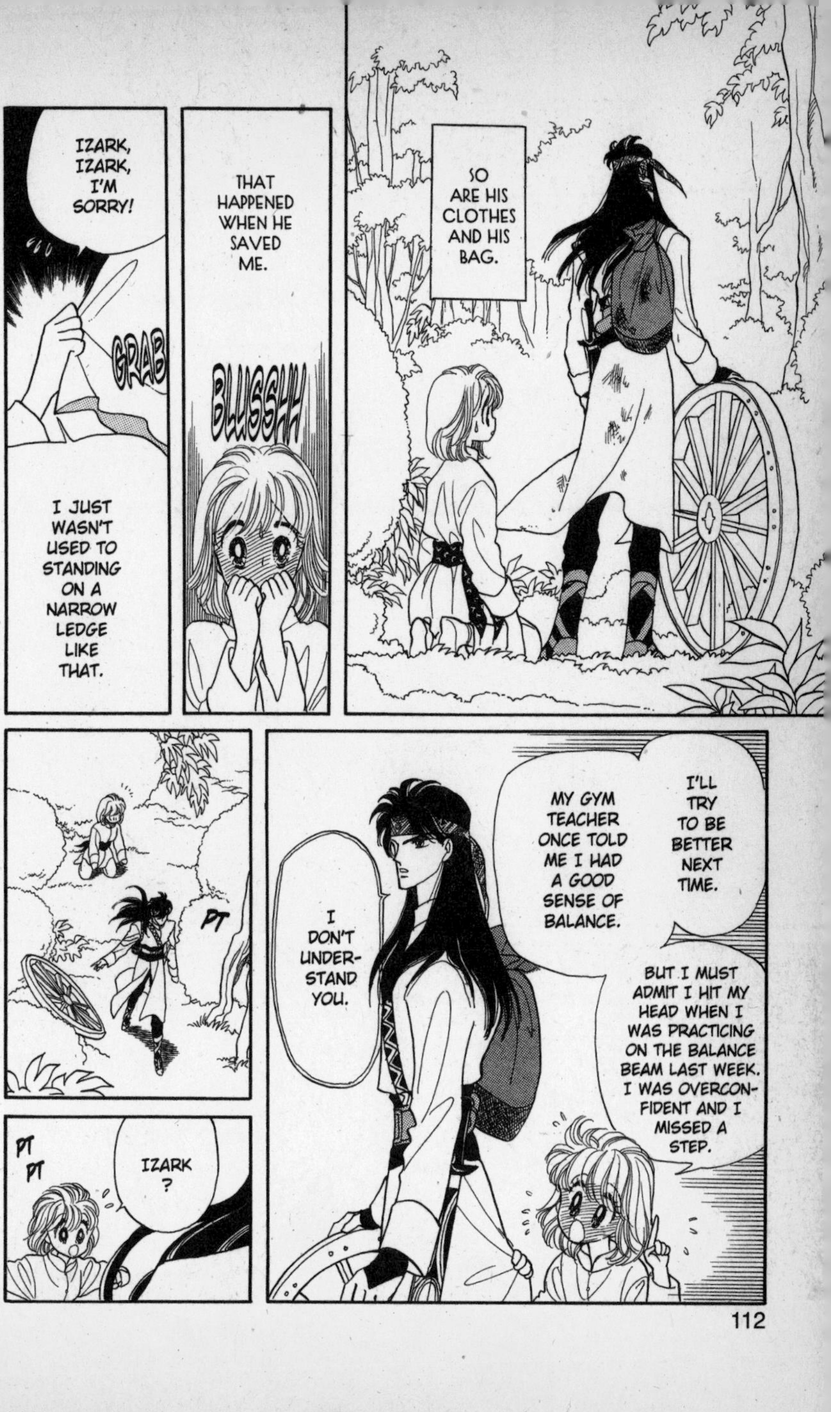
SO ARE HIS CLOTHES AND HIS BAG.
THAT HAPPENED WHEN HE SAVED ME.
BLUSSHH
IZARK, IZARK, I'M SORRY!
GRAB
I JUST WASN'T USED TO STANDING ON A NARROW LEDGE LIKE THAT.
I'LL TRY TO BE BETTER NEXT TIME.
MY GYM TEACHER ONCE TOLD ME I HAD A GOOD SENSE OF BALANCE.
BUT I MUST ADMIT I HIT MY HEAD WHEN I WAS PRACTICING ON THE BALANCE BEAM LAST WEEK. I WAS OVERCON-FIDENT AND I MISSED A STEP.
I DON'T UNDER-STAND YOU.
PT
IZARK ?
PT PT

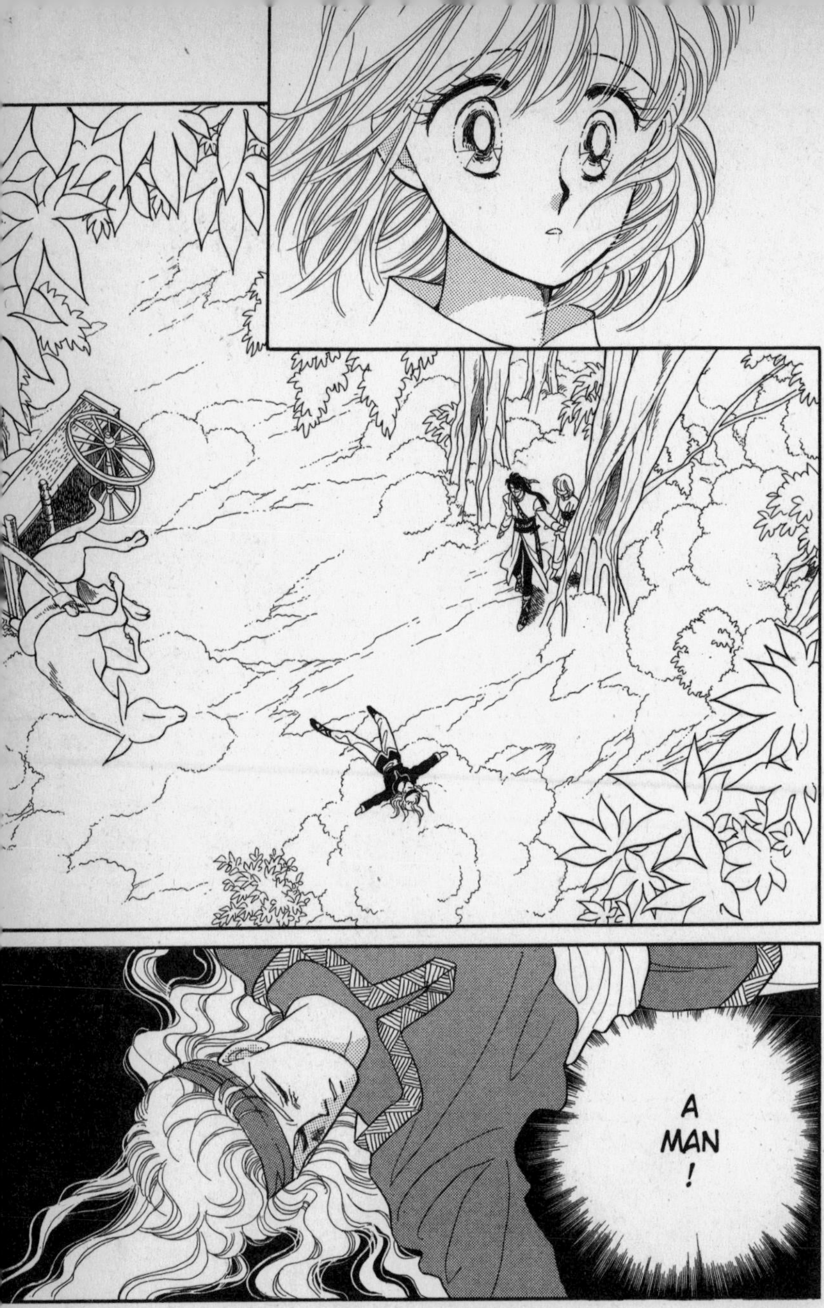
A MAN !

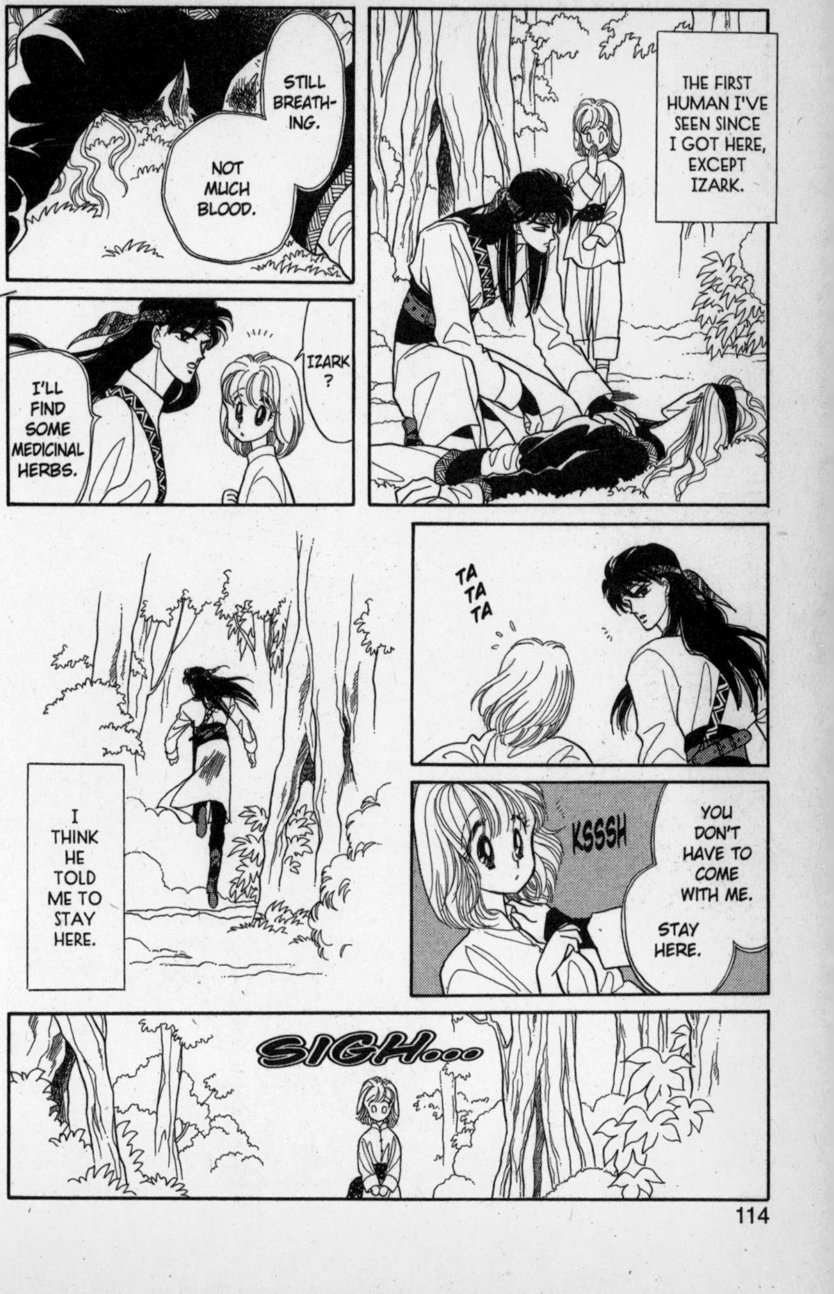
THE FIRST HUMAN I'VE SEEN SINCE I GOT HERE, EXCEPT IZARK.
STILL BREATH-ING.
NOT MUCH BLOOD.
IZARK?
I'LL FIND SOME MEDICINAL HERBS.
TA TA TA
KSSSH
YOU DON'T HAVE TO COME WITH ME.
STAY HERE.
I THINK HE TOLD ME TO STAY HERE.
SIGH...

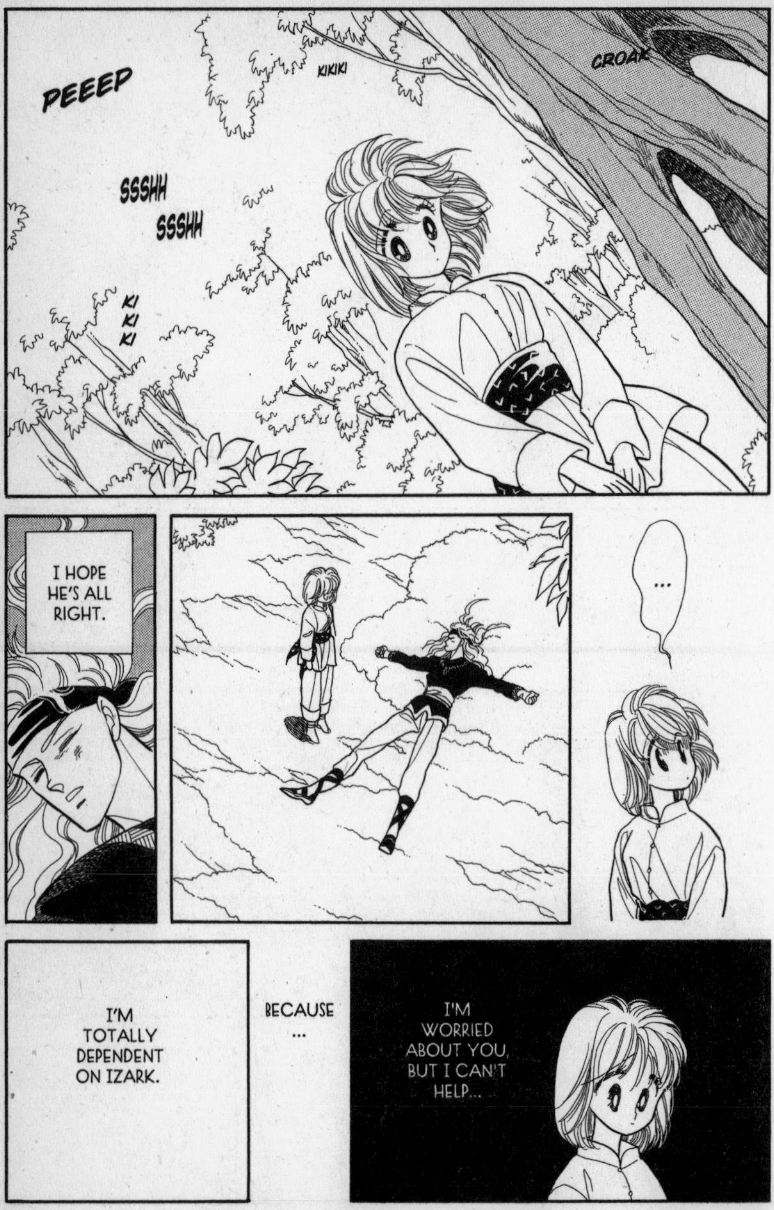
CROAK
KIKIKI
PEEEP
SSSHH
SSSHH
KI KI KI
...
I HOPE HE'S ALL RIGHT.
I'M WORRIED ABOUT YOU, BUT I CAN'T HELP...
BECAUSE ...
I'M TOTALLY DEPENDENT ON IZARK.

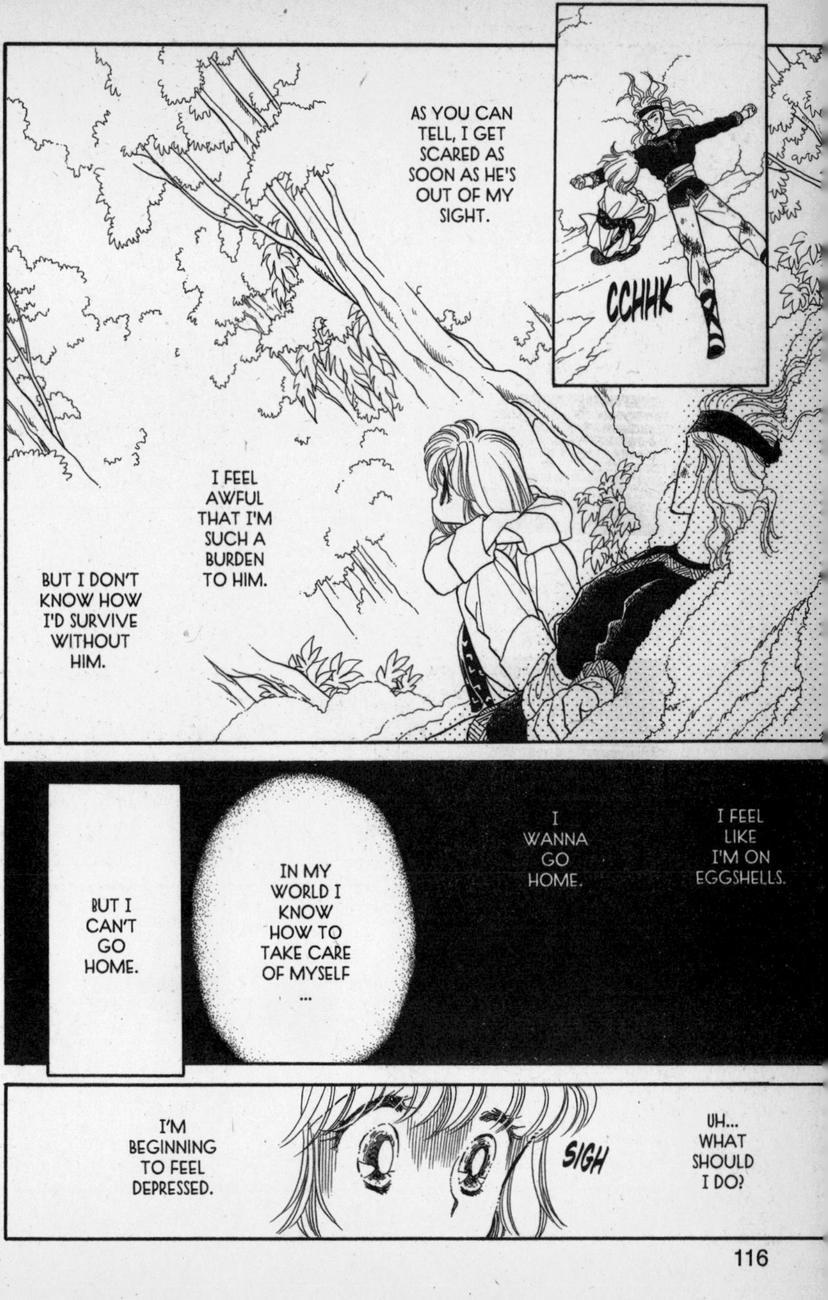
CCHHK
AS YOU CAN TELL, I GET SCARED AS SOON AS HE'S OUT OF MY SIGHT.
I FEEL AWFUL THAT I'M SUCH A BURDEN TO HIM.
BUT I DON'T KNOW HOW I'D SURVIVE WITHOUT HIM.
I FEEL LIKE I'M ON EGGSHELLS.
I WANNA GO HOME.
IN MY WORLD I KNOW HOW TO TAKE CARE OF MYSELF ...
BUT I CAN'T GO HOME.
UH... WHAT SHOULD I DO?
SIGH
I'M BEGINNING TO FEEL DEPRESSED.

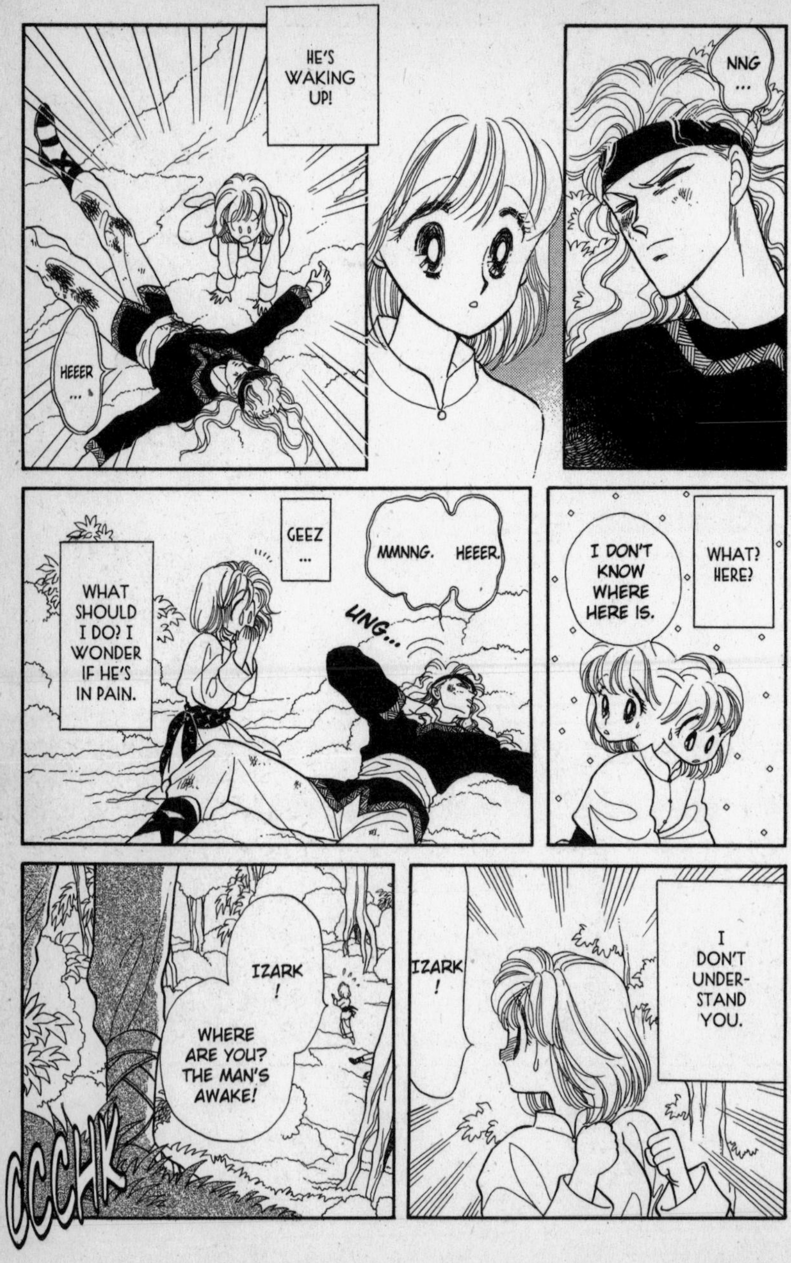
NNG ...
HE'S WAKING UP!
HEEER ...
WHAT? HERE?
I DON'T KNOW WHERE HERE IS.
MMNNG. HEEER.
GEEZ ...
UNG...
WHAT SHOULD I DO? I WONDER IF HE'S IN PAIN.
I DON'T UNDER-STAND YOU.
IZARK !
IZARK !
WHERE ARE YOU? THE MAN'S AWAKE!
CCCHK

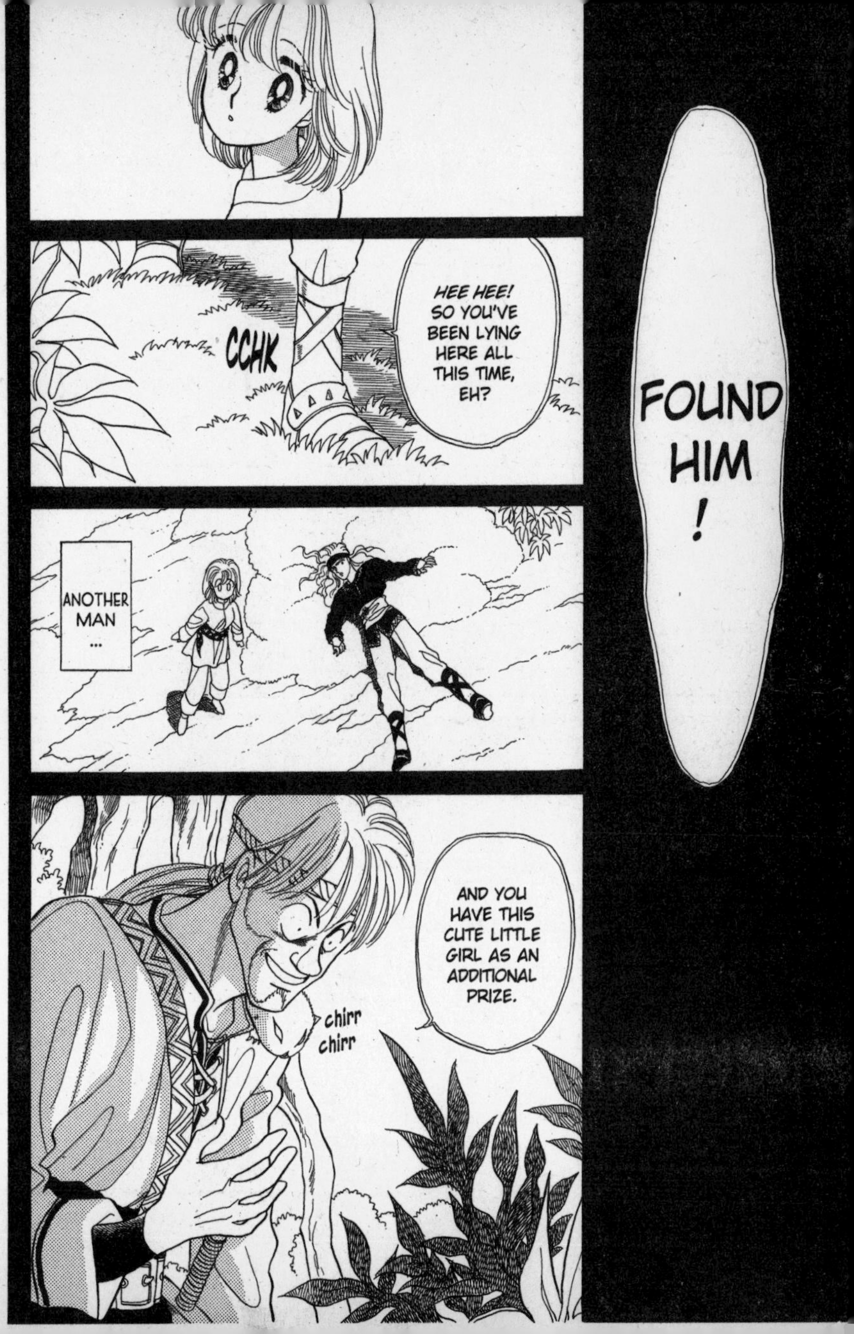
FOUND HIM !
HEE HEE! SO YOU'VE BEEN LYING HERE ALL THIS TIME, EH?
CCHK
ANOTHER MAN ...
AND YOU HAVE THIS CUTE LITTLE GIRL AS AN ADDITIONAL PRIZE.
chirr chirr

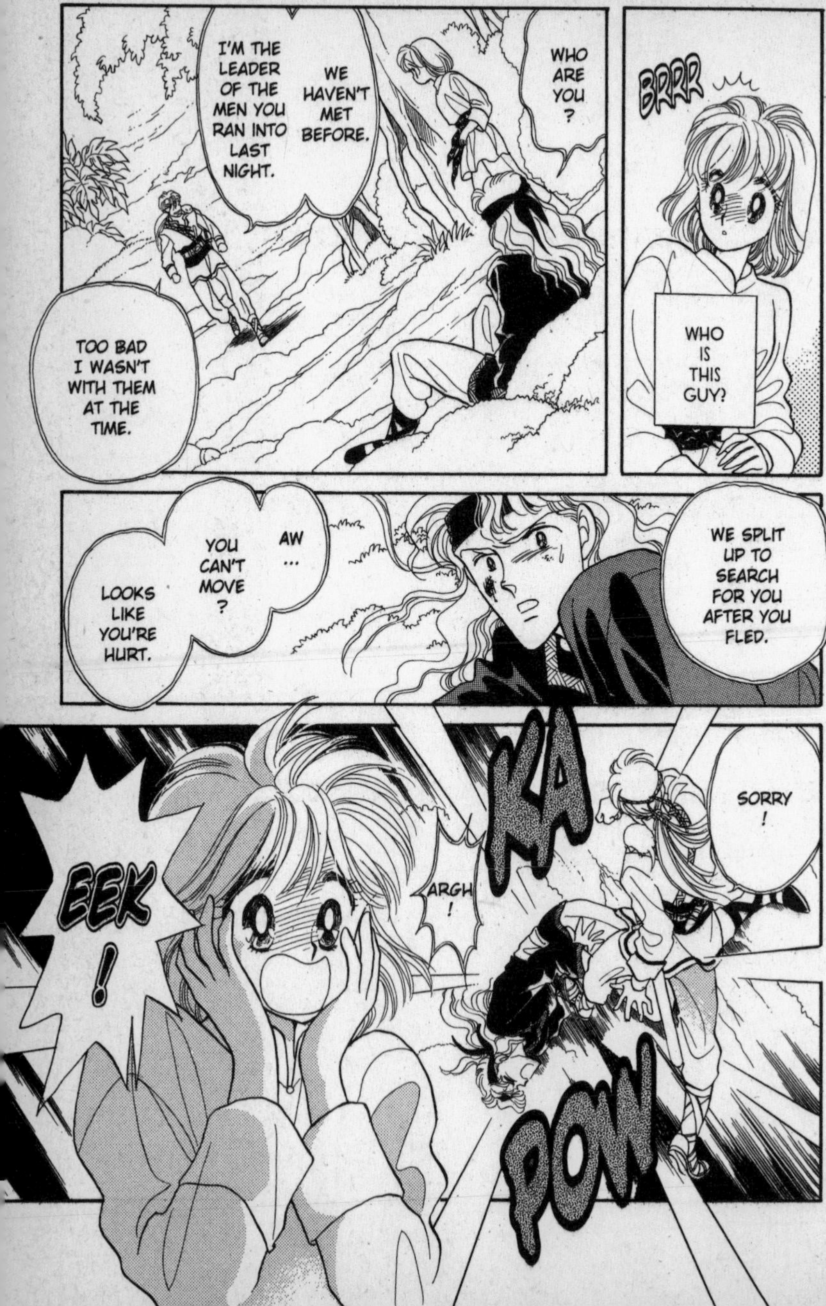
BRRR
WHO IS THIS GUY?
WHO ARE YOU?
WE HAVEN'T MET BEFORE.
I'M THE LEADER OF THE MEN YOU RAN INTO LAST NIGHT.
TOO BAD I WASN'T WITH THEM AT THE TIME.
WE SPLIT UP TO SEARCH FOR YOU AFTER YOU FLED.
AW...
YOU CAN'T MOVE?
LOOKS LIKE YOU'RE HURT.
SORRY!
KA
POW
ARGH!
EEK!

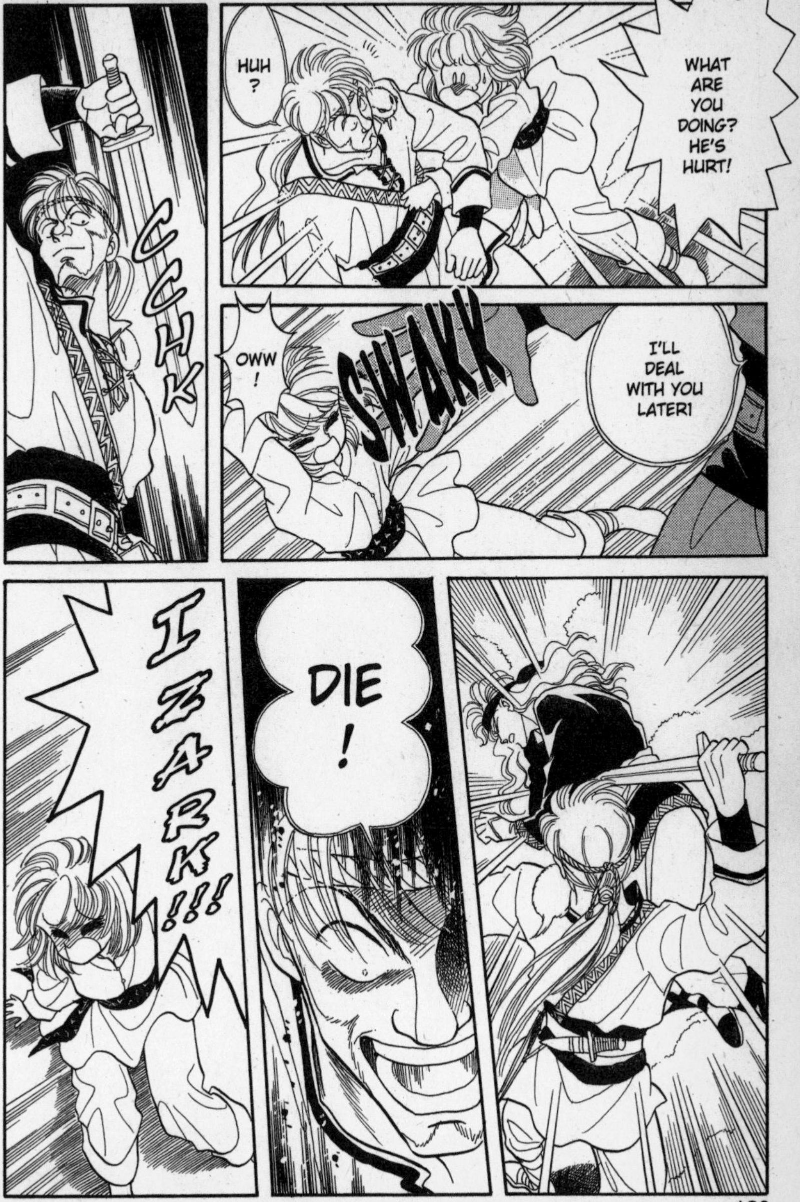
WHAT ARE YOU DOING? HE'S HURT!
HUH ?
I'LL DEAL WITH YOU LATER!
SWAKK
OWW !
CCHK
DIE !
IZARK!!!

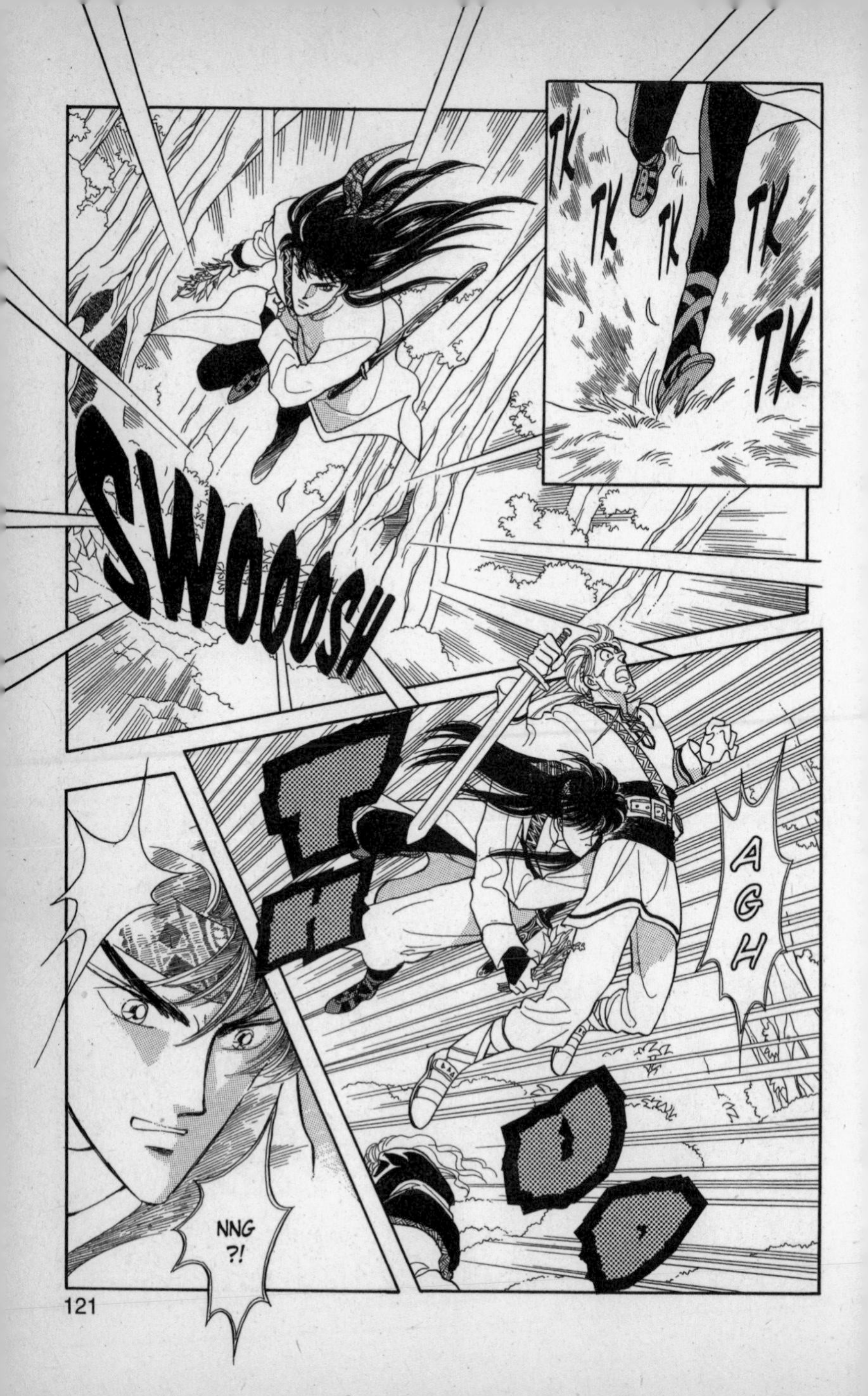
TK TK TK TK TK
SWOOOSH
AGH
NNG ?!

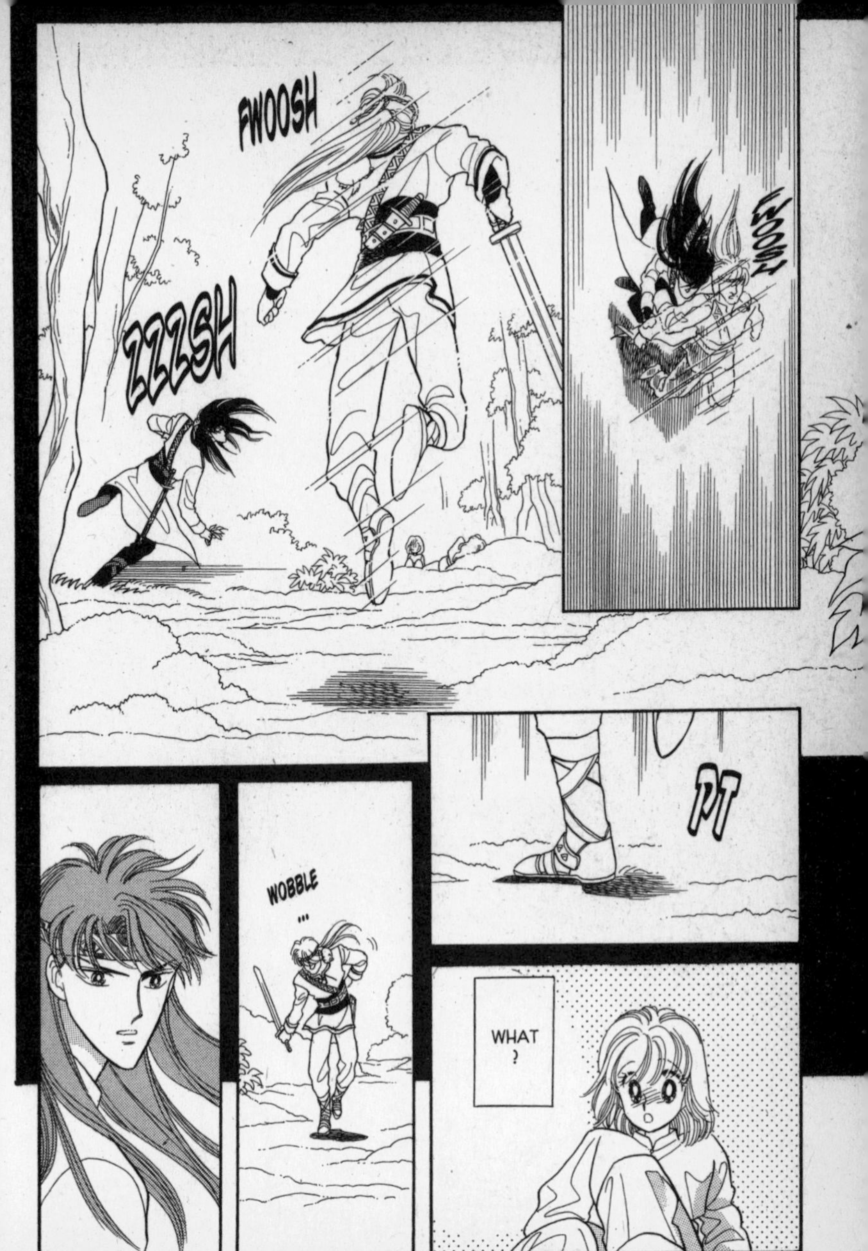
WOOSH
FWOOSH
ZZZSH
PT
WHAT
?
WOBBLE
...

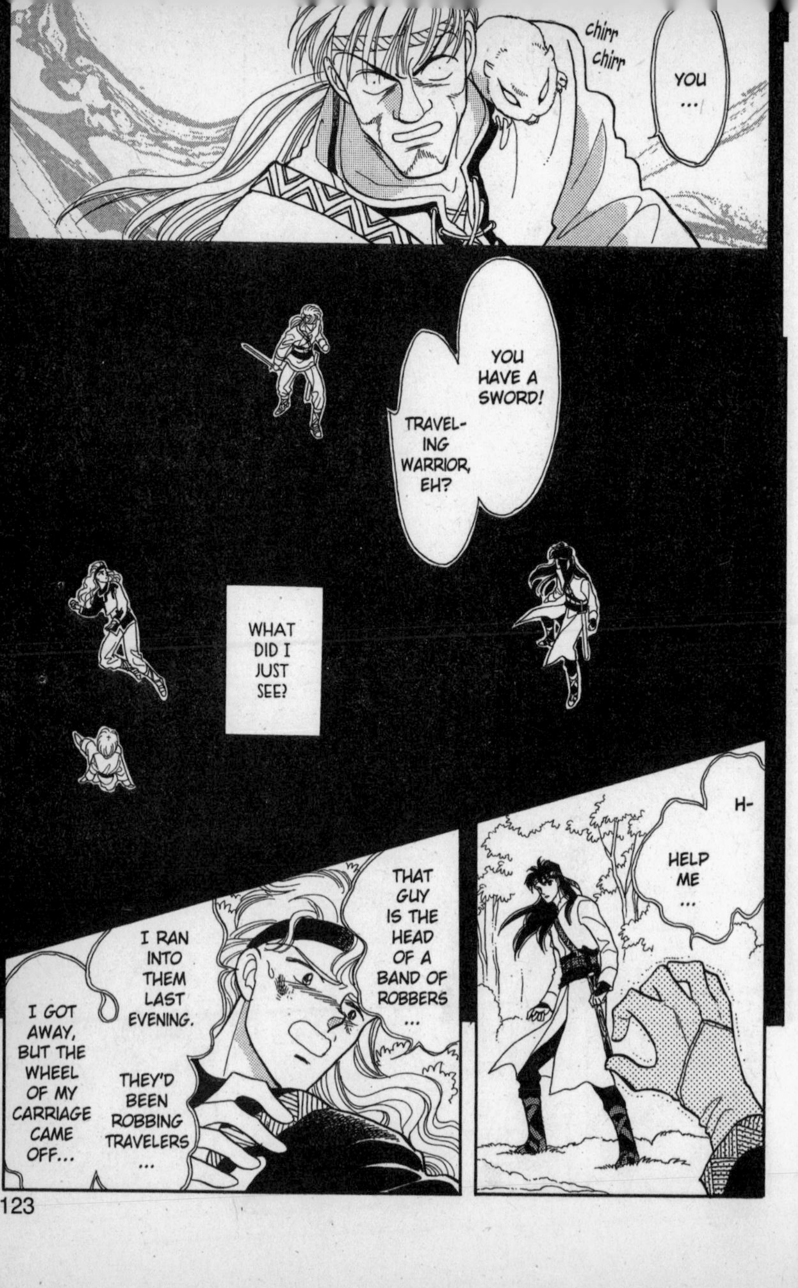

chirr chirr
YOU ...
YOU HAVE A SWORD!
TRAVELING WARRIOR, EH?
WHAT DID I JUST SEE?
H-
HELP ME ...
THAT GUY IS THE HEAD OF A BAND OF ROBBERS ...
I RAN INTO THEM LAST EVENING.
THEY'D BEEN ROBBING TRAVELERS ...
I GOT AWAY, BUT THE WHEEL OF MY CARRIAGE CAME OFF...

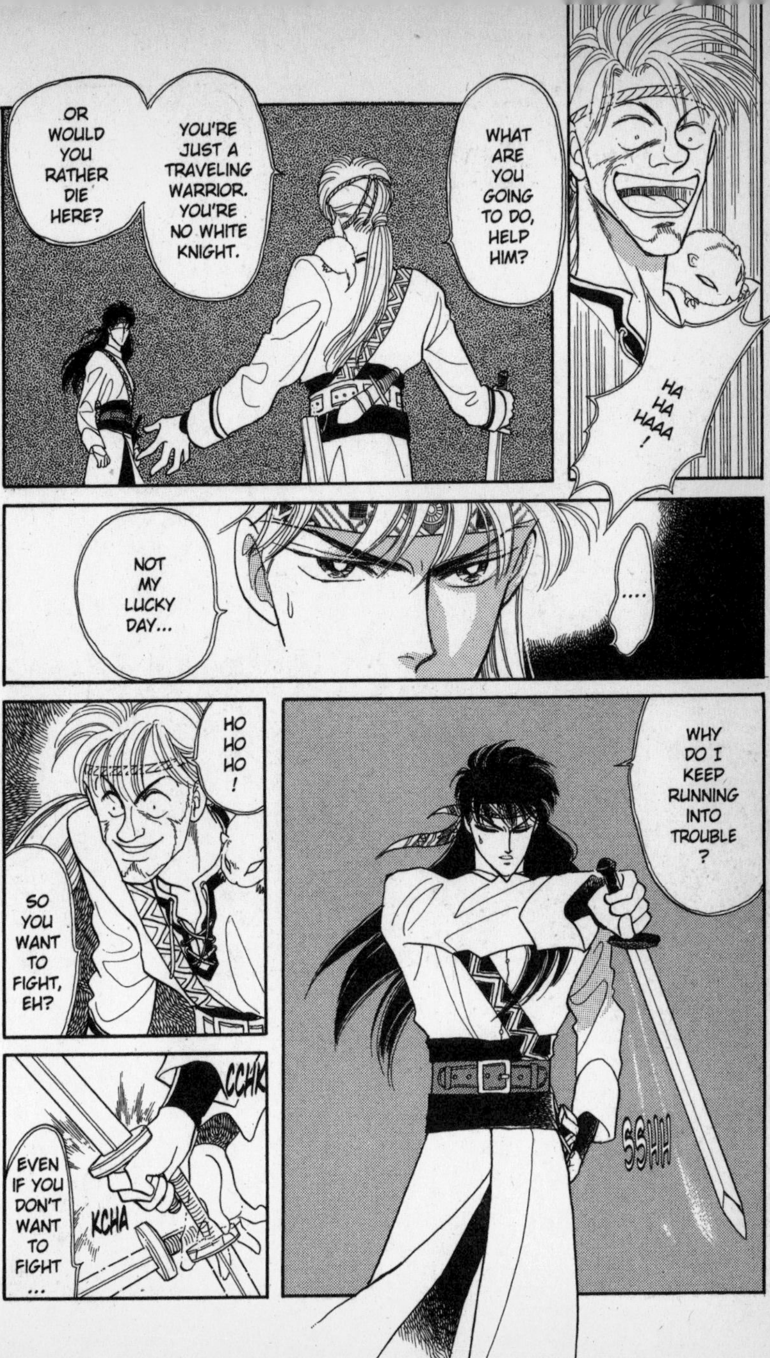
HA HA HAAA!
WHAT ARE YOU GOING TO DO, HELP HIM?
YOU'RE JUST A TRAVELING WARRIOR. YOU'RE NO WHITE KNIGHT.
OR WOULD YOU RATHER DIE HERE?
....
NOT MY LUCKY DAY...
WHY DO I KEEP RUNNING INTO TROUBLE?
SSHH
HO HO HO!
SO YOU WANT TO FIGHT, EH?
CCHK
EVEN IF YOU DON'T WANT TO FIGHT...
KCHA

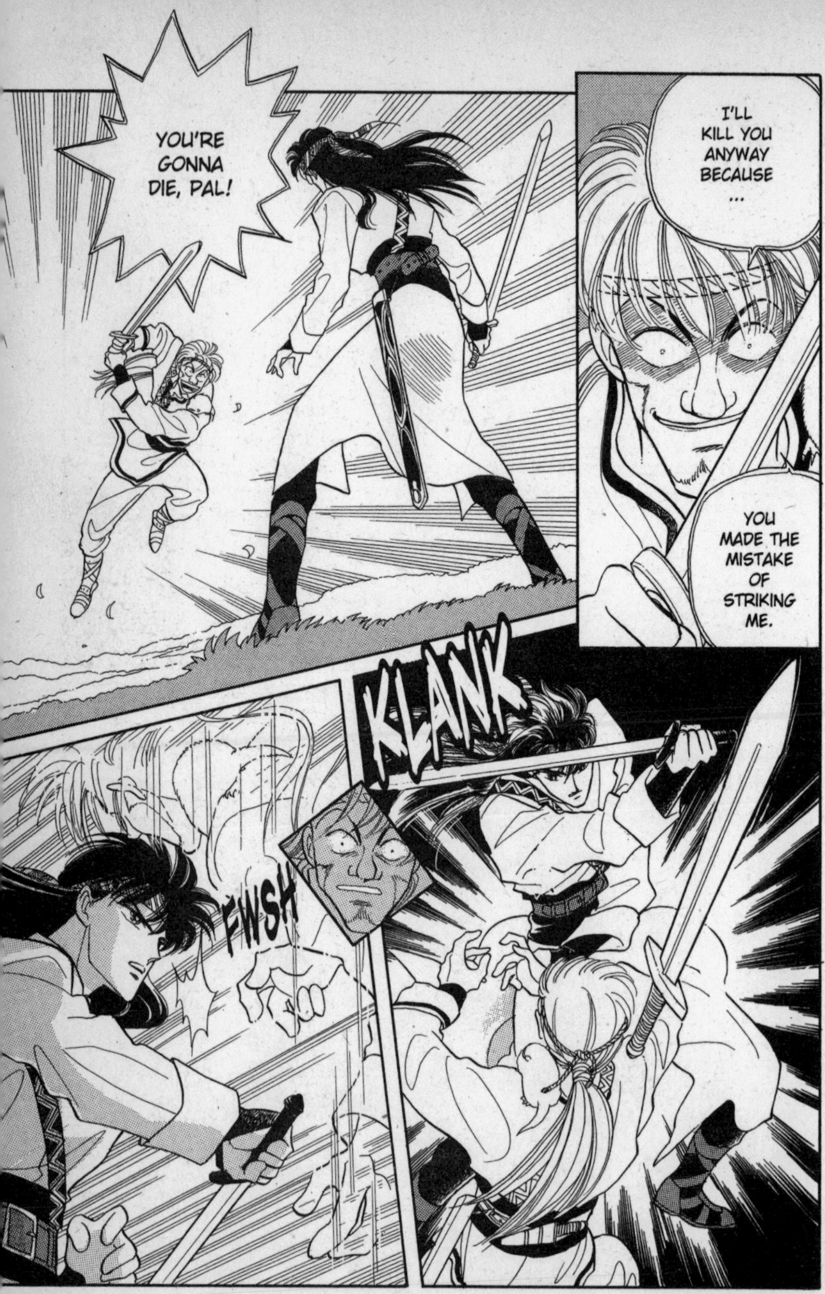
I'LL KILL YOU ANYWAY BECAUSE ...
YOU MADE THE MISTAKE OF STRIKING ME.
YOU'RE GONNA DIE, PAL!
KLANK
FWSH

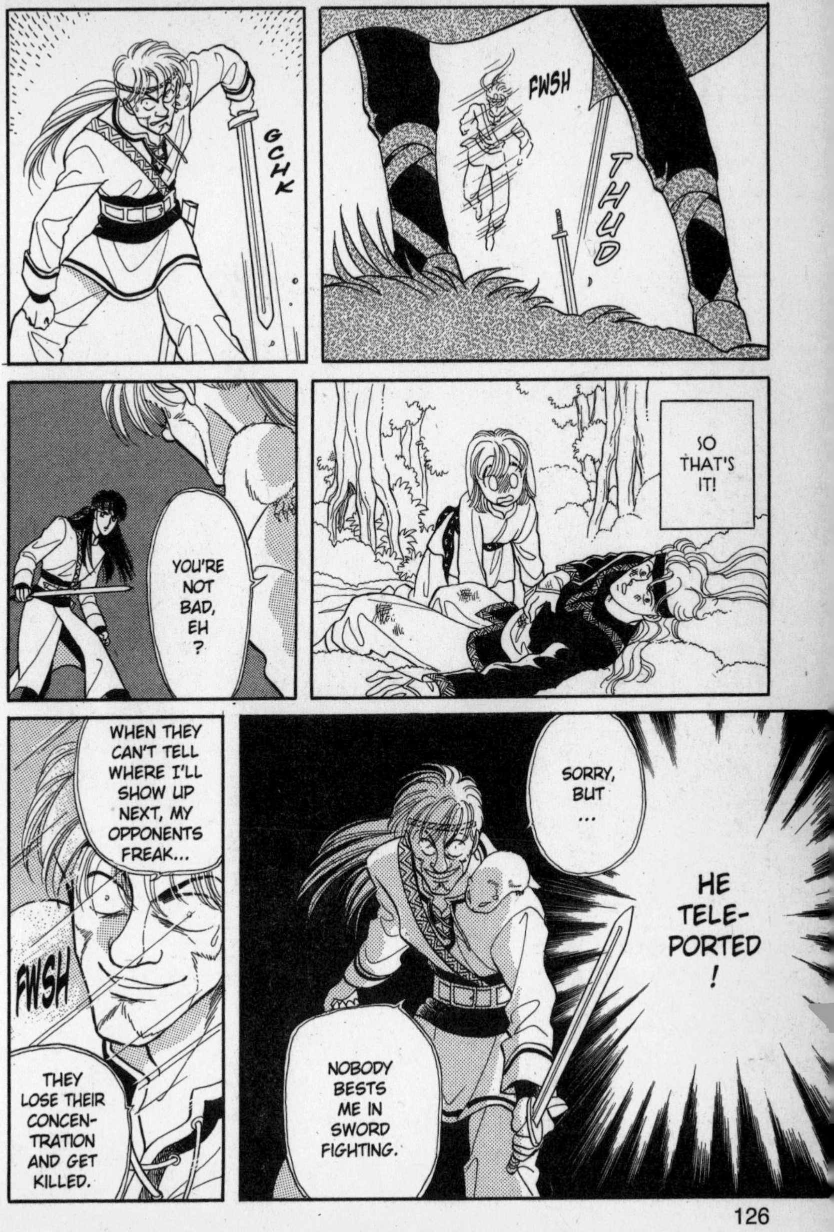
FWSH
THUD
GCHK
SO THAT'S IT!
YOU'RE NOT BAD, EH?
SORRY, BUT...
HE TELE-PORTED!
NOBODY BESTS ME IN SWORD FIGHTING.
WHEN THEY CAN'T TELL WHERE I'LL SHOW UP NEXT, MY OPPONENTS FREAK...
FWSH
THEY LOSE THEIR CONCEN-TRATION AND GET KILLED.

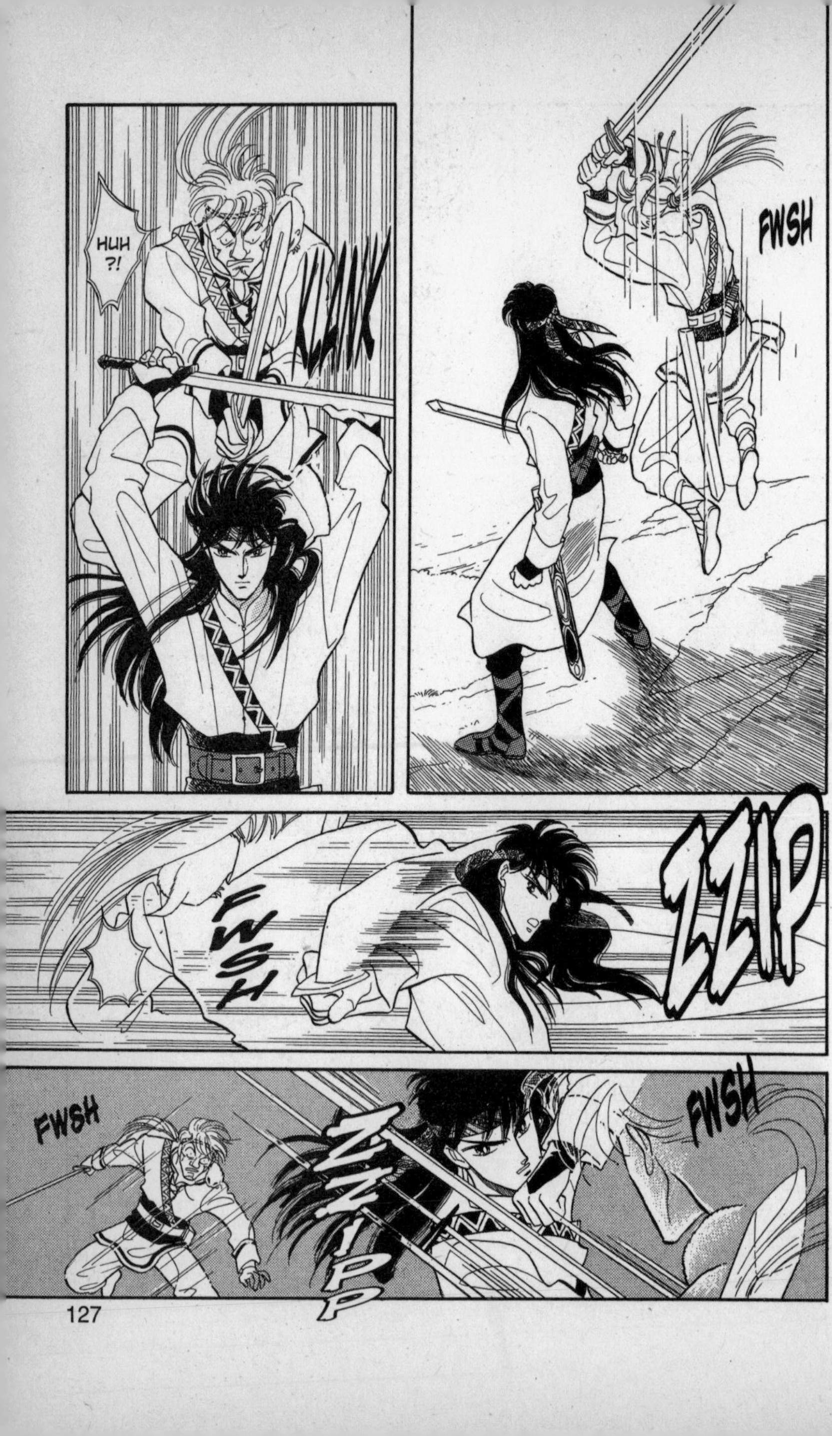
FWSH
HUH ?!
KLANK
ZZIP
FWSH
FWSH
ZWIPP
FWSH

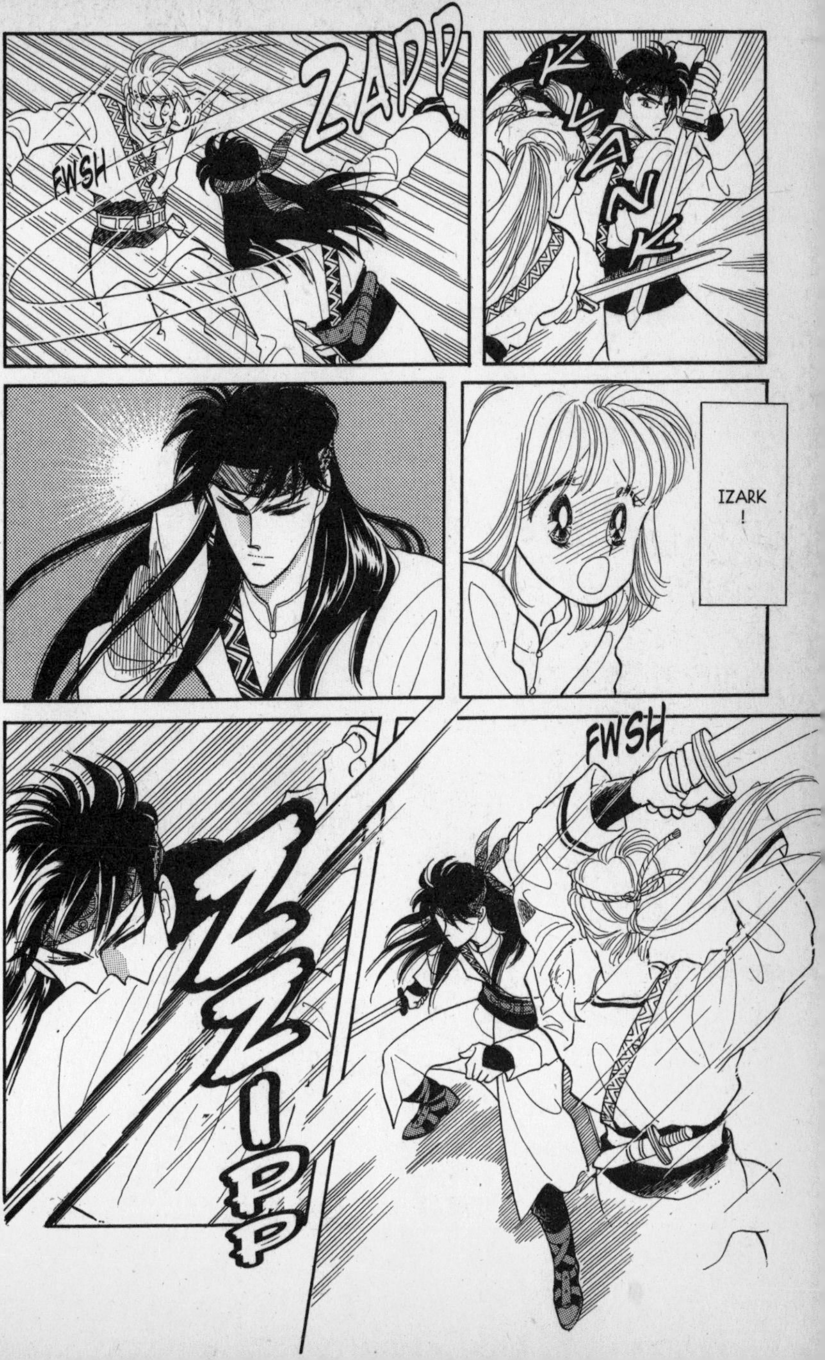
KLANK
ZAPP
FWSH
IZARK
!
FWSH
ZZIPP

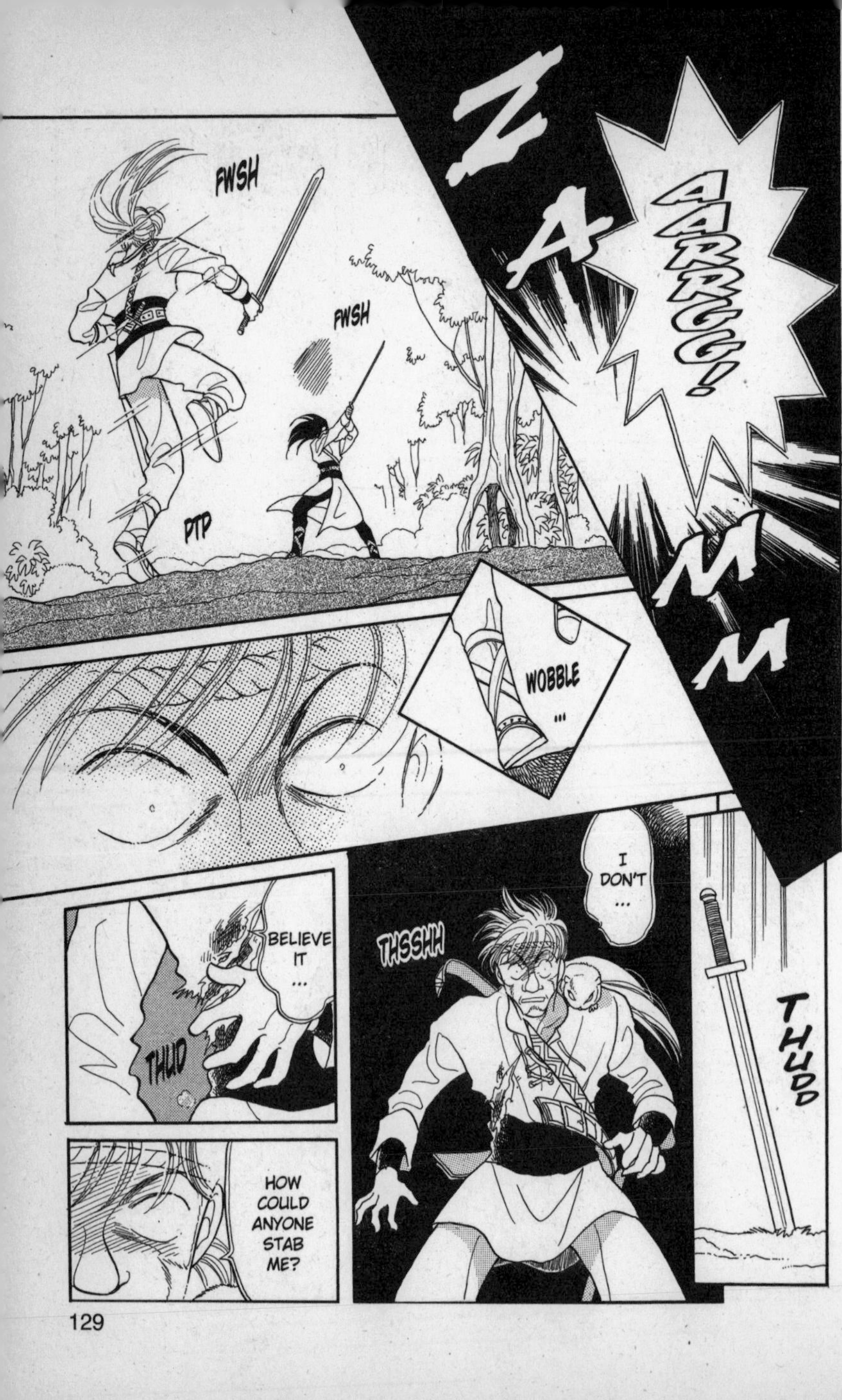
ZAMM
AARRGG!
FWSH
FWSH
PTP
WOBBLE ...
THUDD
I DON'T ...
THSSHH
BELIEVE IT ...
THUD
HOW COULD ANYONE STAB ME?

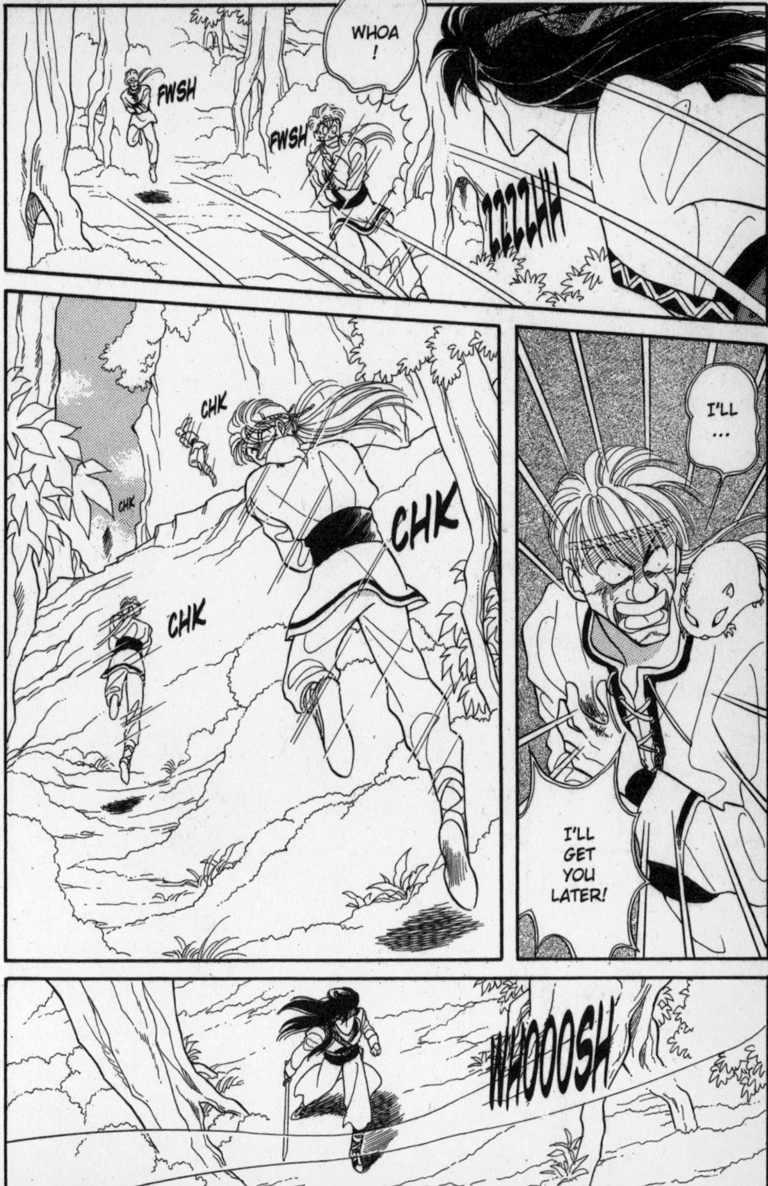
WHOA!
FWSH
FWSH
ZZZZHH
I'LL ...
I'LL GET YOU LATER!
CHK
CHK
CHK
CHK
WHOOOSH

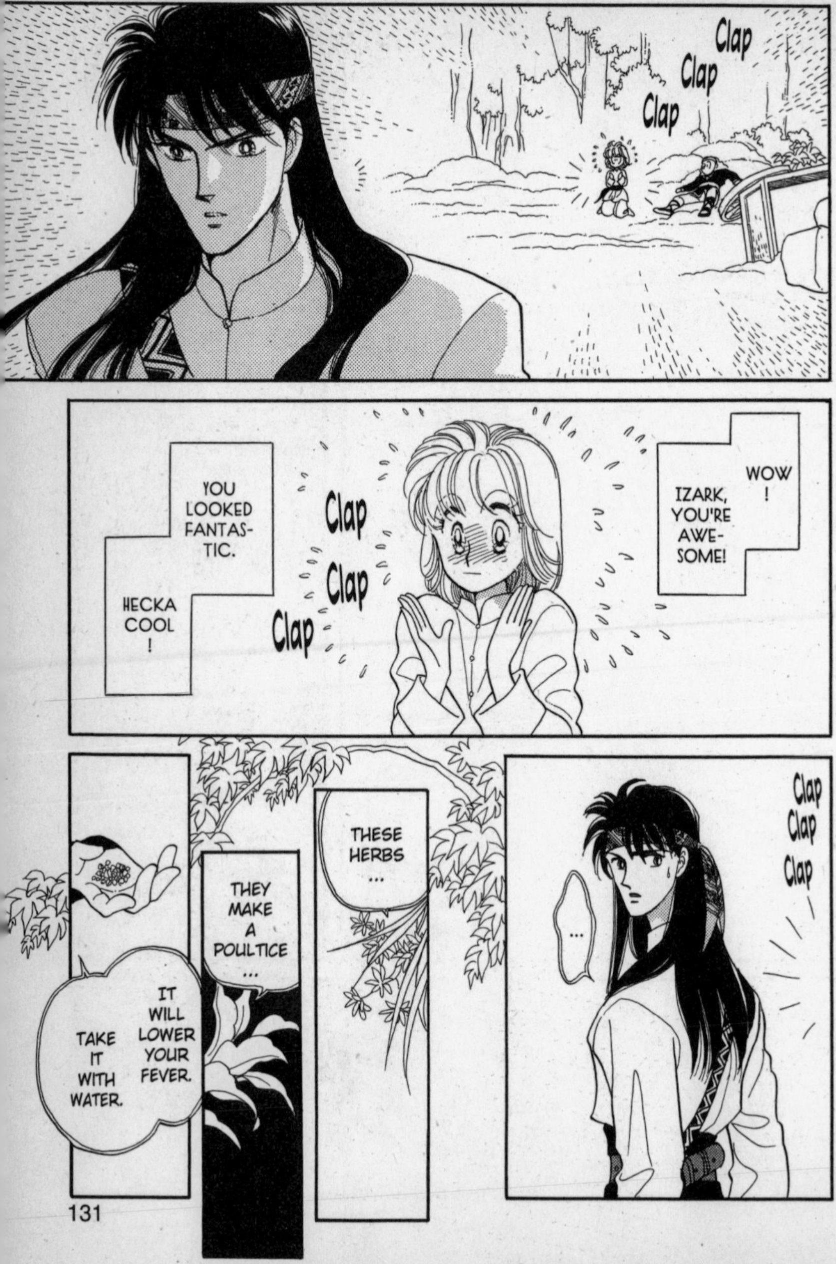
Clap
Clap
Clap
WOW!
IZARK, YOU'RE AWESOME!
Clap
Clap
Clap
YOU LOOKED FANTASTIC.
HECKA COOL!
Clap
Clap
Clap
...
THESE HERBS ...
THEY MAKE A POULTICE ...
IT WILL LOWER YOUR FEVER.
TAKE IT WITH WATER.

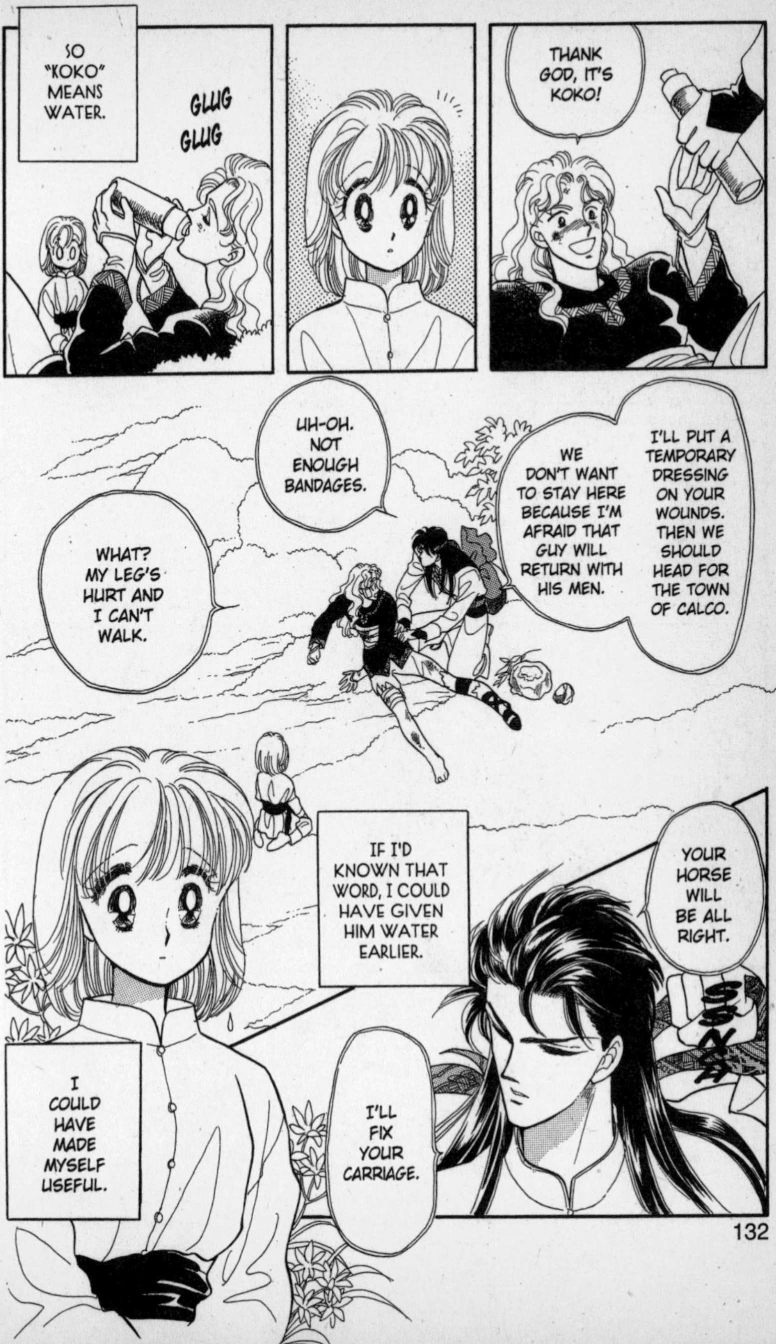
THANK GOD, IT'S KOKO!
SO "KOKO" MEANS WATER.
GLUG GLUG
I'LL PUT A TEMPORARY DRESSING ON YOUR WOUNDS. THEN WE SHOULD HEAD FOR THE TOWN OF CALCO.
WE DON'T WANT TO STAY HERE BECAUSE I'M AFRAID THAT GUY WILL RETURN WITH HIS MEN.
UH-OH. NOT ENOUGH BANDAGES.
WHAT? MY LEG'S HURT AND I CAN'T WALK.
YOUR HORSE WILL BE ALL RIGHT.
I'LL FIX YOUR CARRIAGE.
IF I'D KNOWN THAT WORD, I COULD HAVE GIVEN HIM WATER EARLIER.
I COULD HAVE MADE MYSELF USEFUL.

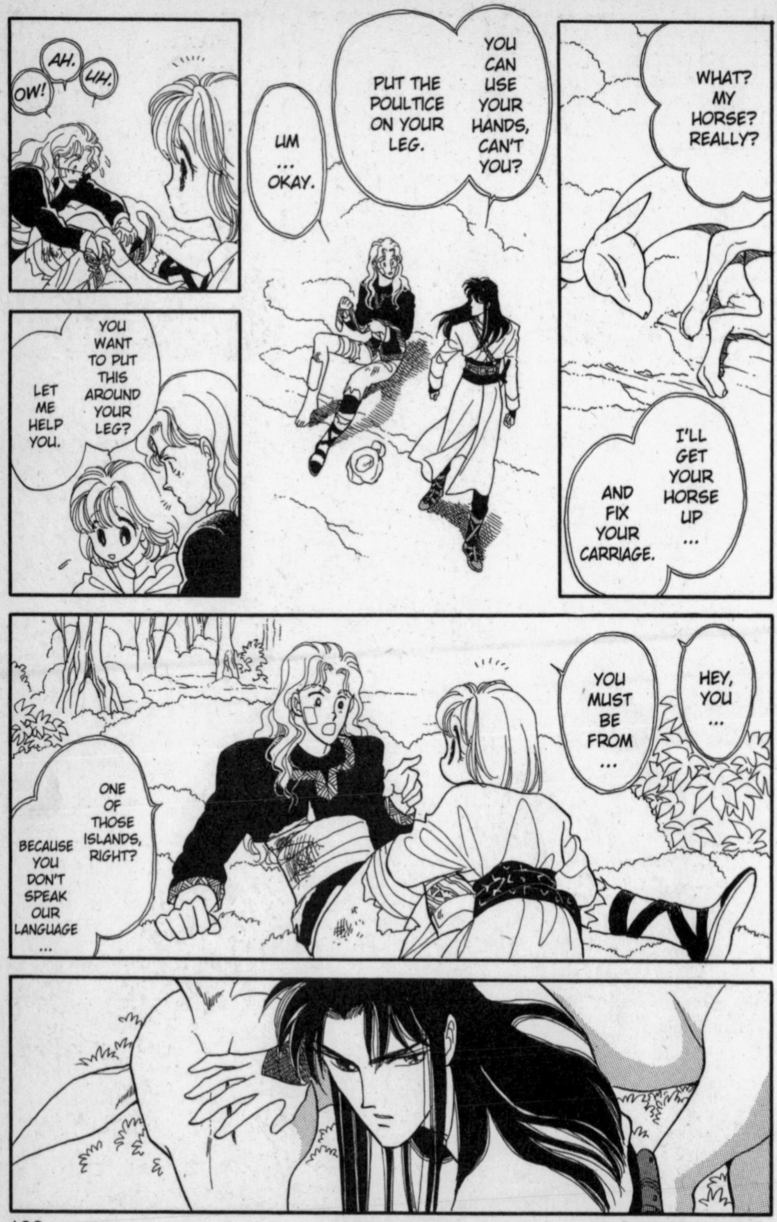
WHAT? MY HORSE? REALLY?
I'LL GET YOUR HORSE UP ... AND FIX YOUR CARRIAGE.
YOU CAN USE YOUR HANDS, CAN'T YOU?
PUT THE POULTICE ON YOUR LEG.
UM ... OKAY.
UH.
AH.
OW!
YOU WANT TO PUT THIS AROUND YOUR LEG?
LET ME HELP YOU.
HEY, YOU ...
YOU MUST BE FROM ...
ONE OF THOSE ISLANDS, RIGHT?
BECAUSE YOU DON'T SPEAK OUR LANGUAGE ...

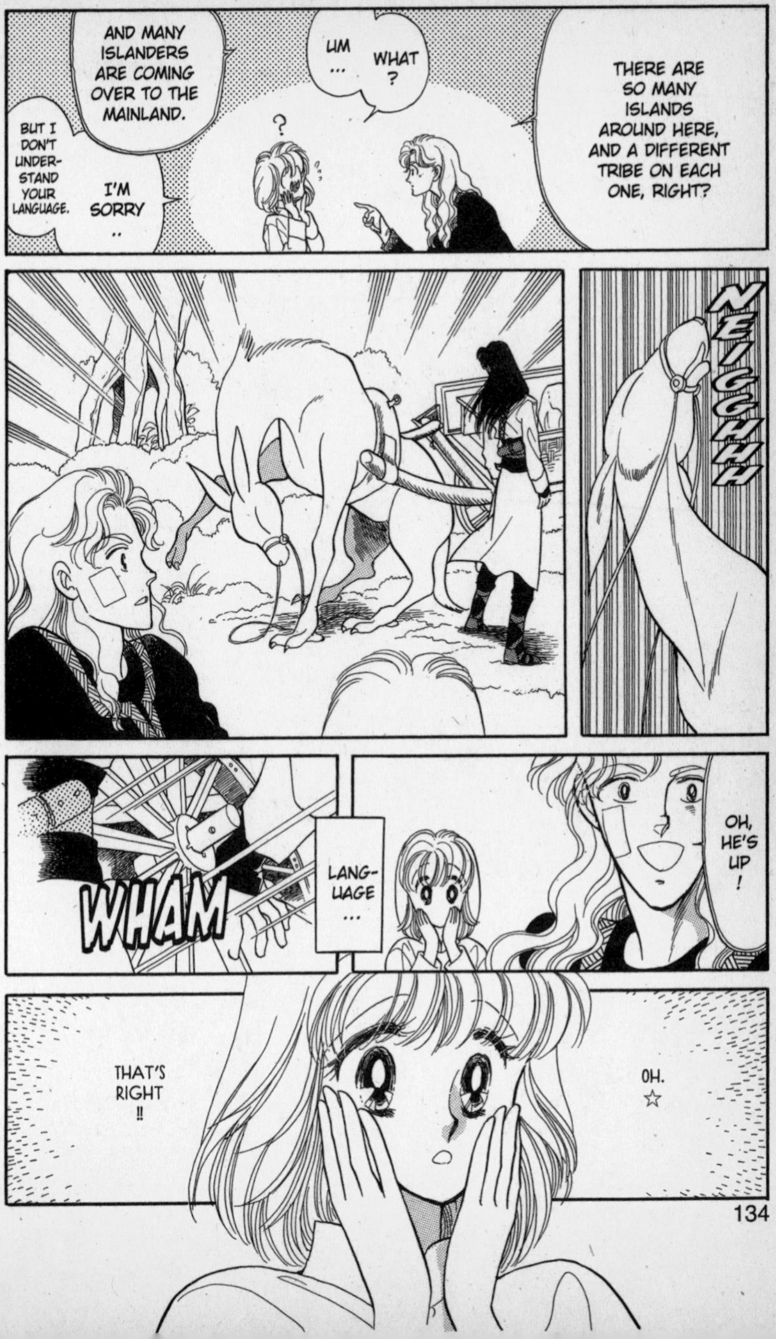
THERE ARE SO MANY ISLANDS AROUND HERE, AND A DIFFERENT TRIBE ON EACH ONE, RIGHT?
AND MANY ISLANDERS ARE COMING OVER TO THE MAINLAND.
UM ...
WHAT ?
?
I'M SORRY ..
BUT I DON'T UNDER-STAND YOUR LANGUAGE.
NEIGCHHH
OH, HE'S UP !
LANG-UAGE ...
WHAM
OH. ☆
THAT'S RIGHT !!

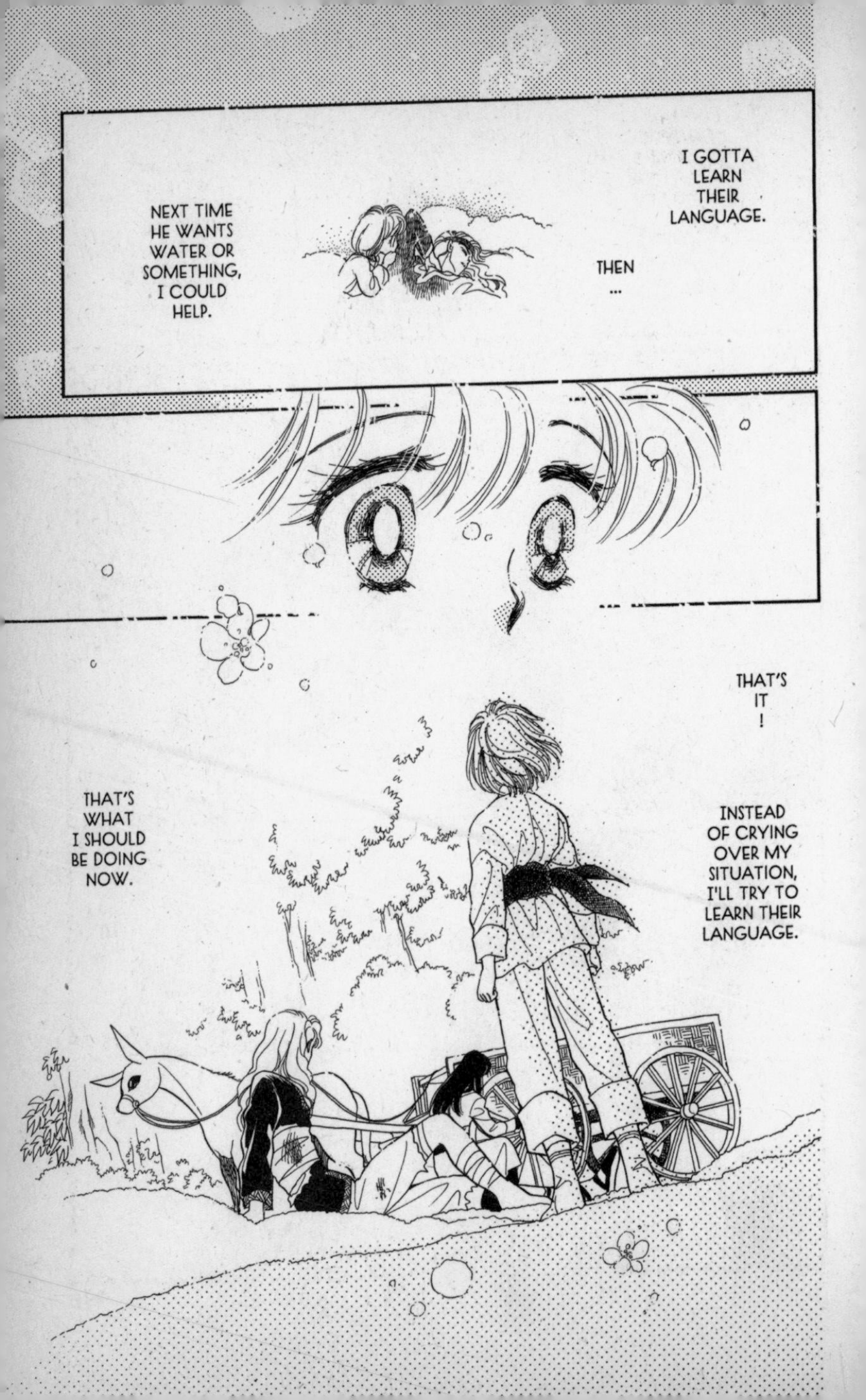
I GOTTA LEARN THEIR LANGUAGE.
THEN ...
NEXT TIME HE WANTS WATER OR SOMETHING, I COULD HELP.
THAT'S IT !
INSTEAD OF CRYING OVER MY SITUATION, I'LL TRY TO LEARN THEIR LANGUAGE.
THAT'S WHAT I SHOULD BE DOING NOW.

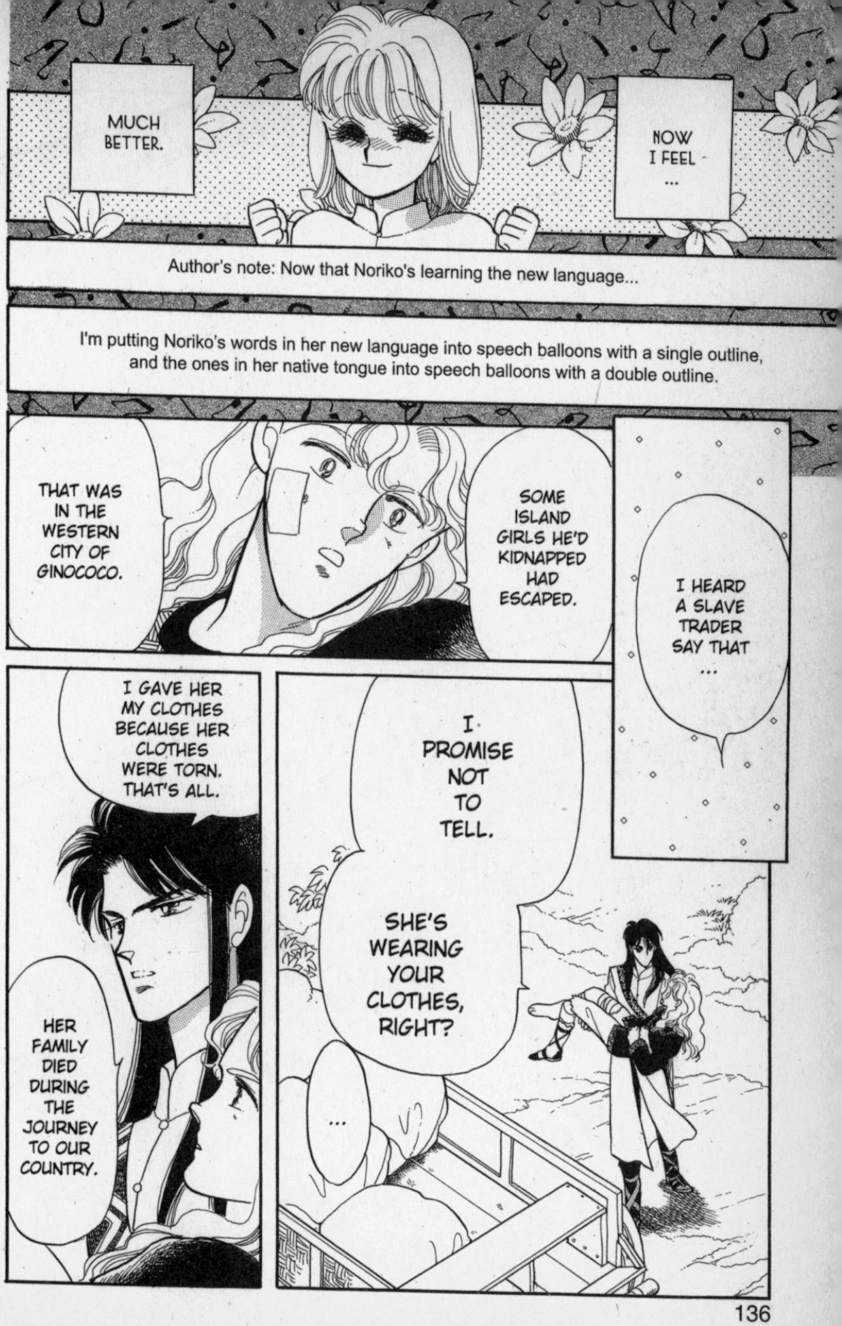
NOW I FEEL ...
MUCH BETTER.
Author's note: Now that Noriko's learning the new language...
I'm putting Noriko's words in her new language into speech balloons with a single outline, and the ones in her native tongue into speech balloons with a double outline.
I HEARD A SLAVE TRADER SAY THAT ...
SOME ISLAND GIRLS HE'D KIDNAPPED HAD ESCAPED.
THAT WAS IN THE WESTERN CITY OF GINOCOCO.
SHE'S WEARING YOUR CLOTHES, RIGHT?
I PROMISE NOT TO TELL.
...
I GAVE HER MY CLOTHES BECAUSE HER CLOTHES WERE TORN. THAT'S ALL.
HER FAMILY DIED DURING THE JOURNEY TO OUR COUNTRY.

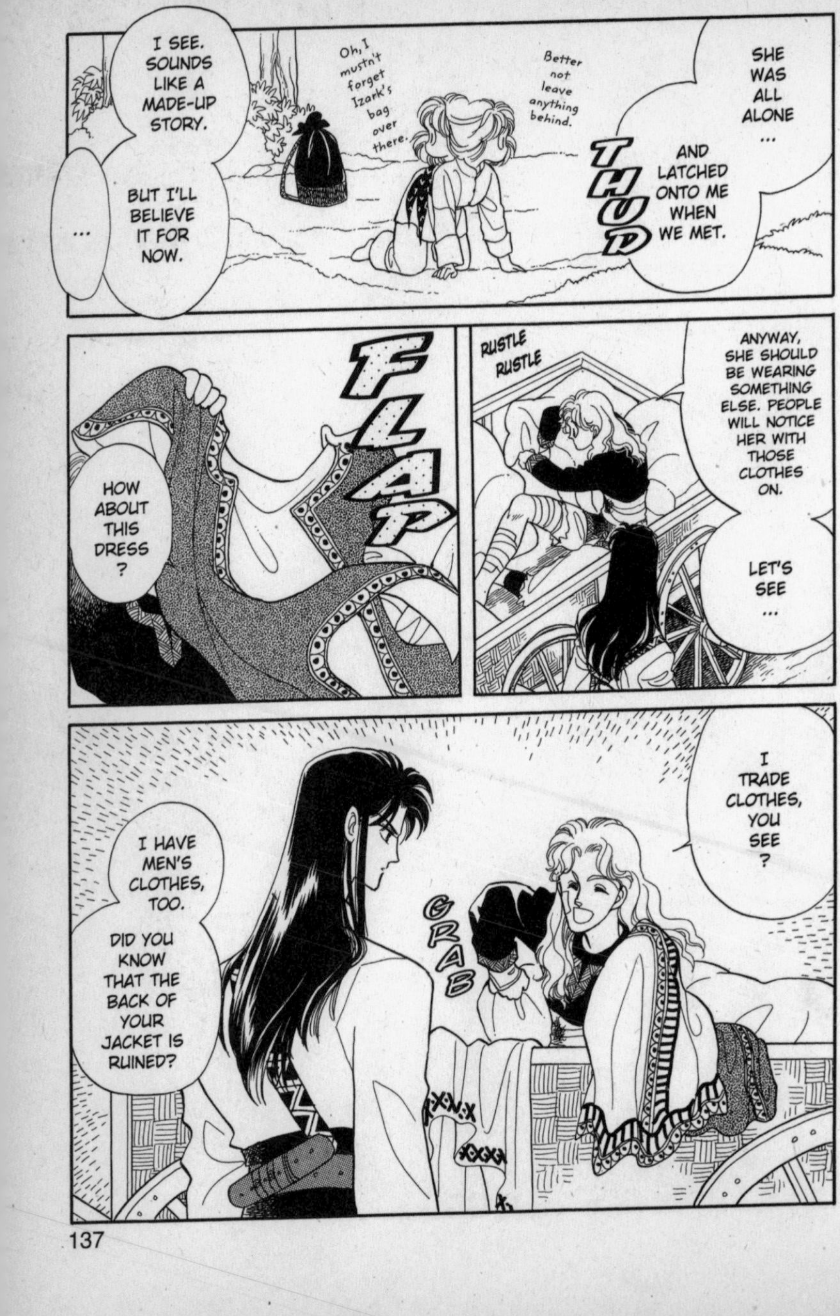
SHE WAS ALL ALONE ...
AND LATCHED ONTO ME WHEN WE MET.
THUD
Better not leave anything behind.
Oh, I mustn't forget Izark's bag over there.
I SEE. SOUNDS LIKE A MADE-UP STORY.
BUT I'LL BELIEVE IT FOR NOW.
...
RUSTLE RUSTLE
ANYWAY, SHE SHOULD BE WEARING SOMETHING ELSE. PEOPLE WILL NOTICE HER WITH THOSE CLOTHES ON.
LET'S SEE ...
FLAP
HOW ABOUT THIS DRESS ?
I TRADE CLOTHES, YOU SEE ?
GRAB
I HAVE MEN'S CLOTHES, TOO.
DID YOU KNOW THAT THE BACK OF YOUR JACKET IS RUINED?

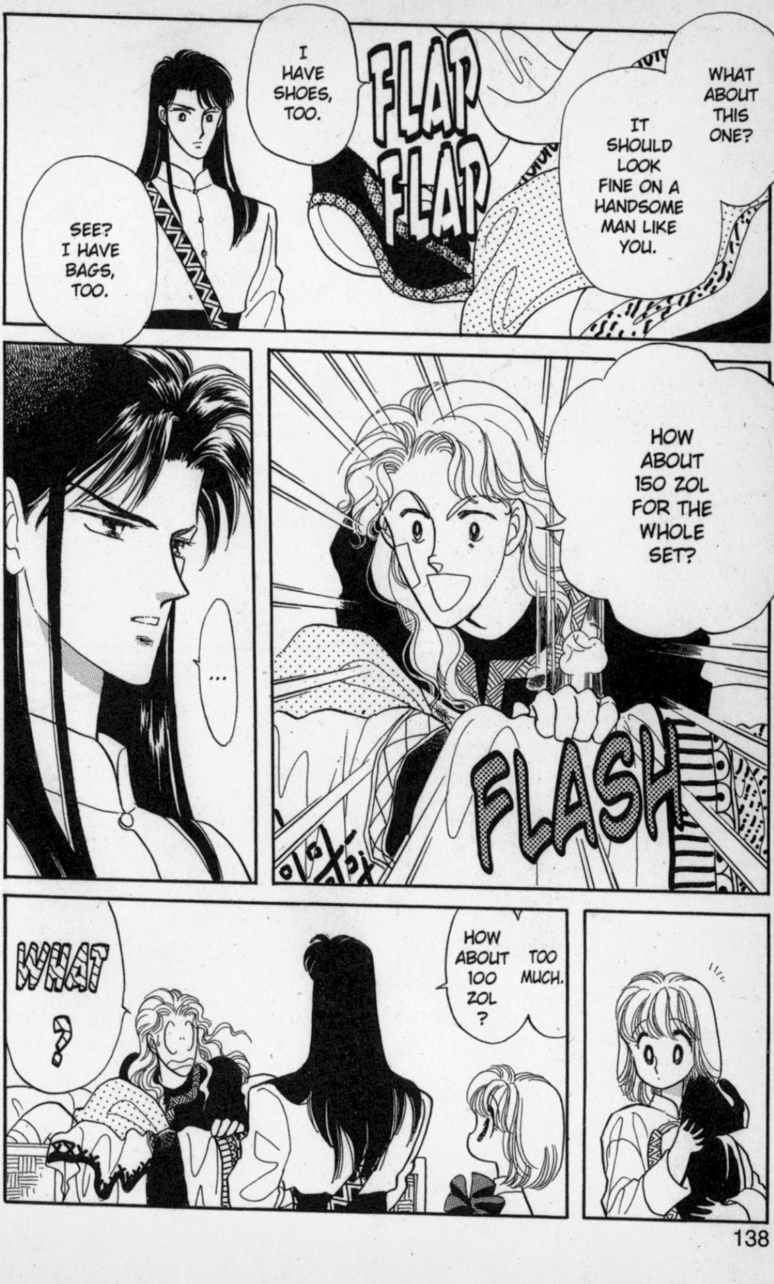
WHAT ABOUT THIS ONE?
IT SHOULD LOOK FINE ON A HANDSOME MAN LIKE YOU.
FLAP FLAP
I HAVE SHOES, TOO.
SEE? I HAVE BAGS, TOO.
HOW ABOUT 150 ZOL FOR THE WHOLE SET?
FLASH
...
TOO MUCH.
HOW ABOUT 100 ZOL ?
WHAT ?

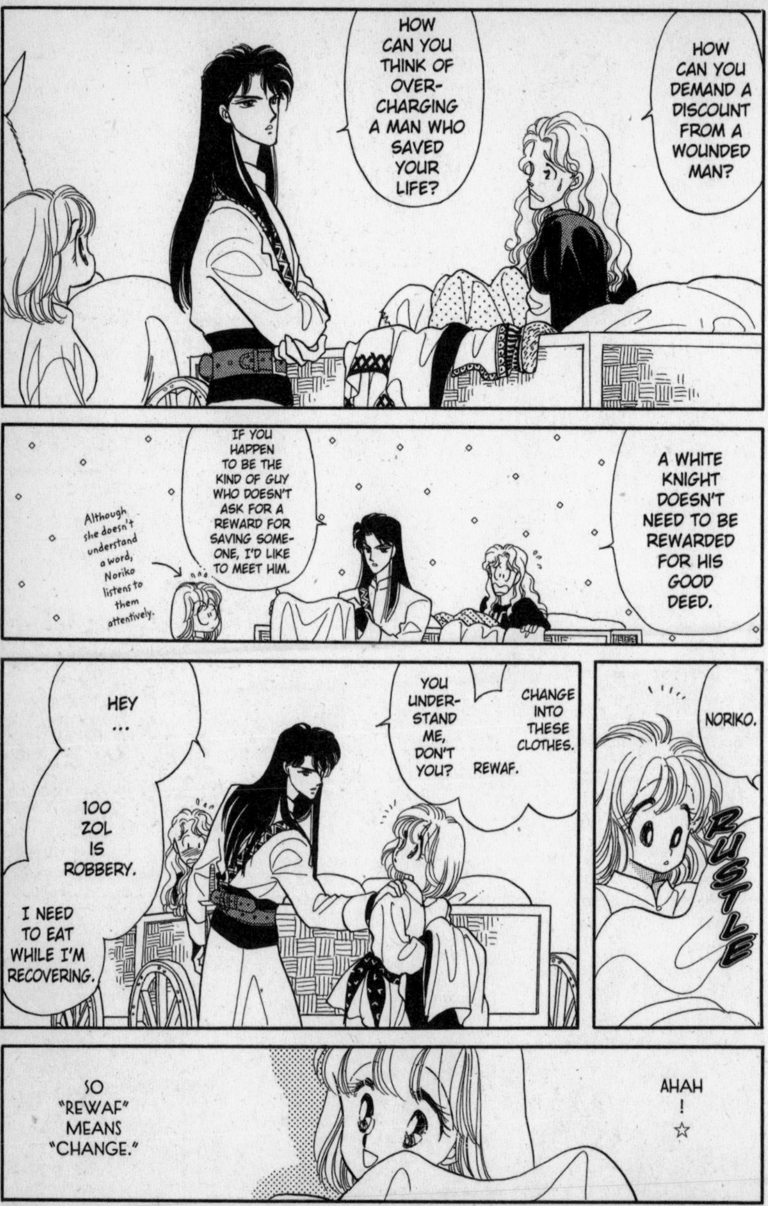
HOW CAN YOU DEMAND A DISCOUNT FROM A WOUNDED MAN?
HOW CAN YOU THINK OF OVER-CHARGING A MAN WHO SAVED YOUR LIFE?
A WHITE KNIGHT DOESN'T NEED TO BE REWARDED FOR HIS GOOD DEED.
IF YOU HAPPEN TO BE THE KIND OF GUY WHO DOESN'T ASK FOR A REWARD FOR SAVING SOME-ONE, I'D LIKE TO MEET HIM.
Although she doesn't understand a word, Noriko listens to them attentively.
NORIKO.
RUSTLE
CHANGE INTO THESE CLOTHES.
REWAF.
YOU UNDER-STAND ME, DON'T YOU?
HEY ...
100 ZOL IS ROBBERY.
I NEED TO EAT WHILE I'M RECOVERING.
AHAH ! ☆
SO "REWAF" MEANS "CHANGE."

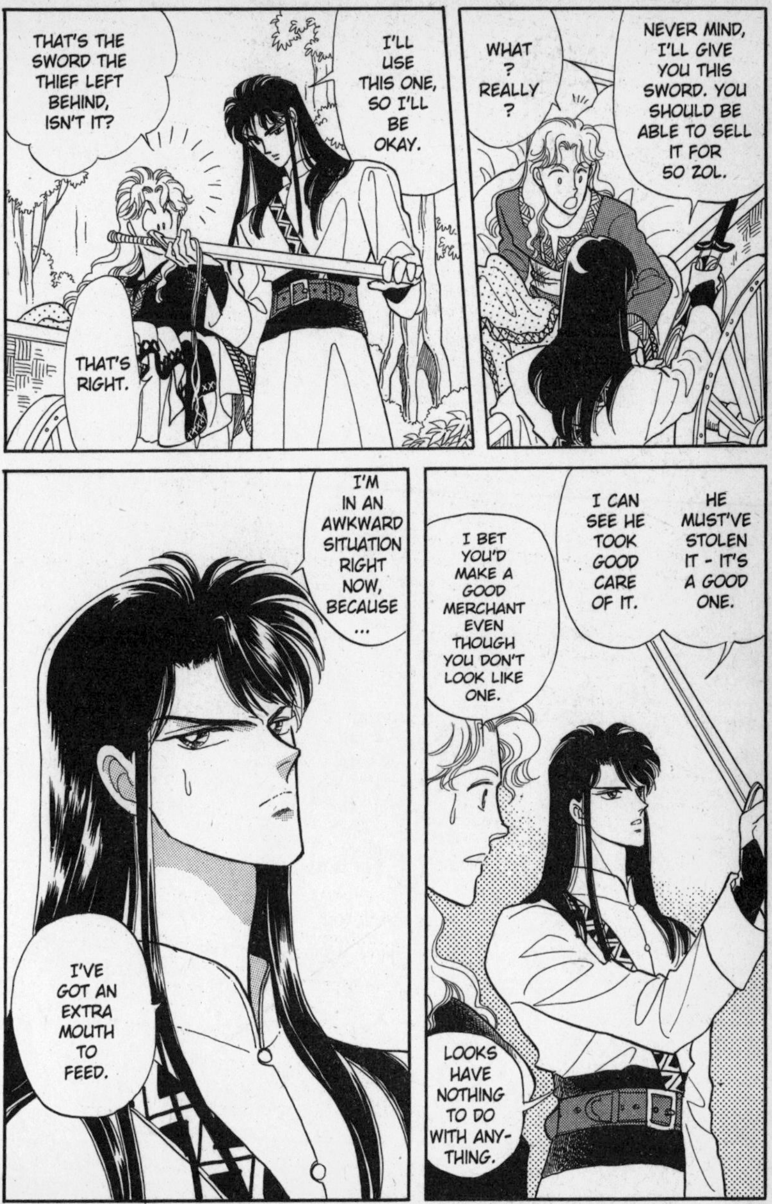
NEVER MIND, I'LL GIVE YOU THIS SWORD. YOU SHOULD BE ABLE TO SELL IT FOR 50 ZOL.
WHAT? REALLY?
I'LL USE THIS ONE, SO I'LL BE OKAY.
THAT'S THE SWORD THE THIEF LEFT BEHIND, ISN'T IT?
THAT'S RIGHT.
HE MUST'VE STOLEN IT - IT'S A GOOD ONE.
I CAN SEE HE TOOK GOOD CARE OF IT.
I BET YOU'D MAKE A GOOD MERCHANT EVEN THOUGH YOU DON'T LOOK LIKE ONE.
LOOKS HAVE NOTHING TO DO WITH ANY-THING.
I'M IN AN AWKWARD SITUATION RIGHT NOW, BECAUSE ...
I'VE GOT AN EXTRA MOUTH TO FEED.

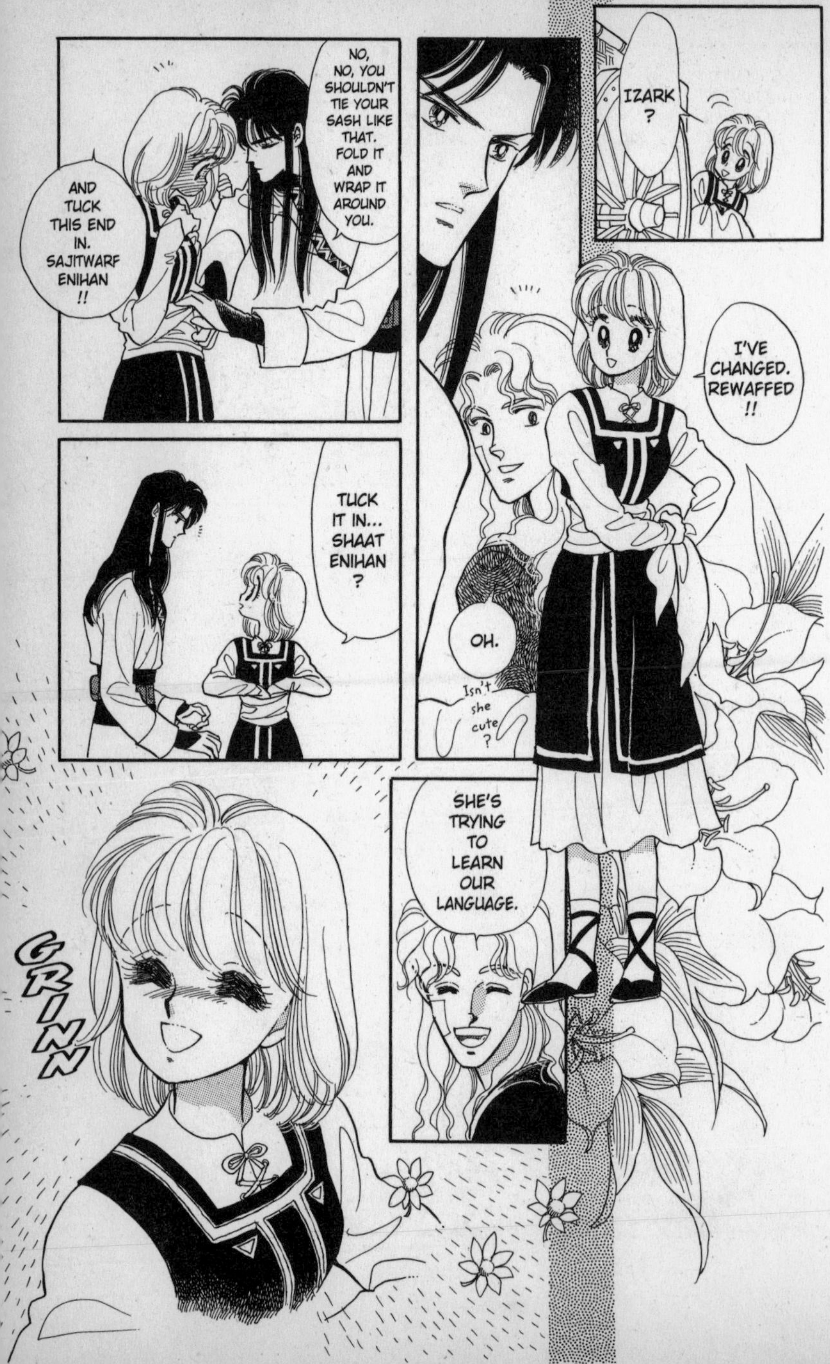
IZARK ?
I'VE CHANGED. REWAFFED !!
OH.
Isn't she cute ?
NO, NO, YOU SHOULDN'T TIE YOUR SASH LIKE THAT. FOLD IT AND WRAP IT AROUND YOU.
AND TUCK THIS END IN. SAJITWARF ENIHAN !!
TUCK IT IN... SHAAT ENIHAN ?
SHE'S TRYING TO LEARN OUR LANGUAGE.
GRINN

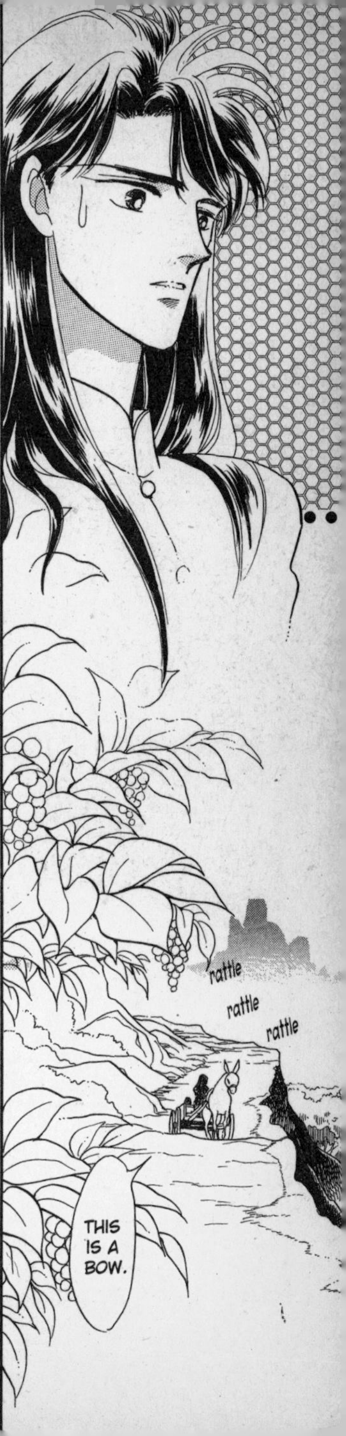
rattle
rattle
rattle
THIS IS A BOW.

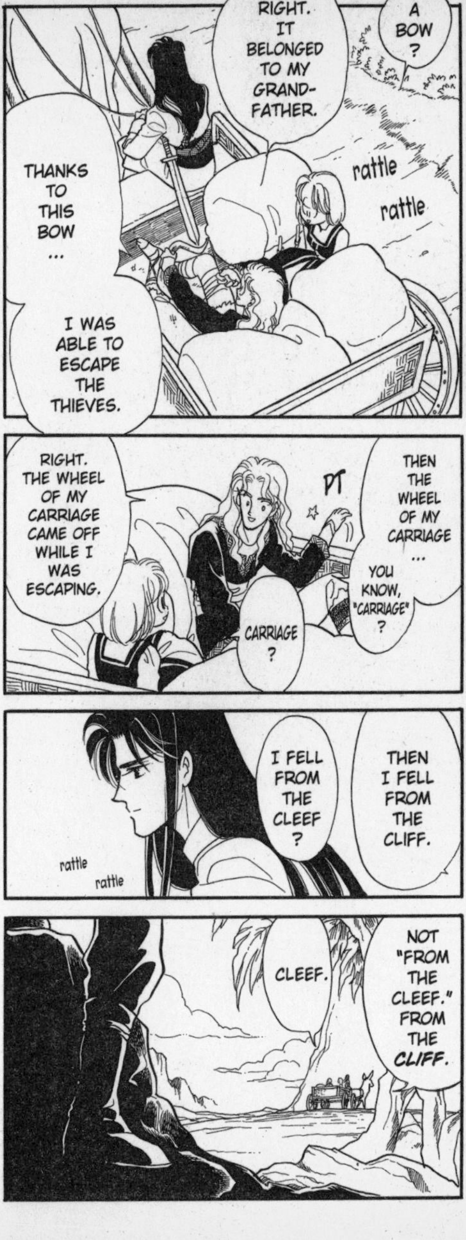
A BOW?
RIGHT. IT BELONGED TO MY GRANDFATHER.
rattle
rattle
THANKS TO THIS BOW ...
I WAS ABLE TO ESCAPE THE THIEVES.
THEN THE WHEEL OF MY CARRIAGE ...
YOU KNOW, "CARRIAGE"?
PT
CARRIAGE?
RIGHT. THE WHEEL OF MY CARRIAGE CAME OFF WHILE I WAS ESCAPING.
THEN I FELL FROM THE CLIFF.
I FELL FROM THE CLEEF?
rattle
rattle
NOT "FROM THE CLEEF." FROM THE *CLIFF*.
CLEEF.

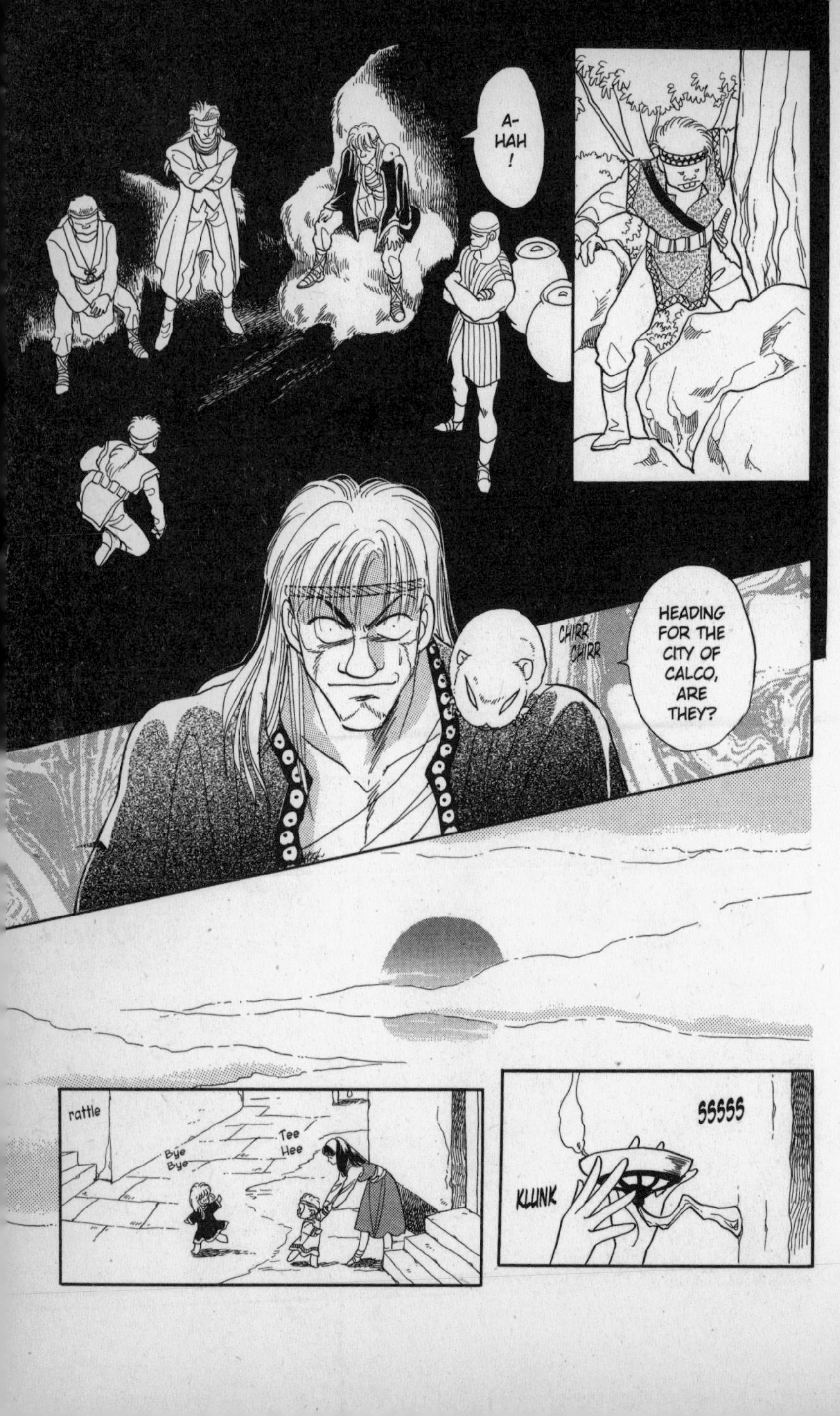
A-HAH!
CHIRR CHIRR
HEADING FOR THE CITY OF CALCO, ARE THEY?
SSSSS
KLUNK
rattle
Tee Hee
Bye Bye

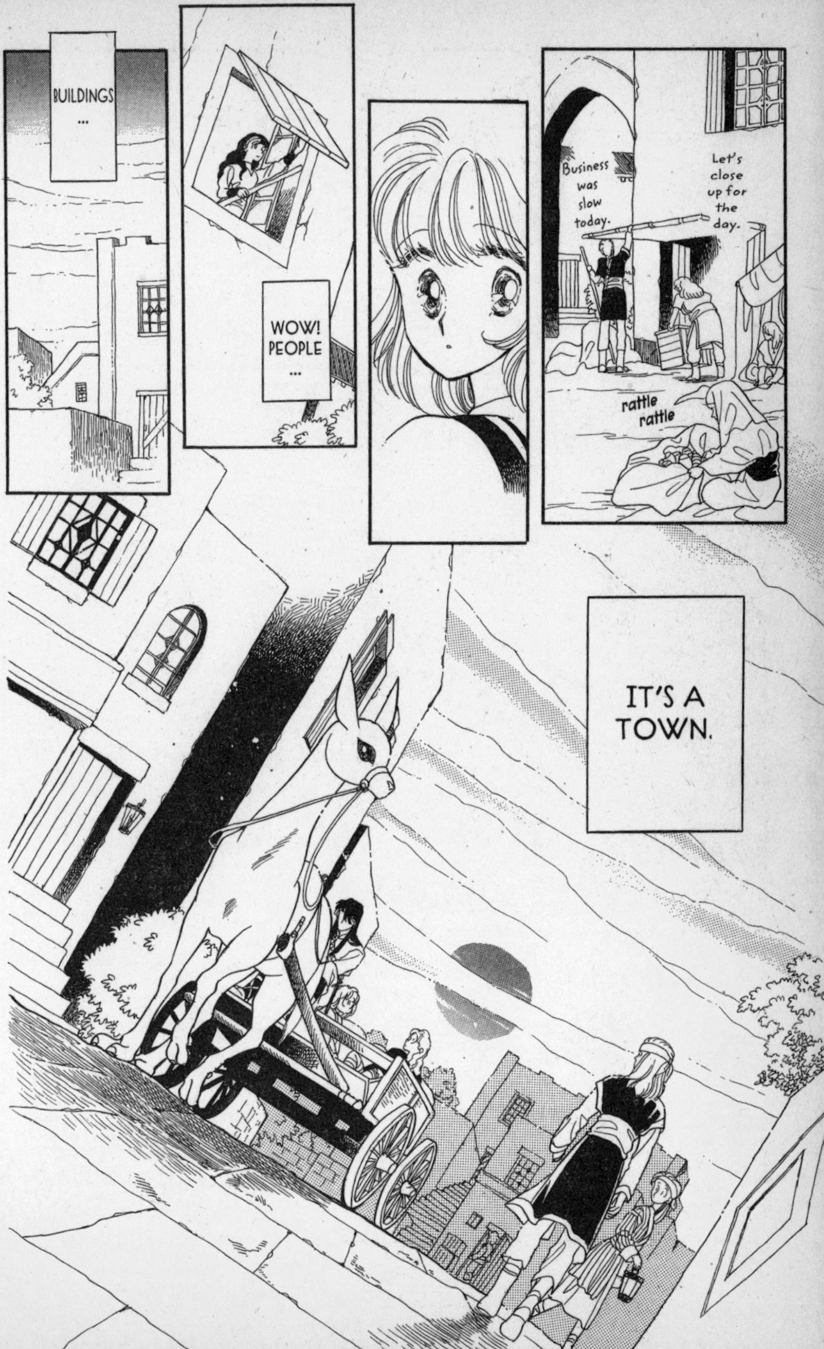
Let's close up for the day.
Business was slow today.
rattle rattle
WOW! PEOPLE ...
BUILDINGS ...
IT'S A TOWN.

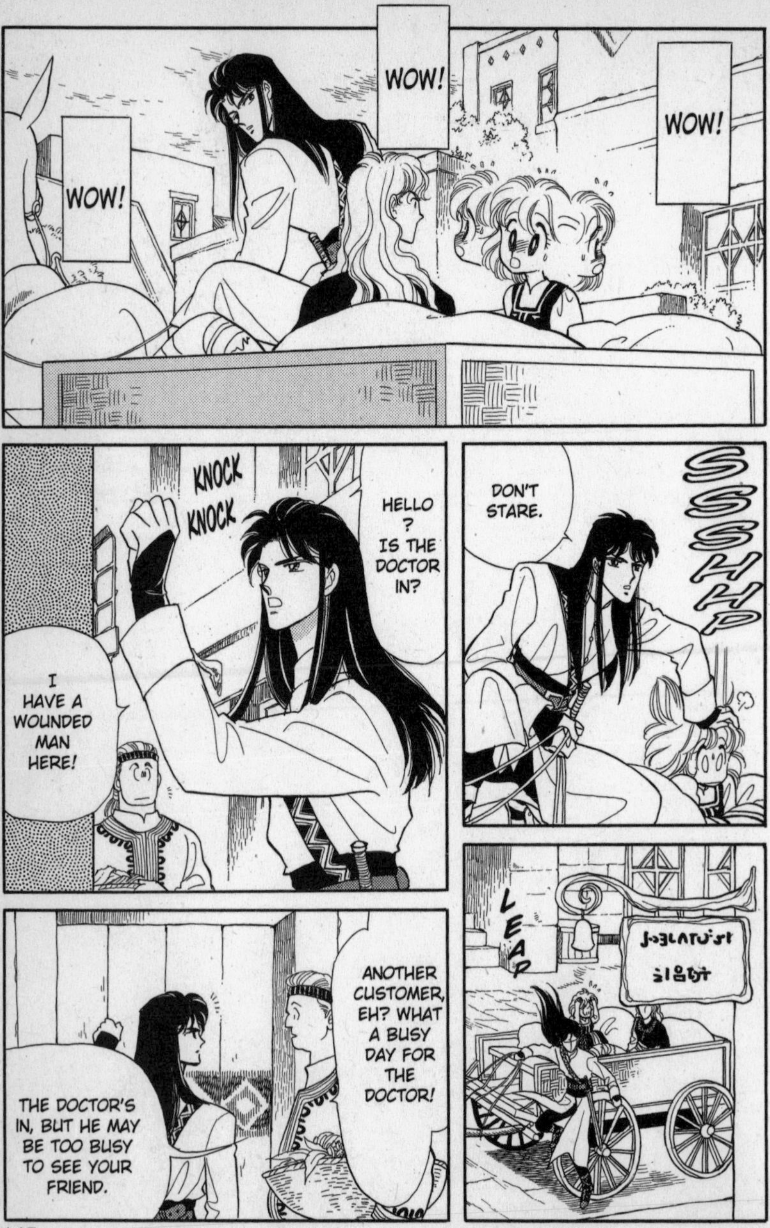
WOW!
WOW!
WOW!
SSSHHP
DON'T STARE.
KNOCK KNOCK
HELLO? IS THE DOCTOR IN?
I HAVE A WOUNDED MAN HERE!
LEAP
ANOTHER CUSTOMER, EH? WHAT A BUSY DAY FOR THE DOCTOR!
THE DOCTOR'S IN, BUT HE MAY BE TOO BUSY TO SEE YOUR FRIEND.

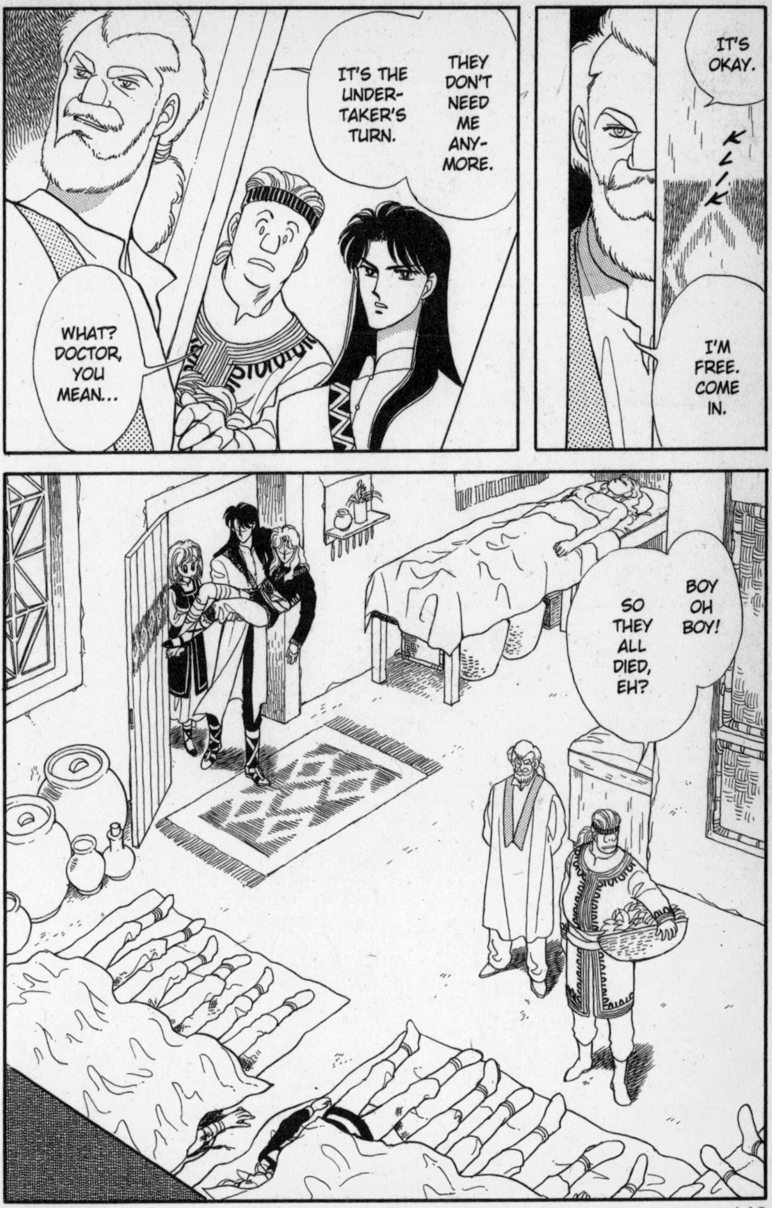
IT'S OKAY.
KLIK
I'M FREE. COME IN.
THEY DON'T NEED ME ANYMORE.
IT'S THE UNDER-TAKER'S TURN.
WHAT? DOCTOR, YOU MEAN...
BOY OH BOY!
SO THEY ALL DIED, EH?

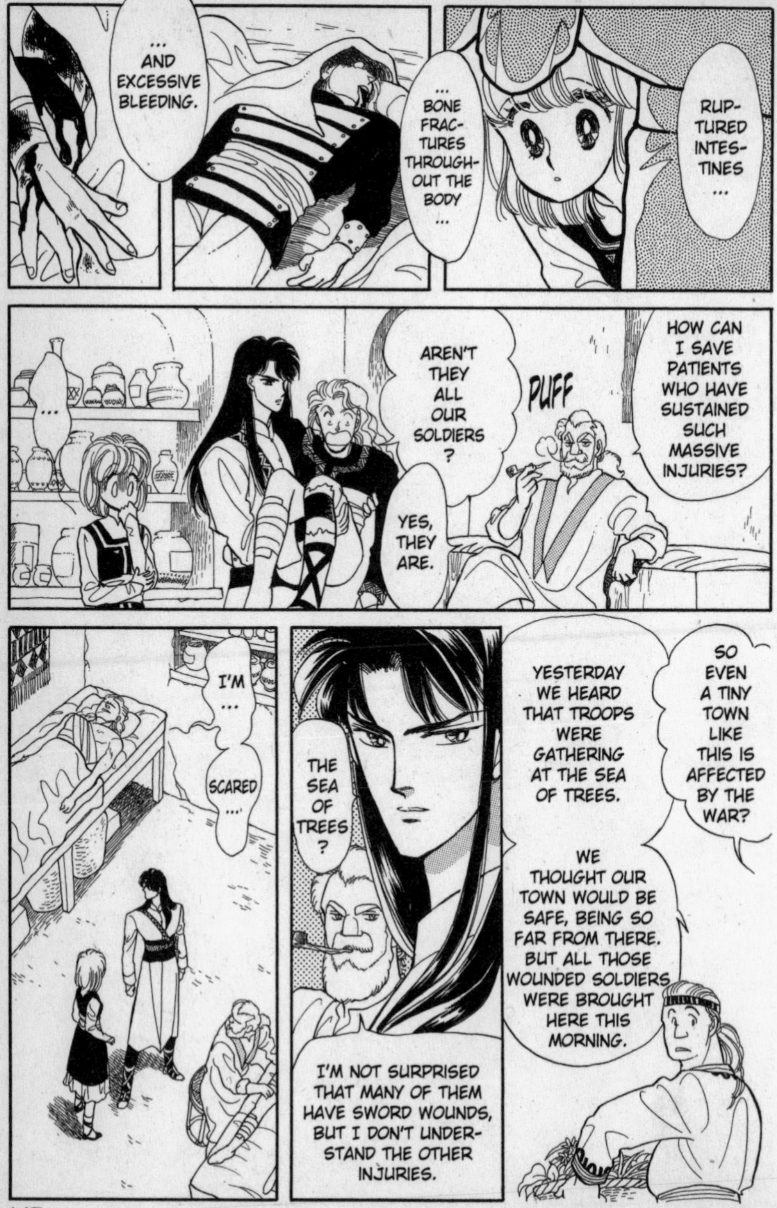

RUP-TURED INTES-TINES ...
... BONE FRAC-TURES THROUGH-OUT THE BODY ...
... AND EXCESSIVE BLEEDING.
HOW CAN I SAVE PATIENTS WHO HAVE SUSTAINED SUCH MASSIVE INJURIES?
PUFF
AREN'T THEY ALL OUR SOLDIERS?
YES, THEY ARE.
...
SO EVEN A TINY TOWN LIKE THIS IS AFFECTED BY THE WAR?
YESTERDAY WE HEARD THAT TROOPS WERE GATHERING AT THE SEA OF TREES.
WE THOUGHT OUR TOWN WOULD BE SAFE, BEING SO FAR FROM THERE. BUT ALL THOSE WOUNDED SOLDIERS WERE BROUGHT HERE THIS MORNING.
THE SEA OF TREES?
I'M NOT SURPRISED THAT MANY OF THEM HAVE SWORD WOUNDS, BUT I DON'T UNDER-STAND THE OTHER INJURIES.
I'M ... SCARED ...!

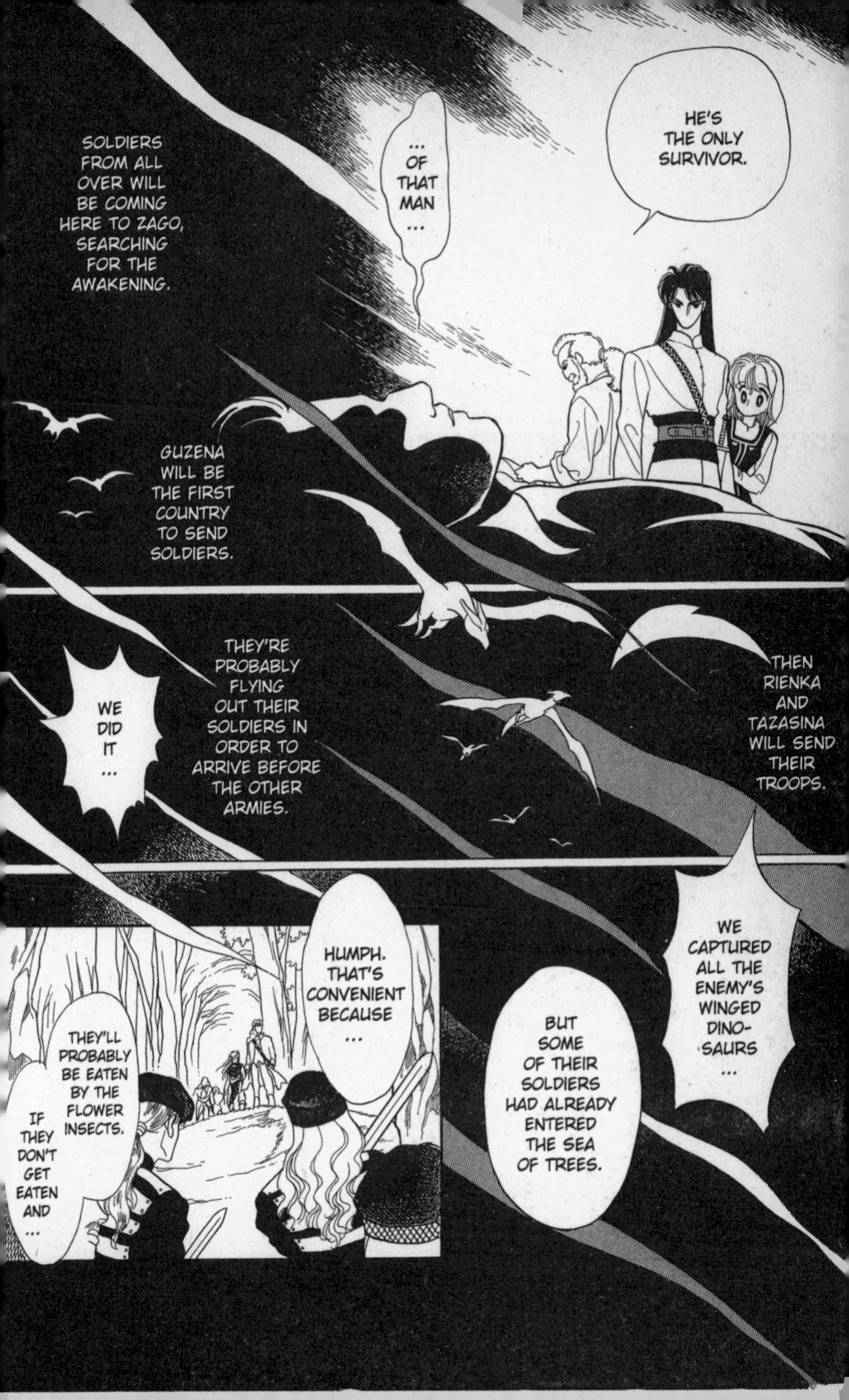
HE'S THE ONLY SURVIVOR.
... OF THAT MAN ...
SOLDIERS FROM ALL OVER WILL BE COMING HERE TO ZAGO, SEARCHING FOR THE AWAKENING.
GUZENA WILL BE THE FIRST COUNTRY TO SEND SOLDIERS.
THEN RIENKA AND TAZASINA WILL SEND THEIR TROOPS.
THEY'RE PROBABLY FLYING OUT THEIR SOLDIERS IN ORDER TO ARRIVE BEFORE THE OTHER ARMIES.
WE DID IT ...
WE CAPTURED ALL THE ENEMY'S WINGED DINO-SAURS ...
BUT SOME OF THEIR SOLDIERS HAD ALREADY ENTERED THE SEA OF TREES.
HUMPH. THAT'S CONVENIENT BECAUSE ...
THEY'LL PROBABLY BE EATEN BY THE FLOWER INSECTS.
IF THEY DON'T GET EATEN AND ...

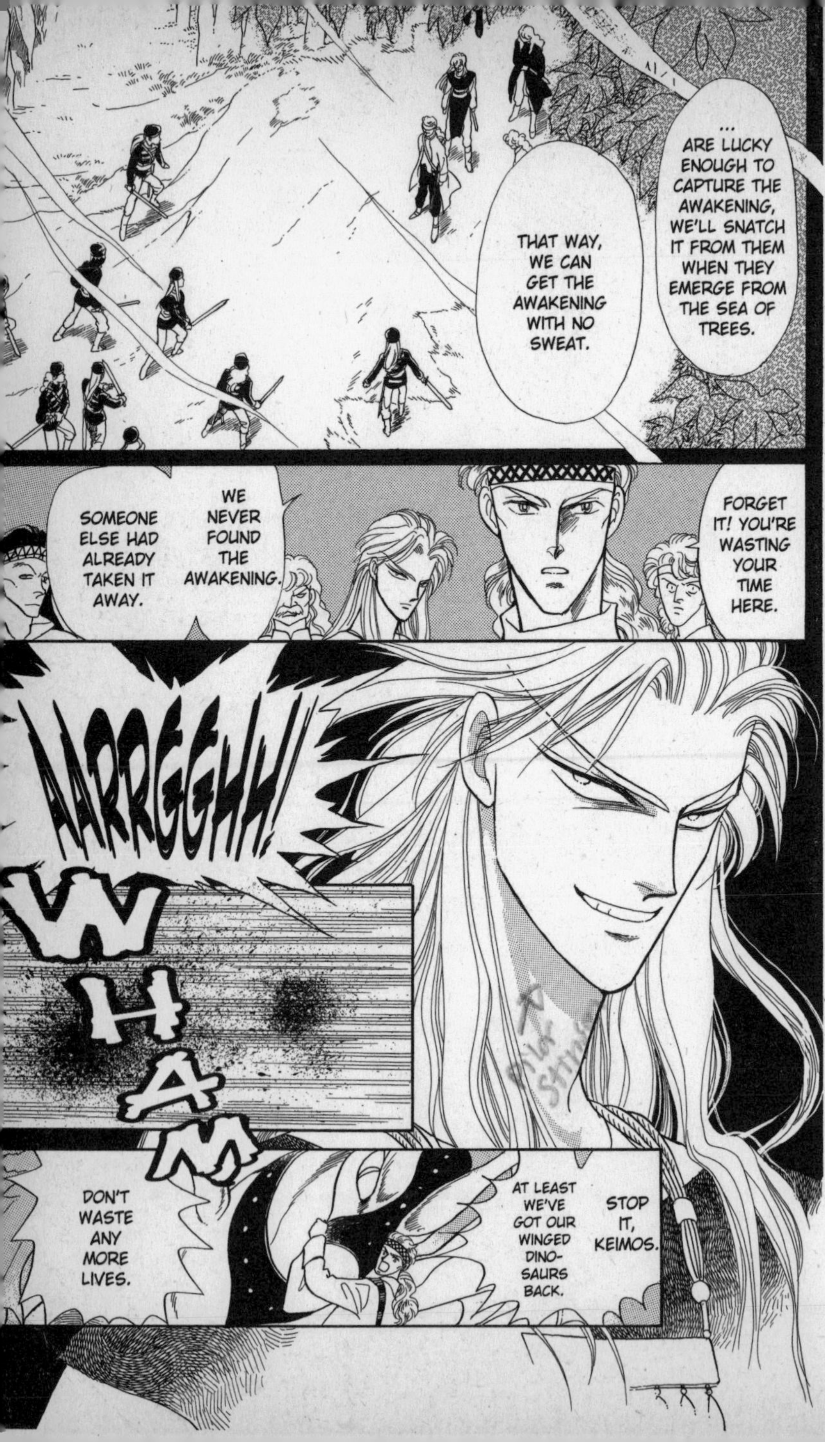
... ARE LUCKY ENOUGH TO CAPTURE THE AWAKENING, WE'LL SNATCH IT FROM THEM WHEN THEY EMERGE FROM THE SEA OF TREES.
THAT WAY, WE CAN GET THE AWAKENING WITH NO SWEAT.
FORGET IT! YOU'RE WASTING YOUR TIME HERE.
WE NEVER FOUND THE AWAKENING.
SOMEONE ELSE HAD ALREADY TAKEN IT AWAY.
AARRGGHH!
WHAM
STOP IT, KEIMOS.
AT LEAST WE'VE GOT OUR WINGED DINOSAURS BACK.
DON'T WASTE ANY MORE LIVES.

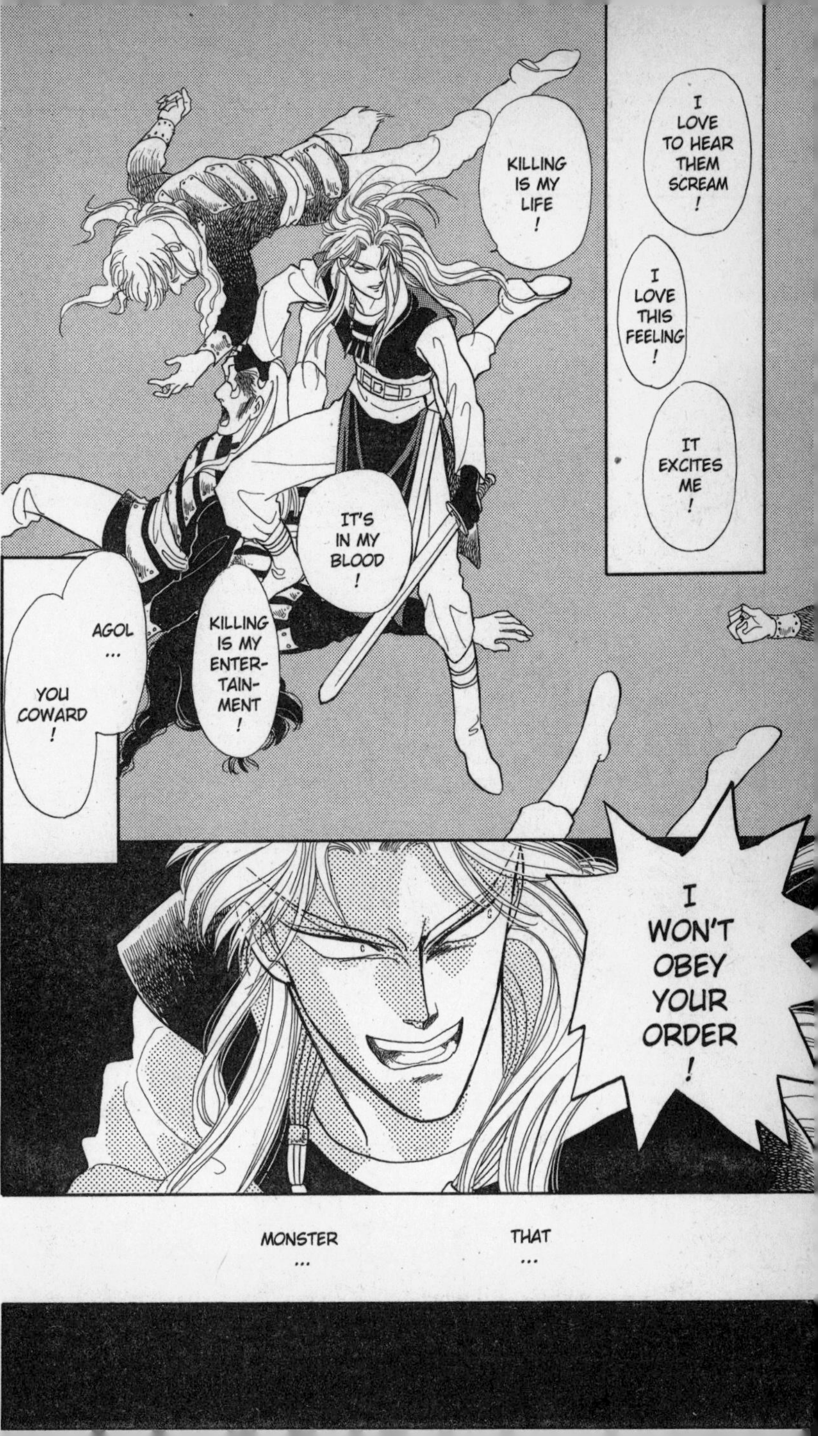
I LOVE TO HEAR THEM SCREAM!
I LOVE THIS FEELING!
IT EXCITES ME!
KILLING IS MY LIFE!
IT'S IN MY BLOOD!
KILLING IS MY ENTER-TAIN-MENT!
AGOL... YOU COWARD!
I WON'T OBEY YOUR ORDER!
THAT...
MONSTER...

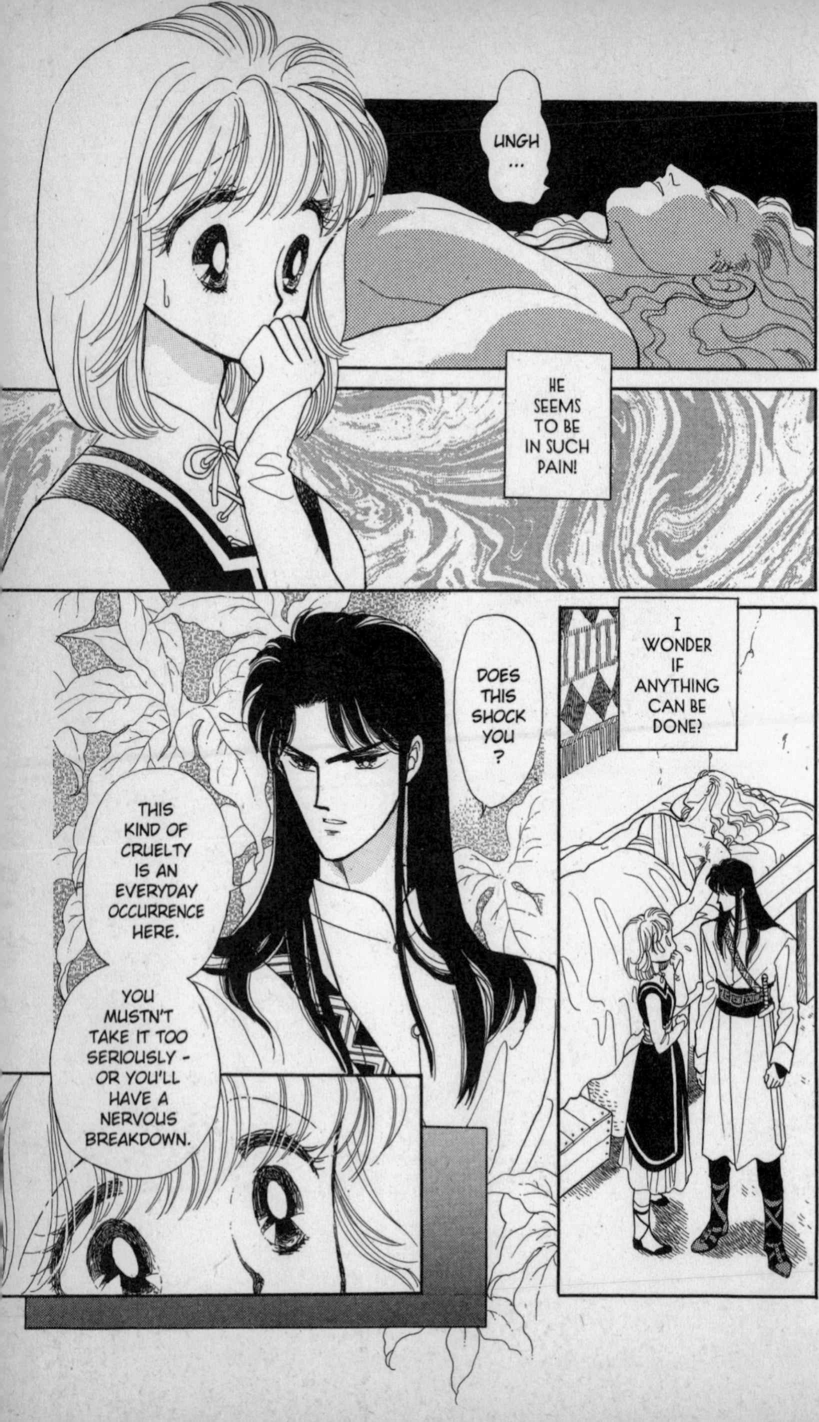
UNGH ...
HE SEEMS TO BE IN SUCH PAIN!
I WONDER IF ANYTHING CAN BE DONE?
DOES THIS SHOCK YOU ?
THIS KIND OF CRUELTY IS AN EVERYDAY OCCURRENCE HERE.
YOU MUSTN'T TAKE IT TOO SERIOUSLY - OR YOU'LL HAVE A NERVOUS BREAKDOWN.

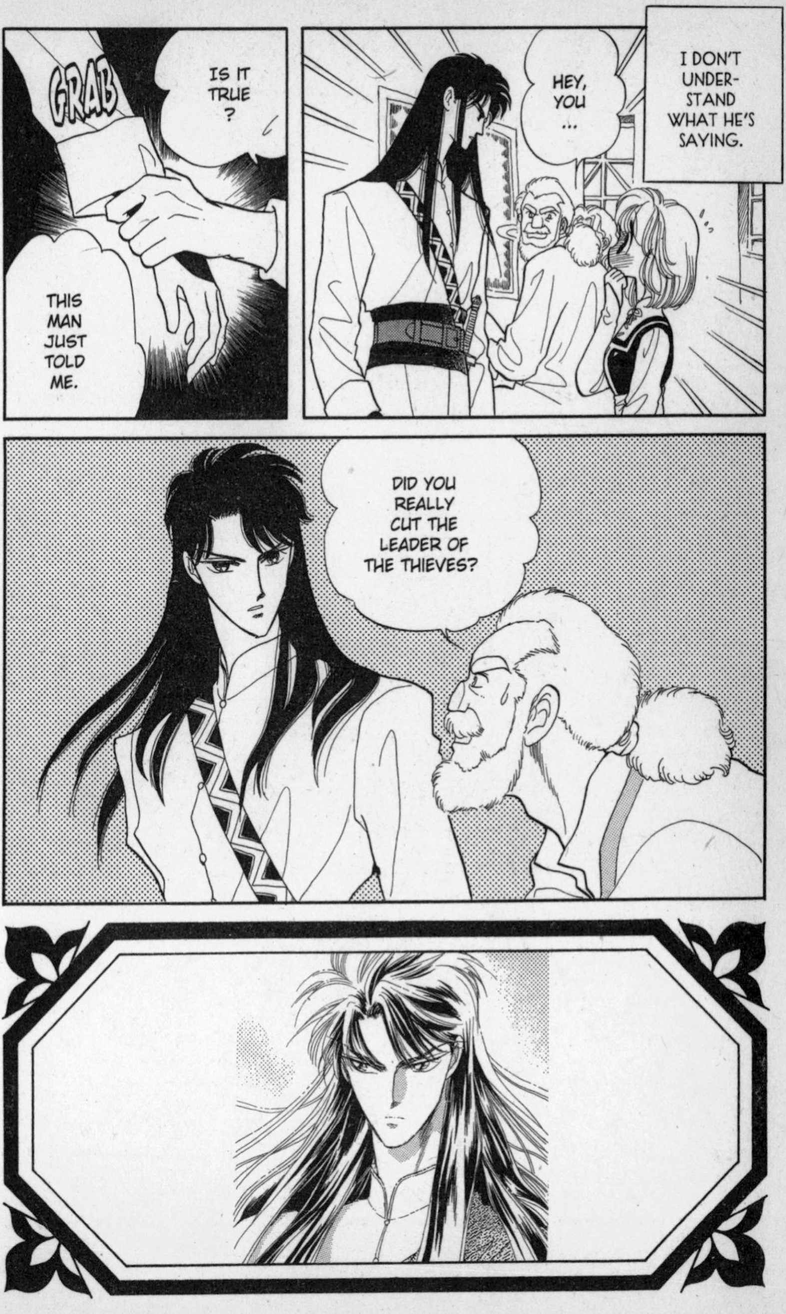
I DON'T UNDER-STAND WHAT HE'S SAYING.
HEY, YOU ...
IS IT TRUE?
GRAB
THIS MAN JUST TOLD ME.
DID YOU REALLY CUT THE LEADER OF THE THIEVES?

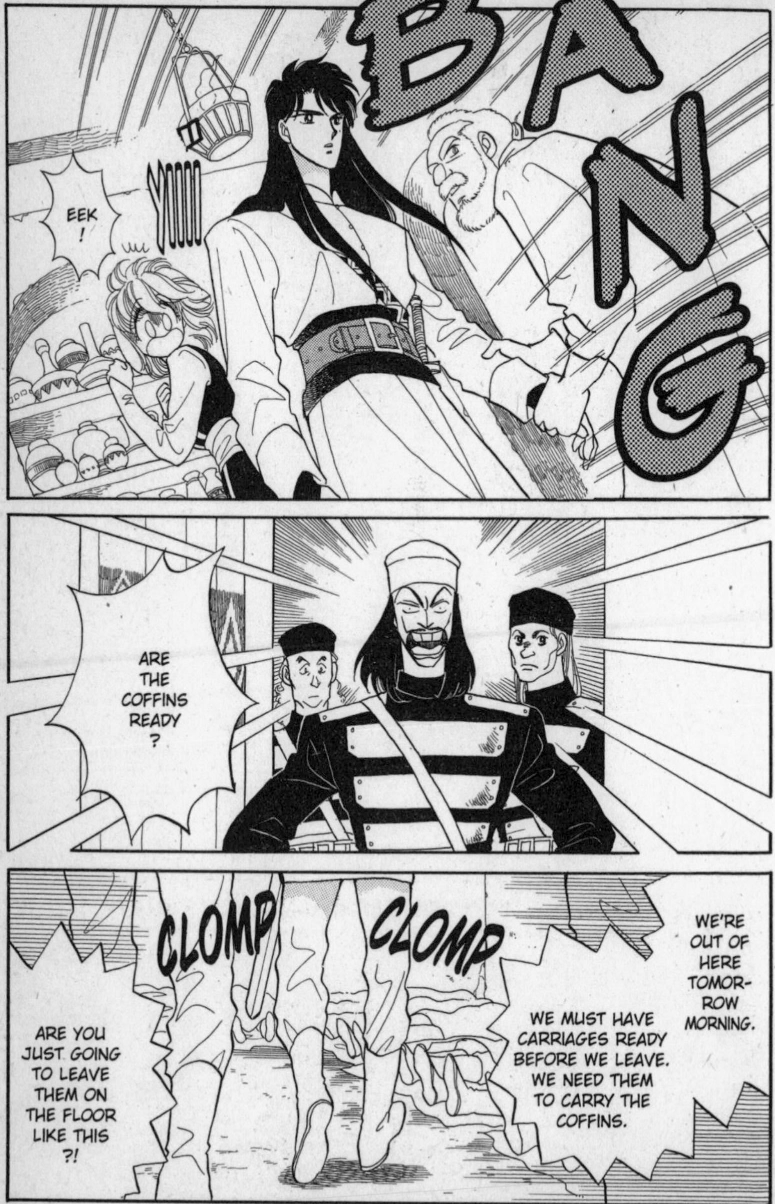
BANG
EEK!
ARE THE COFFINS READY?
WE'RE OUT OF HERE TOMOR-ROW MORNING.
WE MUST HAVE CARRIAGES READY BEFORE WE LEAVE. WE NEED THEM TO CARRY THE COFFINS.
CLOMP
CLOMP
ARE YOU JUST GOING TO LEAVE THEM ON THE FLOOR LIKE THIS?!

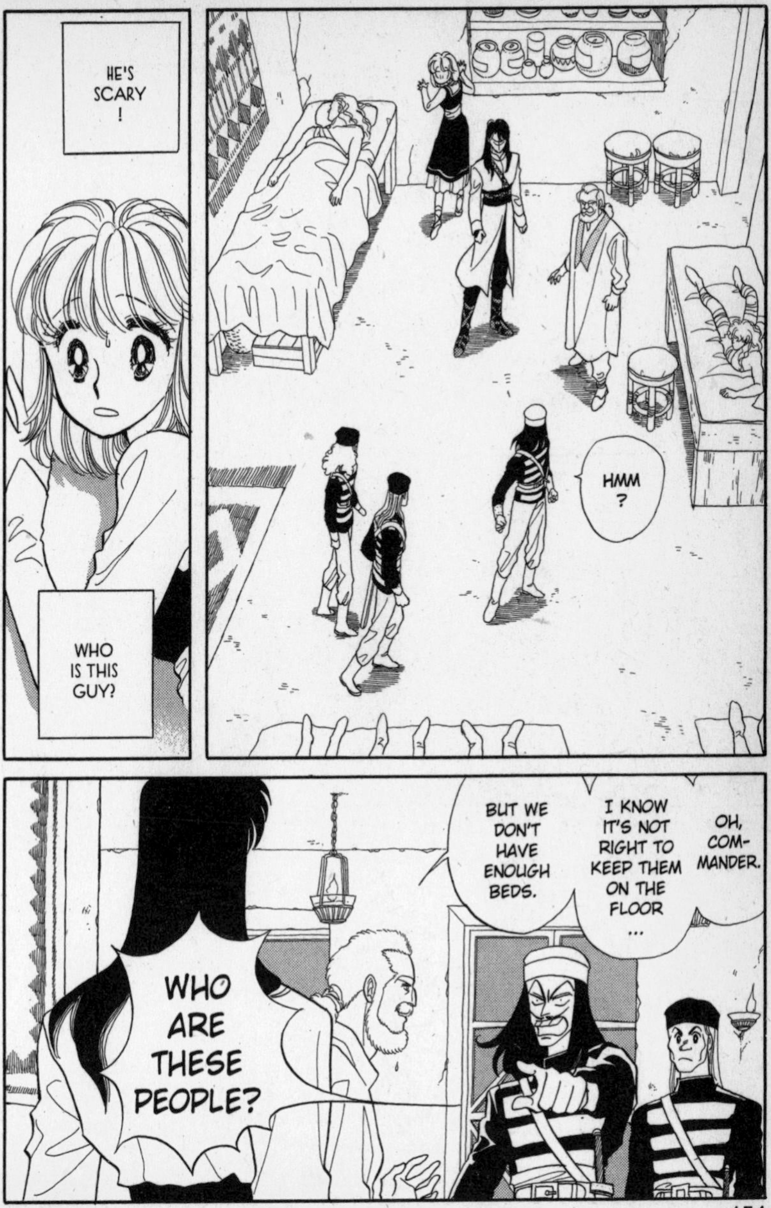
HMM ?
HE'S SCARY !
WHO IS THIS GUY?
OH, COM-MANDER.
I KNOW IT'S NOT RIGHT TO KEEP THEM ON THE FLOOR ...
BUT WE DON'T HAVE ENOUGH BEDS.
WHO ARE THESE PEOPLE?

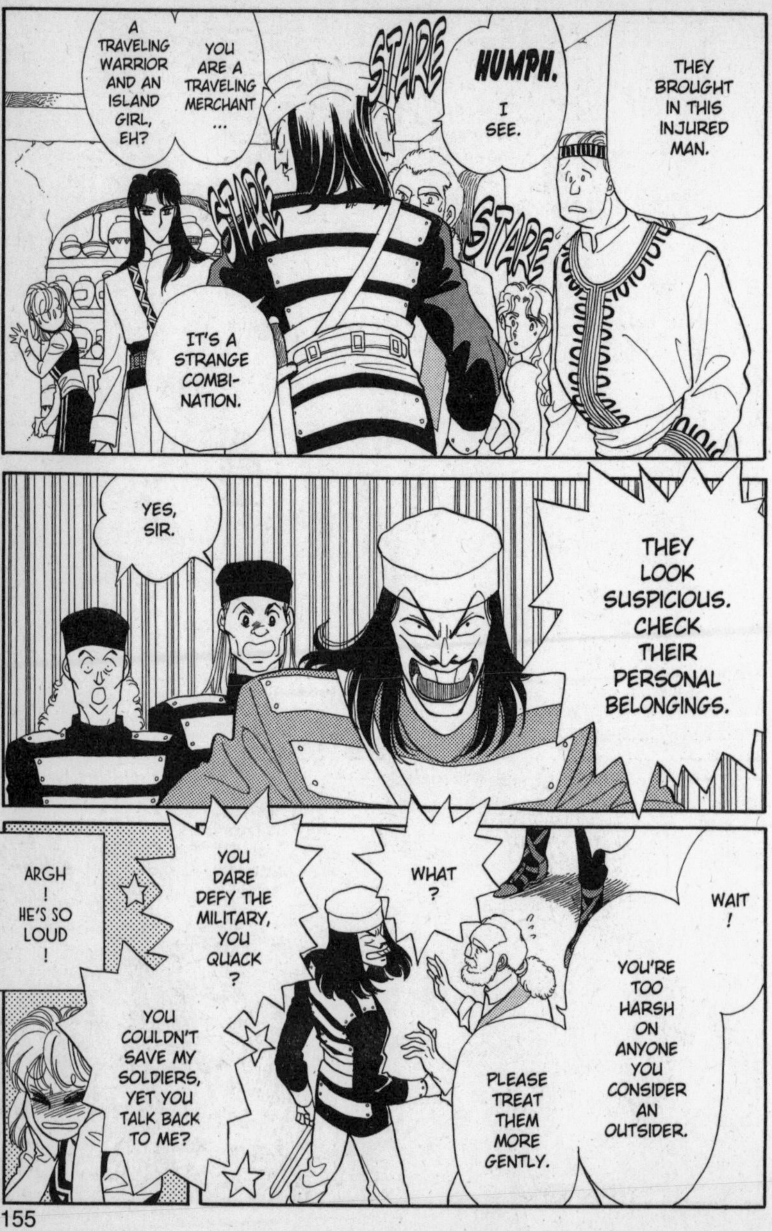
THEY BROUGHT IN THIS INJURED MAN.
HUMPH. I SEE.
STARE
STARE
YOU ARE A TRAVELING MERCHANT ...
A TRAVELING WARRIOR AND AN ISLAND GIRL, EH?
STARE
IT'S A STRANGE COMBINATION.
THEY LOOK SUSPICIOUS. CHECK THEIR PERSONAL BELONGINGS.
YES, SIR.
WAIT! YOU'RE TOO HARSH ON ANYONE YOU CONSIDER AN OUTSIDER.
PLEASE TREAT THEM MORE GENTLY.
WHAT?
YOU DARE DEFY THE MILITARY, YOU QUACK?
YOU COULDN'T SAVE MY SOLDIERS, YET YOU TALK BACK TO ME?
ARGH! HE'S SO LOUD!

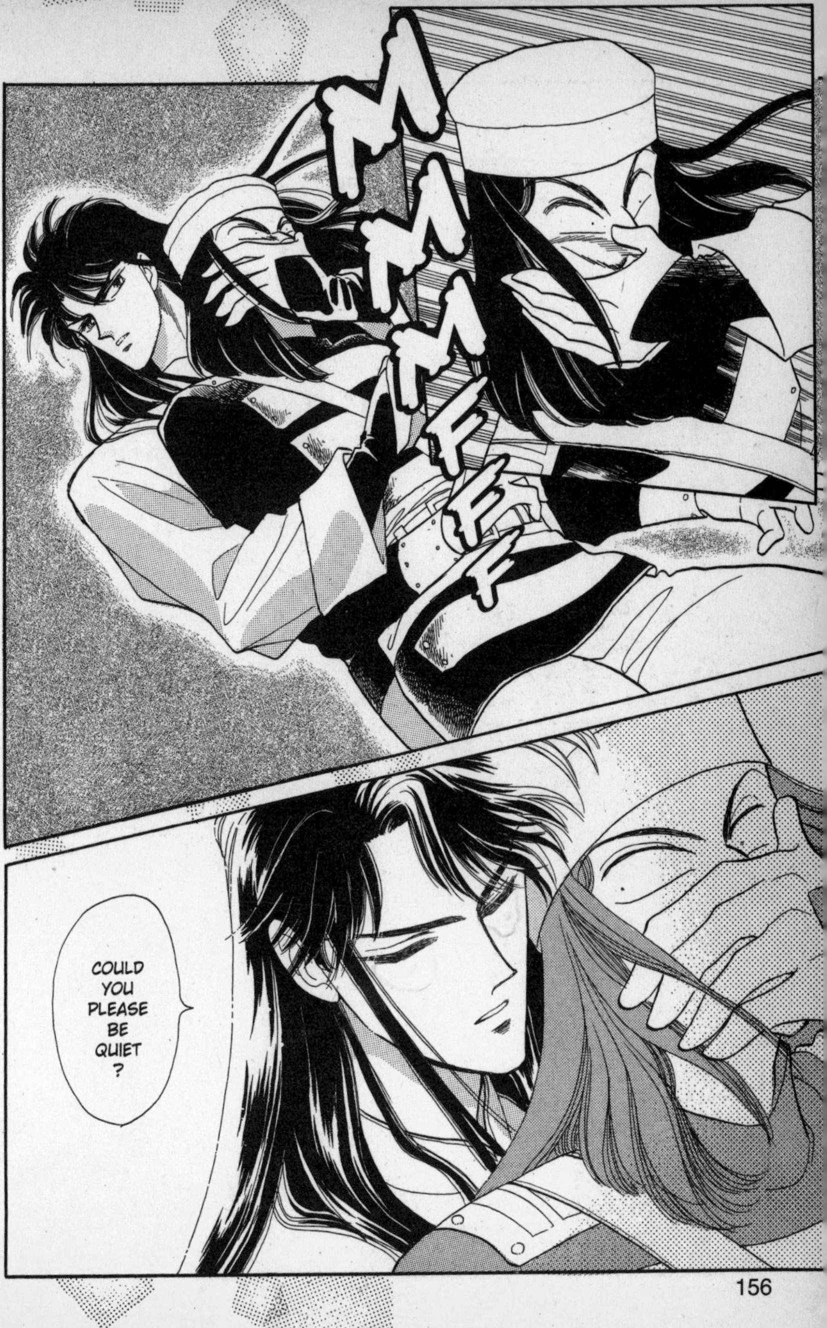
MMMFFF
COULD YOU PLEASE BE QUIET ?

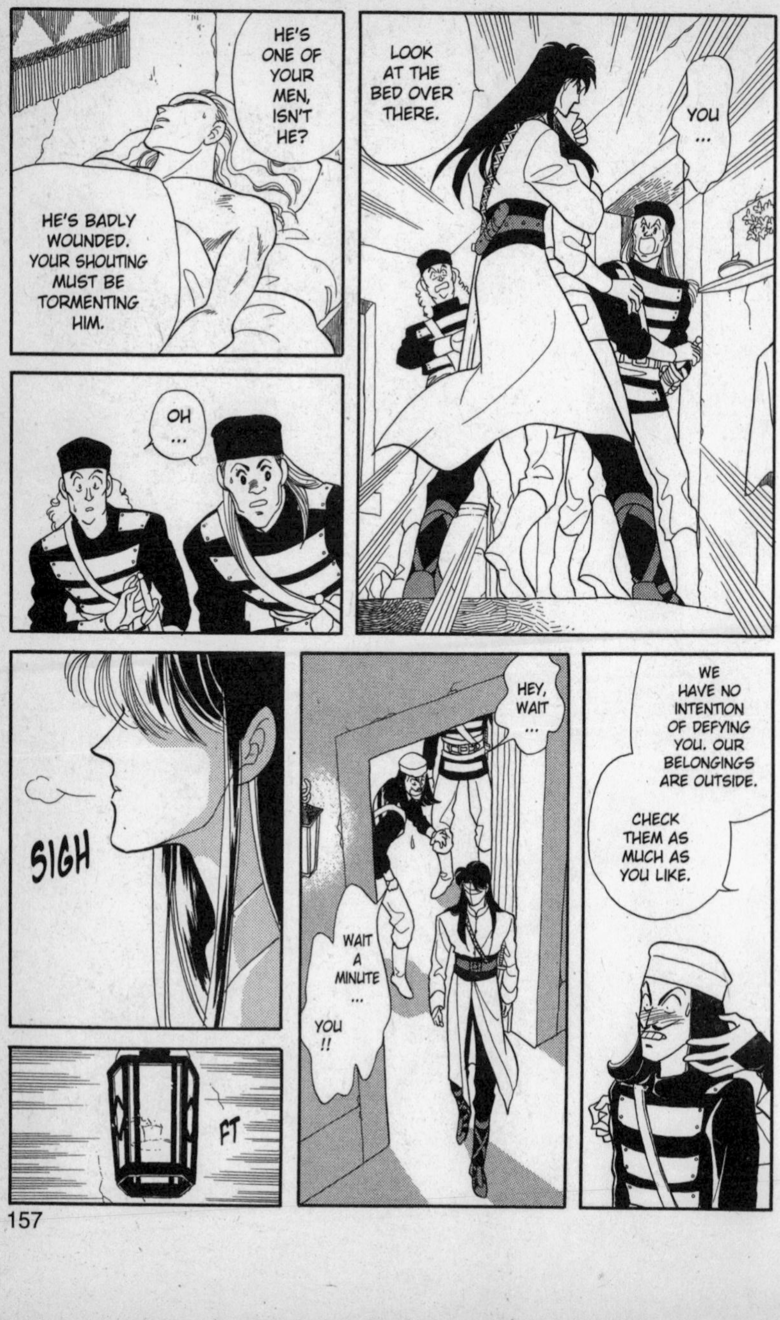
YOU ...
LOOK AT THE BED OVER THERE.
HE'S ONE OF YOUR MEN, ISN'T HE?
HE'S BADLY WOUNDED. YOUR SHOUTING MUST BE TORMENTING HIM.
OH ...
WE HAVE NO INTENTION OF DEFYING YOU. OUR BELONGINGS ARE OUTSIDE.
CHECK THEM AS MUCH AS YOU LIKE.
HEY, WAIT ...
WAIT A MINUTE ...
YOU !!
SIGH
FT

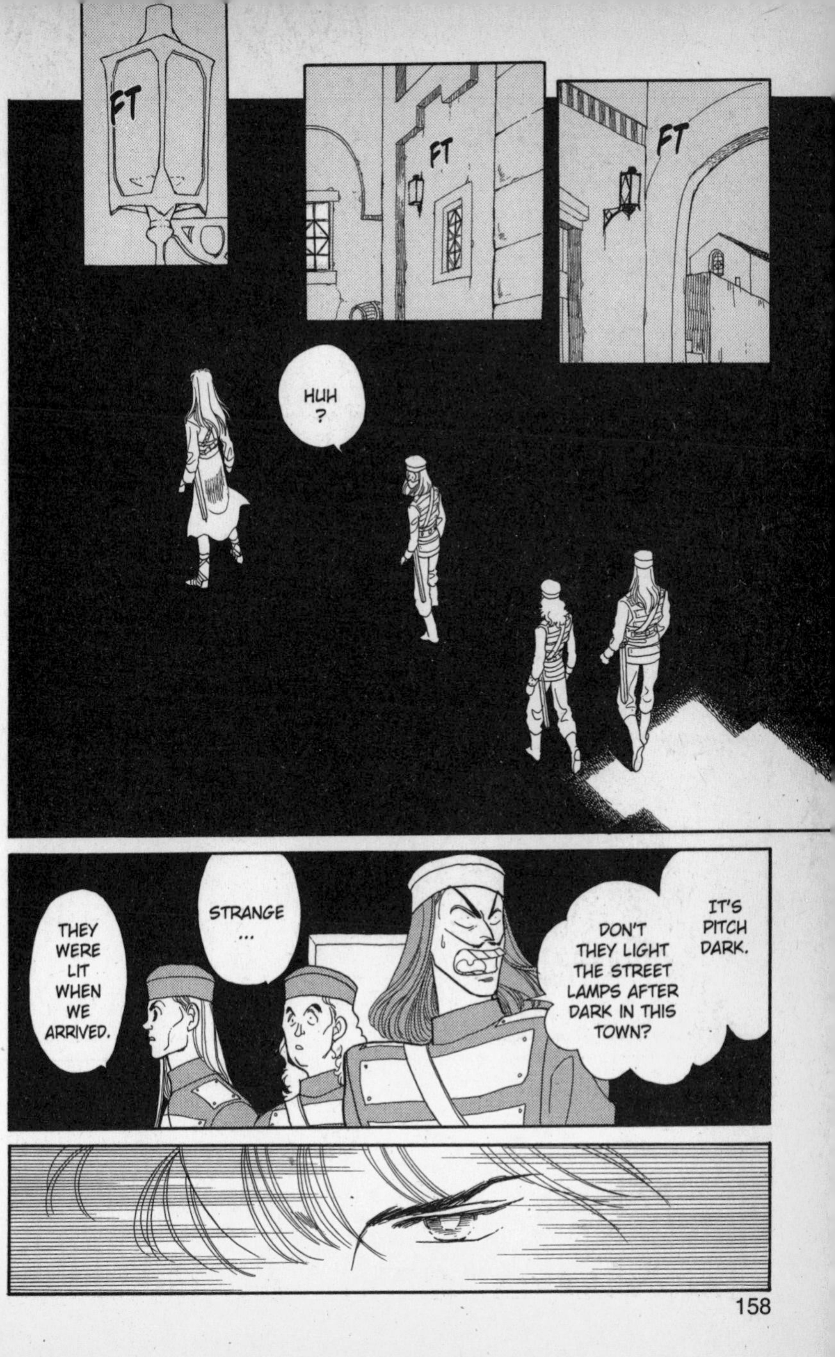
FT
FT
FT
HUH ?
IT'S PITCH DARK.
DON'T THEY LIGHT THE STREET LAMPS AFTER DARK IN THIS TOWN?
STRANGE ...
THEY WERE LIT WHEN WE ARRIVED.

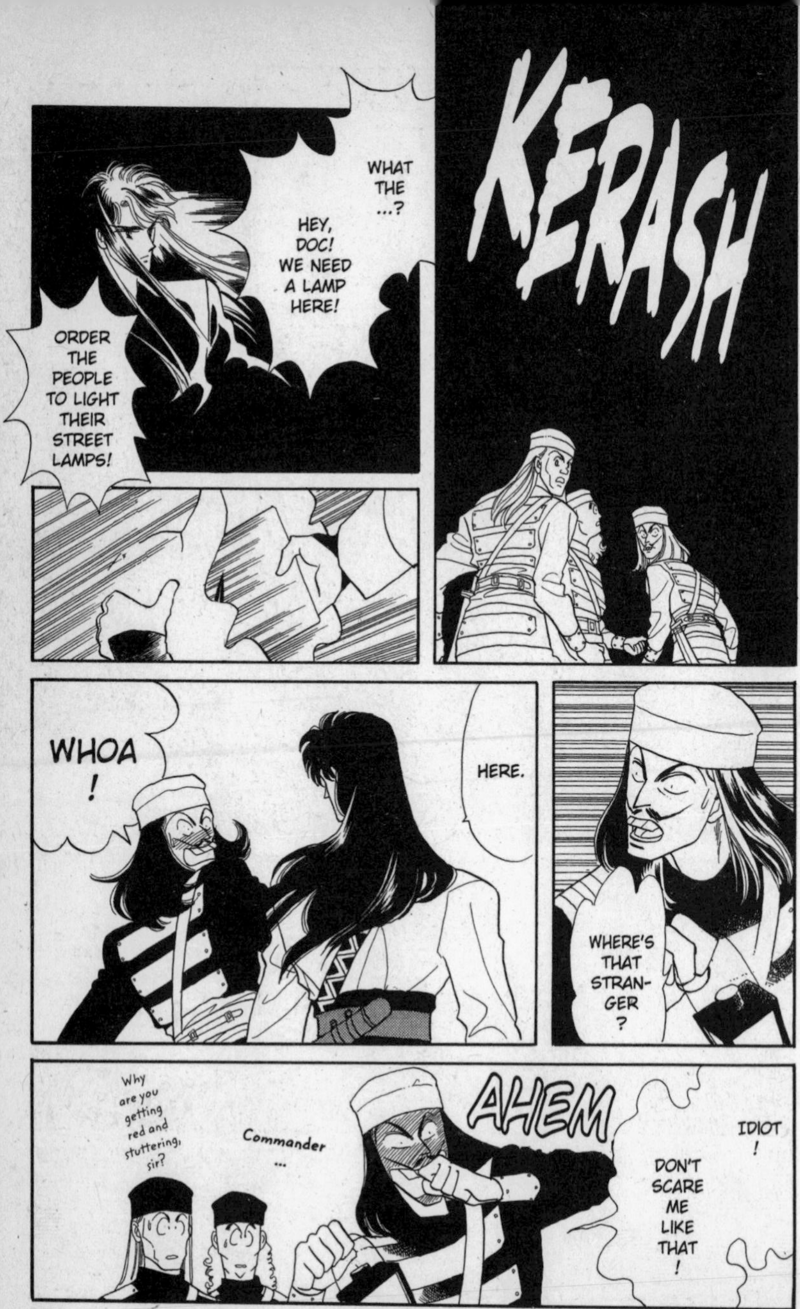
KERASH
WHAT THE ...?
HEY, DOC! WE NEED A LAMP HERE!
ORDER THE PEOPLE TO LIGHT THEIR STREET LAMPS!
WHERE'S THAT STRANGER?
HERE.
WHOA!
IDIOT! DON'T SCARE ME LIKE THAT!
AHEM
Commander ...
Why are you getting red and stuttering, sir?

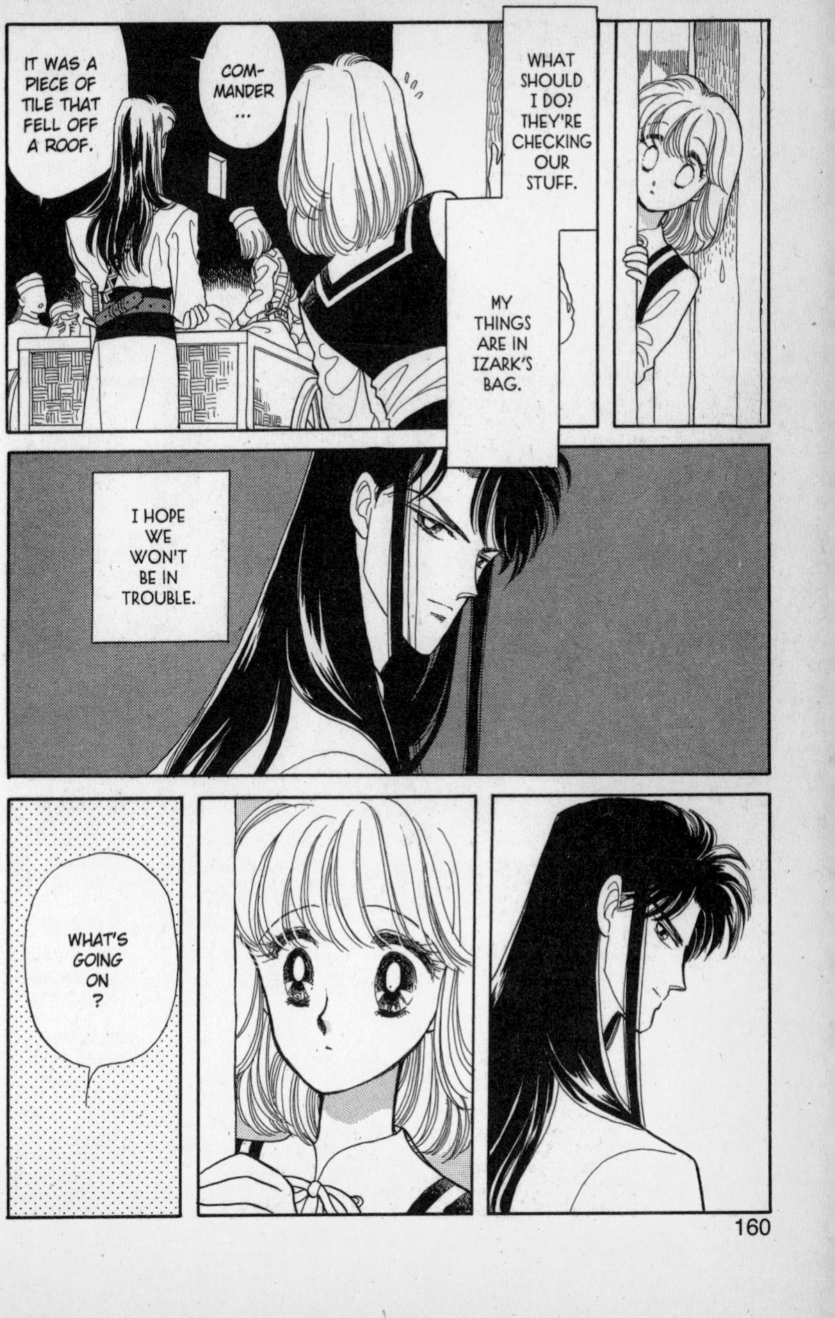
WHAT SHOULD I DO? THEY'RE CHECKING OUR STUFF.
MY THINGS ARE IN IZARK'S BAG.
COM-MANDER ...
IT WAS A PIECE OF TILE THAT FELL OFF A ROOF.
I HOPE WE WON'T BE IN TROUBLE.
WHAT'S GOING ON ?

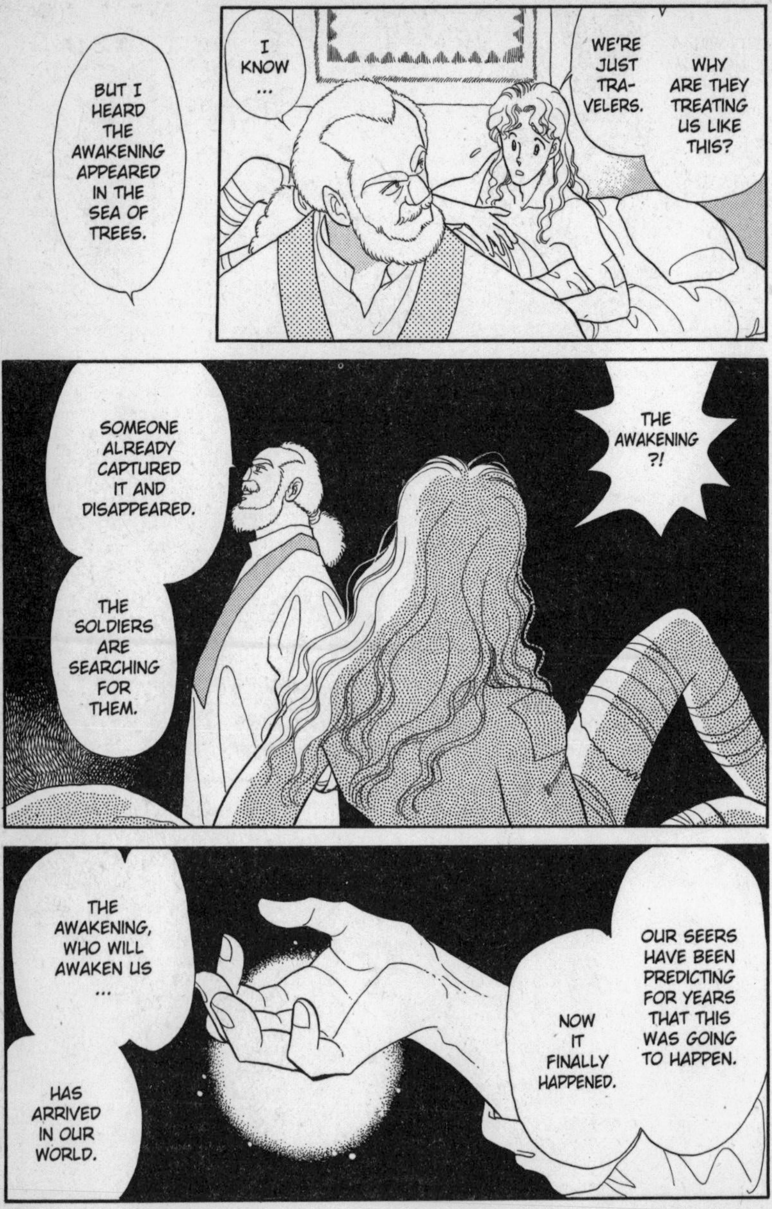
WE'RE JUST TRA-VELERS.
WHY ARE THEY TREATING US LIKE THIS?
I KNOW ...
BUT I HEARD THE AWAKENING APPEARED IN THE SEA OF TREES.
THE AWAKENING ?!
SOMEONE ALREADY CAPTURED IT AND DISAPPEARED.
THE SOLDIERS ARE SEARCHING FOR THEM.
OUR SEERS HAVE BEEN PREDICTING FOR YEARS THAT THIS WAS GOING TO HAPPEN.
NOW IT FINALLY HAPPENED.
THE AWAKENING, WHO WILL AWAKEN US ...
HAS ARRIVED IN OUR WORLD.

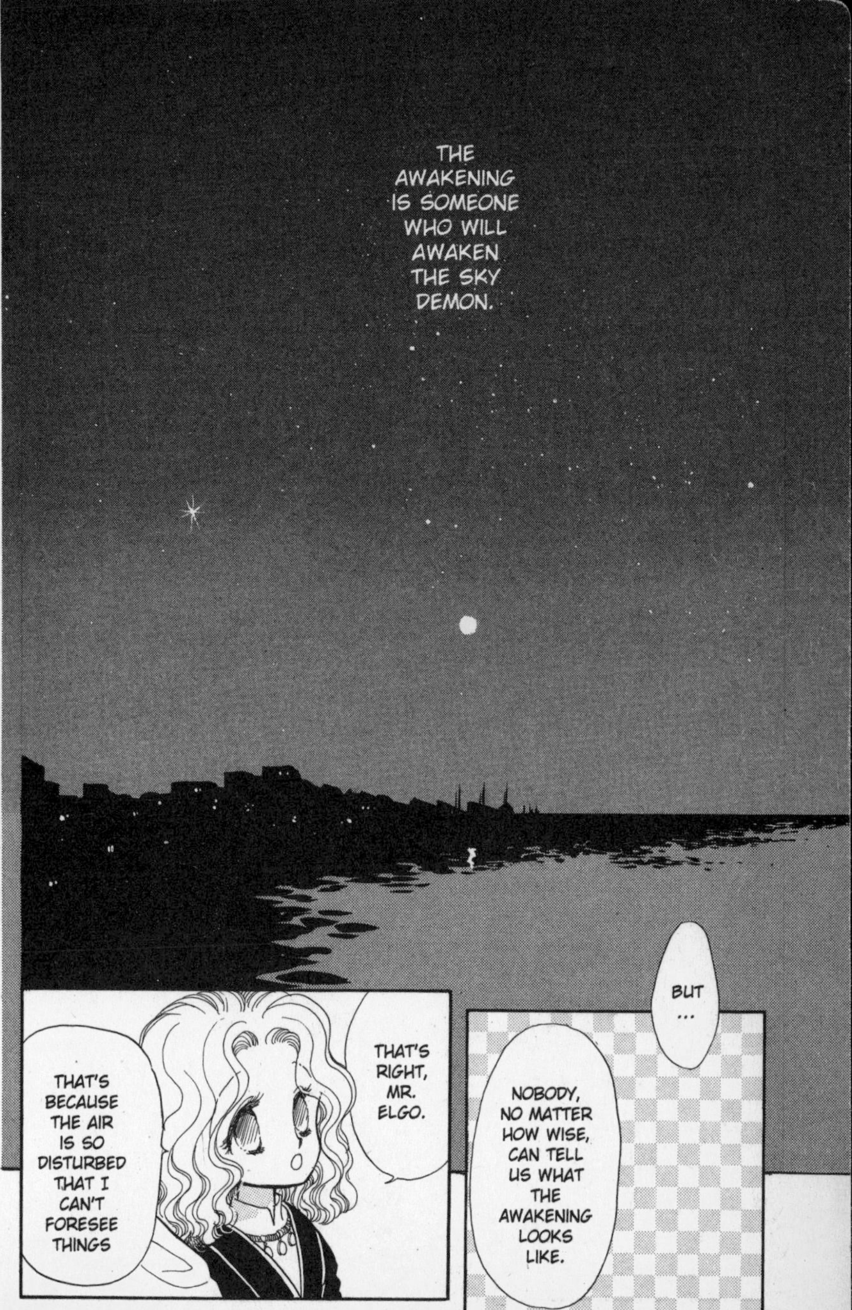

THE AWAKENING IS SOMEONE WHO WILL AWAKEN THE SKY DEMON.
BUT ...
NOBODY, NO MATTER HOW WISE, CAN TELL US WHAT THE AWAKENING LOOKS LIKE.
THAT'S RIGHT, MR. ELGO.
THAT'S BECAUSE THE AIR IS SO DISTURBED THAT I CAN'T FORESEE THINGS

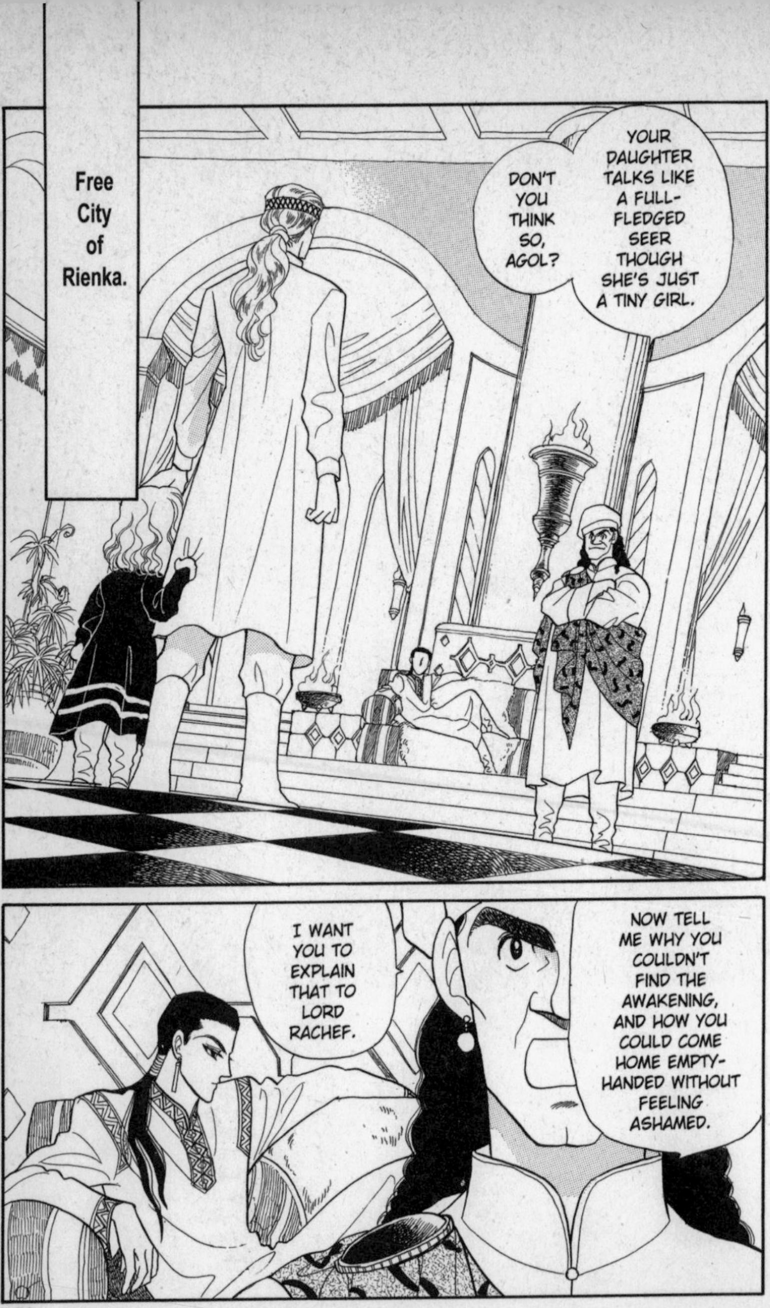
YOUR DAUGHTER TALKS LIKE A FULL-FLEDGED SEER THOUGH SHE'S JUST A TINY GIRL.
DON'T YOU THINK SO, AGOL?
Free City of Rienka.
NOW TELL ME WHY YOU COULDN'T FIND THE AWAKENING, AND HOW YOU COULD COME HOME EMPTY-HANDED WITHOUT FEELING ASHAMED.
I WANT YOU TO EXPLAIN THAT TO LORD RACHEF.

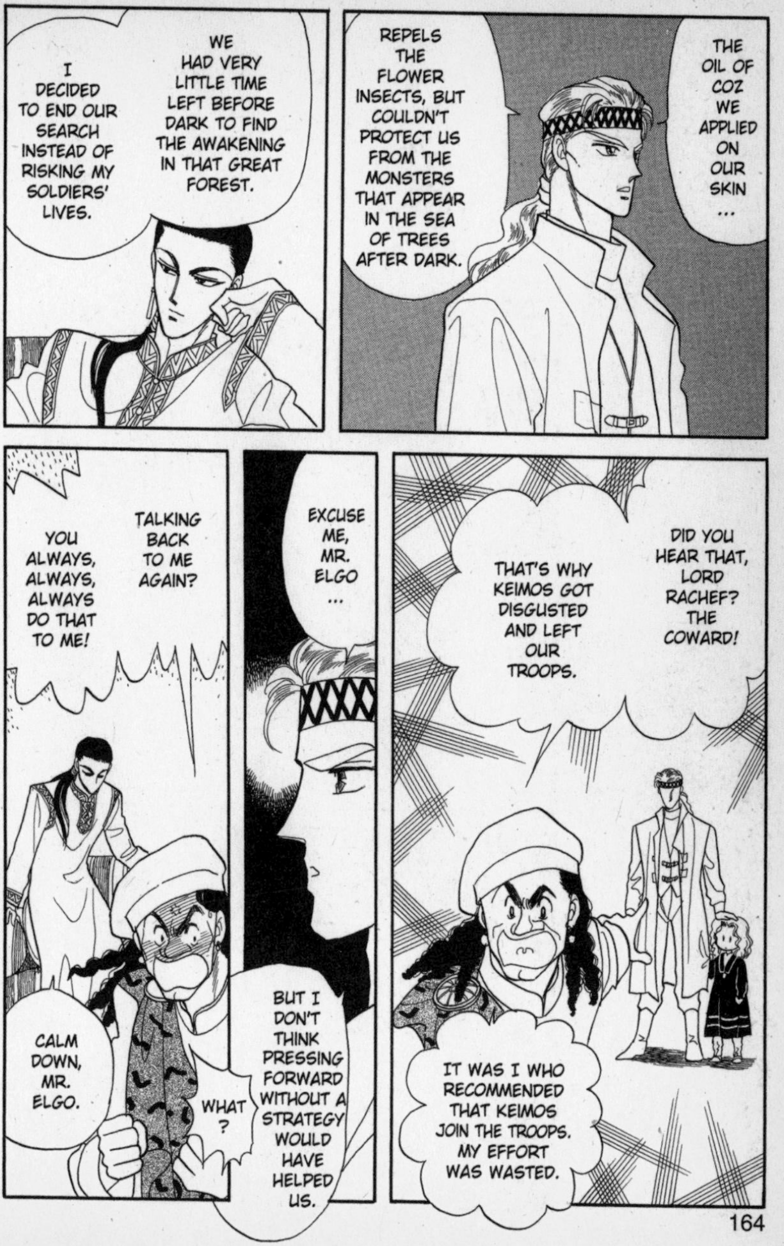
THE OIL OF COZ WE APPLIED ON OUR SKIN ...
REPELS THE FLOWER INSECTS, BUT COULDN'T PROTECT US FROM THE MONSTERS THAT APPEAR IN THE SEA OF TREES AFTER DARK.
WE HAD VERY LITTLE TIME LEFT BEFORE DARK TO FIND THE AWAKENING IN THAT GREAT FOREST.
I DECIDED TO END OUR SEARCH INSTEAD OF RISKING MY SOLDIERS' LIVES.
DID YOU HEAR THAT, LORD RACHEF? THE COWARD!
THAT'S WHY KEIMOS GOT DISGUSTED AND LEFT OUR TROOPS.
IT WAS I WHO RECOMMENDED THAT KEIMOS JOIN THE TROOPS. MY EFFORT WAS WASTED.
EXCUSE ME, MR. ELGO ...
BUT I DON'T THINK PRESSING FORWARD WITHOUT A STRATEGY WOULD HAVE HELPED US.
WHAT ?
TALKING BACK TO ME AGAIN?
YOU ALWAYS, ALWAYS, ALWAYS DO THAT TO ME!
CALM DOWN, MR. ELGO.

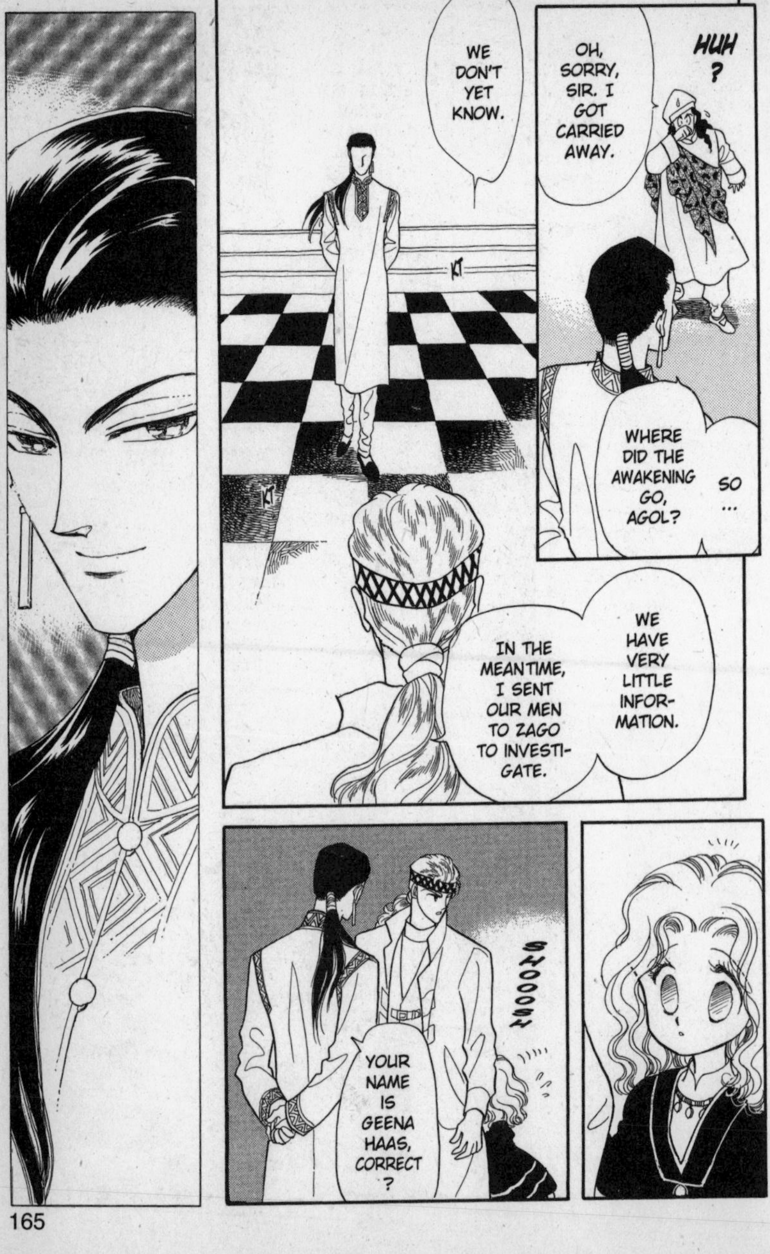
HUH ?
OH, SORRY, SIR. I GOT CARRIED AWAY.
SO ...
WHERE DID THE AWAKENING GO, AGOL?
WE DON'T YET KNOW.
KT
KT
WE HAVE VERY LITTLE INFOR-MATION.
IN THE MEANTIME, I SENT OUR MEN TO ZAGO TO INVESTI-GATE.
SHOOOOSH
YOUR NAME IS GEENA HAAS, CORRECT ?

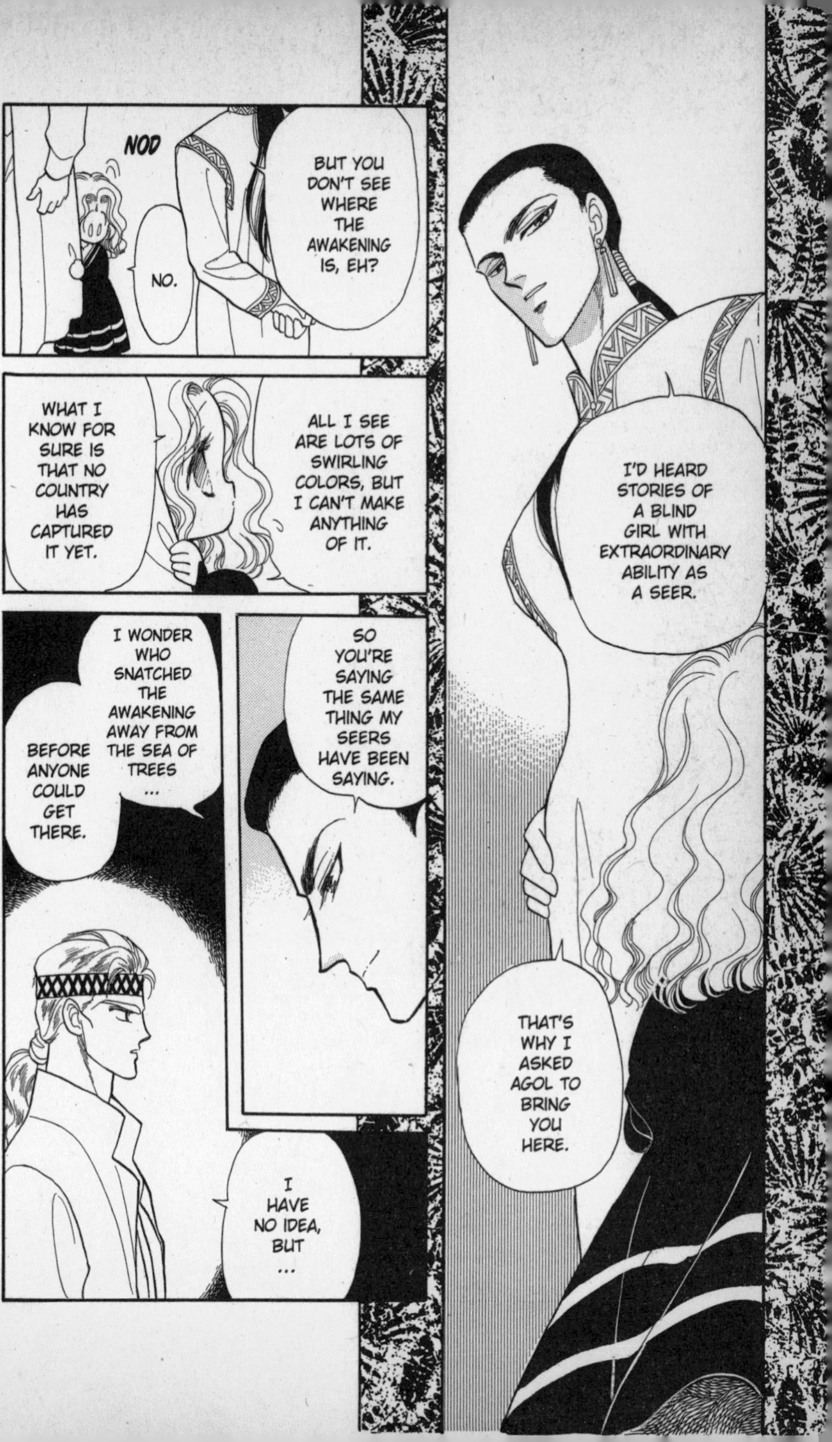
I'D HEARD STORIES OF A BLIND GIRL WITH EXTRAORDINARY ABILITY AS A SEER.
THAT'S WHY I ASKED AGOL TO BRING YOU HERE.
BUT YOU DON'T SEE WHERE THE AWAKENING IS, EH?
NOD
NO.
ALL I SEE ARE LOTS OF SWIRLING COLORS, BUT I CAN'T MAKE ANYTHING OF IT.
WHAT I KNOW FOR SURE IS THAT NO COUNTRY HAS CAPTURED IT YET.
SO YOU'RE SAYING THE SAME THING MY SEERS HAVE BEEN SAYING.
I WONDER WHO SNATCHED THE AWAKENING AWAY FROM THE SEA OF TREES ...
BEFORE ANYONE COULD GET THERE.
I HAVE NO IDEA, BUT ...

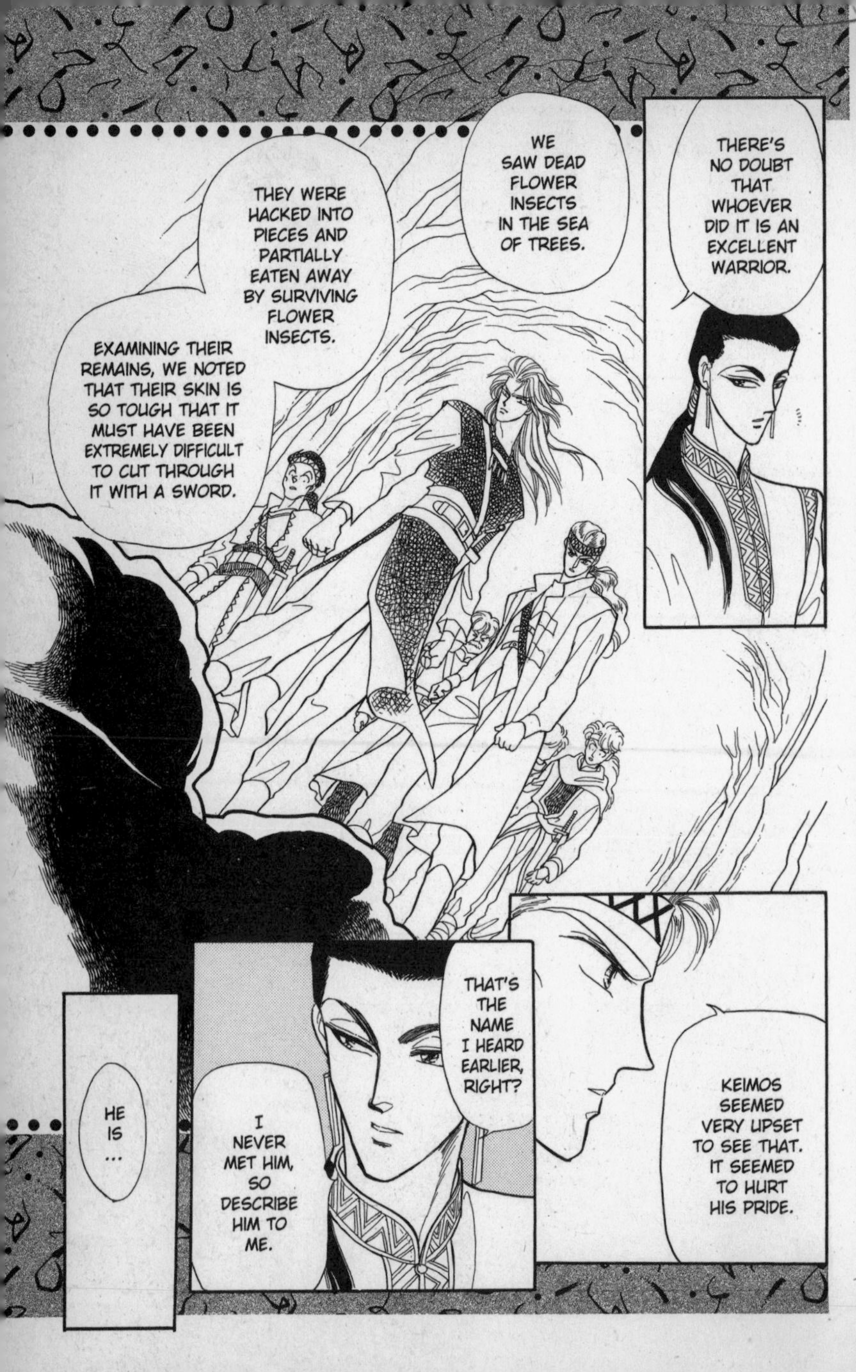
THERE'S NO DOUBT THAT WHOEVER DID IT IS AN EXCELLENT WARRIOR.
WE SAW DEAD FLOWER INSECTS IN THE SEA OF TREES.
THEY WERE HACKED INTO PIECES AND PARTIALLY EATEN AWAY BY SURVIVING FLOWER INSECTS.
EXAMINING THEIR REMAINS, WE NOTED THAT THEIR SKIN IS SO TOUGH THAT IT MUST HAVE BEEN EXTREMELY DIFFICULT TO CUT THROUGH IT WITH A SWORD.
KEIMOS SEEMED VERY UPSET TO SEE THAT. IT SEEMED TO HURT HIS PRIDE.
THAT'S THE NAME I HEARD EARLIER, RIGHT?
I NEVER MET HIM, SO DESCRIBE HIM TO ME.
HE IS ...

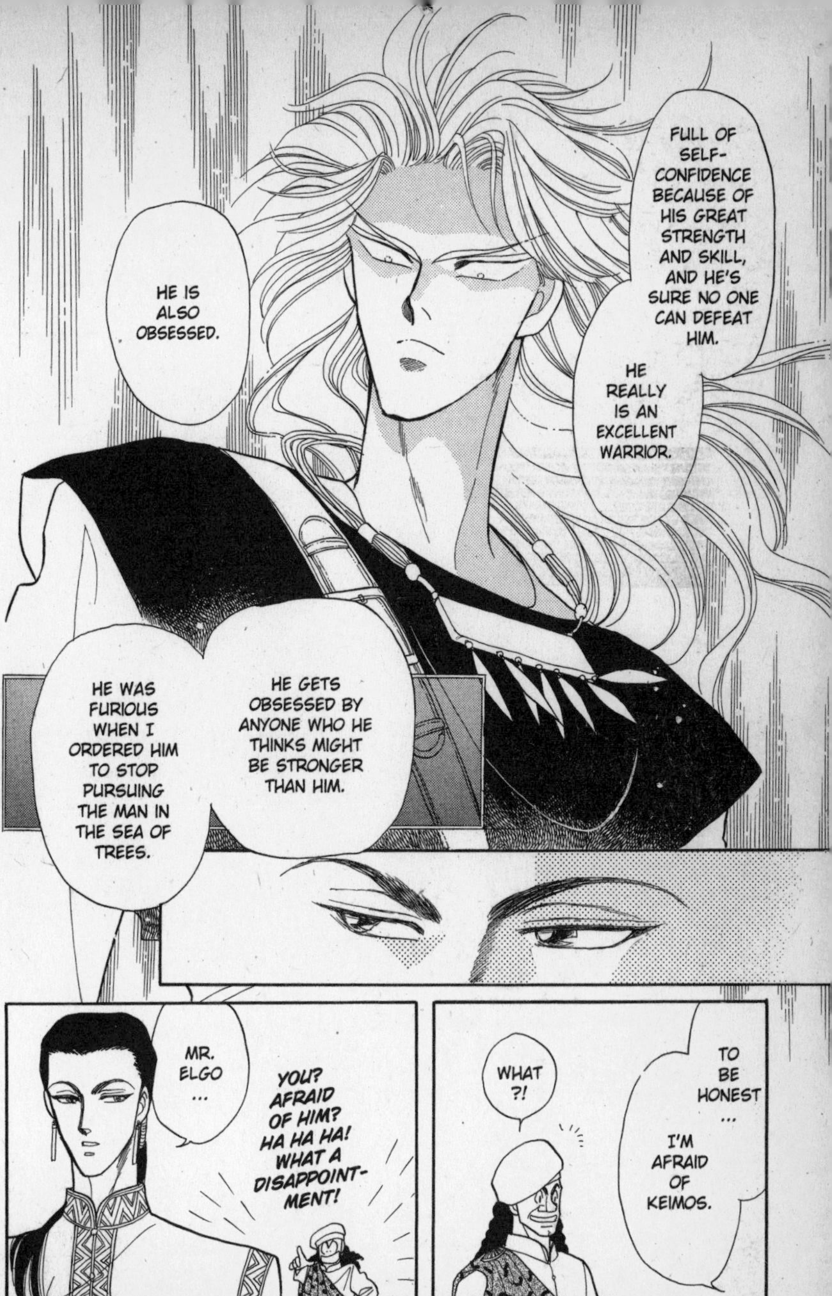
FULL OF SELF-CONFIDENCE BECAUSE OF HIS GREAT STRENGTH AND SKILL, AND HE'S SURE NO ONE CAN DEFEAT HIM.
HE REALLY IS AN EXCELLENT WARRIOR.
HE IS ALSO OBSESSED.
HE GETS OBSESSED BY ANYONE WHO HE THINKS MIGHT BE STRONGER THAN HIM.
HE WAS FURIOUS WHEN I ORDERED HIM TO STOP PURSUING THE MAN IN THE SEA OF TREES.
TO BE HONEST...
I'M AFRAID OF KEIMOS.
WHAT?!
YOU? AFRAID OF HIM? HA HA HA! WHAT A DISAPPOINTMENT!
MR. ELGO...

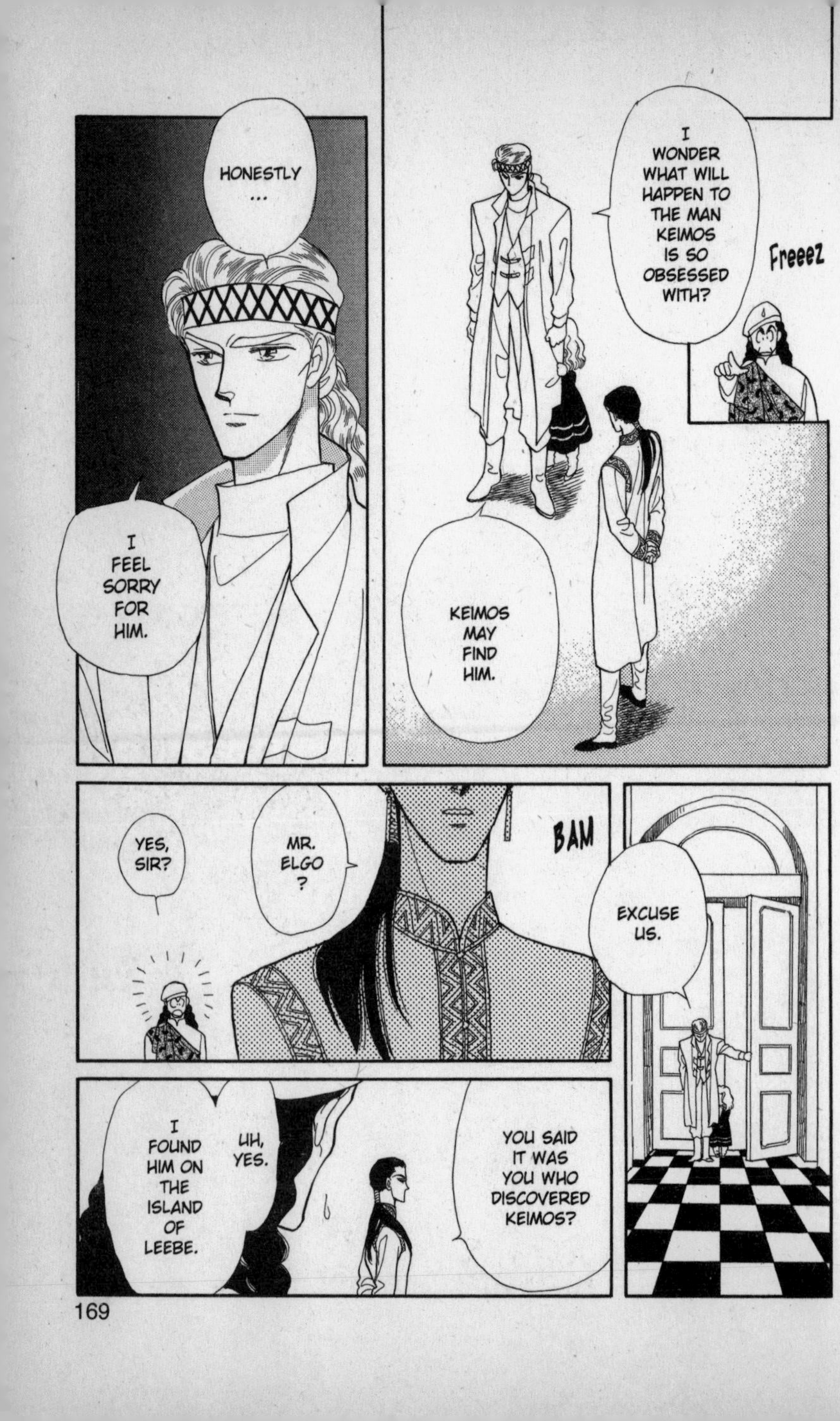
I WONDER WHAT WILL HAPPEN TO THE MAN KEIMOS IS SO OBSESSED WITH?
Freeez
KEIMOS MAY FIND HIM.
HONESTLY ...
I FEEL SORRY FOR HIM.
EXCUSE US.
BAM
MR. ELGO ?
YES, SIR?
YOU SAID IT WAS YOU WHO DISCOVERED KEIMOS?
UH, YES.
I FOUND HIM ON THE ISLAND OF LEEBE.

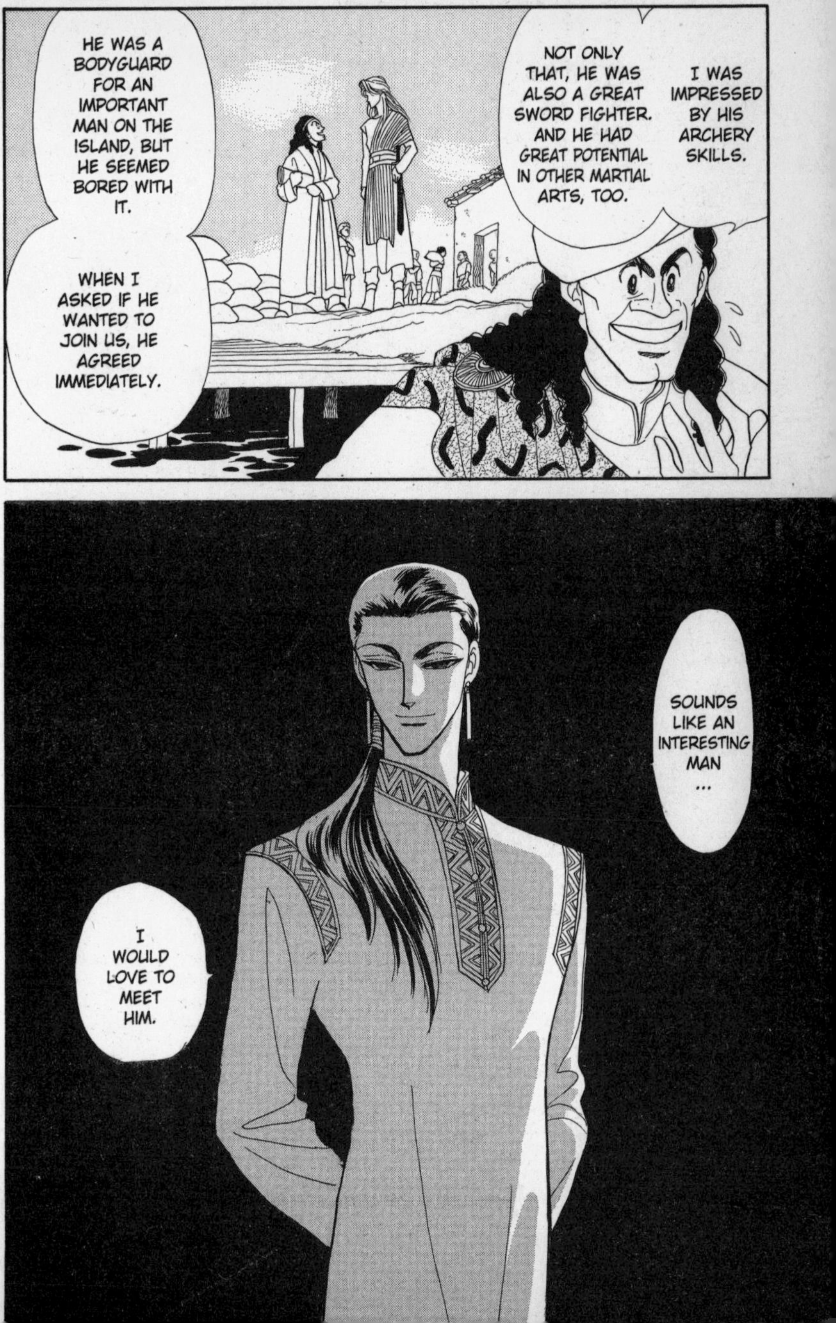
I WAS IMPRESSED BY HIS ARCHERY SKILLS.
NOT ONLY THAT, HE WAS ALSO A GREAT SWORD FIGHTER. AND HE HAD GREAT POTENTIAL IN OTHER MARTIAL ARTS, TOO.
HE WAS A BODYGUARD FOR AN IMPORTANT MAN ON THE ISLAND, BUT HE SEEMED BORED WITH IT.
WHEN I ASKED IF HE WANTED TO JOIN US, HE AGREED IMMEDIATELY.
SOUNDS LIKE AN INTERESTING MAN ...
I WOULD LOVE TO MEET HIM.

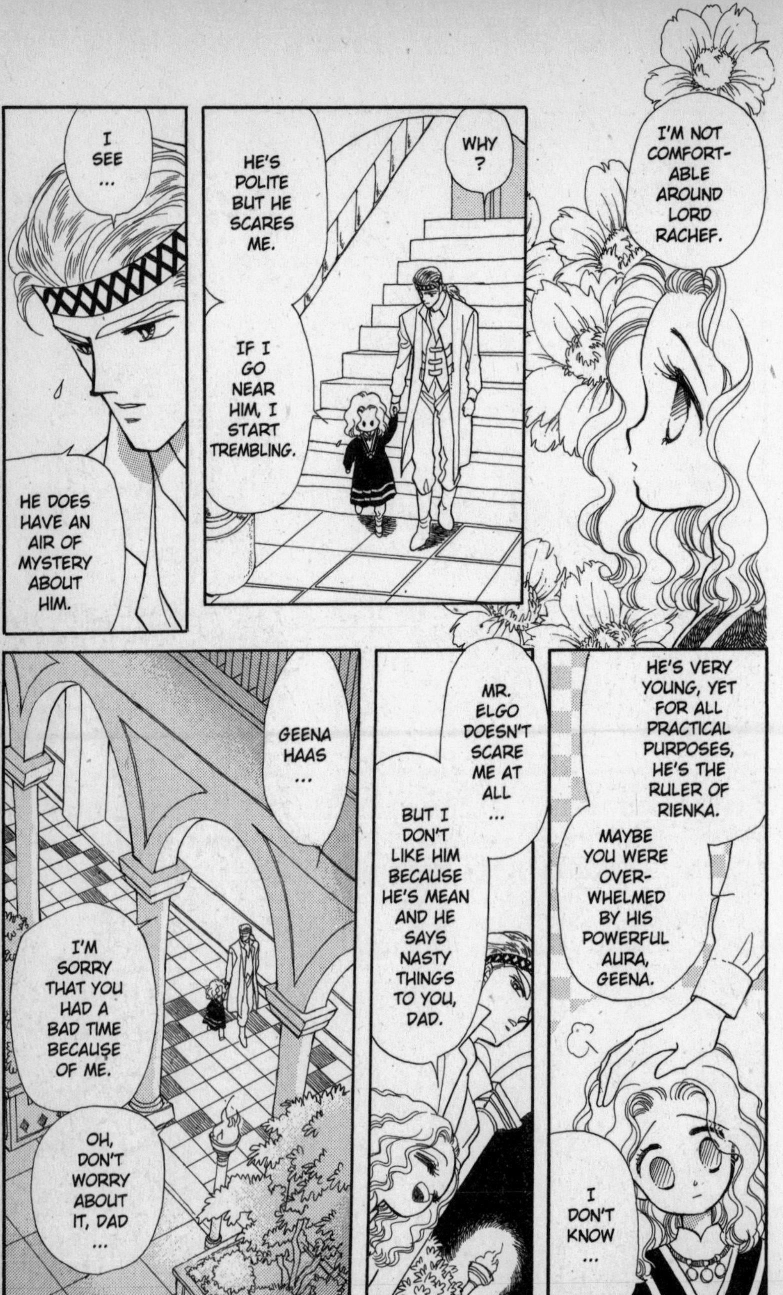
I'M NOT COMFORT-ABLE AROUND LORD RACHEF.
WHY?
HE'S POLITE BUT HE SCARES ME.
IF I GO NEAR HIM, I START TREMBLING.
I SEE ...
HE DOES HAVE AN AIR OF MYSTERY ABOUT HIM.
HE'S VERY YOUNG, YET FOR ALL PRACTICAL PURPOSES, HE'S THE RULER OF RIENKA.
MAYBE YOU WERE OVER-WHELMED BY HIS POWERFUL AURA, GEENA.
I DON'T KNOW ...
MR. ELGO DOESN'T SCARE ME AT ALL ...
BUT I DON'T LIKE HIM BECAUSE HE'S MEAN AND HE SAYS NASTY THINGS TO YOU, DAD.
GEENA HAAS ...
I'M SORRY THAT YOU HAD A BAD TIME BECAUSE OF ME.
OH, DON'T WORRY ABOUT IT, DAD ...

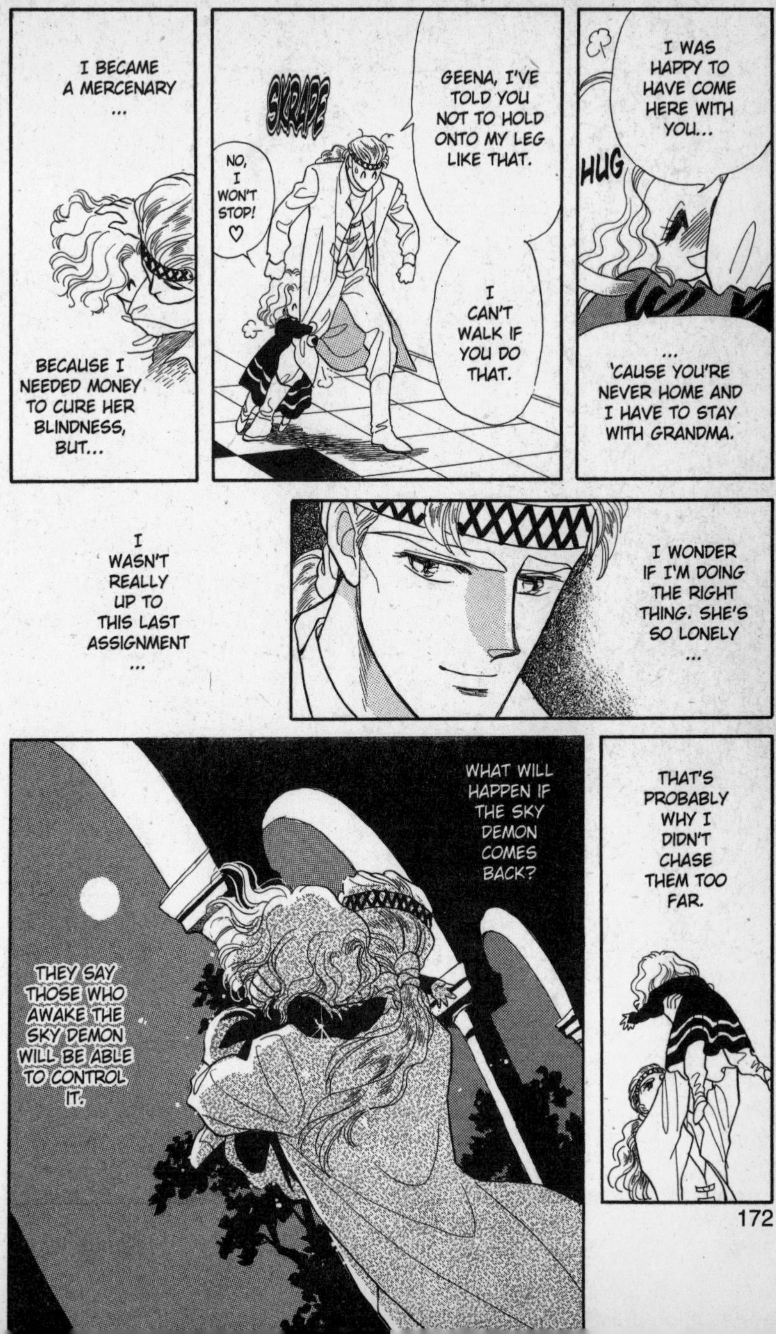

I WAS HAPPY TO HAVE COME HERE WITH YOU...
HUG
... 'CAUSE YOU'RE NEVER HOME AND I HAVE TO STAY WITH GRANDMA.
GEENA, I'VE TOLD YOU NOT TO HOLD ONTO MY LEG LIKE THAT.
SKRAPE
NO, I WON'T STOP! ♡
I CAN'T WALK IF YOU DO THAT.
I BECAME A MERCENARY ...
BECAUSE I NEEDED MONEY TO CURE HER BLINDNESS, BUT...
I WONDER IF I'M DOING THE RIGHT THING. SHE'S SO LONELY ...
I WASN'T REALLY UP TO THIS LAST ASSIGNMENT ...
THAT'S PROBABLY WHY I DIDN'T CHASE THEM TOO FAR.
WHAT WILL HAPPEN IF THE SKY DEMON COMES BACK?
THEY SAY THOSE WHO AWAKE THE SKY DEMON WILL BE ABLE TO CONTROL IT.

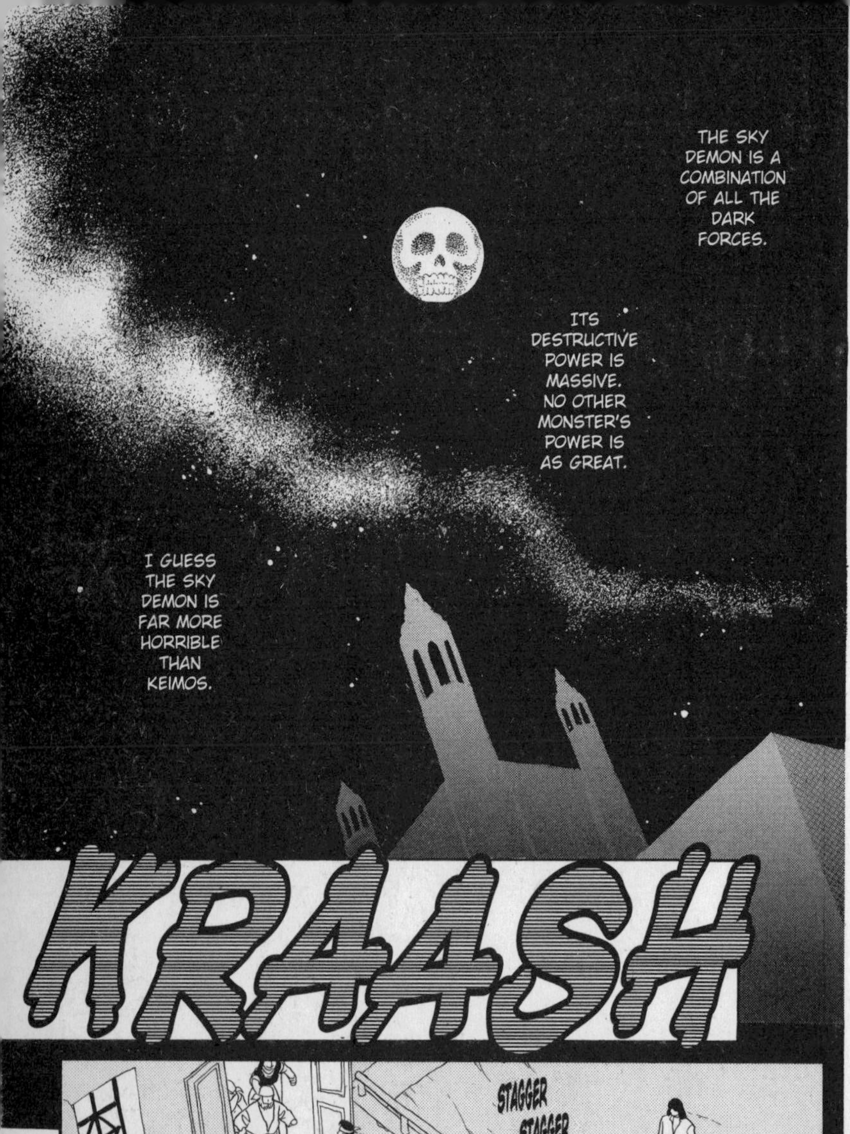
THE SKY DEMON IS A COMBINATION OF ALL THE DARK FORCES.
ITS DESTRUCTIVE POWER IS MASSIVE. NO OTHER MONSTER'S POWER IS AS GREAT.
I GUESS THE SKY DEMON IS FAR MORE HORRIBLE THAN KEIMOS.
KRAASH

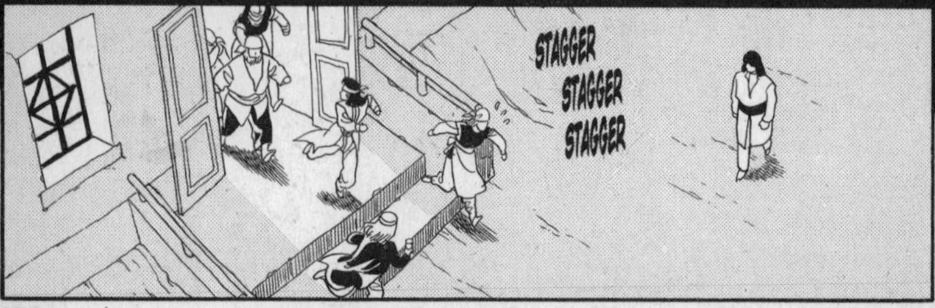
STAGGER STAGGER STAGGER

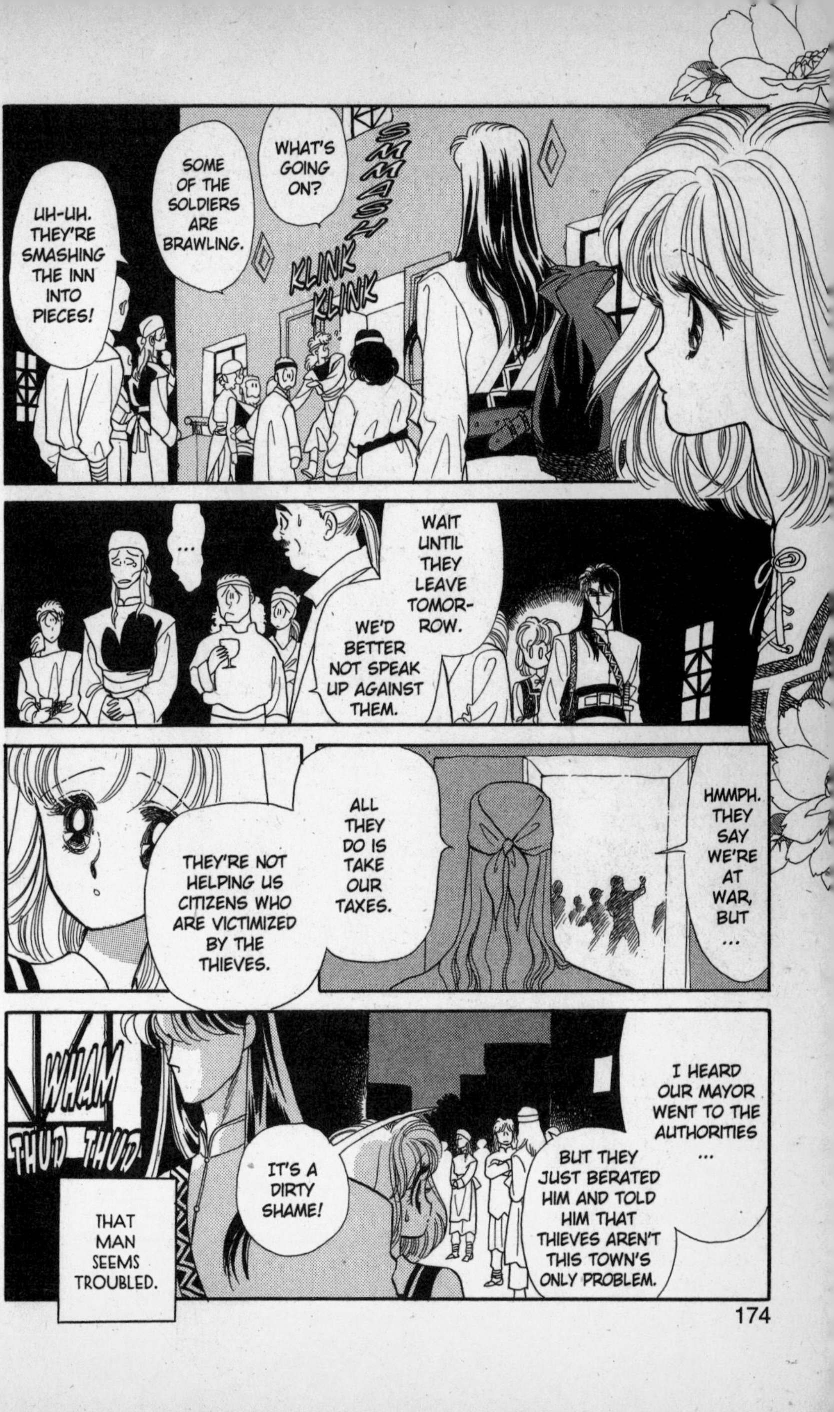
WHAT'S GOING ON?
SMMMASH
SOME OF THE SOLDIERS ARE BRAWLING.
KLINK KLINK
UH-UH. THEY'RE SMASHING THE INN INTO PIECES!
WAIT UNTIL THEY LEAVE TOMORROW.
WE'D BETTER NOT SPEAK UP AGAINST THEM.
...
HMMPH. THEY SAY WE'RE AT WAR, BUT ...
ALL THEY DO IS TAKE OUR TAXES.
THEY'RE NOT HELPING US CITIZENS WHO ARE VICTIMIZED BY THE THIEVES.
I HEARD OUR MAYOR WENT TO THE AUTHORITIES ...
BUT THEY JUST BERATED HIM AND TOLD HIM THAT THIEVES AREN'T THIS TOWN'S ONLY PROBLEM.
IT'S A DIRTY SHAME!
WHAM
THUD THUD
THAT MAN SEEMS TROUBLED.

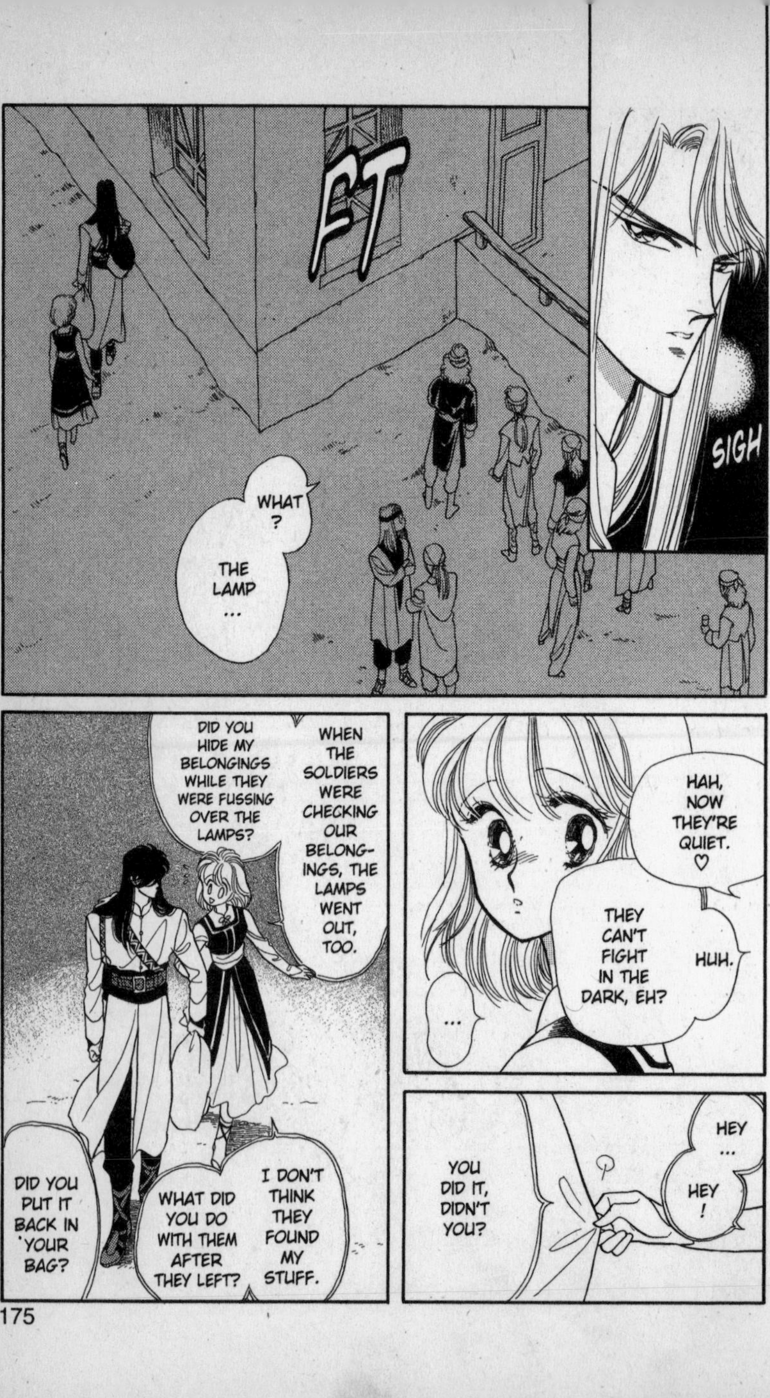
SIGH
FT
WHAT ?
THE LAMP ...
HAH, NOW THEY'RE QUIET. ♡
HUH.
THEY CAN'T FIGHT IN THE DARK, EH?
...
HEY ... HEY !
YOU DID IT, DIDN'T YOU?
WHEN THE SOLDIERS WERE CHECKING OUR BELONGINGS, THE LAMPS WENT OUT, TOO.
DID YOU HIDE MY BELONGINGS WHILE THEY WERE FUSSING OVER THE LAMPS?
I DON'T THINK THEY FOUND MY STUFF.
WHAT DID YOU DO WITH THEM AFTER THEY LEFT?
DID YOU PUT IT BACK IN YOUR BAG?

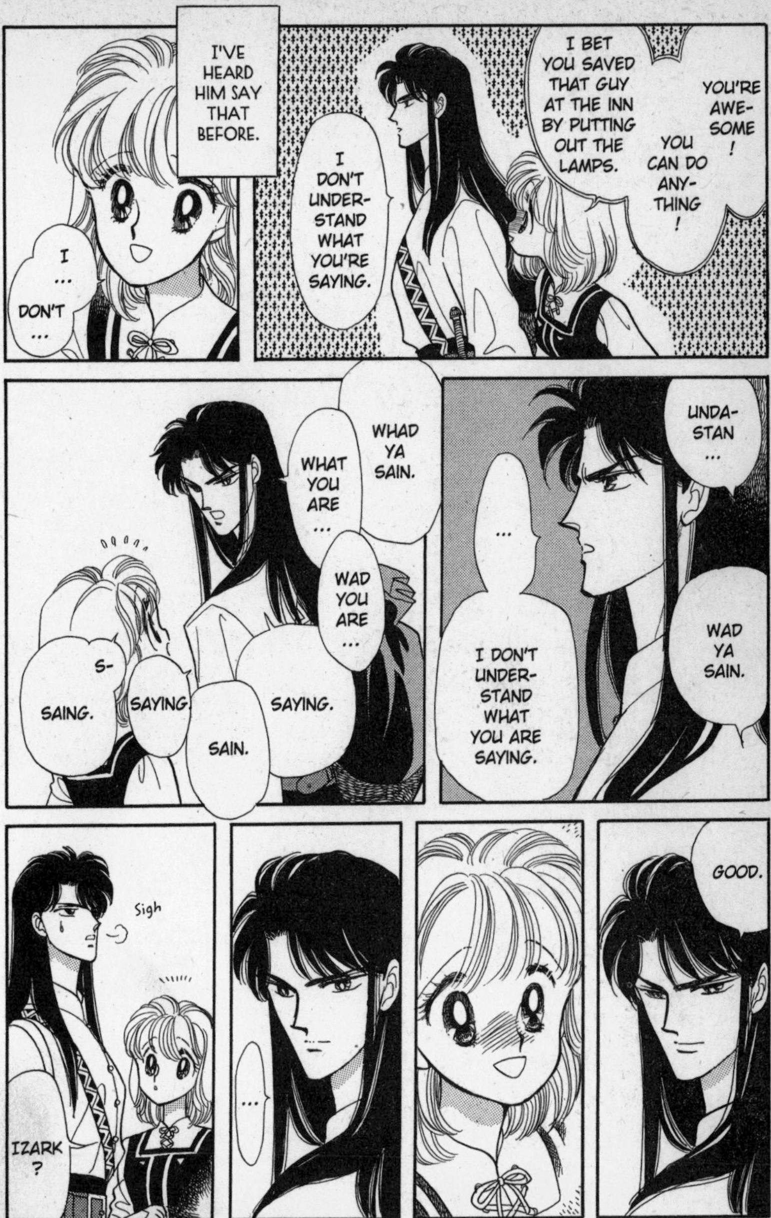
YOU'RE AWE-SOME!
YOU CAN DO ANY-THING!
I BET YOU SAVED THAT GUY AT THE INN BY PUTTING OUT THE LAMPS.
I DON'T UNDER-STAND WHAT YOU'RE SAYING.
I'VE HEARD HIM SAY THAT BEFORE.
I ... DON'T ...
UNDA-STAN ...
...
WAD YA SAIN.
I DON'T UNDER-STAND WHAT YOU ARE SAYING.
WHAD YA SAIN.
WHAT YOU ARE ...
WAD YOU ARE ...
SAYING.
S- SAING.
SAYING.
SAIN.
GOOD.
...
Sigh
IZARK ?

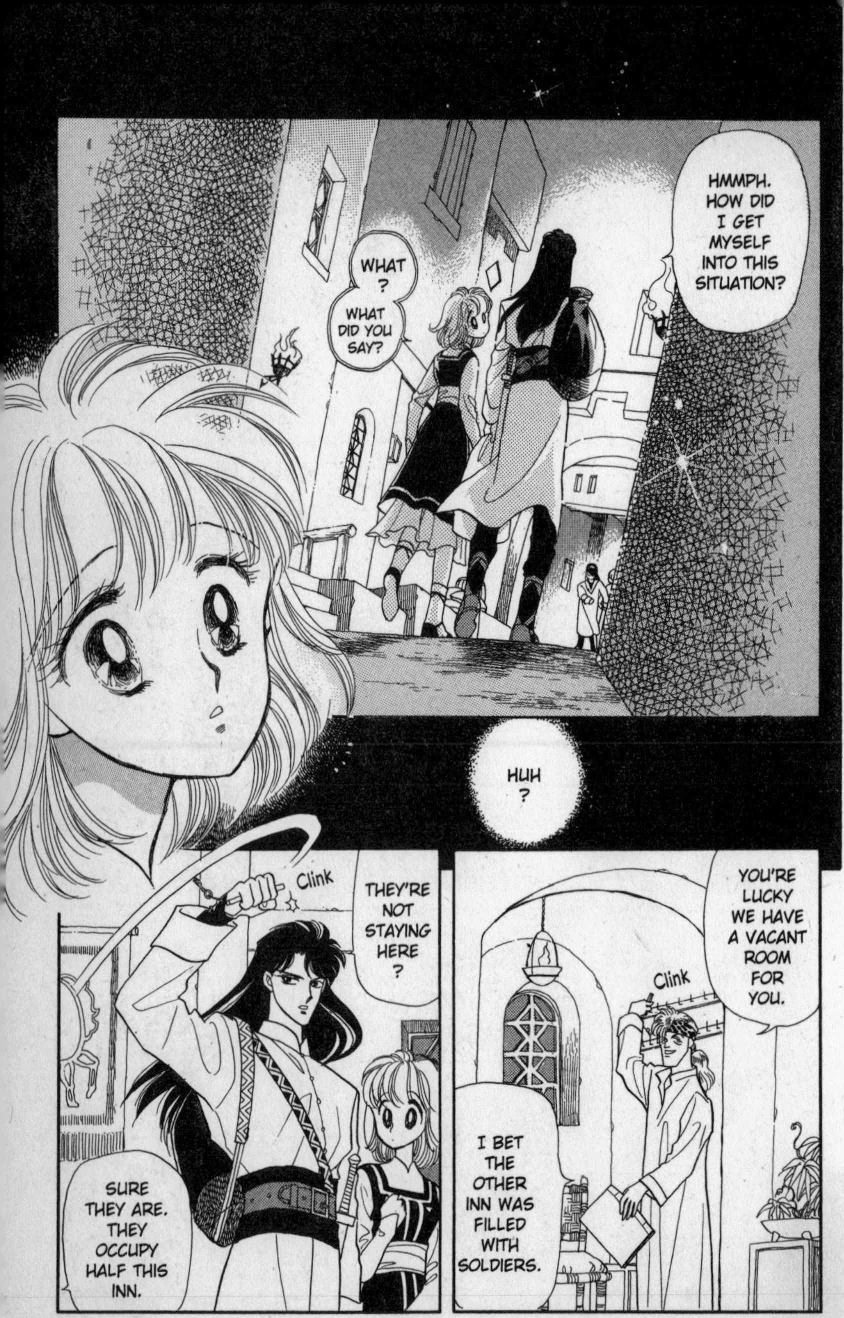
HMMPH. HOW DID I GET MYSELF INTO THIS SITUATION?
WHAT? WHAT DID YOU SAY?
HUH?
YOU'RE LUCKY WE HAVE A VACANT ROOM FOR YOU.
Clink
I BET THE OTHER INN WAS FILLED WITH SOLDIERS.
THEY'RE NOT STAYING HERE?
Clink
SURE THEY ARE. THEY OCCUPY HALF THIS INN.

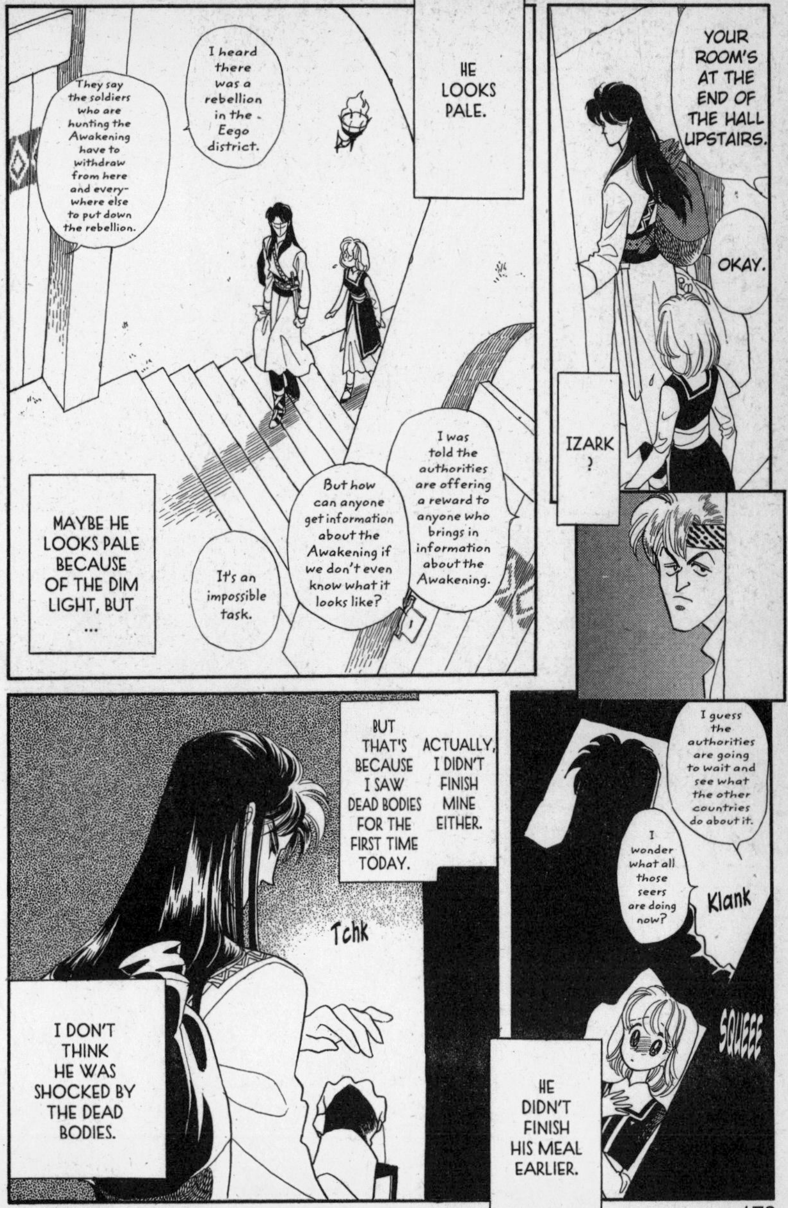

YOUR ROOM'S AT THE END OF THE HALL UPSTAIRS.
OKAY.
IZARK ?
HE LOOKS PALE.
I heard there was a rebellion in the Eego district.
They say the soldiers who are hunting the Awakening have to withdraw from here and everywhere else to put down the rebellion.
I was told the authorities are offering a reward to anyone who brings in information about the Awakening.
But how can anyone get information about the Awakening if we don't even know what it looks like?
It's an impossible task.
MAYBE HE LOOKS PALE BECAUSE OF THE DIM LIGHT, BUT ...
I guess the authorities are going to wait and see what the other countries do about it.
I wonder what all those seers are doing now?
Klank
SQUEEE
HE DIDN'T FINISH HIS MEAL EARLIER.
ACTUALLY, I DIDN'T FINISH MINE EITHER.
BUT THAT'S BECAUSE I SAW DEAD BODIES FOR THE FIRST TIME TODAY.
Tchk
I DON'T THINK HE WAS SHOCKED BY THE DEAD BODIES.

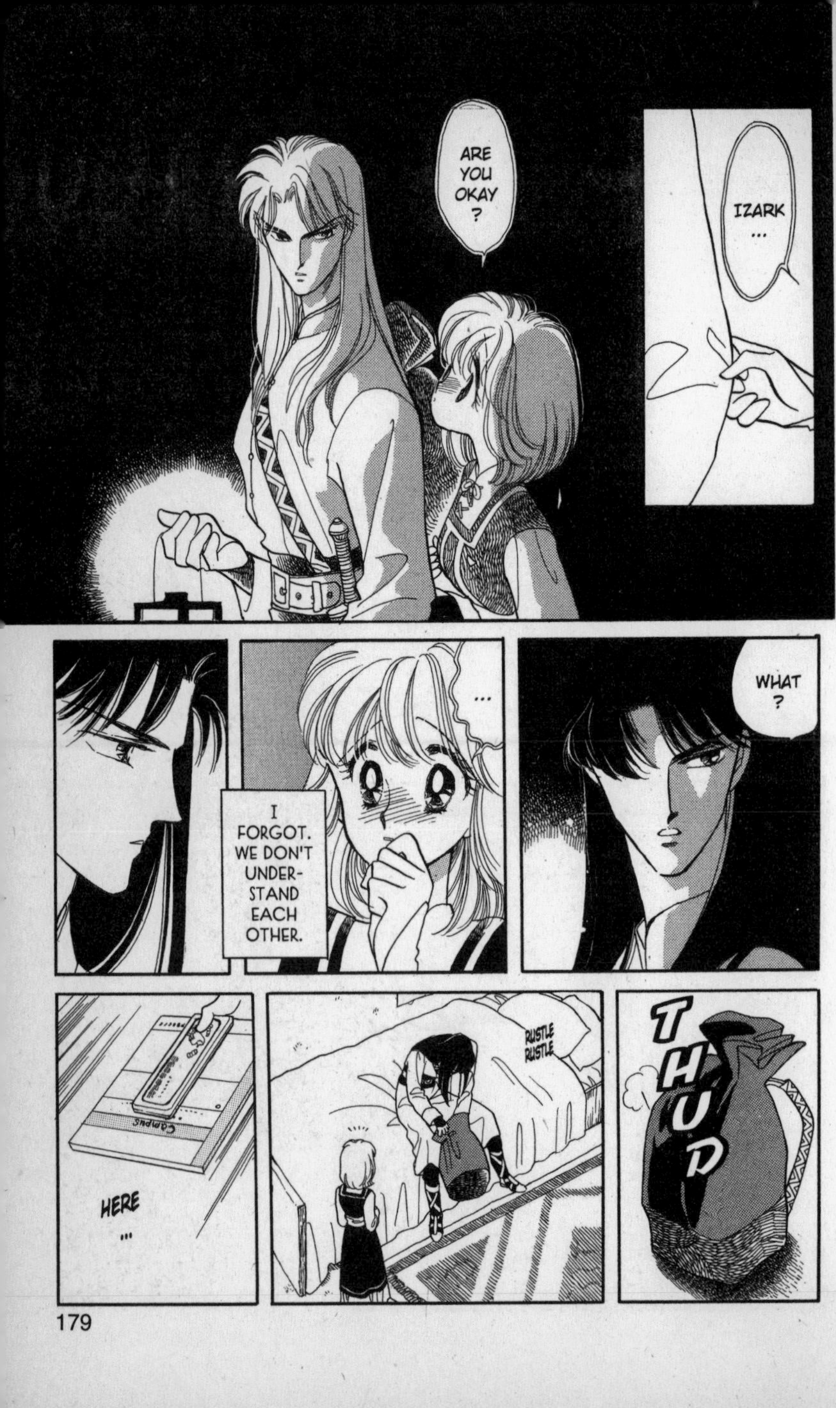
IZARK ...
ARE YOU OKAY ?
WHAT ?
...
I FORGOT. WE DON'T UNDER-STAND EACH OTHER.
THUD
RUSTLE RUSTLE
HERE ...

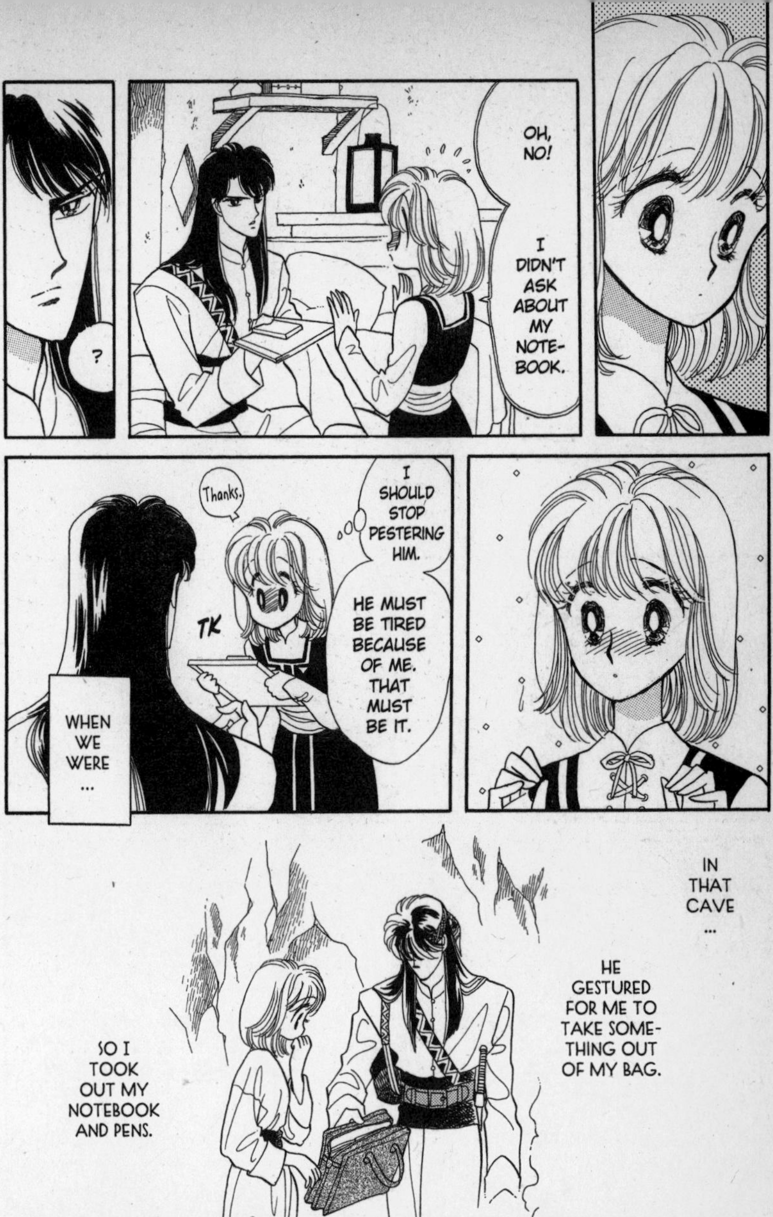
OH, NO!
I DIDN'T ASK ABOUT MY NOTE-BOOK.
?
I SHOULD STOP PESTERING HIM.
HE MUST BE TIRED BECAUSE OF ME. THAT MUST BE IT.
Thanks.
TK
WHEN WE WERE ...
IN THAT CAVE ...
HE GESTURED FOR ME TO TAKE SOME-THING OUT OF MY BAG.
SO I TOOK OUT MY NOTEBOOK AND PENS.

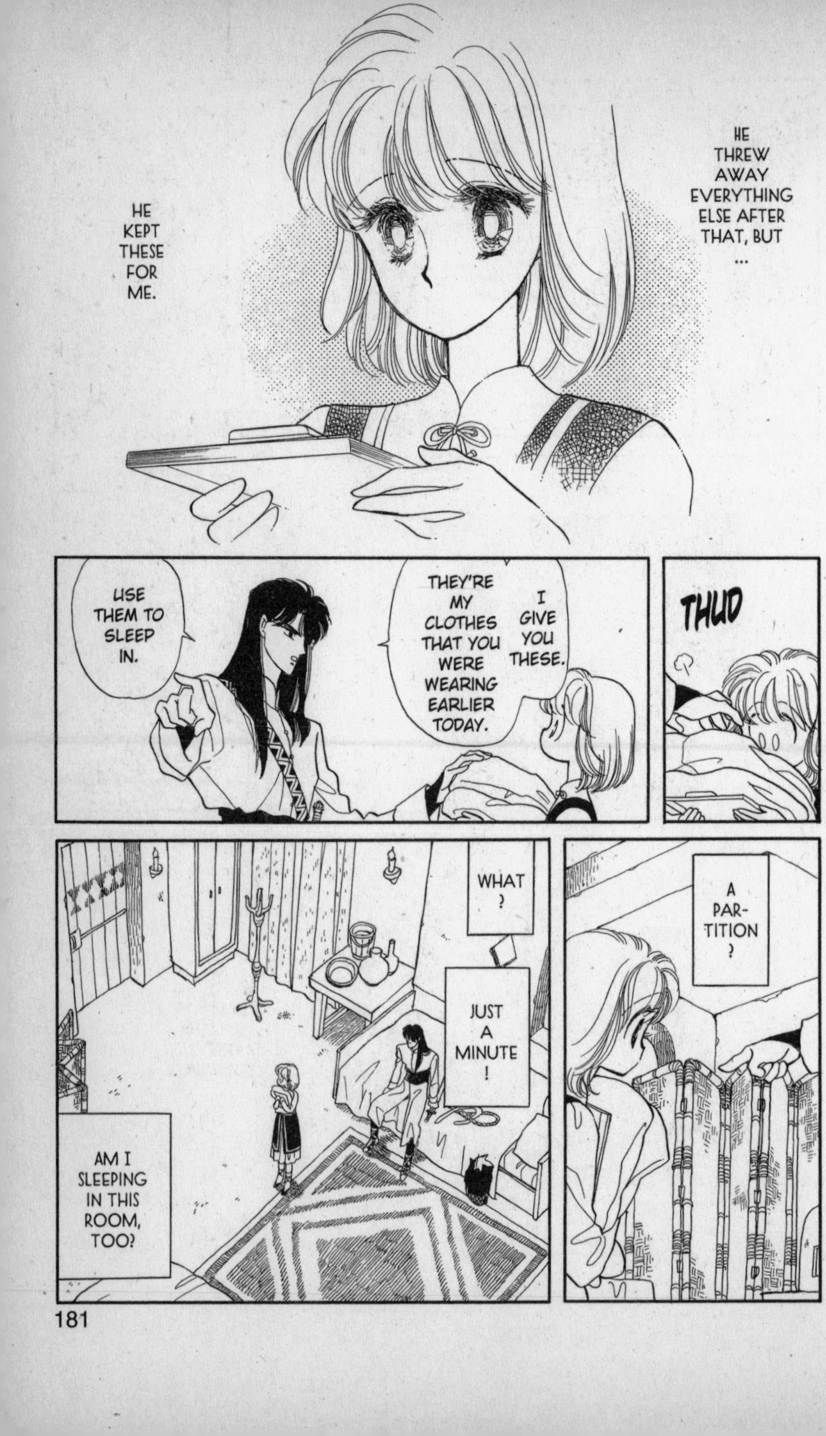
HE THREW AWAY EVERYTHING ELSE AFTER THAT, BUT ...
HE KEPT THESE FOR ME.
THUD
I GIVE YOU THESE.
THEY'RE MY CLOTHES THAT YOU WERE WEARING EARLIER TODAY.
USE THEM TO SLEEP IN.
A PAR-TITION?
WHAT?
JUST A MINUTE!
AM I SLEEPING IN THIS ROOM, TOO?

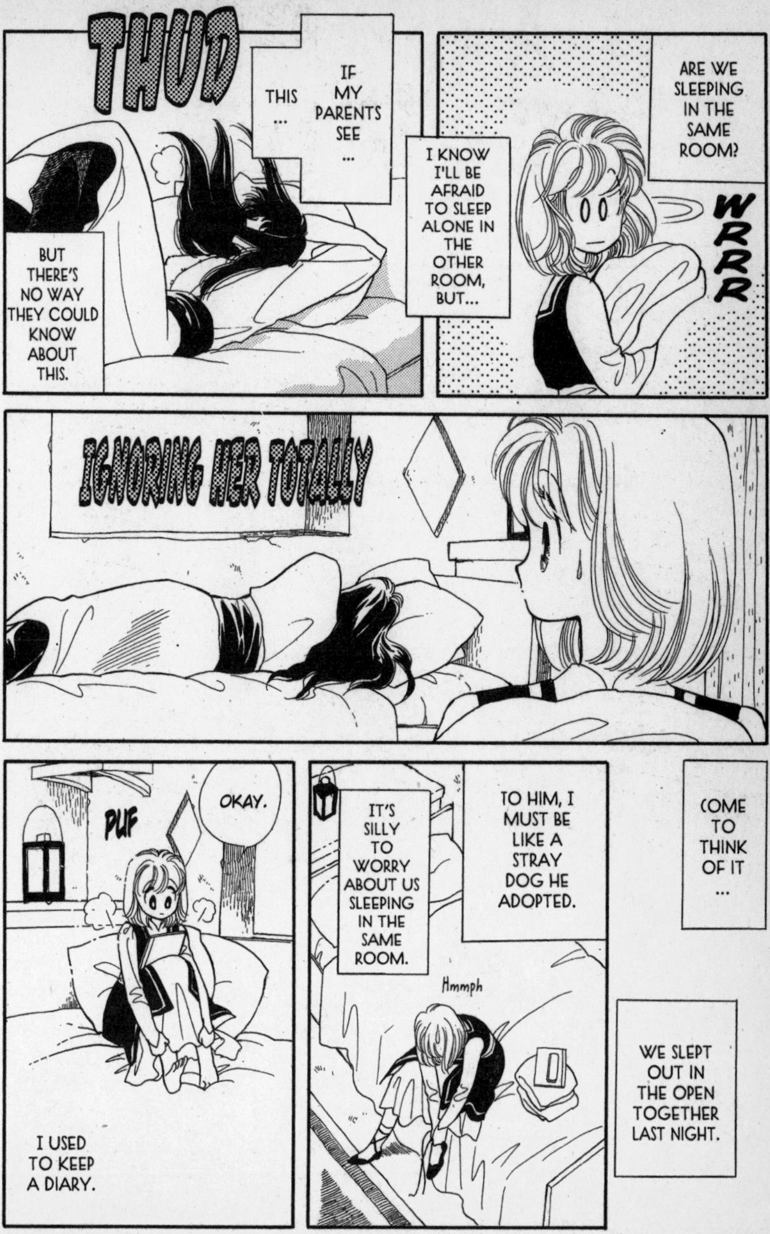

ARE WE SLEEPING IN THE SAME ROOM?
WRRR
I KNOW I'LL BE AFRAID TO SLEEP ALONE IN THE OTHER ROOM, BUT...
IF MY PARENTS SEE ...
THIS ...
THUD
BUT THERE'S NO WAY THEY COULD KNOW ABOUT THIS.
IGNORING HER TOTALLY
COME TO THINK OF IT ...
WE SLEPT OUT IN THE OPEN TOGETHER LAST NIGHT.
TO HIM, I MUST BE LIKE A STRAY DOG HE ADOPTED.
IT'S SILLY TO WORRY ABOUT US SLEEPING IN THE SAME ROOM.
Hmmph
OKAY.
PUF
I USED TO KEEP A DIARY.

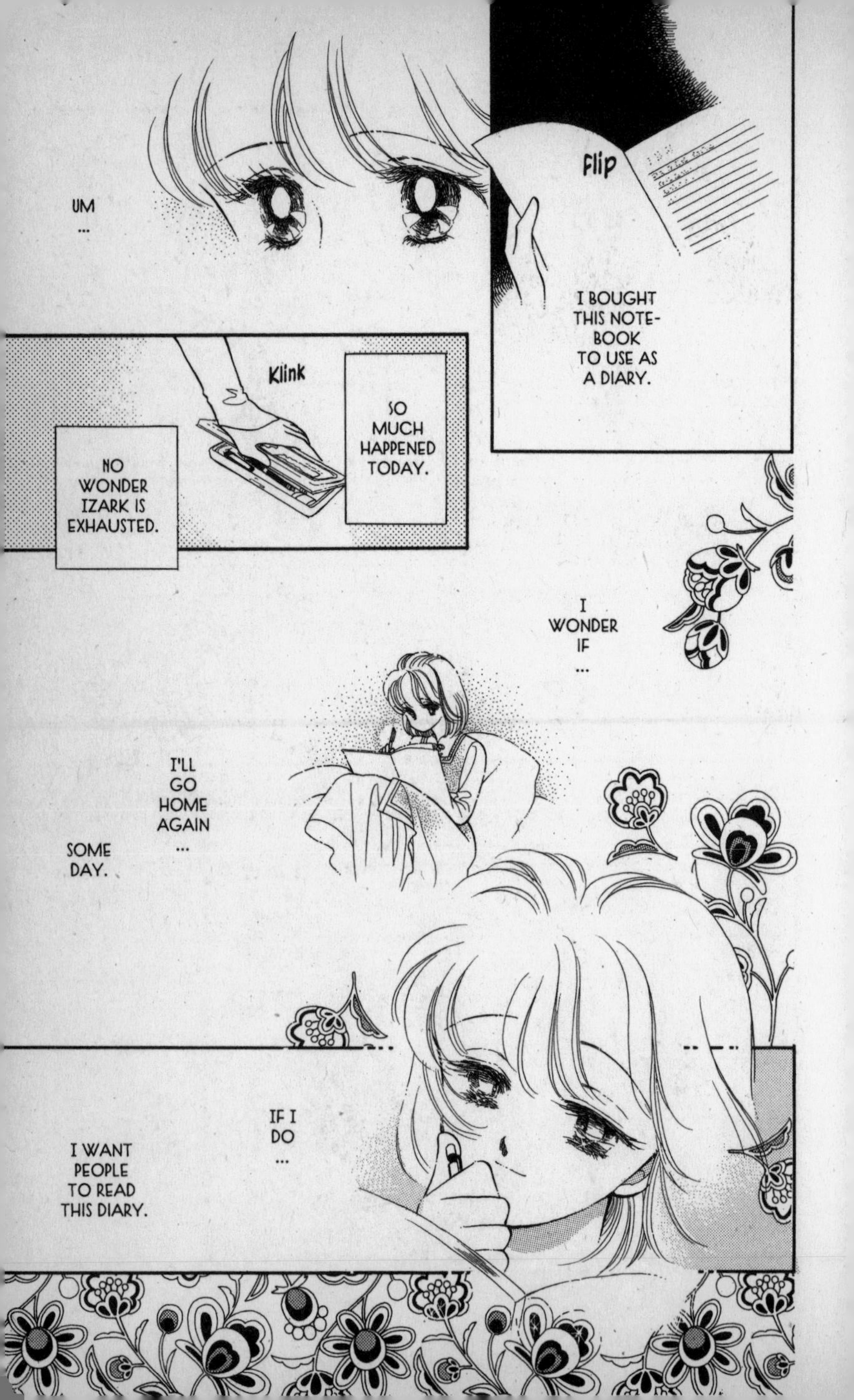
Flip
I BOUGHT THIS NOTE-BOOK TO USE AS A DIARY.
UM ...
Klink
SO MUCH HAPPENED TODAY.
NO WONDER IZARK IS EXHAUSTED.
I WONDER IF ...
I'LL GO HOME AGAIN ...
SOME DAY.
IF I DO ...
I WANT PEOPLE TO READ THIS DIARY.

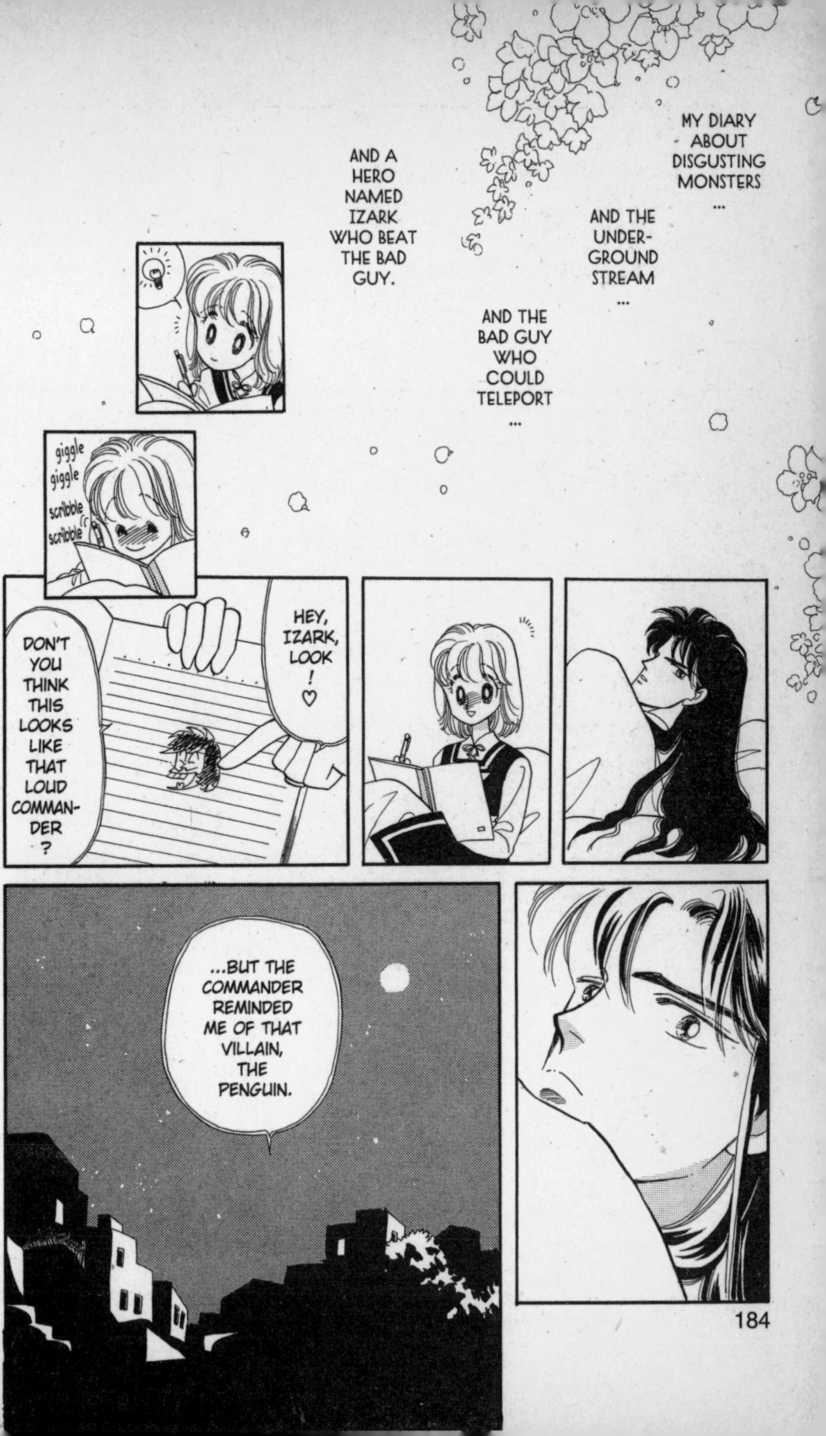
MY DIARY ABOUT DISGUSTING MONSTERS ...
AND THE UNDER-GROUND STREAM ...
AND THE BAD GUY WHO COULD TELEPORT ...
AND A HERO NAMED IZARK WHO BEAT THE BAD GUY.
giggle giggle
scribble scribble
HEY, IZARK, LOOK! ♡
DON'T YOU THINK THIS LOOKS LIKE THAT LOUD COMMAN-DER?
...BUT THE COMMANDER REMINDED ME OF THAT VILLAIN, THE PENGUIN.

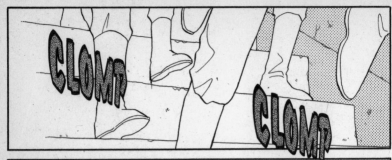

CLOMP

CLOMP

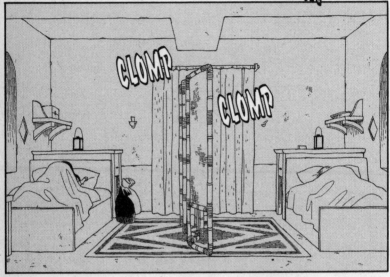

CLOMP

CLOMP

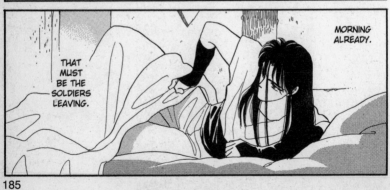

MORNING ALREADY.

THAT MUST BE THE SOLDIERS LEAVING.

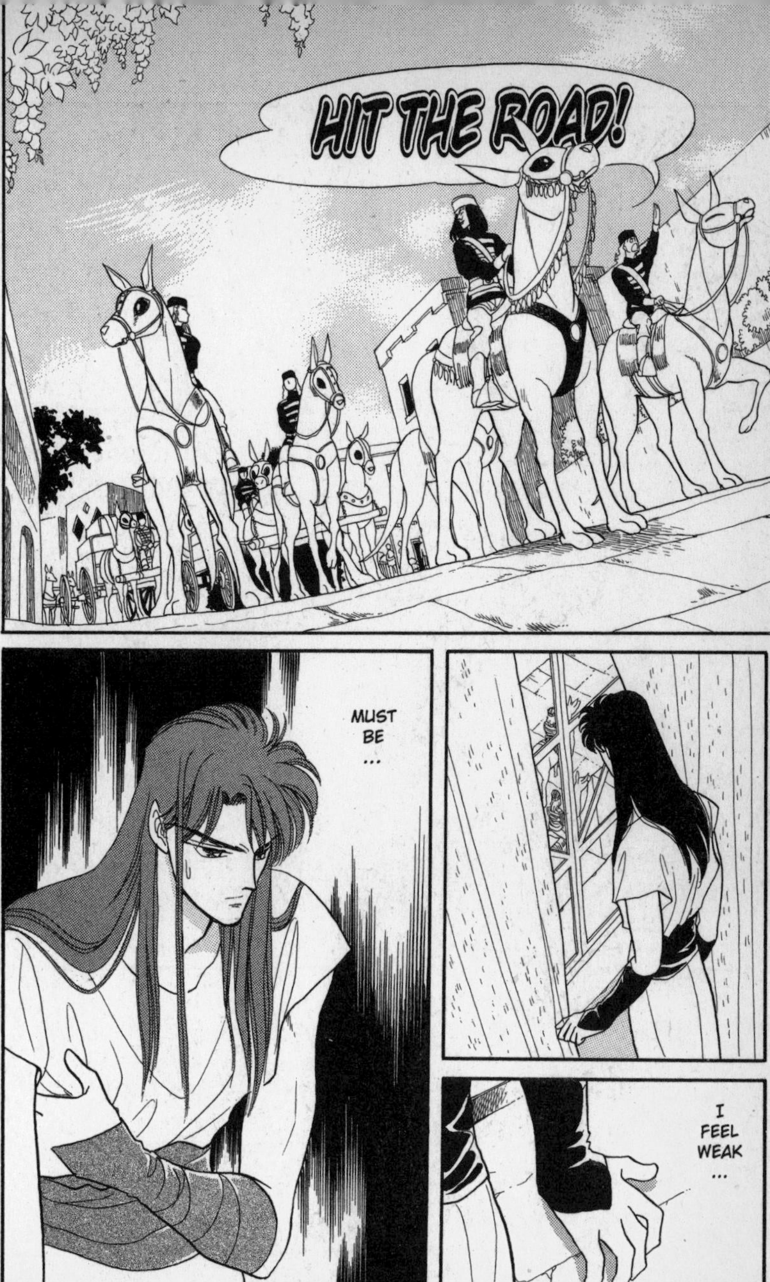
HIT THE ROAD!
I FEEL WEAK ...
MUST BE ...

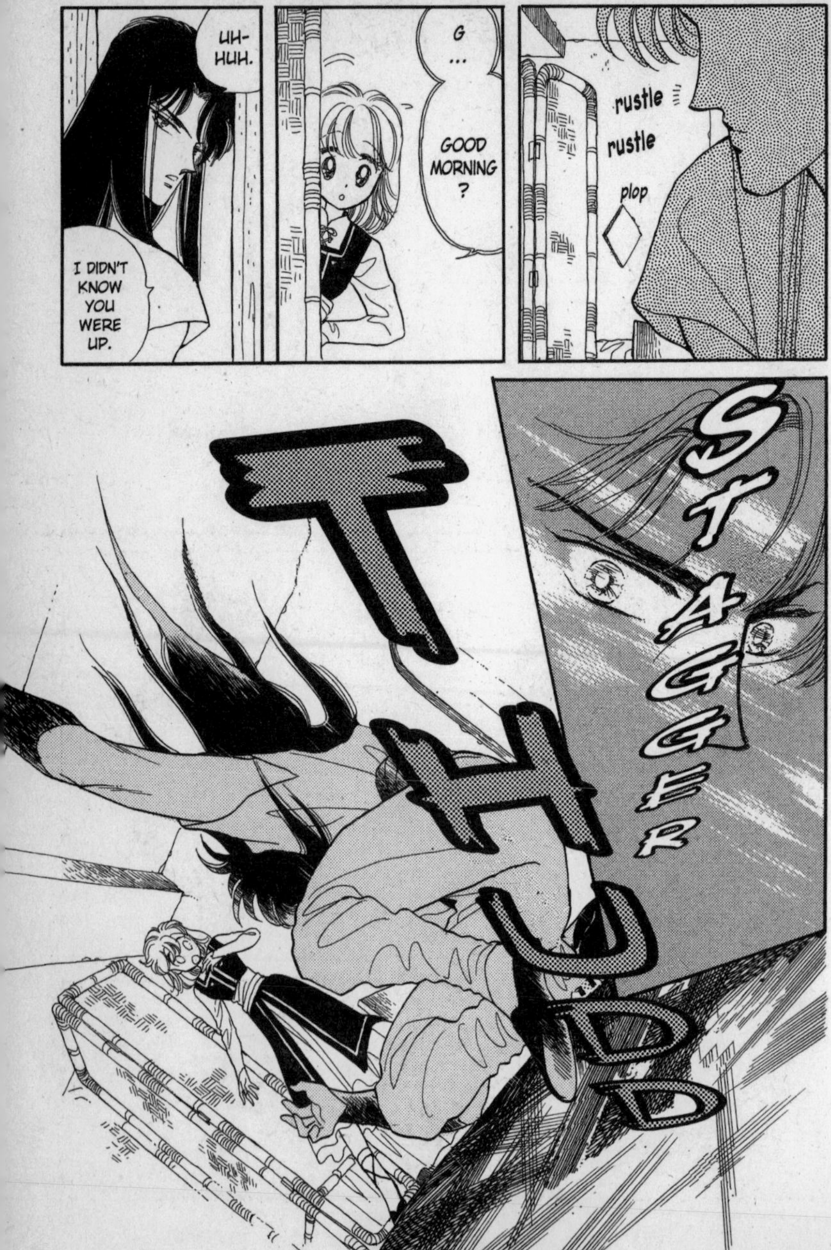
rustle
rustle
plop
G ...
GOOD MORNING ?
UH-HUH.
I DIDN'T KNOW YOU WERE UP.
STAGGER
THUDD

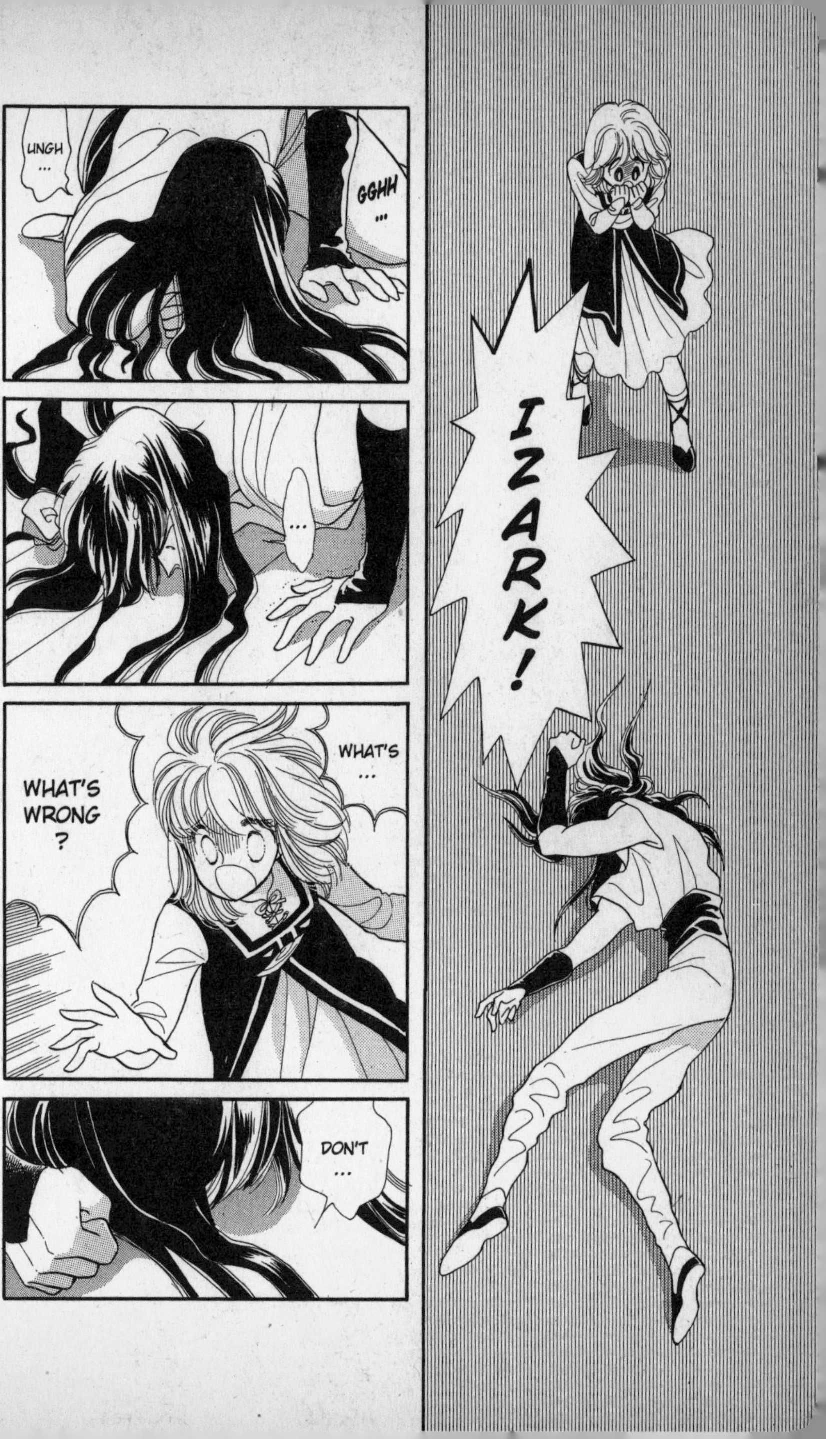
IZARK!
UNGH ...
GGHH ...
...
WHAT'S ...
WHAT'S WRONG ?
DON'T ...

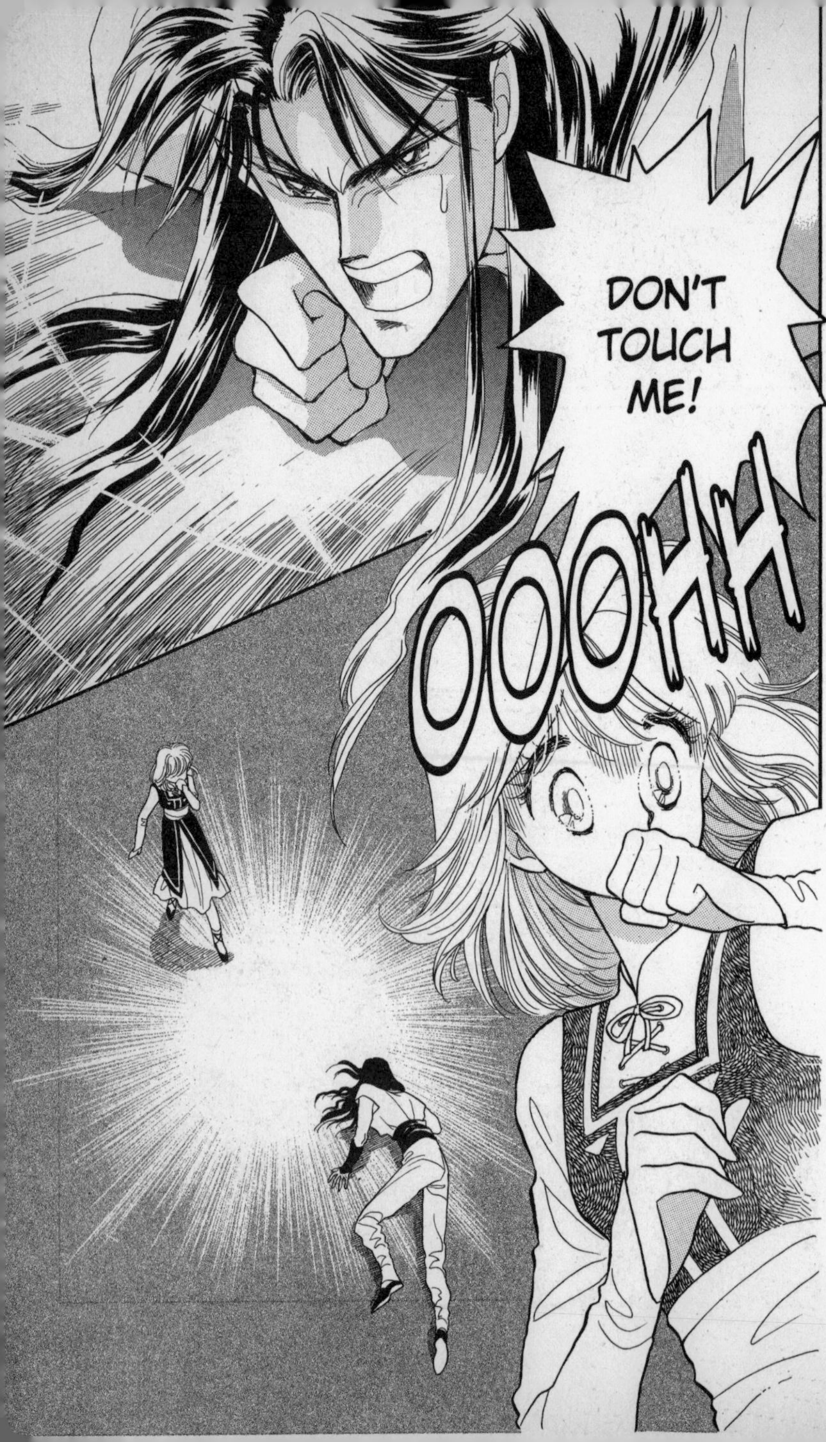
DON'T TOUCH ME!
OOOOHH

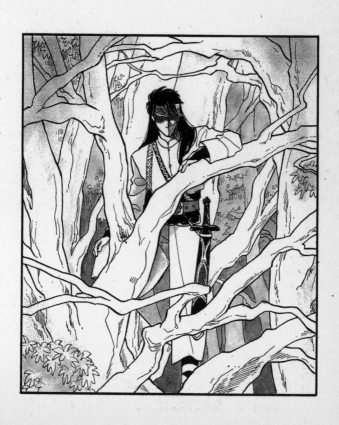

From Far Away
Vol. 1

Shôjo Edition

Story and Art by
Kyoko Hikawa

English Adaptation/Trina Robbins
Translation/Yuko Sawada
Touch-Up Art & Lettering/Walden Wong
Cover Design/Carolina Ugalde
Graphic Design/Andrea Rice
Editor/Eric Searleman

Managing Editor/Annette Roman
Director of Production/Noboru Watanabe
Editorial Director/Alvin Lu
Sr. Director of Licensing & Acquisitions/Rika Inouye
Vice President of Sales & Marketing/Liza Coppola
Executive Vice President/Hyoe Narita
Publisher/Seiji Horibuchi

Published by VIZ, LLC
P.O. Box 77010
San Francisco, CA 94107

10 9 8 7 6 5 4 3 2 1
First printing, October 2004

www.viz.com

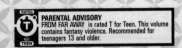

store.viz.com

EDITOR'S RECOMMENDATIONS

If you enjoyed this volume of ***FROM FAR AWAY*** then here's some more manga you might be interested in.

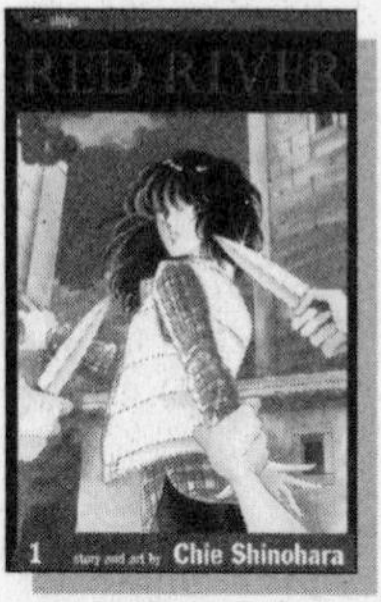
RED RIVER
1
Chie Shinohara

Red River by Chie Shinohara: All Yuri wants to do is go to high school and fall in love. Her life changes dramatically when she suddenly gets whisked away to a magical Middle-Eastern village. Added bonus: lots of sex and romance!

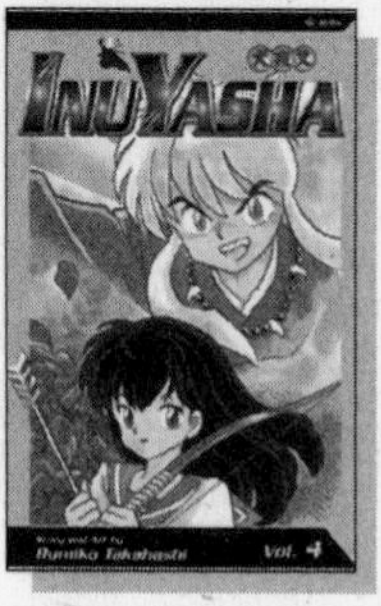
InuYasha
Rumiko Takahashi
vol. 4

InuYasha by Rumiko Takahashi: World's collide when a teenager suddenly finds herself trapped in an ancient Japanese fairy tale. Historical fantasy from the creator of ***Ranma 1/2***, ***Maison Ikkoku*** and ***Mermaid Saga***.

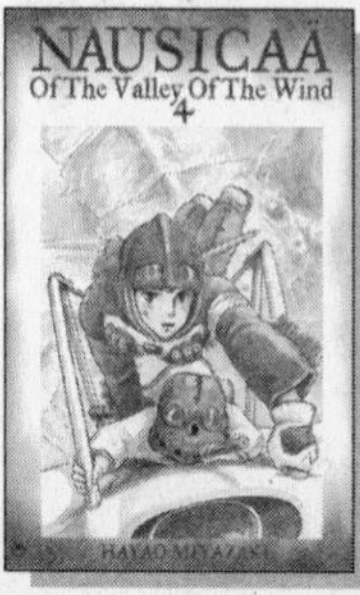
NAUSICAÄ
Of The Valley Of The Wind
4

Nausicaä of the Valley of the Wind by Hayao Miyazaki: A young girl accepts her destiny to save the world from an ecological disaster. Written and drawn by the Academy Award-winning film director. Highly recommended!

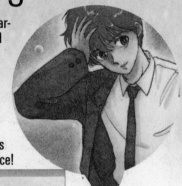

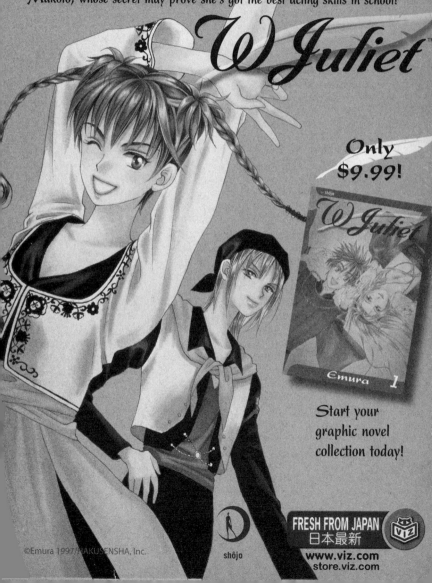

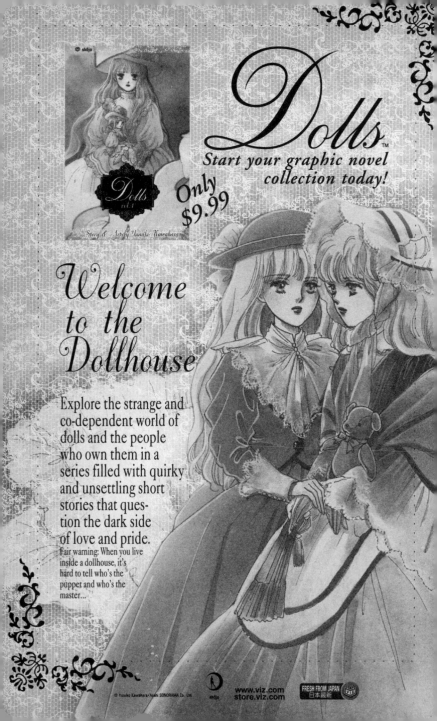

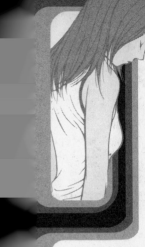
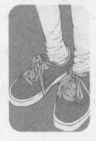 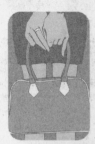

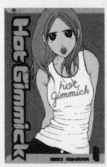

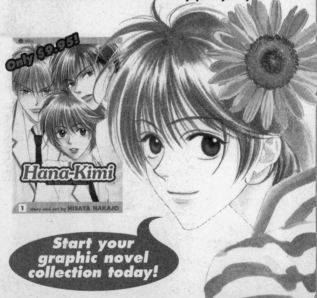

shôjo

AT THE HEART OF THE MATTER

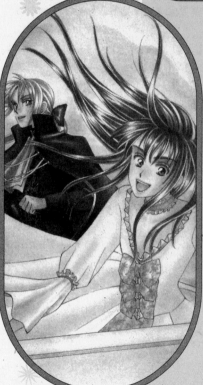

- *Alice 19th*
- *Angel Sanctuary*
- *Banana Fish*
- *Basara*
- *B.B. Explosion*
- *Boys Over Flowers* *
- *Ceres, Celestial Legend* *
- *Descendants of Darkness*
- *Dolls*
- *From Far Away*
- *Fushigi Yûgi*
- *Hana-Kimi*
- *Here Is Greenwood*
- *Hot Gimmick*
- *Imadoki*
- *Kare First Love*
- *Please Save My Earth* *
- *Red River*
- *Revolutionary Girl Utena*
- *Sensual Phrase*
- *W Juliet*
- *Wedding Peach*
- *Wild Com.*
- *X/1999*

Start Your Shôjo Graphic Novel Collection Today!

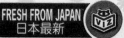

COMPLETE OUR SURVEY AND LET
US KNOW WHAT YOU THINK!

☐ Please do NOT send me information about VIZ products, news and events, special offers, or other information.

☐ Please do NOT send me information from VIZ's trusted business partners.

Name: _____

Address: _____

City: _____ **State:** _____ **Zip:** _____

E-mail: _____

☐ **Male** ☐ **Female** **Date of Birth** (mm/dd/yyyy): ___/___/___ (Under 13? Parental consent required)

What race/ethnicity do you consider yourself? (please check one)

☐ Asian/Pacific Islander ☐ Black/African American ☐ Hispanic/Latino

☐ Native American/Alaskan Native ☐ White/Caucasian ☐ Other: _____

What VIZ product did you purchase? (check all that apply and indicate title purchased)

☐ DVD/VHS _____

☐ Graphic Novel _____

☐ Magazines _____

☐ Merchandise _____

Reason for purchase: (check all that apply)

☐ Special offer ☐ Favorite title ☐ Gift

☐ Recommendation ☐ Other _____

Where did you make your purchase? (please check one)

☐ Comic store ☐ Bookstore ☐ Mass/Grocery Store

☐ Newsstand ☐ Video/Video Game Store ☐ Other: _____

☐ Online (site: _____)

What other VIZ properties have you purchased/own? _____

_____

How many anime and/or manga titles have you pur... VIZ titles? (pleas...

ANIME

- [ ] None
- [ ] 1-4
- [ ] 5-10
- [ ] 11+

I find the pricing of VIZ products to be: (please check one)

- [ ] Cheap
- [ ] Reasonable
- [ ] Expensive

What genre of manga and anime would you like to see from VIZ? (please check two)

- [ ] Adventure
- [ ] Comic Strip
- [ ] Science Fiction
- [ ] Fighting
- [ ] Horror
- [ ] Romance
- [ ] Fantasy
- [ ] Sports

What do you think of VIZ's new look?

- [ ] Love It
- [ ] It's OK
- [ ] Hate It
- [ ] Didn't Notice
- [ ] No Opinion

Which do you prefer? (please check one)

- [ ] Reading right-to-left
- [ ] Reading left-to-right

Which do you prefer? (please check one)

- [ ] Sound effects in English
- [ ] Sound effects in Japanese with English captions
- [ ] Sound effects in Japanese only with a glossary at the back

THANK YOU! Please send the completed form to:

VIZ Survey
42 Catharine St.
Poughkeepsie, NY 12601

All information provided will be used for internal purposes only. We promise not to sell or otherwise divulge your information.